Elusive Rothschild

Also by Kenneth Rose

*Superior Person: a portrait of Curzon and his
circle in late Victorian England*

The Later Cecils

William Harvey: a monograph

King George V

*Kings, Queens and Courtiers:
intimate portraits of the Royal House of Windsor*

Elusive Rothschild

THE LIFE OF VICTOR, THIRD BARON

KENNETH ROSE

Weidenfeld & Nicolson
LONDON

To

Miriam Rothschild

First published in Great Britain in 2003
By Weidenfeld & Nicolson

A CIP catalogue record for this book
is available from the British Library.

ISBN 0 297 81229 7

Typeset in Monotype Garamond by
Selwood Systems, Midsomer Norton

Printed in Great Britain by
Butler & Tanner Ltd,
Frome & London

Weidenfeld & Nicolson

The Orion Publishing Group Ltd
Orion House
5 Upper Saint Martin's Lane
London, WC2H 9EA

Contents

Lord Rothschild's Names

The full name of the subject of this biography was Nathaniel Mayer Victor Rothschild. He was known invariably by the last of his three forenames.

Meyer Amschel Rothschild (1744–1812), the founder of the dynasty, bore the Hebrew name Meyer until 1802, after which date he preferred to use the seemingly more Germanic name of Mayer. (See *Founder: Meyer Amschel Rothschild and his Time* by Amos Elon, p.108).

It was as Mayer that the name persisted through six generations of the family to Nathaniel Mayer Victor, 3rd Baron Rothschild.

Illustrations

Victor in his study at Merton Hall, Cambridge[1]

James de Rothschild, Liberal MP and racehorse owner[4]

Dorothy de Rothschild, the wife of James[1]

Victor with his Central Policy Review Staff in October 1972[6]

JAK's cartoon about the public dispute in 1973 between Edward Heath and Victor Rothschild[7]

Rivals for the chairmanship of NM Rothschild and Sons Ltd, 1975:
Jacob (later 4th Baron) Rothschild, Victor's elder son[8]
Evelyn (later Sir Evelyn) de Rothschild, a cousin[2]

Two more Rothschild smokers: Victor[1] with his favourite French cousin, Baron Henri[1]

The Spycatcher trial in the Supreme Court of New South Wales, 1986:
Peter Wright, the former officer of MI5, whose memoirs infringed the Official Secrets Act and so could not be published in Britain[9]
Malcolm Turnbull, Wright's Australian lawyer[10]
Justice Philip Powell, who heard the case in Sydney[10]
Sir Robert Armstrong, the Cabinet Secretary and principal witness for the British Government[5]

The author and the publishers offer their thanks to the following for their kind permission to reproduce images:

1   The Rothschild family
2   Hulton Archive/Getty Images
3   King's College Library
4   Illustrated London News
5   Camera Press
6   Lord Butler of Brockwell
7   Evening Standard
8   Robin Laurance
9   NI Syndication
10 Popperfoto

Foreword

The life of Victor, third Baron Rothschild (1910–1990) both delights and daunts his biographer. The record of his accomplishments and the diversity of his interests were enough for a dozen men. He was equally at ease in those supposedly rival cultures, science and the arts. A zoologist by choice and training, elected a Fellow of the Royal Society for research into fertilisation, he began even as a Cambridge undergraduate to form the finest collection in private hands of eighteenth-century English books, bindings and manuscripts.

Throughout the war of 1939–45 he served in MI5 as head of counter-sabotage and was awarded the George Medal for dismantling a new type of explosive device hidden by German agents in a cargo of Spanish onions bound for Britain. He was also responsible for examining presents of food, drink and cigars offered by strangers to Winston Churchill in case they contained poison or a miniature bomb.

Having joined the Labour party in 1945, he accumulated public appointments, including the chairmanship of the Agricultural Research Council; in his own right he was an enterprising experimental farmer. He spent nearly ten years with Royal Dutch Shell, rising through the hierarchy to be co-ordinator of research for the group worldwide. On retirement at sixty he was chosen by the new Conservative Prime Minister, Edward Heath, to be the first director-general of the Central Policy Review Staff, popularly known as the Think Tank. Free from civil service pressure, its role was to offer independent advice to the Cabinet on problems as various as race relations, alcohol, Concorde and coal.

He afterwards became chairman of N. M. Rothschild & Sons

Ltd, presided over the Royal Commission on Gambling, was consulted by Margaret Thatcher on the reform of local government finance by the imposition of a poll tax. Rothschild received ten honorary degrees.

As well as innumerable papers of scientific and general interest, he published two monographs of revisionist family history. The first was on N. M. Rothschild, founder of the English line and paymaster of Wellington's armies; the other on the audacity of NM's son Lionel in financing Disraeli's acquisition of the Suez Canal shares in 1875. Both illustrate the dexterity of Victor's forebears in harnessing profit to patriotism.

Such is the solidity of Victor Rothschild's achievement. How robustly he spurned the temptations that beset any youth endowed with money, brains, charm, good looks and a renowned family name; how languidly he might have drifted into the lifelong habits of the dilettante or the playboy, dawdling from country house to country house, from one Mayfair ball to another, migrating with the birds in search of winter warmth.

Those pleasures he did indeed sample, without allowing them to enslave him. There were others, too. He played county cricket, intrepidly facing the body-line bowling of Larwood and earning an obituary tribute in *Wisden Cricketers' Almanack* sixty years later. He was admired for his agility as a jazz pianist and for the records he set scorching between Cambridge and Hyde Park Corner in Mercedes and Bugatti.

Yet all those pursuits were mere diversions. It was the siren call of the laboratory that ruled his life, until in middle age he decided that he had run out of original thought as a research scientist and sought the wider horizons of public service.

Although he found no spiritual satisfaction in Jewish beliefs and observances, he never ceased to be conscious of his inheritance or of the leadership that was expected of the head of the house of Rothschild. It was to spare the Jewish community embarrassment that before his marriage to Barbara Hutchinson in 1933 he persuaded her to convert to Judaism and so ensure that their children should be Jewish too. (After divorce in 1945 and remarriage to Tess Mayor in the following year he made no such request.) He brought compassion and dedication to fund-raising on behalf of the victims of Nazi persecution that culminated in the Holocaust. He was also a generous patron of Israel's scientific and intellectual expansion.

The last decade of his life was clouded by misfortune and ill health. The carefree friendships of his early Cambridge years returned to haunt him. Like many of his contemporaries, he had been mildly left-wing but never a Marxist. Nor had he shared the conviction of such friends as Guy Burgess and Anthony Blunt that the menace of Nazi Germany demanded uncritical adulation of Soviet Russia. But the post-war defection of Burgess to Russia and the unmasking of Blunt as a Soviet agent exposed Victor Rothschild to vilification and innuendo in press and Parliament.

Rather than let his name, his record and his courage speak for themselves, he sought vindication by imprudent means. Ultimately declared innocent by Margaret Thatcher of having spied for Soviet Russia, he escaped prosecution for having breached the Official Secrets Act only after the humiliation of interrogation by the Serious Crimes Squad of Scotland Yard. He was the victim of a cruel and relentless campaign of denigration that temporarily obscured a lifetime of scientific endeavour and public service. I hope that these pages may dispel lingering suspicions.

Some readers may be disturbed that my admiration and affection for Victor Rothschild is occasionally suffused by a sharper but I hope not unfriendly tone. That, however, is how we talked and wrote to each other: an exercise in banter, irony and intellectual competitiveness familiar to his intimates. I like to think that a man of his mental rigour would have despised any cosmetic treatment of his life and character. A year or so before he died he recalled reading in a copy of Clarendon's *History of the Rebellion* from the library of Jonathan Swift a scornful note that his exemplar had pencilled in the margin: 'What a softener is the historian.'

Family Tree of the Rothschild Family
(simplified to include only those mentioned in this book)

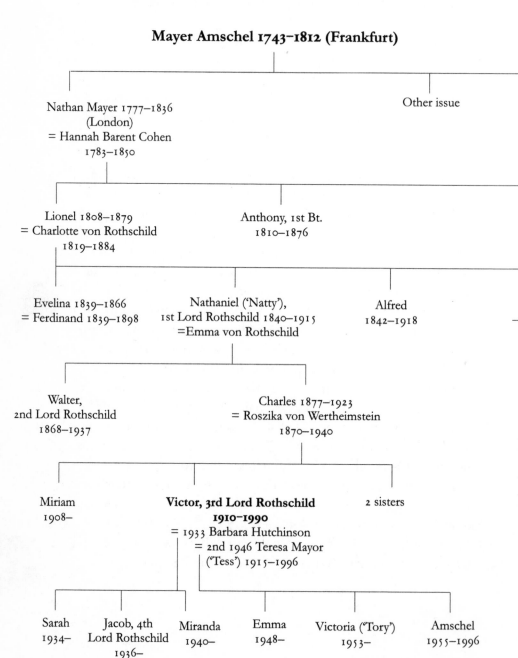

Mayer Amschel 1743-1812 (Frankfurt)

Nathan Mayer 1777–1836
(London)
= Hannah Barent Cohen
1783–1850

Other issue

Lionel 1808–1879
= Charlotte von Rothschild
1819–1884

Anthony, 1st Bt.
1810–1876

Evelina 1839–1866
= Ferdinand 1839–1898

Nathaniel ('Natty'),
1st Lord Rothschild 1840–1915
=Emma von Rothschild

Alfred
1842–1918

Walter,
2nd Lord Rothschild
1868–1937

Charles 1877–1923
= Roszika von Wertheimstein
1870–1940

Miriam
1908–

Victor, 3rd Lord Rothschild
1910-1990
= 1933 Barbara Hutchinson
= 2nd 1946 Teresa Mayor
('Tess') 1915–1996

2 sisters

Sarah
1934–

Jacob, 4th
Lord Rothschild
1936–

Miranda
1940–

Emma
1948–

Victoria ('Tory')
1953–

Amschel
1955–1996

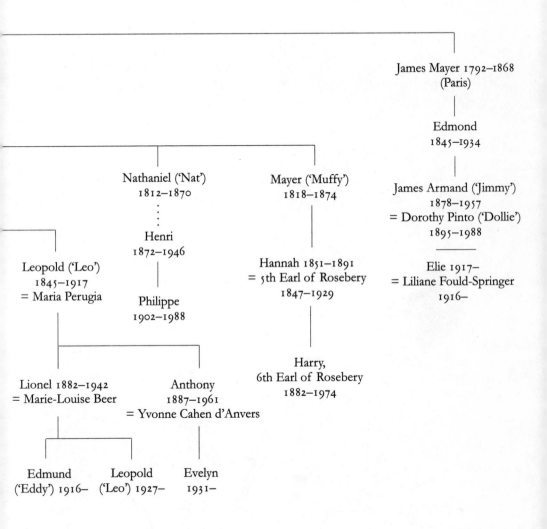

James Mayer 1792–1868
(Paris)

Edmond
1845–1934

Nathaniel ('Nat')
1812–1870

Mayer ('Muffy')
1818–1874

James Armand ('Jimmy')
1878–1957
= Dorothy Pinto ('Dollie')
1895–1988

Henri
1872–1946

Hannah 1851–1891
= 5th Earl of Rosebery
1847–1929

Elie 1917–
= Liliane Fould-Springer
1916–

Leopold ('Leo')
1845–1917
= Maria Perugia

Philippe
1902–1988

Lionel 1882–1942
= Marie-Louise Beer

Anthony
1887–1961
= Yvonne Cahen d'Anvers

Harry,
6th Earl of Rosebery
1882–1974

Edmund
('Eddy') 1916–

Leopold
('Leo') 1927–

Evelyn
1931–

..... signifies more than one generation

Introduction

Victor, third Baron Rothschild, born on 31 October 1910, was the heir to both history and legend. He belonged to the sixth generation of a family renowned throughout Europe and beyond for its financial flair. From the obscurity of a Frankfurt ghetto, the sons of Meyer Amschel Rothschild established branches of his banking business in London, Paris, Vienna and Naples. Their private intelligence service was swift, secret and accurate; they used it to control a multinational organisation a century and a half before such a concept became commonplace. By the early years of the nineteenth century the five symbolic arrows of their armorial bearings had penetrated deeply into the money markets of Europe. In war and peace alike they fuelled that bonfire of expenditure which the antiquated fiscal system of the Great Powers could no longer sustain. They financed armies, yet had the vision to underwrite a growing network of railways that would transform the economic and social fabric of the West. They were Tennysonian in their optimism a generation before the poet forged his iron metaphor:

> *Forward, forward let us range*
> *Let the great world spin for ever*
> *down the ringing grooves of change.*

Not quite for ever, as it turned out. Steam gave way to the carburettor and today the ghetto that once displayed the red shield of the Rothschilds lies buried beneath a Frankfurt motorway.

The founder of the English branch, Nathan Mayer Rothschild, arrived in Manchester in 1798 without a word of English but far from penniless. His father, Meyer Amschel, dealer in coins and banker to the Elector of Hesse-Cassel, had entrusted him with the substantial working capital of £20,000. He applied it skilfully to the textile trade, then to finance. Throughout the later Napoleonic wars he was the trusted agent of the Treasury and paymaster of Wellington's armies. In 1806 he married Hannah Berent Cohen, daughter of a prosperous and well-connected linen merchant of Dutch origin; a sister and a son both married into the Montefiore family, Sephardic Jews considered socially superior to the Ashkenazic Rothschilds. His own daughters he counselled to marry only cousins; not to keep the money in the family, as has been vulgarly supposed, but because Rothschild women were brought up not to chatter about their husbands' business. Of the twelve marriages contracted by the sons of the five brothers, nine were with Rothschild girls.

Victor Rothschild was much attracted to the memory of his great-great-grandfather's irascible temper and soaring fortune (though it scarcely compared with the Croesus-like wealth of Nathan Mayer's brother James, founder of the French branch of the family) and in 1982 published a monograph entitled *The Shadow of a Great Man*. The author found himself handicapped in his pursuit of NM (as he was known) by a paucity of written records: partly because NM preferred his head to any ledger, partly because the Rothschilds have felt little obligation towards their future historians and biographers. It was epitomised by NM's daunting reply to the man who asked him for the secret of his extraordinary success. 'To minding my own business,' he said. There were, however, Victor found, as many anecdotes about NM as there were red hairs on his head. Some are harmless enough. When the Prussian traveller Prince Pückler Muskau was announced at New Court, St Swithin's Lane, NM looked up briefly from his papers, asked him to take a chair and went on writing.

'I do not think you know who I am,' the intruder persisted. 'I am Prince Pückler Muskau.'

NM gave him a second glance. 'Then take two chairs.'

Other stories are less amiable. He told his friend Sir Thomas Buxton, the anti-slavery leader, 'Sometimes to amuse myself I give a beggar a guinea. He thinks I have made a mistake, and for fear that I should find out, off he runs as hard as he can. I advise you to give a beggar a guinea sometimes; it is very amusing.'

The most persistent legend about NM is that he was present on the field of Waterloo on 18 June 1815 and subsequently made a fortune by putting his early knowledge of Wellington's victory to dishonourable use. It was the invention of a French journalist, Georges Marie Mathieu-Dairnvaell, who in 1846 published it in a scurrilous pamphlet, *Rothschild 1er, Roi des Juifs*. Embroidered down the ages, it ultimately alleged that NM, having lingered at Waterloo long enough to be sure of Napoleon's defeat, dashed to Ostend and so across the Channel to London. That morning he stood on his usual place on the Stock Exchange, but apparently broken in health and spirits as if overwhelmed by some calamity. Then it was whispered that Rothschild's agents were selling, presumably on early intelligence of Wellington's defeat. An already depressed market took fright and the Funds plunged. Some hours later, when official news of the British victory reached London, prices rose sharply and the City spoke excitedly of NM's enormous losses. What the City did not know (the tale continues) is that while a few of his agents had been selling openly, others had secretly bought up every piece of scrip they could secure. Far from making a loss, NM had artfully pocketed a million sterling. And the figures grew with the years.

Point by point, Nathan Rothschild's great-great-grandson demolishes the myth in his monograph. The letter-book in the bank archives reveals that at the time of Waterloo NM was at his desk in London. And although there is documentary evidence – but not much of it – that he received early news of the battle and made money, he seemingly did nothing underhand, much less dishonest. What did happen is that on hearing of the victory from one of his own couriers, he at once went round to Downing Street to inform the Prime Minister. But Lord Liverpool had gone to bed and could not be disturbed. The following morning, NM did see the Prime Minister, but could not persuade him of the truth; for the latest official news was of enemy pressure on Quatre Bras and Ligny, buttressed by depressing rumours from Brussels. So NM felt free to take himself off to the Stock Exchange, where he bought heavily, perhaps through agents, in an already depressed market. Then the official news of Waterloo did indeed reach the City, prices soared and NM certainly had his reward. But the constricted size of the market, Victor Rothschild demonstrated, could not possibly have allowed him to make a profit of anything approaching £1 million, let alone millions.

It both pleased and amused Victor to have disproved at least one of the disobliging tales that for almost a century and a half had cast a shadow over his ancestor's probity. He also showed how unlikely it was that the first news of Waterloo had reached NM by carrier pigeon – another colourful detail that has long appealed to a nation of bird fanciers.

NM continued to live modestly. In 1816 he acquired a small suburban retreat, but it was not until 1835 that he bought the country house and estate of Gunnersbury Park. In 1825, however, the year in which Rothschild saved the Bank of England from collapse, he did move from New Court, in the City, to an imposing town house in Piccadilly. By then, in common with his four brothers, he had been created a baron of the Austrian Empire; he alone of them did not use the title, although his wife did. He remained a counting-house man. He died aged sixty in Frankfurt while attending the wedding of his eldest son, Lionel. The victim of an acutely painful internal abscess that failed to respond to surgery, he controlled his enterprises to the very end: sell Exchequer bills and Consols, ship 100,000 sovereigns to Paris, purchase 200 Danube shares, send 100 bottles of soda water, 200 bottles of lavender water and a chest of good oranges – and do not allow the gardener at Gunnersbury to do as he pleases.

His Will was proved at a little over £1 million; but there is reason to think that the true value of his estate was £5 million, or something near to £200 million in the currency of the late 1990s.

It is often said that Disraeli took his friend Lionel de Rothschild, NM's eldest son, as his model for Sidonia, the wise, enigmatic old Jew in *Coningsby*, and later in *Tancred*. The resemblance is superficial. Lionel's mother certainly saw nothing of her son in Disraeli's romantic creation. Lionel was serious, conscientious and shrewd; he was arrogant, too. In 1846 he not only declined the baronetcy

4

offered to him by the Prime Minister, Lord John Russell, but with patrician hauteur asked that it be given to his younger brother Anthony, together with a special remainder to his own sons should Anthony have no male heir of his own. 'I do not think it good taste to refuse it,' his mother wrote to him; nor did the rest of the family. But the Prime Minister was obliging and Anthony's baronetcy passed eventually to Lionel's son Natty and, two generations later, to the subject of this biography.

Lionel did not object in principle to titles. Six years earlier, as was required of a British subject, he had applied for and received a royal licence to style himself a baron of the Austrian Empire, a dignity inherited from his father which he used for the rest of his life. What led him to disdain the proffered honour of November 1846 was that baronetcies had already been bestowed on two other Jews: Sir Isaac Goldsmid in 1841 and Sir Moses Montefiore, Lionel's uncle by marriage, as recently as July 1846. He would of course willingly have become the first Jewish peer; but that distinction eluded the family until his eldest son was created Lord Rothschild nearly forty years later.

Within a few months of refusing a baronetcy, Baron Lionel was embroiled in a more historic controversy. He stood for the House of Commons, well aware that if elected he would by law be required to swear allegiance to the Crown 'upon the faith of a Christian': a betrayal of conscience he could not even contemplate. Charles Greville, Clerk of the Privy Council, called it, 'a great piece of impertinence when he knows he can't take his seat'. The City of London, the most important constituency in the country, thought otherwise. Elected in 1847, he was re-elected in 1849, 1852 and twice in 1857, each time being excluded from the chamber. His persistence at length moved the government to change the law, so that Jews should be relieved of taking a Christian oath. He sat in the House of Commons from 1858 until defeated at the general election of 1874. Sat was in fact all he did do during those sixteen years, never once rising to his feet to speak. His silent presence at Westminster was victory enough.

The admittance of Jews to Parliament was not the only imprint which Baron Lionel left on the history of his times. In 1875 he caught the imagination of Queen and country by financing the British government's purchase of Suez Canal Company shares from the bankrupt Khedive of Egypt. Rothschild's loan of so large a sum as £4 million at a moment's notice has sometimes been seen as a conspiracy between two old friends, each with an interest to pursue. Disraeli and Baron Lionel had indeed known each other well for more than thirty years. But their esteem for each other glowed at different temperatures. The future prime minister fawned and flattered, sought guidance in his tangled financial affairs, thanked the baroness for 'delicacies which Epicurus never tasted and a pine apple which was worthy of the desserts of Paul Veronese'.

Baron Lionel, prickly by temperament, was irritated by Disraeli's youthful pretensions and suspicious of his motives. 'You write about Mrs Dizzy,' he instructed his wife from Paris in 1848, 'do me a great favour and the next time you see her pray ask her why Mr Dizzy cannot come up to speak with me whenever he sees me, is there any reason why I have to cross the room always to speak with him.' The next generation of Rothschilds also had their misgivings. 'I am not sorry that Dizzy has made so many mistakes,' young Natty wrote home from Cambridge, 'it is the natural consequence of hypocrisy.' The Suez Canal loan was no exchange of favours but a business transaction: no more, no less.

Victor, attracted by the scale and audacity of his great-grandfather's operation, wrote a sixty-two-page monograph on it. The title, *You have it, Madam*, is a quotation from the letter of 23 November 1875 in which Disraeli congratulated both himself and the Queen on having acquired nearly half the shares of the Suez Canal Company and so safeguarded the route to India:

It is just settled: you have it, Madam. The French Government has been outgeneraled. They tried too much, offering loans at an usurious rate, & with conditions wh: would have virtually given them the government of Egypt.

The Khedive, in despair & disgust, offered Yr Majesty's Government to purchase his shares outright – he never would listen to such a proposition before.

Four millions sterling! and almost immediately. There was

only one firm that cd do it – Rothschilds. They behaved admirably; advanced the money at a low rate, and the entire interest of the Khedive is now yours, Madam.

That was one of the hyperbolic documents which Victor insisted on scrutinising with an historian's eye. The other was the account left by Montagu Corry, Disraeli's private secretary, of his conversation with Baron Lionel immediately after the Cabinet had approved an overture to New Court:

'How much?'
  'Four million pounds.'
  'When?'
  'Tomorrow.'
  'What is your security?'
  'The British Government.'
  'You shall have it.'

Disraeli and Baron Lionel, Victor noted, had almost certainly discussed the deal before the Cabinet meeting. The number of the Khedive's shares was known; and, given his acute shortage of money, an estimate of what he would accept for them. Corry had neither the need, nor indeed the authority, to negotiate with the most powerful banker in the City of London. But, like the prime minister he served with such devotion, he was a master of the colourful anecdote. As for his assertion that Baron Lionel spat out grape pips between sentences, Victor consigned them, like King Henry VIII's peripatetic chicken legs, to the dustbin of history.

That Rothschild 'advanced the money at a low rate', as Disraeli told the Queen, may also be disputed. The bank charged not only interest on the loan at 5 per cent but also a commission of 2½ per cent, much criticised by that guardian of public expenditure Mr Gladstone. Baron Lionel justified the additional charge to the government of £100,000 by pleading that not even Rothschild's could afford to deplete their reserves by £4 million without covering the risk to their usual business, particularly if the Khedive should demand to be paid in gold.

For the House of Rothschild, profit and patriotism had gone hand in hand; but for the British government, the investment proved financially unspectacular, whatever its political and strategic rewards. It is true that throughout the next hundred years the Suez Canal shares paid about £3 million in dividends, thus covering 75 per cent of the purchase price. Yet in 1979, the centenary year, as it happened, of Baron Lionel's death, the government sold them for £22 million, or only a little more than £3 million in the currency of 1875. 'N. M. Rothschild & Sons', Baron Lionel's great-grandson noted with satisfaction, 'were not involved in the transaction.'

With wealth came assimilation. In London the Rothschilds formed a family enclave in Piccadilly, where Lionel knocked two mansions together next door to Apsley House, the Duke of Wellington's residence. For their country pursuits they bought or built a chain of palaces across the Vale of Aylesbury. The brothers and their children hunted and shot, bred prize cattle and racehorses, entertained royalty and quarrelled with their neighbours. NM's third son, Nat, hearing that his brothers had been out with the Royal Buckhounds at Windsor, cheered them on from France. 'Ride like trumps,' he urged, 'and do not let the Queen's people fancy we are all tailors.' Mayer commissioned Joseph Paxton, architect of the Crystal Palace, to build Mentmore in the Jacobean style, won the Derby, but died before the marriage of his daughter to the future prime minister, Lord Rosebery. 'If the flame seize on the cedars,' the *Jewish Chronicle* lamented, 'how will fare the hyssop on the wall: if the leviathan is brought up with a hook, how will the minnows escape?' But the bride's aunt and namesake, Hannah Rothschild, had already broken the tradition of centuries by marrying out of the faith; her husband was the Hon. Henry FitzRoy, a younger brother of Lord Southampton. The two daughters of Sir Anthony, the windfall baronet, also married Gentiles.

The declining fortunes of great landowners like the Dukes of Buckingham and Marlborough enabled the new men to buy their country estates at moderate cost. The revolutionary ferment of Europe, too, continued to flood the market with treasures of fallen dynasties; and the whim of fashion allowed the finest eighteenth-century French furniture to be sold at bargain prices. Baron Mayer used to say that he found it cheaper to buy Louis XV or Louis XVI commodes rather than the modern wash-hand stands sold at Sir Blundell Maple's emporium in the Tottenham Court Road. Not that he had need of such bargains, for his collection rested on a covetable fortune which the family referred to endearingly as 'tin'. Everard Primrose, Rosebery's younger brother, wrote of Mentmore in 1879,

> Amid Venetian furniture, brocades and gilded thrones, tables of tarsia and tortoiseshell, Gobelin hangings and the spoils of Fontainebleau and the Trianon, one sighs for an old armchair, a drugget one need not hesitate to tread on, and a table which will conveniently hold something.

That could also be said of Waddesdon Manor, the home of Baron Ferdinand de Rothschild. A member of the Austrian branch of the family, he became a British subject, married Lionel's daughter Evelina, and put up a grandiose chateau in the French Renaissance style a few miles from Mentmore. In its exotic profusion could be found two immense views of Venice by Guardi, portraits by Reynolds and Gainsborough, carpets from Savonnerie. Three of France's most celebrated families had each lost a panelled room to Waddesdon: Montmorency, Richelieu and Lauzun. It was all too much for Henry James, who lunched there one day with Lady Ottoline Morrell:

> His basilisk gaze had absorbed the company of seven-foot-high footmen that waited on us, the hot-house flowers and the dish of enormous white strawberries that were in front of the plates. He looked up at the footmen, he looked down on the strawberries. 'Murder and rapine', he said, 'would be preferable to this.'

Queen Victoria was a more appreciative guest when in 1890 curiosity drove her to make a rare visit to the home of a subject.

She insisted, however, on having luncheon alone with her daughter Princess Louise while Baron Ferdinand uncomplainingly ate with his other guests next door. She went through the menu, had two helpings of cold roast beef and later sent her own chef to learn a thing or two in the Waddesdon kitchens.

There were earlier links with the royal family. When the Queen was about to visit Germany, the House of Rothschild asked that it might supply her with the money needed on the journey. The request was granted and the role of banker to Her Majesty did nothing to diminish Lionel's considerable prestige. The next generation of the two families established a cordiality that fell just short of friendship when Natty and the future King Edward VII were undergraduates at Trinity College, Cambridge. There was a reason for the choice of university. Hannah, Natty's grandmother, had taken against Oxford. 'The place is too orthodox to be an agreeable residence for any other sect besides Protestants,' she wrote during a visit. 'Bibles and other religious books are placed in the different apartments of the hotel we are in, but the inhabitants are civil and attentive.' In any case, Cambridge was less demanding in its requirement that all undergraduates should attend services in their college chapel.

A generous allowance from his father enabled Natty to move at ease in the Prince's circle. Although he was a frequent guest at Madingley Hall, where the Prince lodged in guarded privacy during his single year at Cambridge, Natty scarcely ever mentioned him when writing home except with mild disparagement. The heir to the throne, it seems, bowled at the legs of his opponents when playing cricket; was the worst loser ever seen at whist; took care to bully only the weak; and expected to buy three hunters for the price of one. 'No wonder', Natty continues, 'that he gets so many falls and is never up. Someone ought to speak to the Master of the Horse about it.' But there must be sympathy for a hot-blooded young prince who 'has rooms at the Lodge where the different Regius Professors come and lecture to him, they say he is not allowed to take any notes but has to write out the lectures when he gets back to Madingley'. In time he became both the friend and the benefactor of the Prince; but as the most English in character of all nineteenth-century Rothschilds he continued to scrutinise the heir to the throne with a Whiggish coolness.

Other members of the family on both sides of the Channel seemed to lose their heads in the royal presence. When the Prince of Wales came to Mentmore for a stag hunt, there were Sèvres plates at breakfast piled high with huge red strawberries; but the month was March, and Baroness Mayer explained that they had loyally ripened early for him. Baron James chose to entertain Napoleon III at Ferrières with a pheasant shoot: birds so tame, a daughter-in-law wrote, that they came to meet the carriages. It was said that the host had persuaded the painter Eugène Lami to disguise parrots as pheasants, so that as the birds fell to Napoleon's gun they cried 'Vive l'Empereur'.

Natty's brothers Alfred and Leo followed him to Cambridge, but neither satisfied their father's ambitions. Alfred sought success only as an amateur actor and Leo amiably shrugged off the paternal rebukes that arrived by every post. 'I am glad to see', Baron Lionel wrote, 'that you are pleased with yourself for having guessed the winners of the great races, your examiners were quite right in saying you were a good hand at guessing.' And, four days later, this daunting enquiry: 'Be so good as to say what you do all day long with yourself if you get up at 12 and go to bed at six.' Young Leo sometimes received a different sort of letter from his father: a request rather than a reproof, but if anything more chilling. 'Enquire *very quietly*', Baron Lionel wrote, 'if some of the colleges would be disposed to sell some of their old silver things – you won't mind how you go to work.' And when Leo was in Venice: 'Ask to be introduced to some of the old Jewish families. Somewhere or other there is some fine old plate.' Natty, Alfred and Leo: all three brothers emerge from the family archives in a more kindly light than does their stern, acquisitive, single-minded papa.

Baron Lionel died in 1879, leaving a prosperous N. M. Rothschild in the hands of his three sons. It was a triumvirate only in name. The story has been handed down of a meeting at New Court to discuss some momentous issue with officials of the Treasury and of the Bank of England. At length the senior partner announced majestically, 'I have decided...' There came a gentle interruption from Alfred: '*We*, Natty, *we* have decided...' That mild remonstrance was the extent to which Natty's authority was resented by his two younger brothers, neither of whom shared his dedication to business or his judgement. Even in the dog days of summer, when other Rothschilds took to the country, Natty would drive each morning from his dust-sheeted mansion in Piccadilly for a full day's work at New Court, habits of industry which his grandson Victor admired and inherited two generations later.

The two younger partners were less assiduous. Leo arrived at New Court at about eleven o'clock, took a leisurely lunch at half past one and went home at five. Alfred did not turn up until two o'clock or so, lunched between half past three and four, then recovered from the exertions of the day by sleeping for an hour or two on a leather sofa; occasionally he had to be roused prematurely to sign a cheque. That placid routine, it must be admitted, was after he had retired as the first Jewish director of the Bank of England, an appointment he held for twenty-one years. It ended unhappily when he showed too curious an interest in the account of an art dealer who, he believed, had not been quite straight with him in some transaction; he talked of it openly at the dinner table and was required to resign.

Yet how much colour and warmth those two great-uncles of Victor brought to the austerity of New Court. Alfred pursued the pleasures of the flesh with nervous diffidence. 'Unmarried', a cousin wrote of him, 'and rather at the mercy of doctors, secretaries and dependants whom he alternately liked and distrusted, he occasionally failed to see the proportion of things.' One secretary, Jules Ayer, persuaded Alfred to become godfather to his son Freddie – later Sir Alfred (A.J.) Ayer, the philosopher. Eighteen months later, Ayer senior speculated in foreign exchange, went bankrupt and was dismissed. For many years Alfred lived contentedly with a mistress, Mrs Wombwell, by whom he had a daughter. Called Almina, a whimsical amalgam of her parents' names, she married the fifth Earl of Carnarvon who used her father's legacy to finance the excavation of the tomb of King Tutankhamun.

Some were amused by the liaison, referring to her as Mrs Rothwell or Mrs Wombchild. Alfred, however, was annoyed that Natty's wife Emma refused ever to invite her either to 148 Piccadilly or to Tring, the family country house in Buckinghamshire. He took a posthumous revenge by leaving his sister-in-law a daring nude by Greuze, which an affronted Emma gave away.

Alfred's own hospitality at Halton, in Buckinghamshire, a house originally belonging to the Dashwood family which he rebuilt with slate roofs, towers and turrets, was exuberant but bizarre. He liked to conduct his own orchestra and act as ringmaster at his own circus of performing dogs. Whole flower beds of potted plants would be brought from London on Friday and returned on Tuesday. (It was a Rothschild dodge. When the King of Spain came to shoot with Baron Edmond at Armainvilliers, he was greeted on arrival by massed beds of pink and blue. He awoke next morning to his national colours of red and yellow.) Neatness was all. Ivy sheds leaves, so Alfred's was made of tin and tinkled in the breeze. The contents of the house reflected his taste as a trustee of the National Gallery and of the Wallace Collection; but his fine pictures were over-varnished, their frames over-gilded. Nor did his love of birds and beasts extend to pheasant poults, whose necks were illegally wrung in July to produce a dish only for the voluptuous: 'poussins Haltonnais'.

Leo never fulfilled the promise foreshadowed for him by Mrs Disraeli: 'My dear,' she gushed to Baroness Lionel, 'that beautiful boy may be the future Messiah whom we are led to expect – who knows? And you will be the most favoured of women.' Neither role was to the liking of the Rothschilds and Leo grew up with worldly tastes tempered by a generous nature. He was genial in negotiation and successful when transacting business across the Atlantic. At New Court he supervised the bank's contributions to charity and the welfare of the staff. Banknotes would readily be pressed into the palms of the meritorious, yet he might also recognise trivial services or none. The luncheon allowance could be worth as much as one-quarter of a young man's salary. I recall visiting New Court just before the demolition of the old cramped building in 1962 to make way for the present marble halls; in contrast to the

Dickensian murk, the desk of each clerk had its own bottle of expensive mineral water and glass.

At Ascott Wing, on the Mentmore estate, Leo matched the sybaritic style of his brother at Halton. Raymond Asquith called him 'the greatest master of luxury of our age': incomparable roses and claret, asparagus in the bedrooms, baths as big as billiard tables, golf and bridge with the Prime Minister. Leo cemented his friendship with the Prince of Wales on the racecourse. Between 1894 and 1909, his cousin Rosebery won the Derby three times, the Prince twice and Leo himself once. 'Are we as welcome as ever?' Max Beerbohm called his cartoon of Edward VII's rich Jewish friends, including Alfred and Leo, making their way apprehensively along a corridor of Buckingham Palace to be received by George V. Certainly there was no abrupt break. On the morning of the new King's coronation in 1911, Leo sent along a display of orchids – tastefully arranged in a Fabergé vase of cut rock crystal inlaid with gold and enamel.

He has his memorial in New Court: a framed letter from Disraeli congratulating him on his engagement to the seventeen-year-old Maria Perugia. 'I have always been of the opinion', the dying statesman wrote, 'that there cannot be too many Rothschilds.'

Darker colours must suffice for a portrait sketch of the eldest brother, Nathanial first Baron Rothschild. That is as he would have wished; indeed, he arranged his affairs that it should be so. He guarded his private and family life, avoided public controversy unless it were forced on him, scarcely ever made use of the parliamentary platform that was his for half a century, neither sought nor rejoiced in his many honours, wrote few letters and saw to it that his papers should be destroyed at death.

Such reticence masked a remarkable career. Rothschild has, of course, his place in history as the first Jew to take his seat in the House of Lords; but here the symbol has overshadowed the man. The last obstacle to Jewish equality of rights would have been removed a generation earlier but for the intransigence of Queen Victoria. Perhaps it was the death of the Prince Consort in 1861 which deprived her of a guiding liberal hand. She had not objected when, as long ago as 1846, Baron Lionel had been recommended for the baronetcy he declined; or expressed dismay when in 1858 he had at last been allowed to sit in the House of Commons without taking an oath offensive to the Jewish conscience. His swift ascent to the House of Lords seemed to be assured. 'The public will have it you, dear Papa, are to be made a peer,' young Natty wrote in 1863. The rumour was premature. Six years later, when Gladstone formally put Lionel's name before the Queen as one of ten proposed peers, she turned it down out of hand. 'To make a *Jew a Peer*', she wrote in a frenzy of italics, 'is a step she *could not* consent to.' Lord Granville, worldly and urbane, then tried his hand:

> The notion of a Jew Peer is startling. *'Rothschild le premier Baron Juif'* does not sound as well as *'Montmorency, le premier Baron Chrétien'* – but he represents a class whose influence is great by their wealth, their intelligence, their literary connections and their numerous seats in the House of Commons. It may be wise to attach them to the Aristocracy, rather than drive them into the Democratic camp.

Once more the Queen rejected the plea, not least because 'it would do the Government harm instead of good': a rare if not unique instance of Her Majesty's concern for the welfare of a Gladstone government. Still the Prime Minister persisted. The Queen continued to object to a Jew in the House of Lords on grounds of religion, but now employed another kind of prejudice:

> She cannot think that one who owes his great wealth to contracts with Foreign Govts for Loans, or to successful speculations on the Stock Exchange can fairly claim a British peerage.
>
> However high Sir L. Rothschild may stand personally in Public Estimation, this seems to her not the less a species of gambling, because it is on a gigantic scale – & far removed from that legitimate trading w^h she *delights* to *honour*, in which men have raised themselves by patient industry & unswerving probity to positions of wealth and influence.

Another sixteen years were to pass before the Queen agreed to a peerage for Lionel's son, who by any measure was qualified to sit in the House of Lords after twenty years in the House of Commons. Perhaps it was that by then the Rothschild millions had acquired a patina of respectability, not least when used to safeguard the route to India. Or perhaps the Queen, who liked to boast that she had more Moslem subjects than the Sultan of Turkey, saw the inconsistency of maintaining against Jews a racial prejudice that she deplored in her Indian empire. On 9 July 1885 the first Baron Rothschild, of Tring in the County of Hertford, took the oath of allegiance in the House of Lords, his head covered according to Jewish custom. Of his two required sponsors of his own rank in the peerage, one was his old Cambridge friend and country neighbour Lord Carrington; the other was his cousin by marriage Lord Rosebery, who although a Scottish earl, was able to introduce a mere baron by virtue of the United Kingdom peerage that alone entitled him to a seat in the Lords. The Queen thereafter smiled upon the Rothschilds. When they dined at Windsor she took care to draw their attention to a ham pie without ham she had specially ordered for her Jewish guests: a more striking compliment than if she had simply omitted the dish from the menu.

With the Prince of Wales, too, he established a growing intimacy and respect. When Carrington had doubts about his old friend's appointment in 1889 to be Lord-Lieutenant of Buckinghamshire, the Prince defended Natty: 'It would have been strange ten years ago, but times change. He is a good fellow and man of business, and he and his family own half the County!' The Squire of Sandringham also admired Natty's knowledgeable enthusiasm for breeding Jersey cattle and shire-horses. Other honours followed. Early in the new reign, King Edward VII appointed him to the Privy Council, a rare honour outside the ranks of senior ministers and officials. He also received at the King's hands the Grand Cross of the Royal Victorian Order; Alfred and Leo, both of whom had earlier ceased to style themselves barons of the Austrian Empire in deference to their brother's peerage, were appointed to be commanders of the order.

Although Natty and Emma did not attempt to emulate the opulence of Halton and Ascott Wing, neither Tring Park nor 148 Piccadilly was exactly a cottage. Built by Wren, rented by N. M. Rothschild as a summer residence and bought by Baron Lionel for £230,000 in 1872, Tring stands in a deer park at the foot of the Chilterns where King Charles II was reputed to have wooed Nell Gwyn. Natty's contribution to its history was less romantic. He enlarged it, encased it in brick and stone, gave it a slate-grey roof and plate-glass windows. Inside the house the worst excesses of art nouveau jostled eighteenth-century French furniture of supreme elegance; Gainsborough's *Morning Walk* and Reynolds's *Mrs Lloyd* vied for attention with modern bas-relief white marble plaques of nude but sexless figures, each set in a pink marble surround. One visitor, a trustee of the National Gallery, noted 'awful inlaid chairs and tables, huge costly fitments, vast Chinese vases of the worst period, sophisticated tapestries, mantelpieces which ruined the whole room – I passed from one monstrous apartment to another with ever growing consternation'. Yet Tring was not without its admirers. 'What a comfortable house this is,' young Winston Churchill wrote, on leave from Sandhurst, 'such a change after the untidy, dilapidated and tobacco-smelling rooms of the RMC.' The food, too, at Tring he no doubt found superior to that at Sandhurst. The elder Grosstephen (he also had a son) was reputed to be the best chef in Europe. Buying smoked salmon at one shilling a pound, Natty's granddaughter Miriam Rothschild tells us, Grosstephen ran up an annual bill at the fishmonger of £5000: the salary of a Cabinet minister. Rothschild himself appreciated that artist of the table and defied his wife by instructing him to stuff foie gras into the game pie. But his favourite meal remained nursery tea.

In his daily routine he was a man of purpose and industry, as much a trustee of an honourable name as of an immense fortune. Some of his decisions have passed into history. He followed in his father's footsteps by saving Egypt from financial collapse seven years after the purchase of the Khedive's Suez Canal shares. He helped to rescue Baring Brothers when the rival bank faced insolvency after reckless speculation in South America. ('Where is the capital of the Rothschilds?' ran the schoolroom riddle. Answer: 'In the Baring straits.') Elected to the Commons as a Liberal, he became a Conservative in all but name after Gladstone had embraced Home Rule for Ireland. He was the intimate friend of Lord Randolph Churchill, who at the time of his death in 1895 owed the bank £66,902; although much of the debt had been incurred after he had ceased to be Chancellor of the Exchequer, there were whispers that Budget secrets had been leaked to his patron. Rothschild had no need of illicit sources. There was scarcely a British government which did not trust and use him. A champion of naval rearmament against Germany, he was asked by Winston Churchill in 1913 if he would consider buying a battleship from Brazil to prevent its sale to Italy. And although he quarrelled openly with Lloyd George over social welfare, housing and taxa-tion, the future prime minister, invited to construct an imaginary Cabinet of all the talents, nominated his adversary as Chancellor of the Exchequer.

There are few recorded instances of his having used the strength of N. M. Rothschild & Sons in pursuit of political ends. He is known, however, to have refused a loan of £100 million to Russia, thus relinquishing a certain profit of £2 million, as long as its gov-ernment encouraged systematic and barbaric anti-Semitism. In 1907, before Edward VII's visit to Russia, he and his brothers pre-vailed on the King to express displeasure to the Tsar at the perse-cution of the Jews. The King's advisers demurred, but Natty's friend insisted on having his say, however ineffective it proved. He cannot have forgotten that in more penurious days Rothschild had lent him £160,000 on undemanding terms against a mortgage on Sandringham.

The English Rothschilds seemed well protected from anti-Semitism. In a letter to his parents from Cambridge, Natty had expressed surprise and dismay at a speech by a Mr Lush in the Union debating society, a reaction suggesting that it was rare for such prejudice to be aired in public:

> My blood boiled with rage when he quoted as a solitary instance
> of the too great power of the House of Commons the passing

of the Jew Bill [for the relief of disabilities]. I had hoped that the day was gone by for all distinctions of this kind.

As the century progressed, bringing waves of impoverished and overtly alien refugees from Russia, the mild, mindless anti-Semitism of all classes turned more violent. Assimilated, patriotic and charitable, the Rothschilds endured no more than an occasional spurt of jealousy at their financial supremacy or a patrician contempt for opulence that did not deter the fastidious critic from accepting their hospitality. Only at the very end of his life did Rothschild look on Zionism with cautious and qualified sympathy. But he never ceased to use his influence both to ensure the acceptance of dispossessed Jewry in England and to relieve their acute poverty. Here, with the voice of liberalism, his first political allegiance, he denounces the Aliens Bill of 1905 introduced by a Conservative government to cut illegal immigration:

It proposes to establish in this country a loathsome system of police interference and espionage, of passports and arbitrary power, exercised by police officers who in all probability will not understand the language of those upon whom they are called to sit in judgment.

Rothschild's practical help to Jewish immigrants was sustained and prodigious. But his charity spread far beyond their particular needs. There was scarcely a national or local appeal for the relief of suffering that did not receive a donation from the House of Rothschild. At New Court an entire department, supervised by Leo, administered these princely benefactions. At the other end of the scale were thousands of personal cases and worthy causes: few went unsatisfied, not least those sponsored by churches or other Christian bodies. Food parcels and cigars raised the morale of whole regiments in the Boer War. Piccadilly policemen were always welcome to a hot meal in the basement of Number 148. Cabbies received a brace of pheasants each Christmas, saluting the donors by tying the Rothschild racing colours of blue and yellow to their whips. At Tring the village children would scramble for handfuls of half-sovereigns thrown by Natty from an open carriage. Emma thought it patronising and insensitive; but Natty – and the children – found it fun. The distribution of charity had become a way of life untinged by cynicism. As Natty lay dying at 148 Piccadilly in the spring of 1915, his old friend Lord Haldane was announced. Before the Lord Chancellor could state his business – a technical problem of stopping a neutral ship believed to be carrying bullion to Germany – Natty had from force of habit reached for his chequebook. 'If Haldane wants £25,000,' was his instinctive thought, 'it's his – and no questions asked of course.' At his death a few days later it was found that every member of the staff at New Court had been left one year's salary.

Men of power with few words attract myths. There are many that cluster round the memory of the first Lord Rothschild, and some have an authentic ring to them. He was once asked how he had made his fortune. NM would reply to the same question: 'By minding my own business.' His grandson's answer was equally shrewd: 'By selling too soon.' No less astringent was his retort to the employee at the bank who complained about his yearly bonus: 'If you are not careful I shall make you a partner.' And there is his gruff comment on hearing a clerk speak casually of a halfpenny. 'That young man', he said, 'does not appear to know much about large transactions.' (Across the Channel a similar tale was told of Baron James. When an error of 5 centimes appeared in his accounts for a whole year, the seven employees who handled his private fortune were set to work for five days and five nights until the cause had been traced.)

Victor Rothschild used to tell of how in 1912 his grandfather's Alliance Marine Assurance Company refused a share of underwriting the supposedly unsinkable *Titanic*. When the liner had gone to the bottom of the sea, the old man was asked why he had declined so lucrative an offer. 'The ship was so large', he replied, 'that I did not believe it would float.' That is the least credible of the Rothschild legends. Or so I thought until in the archives of New Court I came across a letter from Natty to his parents written exactly half a century before. Referring to another maritime disaster in the Atlantic, he said, 'I suppose you know the *Monitor* has foundered and thus there is an end to iron-cased floating batteries.' Nobody ever accused him of not having a good memory.

The most characteristic of all tales concerns the arrival at New Court of a young actuary known to be an able mathematician. Natty sent for him and asked what was 1 per cent of 100 million. He replied, 'One million.'

'Don't guess, boy,' Natty said. 'Go away and work it out.'

Both Lord Rothschild's sons, Walter and Charles, dutifully followed their father into the family bank. Walter's biographical details – as published in any work of reference – suppose a career of conventional decorum. Born in 1868 and educated at the Universities of Bonn and Cambridge, he became Liberal Unionist MP for Aylesbury, a Deputy Lieutenant and Justice of the Peace for Buckinghamshire, a Lieutenant of the City of London and a major in the Royal Buckinghamshire Yeomanry, to whom he made the private benefaction of a Maxim machine-gun. That roll-call of respectability is both deceptive and incomplete. He spent eighteen years in the partners' room of N. M. Rothschild; but no trace remains of either industry or enterprise on his part. He sat for eleven years in the Commons but spoke only on two minor measures; his remaining claim to parliamentary attention rested with the white top hat which he alone wore in the chamber.

His contemporaries looked on him with affectionate tolerance. What they did not know was that this shy, shambling giant of a man, standing six foot three inches and weighing twenty-two stone, was applying knowledge and memory to assemble the largest collection of natural history objects ever made by one person: literally hundreds of thousands of birds, eggs and insects. He loved the animal kingdom at its most bizarre: giant tortoises, cassowaries, giraffes with five horns instead of four, emus which attacked his father at Tring, zebras which he harnessed to a carriage and drove into the forecourt of Buckingham Palace, a pair of brown bears which would wait patiently for their owner outside New Court, occasionally rattling their chains. With practised cunning he would work surreptitiously on his collection in the bank, then put in a token appearance at Westminster before escaping to the Natural History Museum, of which he was a trustee for thirty years; or to his own ever-growing museum at Tring. But for all his erudition, the professionals persisted in regarding him as an amateur. He was elected a Fellow of the Royal Society in 1911, not for scientific achievement but for services to zoology: as if he had merely financed his worldwide expeditions. It was one of several slights inflicted on him by the scientific elite of the day.

Walter's private life, too, proved unexpectedly untidy. Lord Rothschild might have continued to tolerate a son whose heart was not in banking had not two grotesque failings come to light. For the past two years, it suddenly emerged in 1908, Walter had not attended to his mail. Instead, he had daily tossed it unopened into a large wicker laundry basket; and when that was full, he padlocked it, pushed it into a corner and set to work filling a second and a third and a fourth. When Lord Rothschild got wind of it, he summoned the confidential staff that dealt with the family's private affairs: known to the irreverent as the Department of Whores and Jockeys. His reliable son Charles and four clerks set to work, opening and sorting the accumulated correspondence. Labouring all day and some of the night, it took them six weeks. Then a shocked chief clerk reported to the senior partner that Walter's portfolio of investments consisted largely of worthless shares in obscure companies and that their owner was heavily in debt. The debts were paid but it was the end of his career as a banker. Although he continued to live on at Tring to the end of his life, his father treated him with cold, silent contempt and ultimately disinherited him except for a small annuity.

The cause of Walter's retreat from reality was probably unknown to his parents. For years, it emerges from the sympathetic biography of him written by his niece Miriam Rothschild, his emotional life had been of labyrinthine disorder. Two mistresses, by one of whom he had a child, fought each other for his favours. A third, a peeress, systematically blackmailed him for thirty years by threatening to tell his strait-laced mother of their defunct liaison. Only Lady Rothschild's death in 1935, two years before his own, defused that aristocratic conspiracy. In 1931 he was obliged to sell his collection of bird skins to the American Museum of Natural History for $225,000, a little less than a dollar apiece; but his learned publications and the Tring museum itself lived on.

Walter achieved fame of another sort when in 1917, two years after he had succeeded to his father's peerage as the second Lord Rothschild, he became the unexpected recipient of the Balfour Declaration: the British government's qualified expression of sympathy with Zionist aspirations that ensured the foundation of the State of Israel thirty-one years later. Chaim Weizmann, who was to become the first president of Israel, wrote to Walter, 'It will be rightly said that the name of the greatest house in Jewry was associated with the granting of the Magna Carta of Jewish liberation.' Thus did the black sheep of the family, a recent recruit to Zionism, assume a place in Jewish history that he had neither sought nor allowed to displace his lifelong passion for natural history.

Walter's younger brother Charles, the father of Victor, like many well-established English Jews of his time, was unmoved by Zionism. He was assimilationist, rationalist, cautiously left-wing. He did, however, share two traits of his elder brother: the instincts of a naturalist and a distaste for the restrictive routine of N. M. Rothschild & Sons. Unlike Walter, he felt obliged to subordinate them to the wishes of his father. There was not room for two cuckoos in the New Court nest. After Harrow and Cambridge, he dutifully went to work each day in the City from nine to five. Like his French cousin and fellow naturalist Henri de Rothschild, who developed instant chocolate powder and toothpaste tubes containing jam for use in the trenches during the First World War, Charles had an ingenious mind. He tried to enliven the staid practices and traditions of the family bank, but few of his suggestions found favour with the older partners. They turned down plans to finance a new invention called the gramophone disc; to process copper as well as gold and silver bullion; to open a branch in Japan. In 1915 Charles succeeded his father as senior partner, not without dissent from his hidebound uncles. But by then it was too late. In 1916 he was struck down by an epidemic of St Louis encephalitis, or inflammation of the brain, that killed 26,000 people in Britain alone; and although he lingered on until 1923, the intervening years were clouded by depression and increasing debility.

It makes the extent of Charles's studies as a naturalist all the more remarkable; for unlike his brother he had to confine them to evenings, weekends and six weeks of holiday a year. Only forty-six when he died, he had already become the pioneer of conservation, identifying and grading nature reserves throughout the country and founding a society for their upkeep and protection. His early death put back the cause by at least a generation, and it was not until sixty years later that his daughter Miriam won official approval of Capital Transfer Tax concessions for donors of nature reserves. He loved butterflies. Even as a schoolboy he published *The Lepidoptera of Harrow*, and in 1900 he fled the Rothschild belt in Buckinghamshire to restore the butterfly-haunted village of Ashton Wold, in Northamptonshire. He insisted in his Will on the destruction of all his maps showing where rare butterflies such as the Large Copper and the Swallowtail were to be found. He made a fine collection of the Iris and published more than 150 scientific papers.

On an expedition to the Nile he collected wild donkeys for Walter and made his own most important find: the plague-carrying flea which he called *Xendpsylla cheopis*, after the Pharoah Cheops. He went in for a little anthropology too: 'The faalin Arabs are weird folk and candidly I do not like them. They SEW their unmarried women folk up to ensure their keeping virtuous. They also preserve the penis of the crocodile in honey and eat it as an aphrodisiac.' His expeditions were on a spacious scale. Raymond Asquith, son of the future prime minister, spent a week in the Egyptian desert with him: 'We had twenty-two camels, 30 black men of various nations, and one Cingalese boy of 15 brought by Rothschild from Colombo on account of his skill in taxidermy.'

It was in pursuit of butterflies and the flea-bearing mice in the Carpathian mountains that Charles met his future wife, Rozsika von Wertheimstein, of a well-born but impoverished Jewish family. At their wedding in 1907, the bride's brother, Victor, turned up late after fighting a duel with rapiers. He was unscathed; his opponent lost an ear. In 1910, Charles and Rozsika called their only son after him. It was a portent.

CHAPTER I

Youth

Victor Rothschild's earliest recollection was of being sent into the garden by his father at the age of four to catch a gynandromorph Orange Tip: a rare butterfly, half male and half female, with its orange tip, therefore, on only one wing. Brought up, as he put it, with butterflies, birds, bees and insects instead of with human beings, he acquired that eye for accurate observation essential to any scientist. But there was nursery humour, too, at Ashton Wold. Like the architect Lutyens with his ritual breakfast refrain of 'Butter late than never', Charles had a limitless store of those puns and quips which delight children however often they are repeated. 'Mutton was cheap and venison was dear,' he would intone; or explain to an ecstatic audience that two mustelids were 'weasely distinguished and stoatly different'.

The idyll did not last. The outbreak of war in 1914 restricted international banking; and the death of Lord Rothschild in the following year left his son to bear an even heavier burden with only limited help from his ageing uncles and none from the younger members of the family on active service. He also became financial adviser to the Ministry of Munitions. On medical advice he left for Switzerland in 1916 to seek treatment for nervous instability and at times madness. His wife reluctantly remained in England to manage his affairs and to bring up four young children, all under ten years of age. In 1919 Charles returned to Tring; but his improvement was illusory. In 1923 he killed himself.

Victor, denied the firm guidance of a father from the age of six, proved more than a match for the governesses and tutors who seemed to fill the house. He even dared to take on his uncles. One of them was Major Charles Behrens, who married Charles Rothschild's sister, Evelina. When the Tring brass band came to play outside the house on public holidays, he would briskly spring to attention for the National Anthem. Victor used to pretend that every piece was the National Anthem, and punctiliously froze into an insolent parody of the soldier. Walter too was aware that his nephew mocked him. At luncheon one day, even his good nature could take no more. 'Mister Victor,' he bellowed, 'Mister Victor. You will be painted blue and yellow and exposed in the High Street.'

He faced more formidable resistance when sent away to school on the eve of his ninth birthday. 'Stanmore Park, I am convinced, was a hell hole,' Victor wrote in later years. It was a plausible complaint. The headmaster, the Reverend Vernon Royle, had played cricket for England and chose his teaching staff by their competence at the game. They belonged to the world of Evelyn Waugh's Captain Grimes. One of them could at will pepper the nose, cheeks and forehead of inattentive pupils with lumps of chalk, but always spared their eyes. Another dangled a delinquent by his hair from a second-floor classroom window. A third tried to remove a boy's appendix with a penknife, but only when he was drunk. A fourth, a kindly man, could no longer compete with school life and laid his head on a railway line.

Perhaps Victor was not on oath when telling these lurid tales in a short essay written more than half a century later. In any case, children are not always as easily shocked as their parents and can be as fiendishly unkind to each other as any schoolmaster. Victor was made aware of anti-Semitism for the first time soon after his arrival at Stanmore when another boy kicked his shins and called him 'a dirty little Jew'. It was all the more bewildering to a child brought up in an utterly assimilated family circle. If such bullying was common practice, he was too stoical to tell his parents. The letters he wrote home are no different from those of thousands of other small exiles, with their staple fare of football, cricket, food, aeroplanes, chilblains and foreign stamps.

His spelling was eccentric yet not without charm. 'I like the Jim very much and I have climbed a rope very nearly to the top...Thank you for the fruit which I apreshiate greatly and so do my friends.' One letter concludes abruptly, 'Now I must end up as I have no more to say.' That attachment to brevity was to remain with him for the next seventy years, both in correspondence and on the telephone.

A child of deceptively angelic countenance, Victor established an easy ascendancy over his three sisters. Miriam was two years older; Elizabeth, known as Liberty, and Kathleen, known as Nica, were each a year or two younger. It was no doubt to impress them that he performed some of his wildest escapades, hurling sausages down the lift shaft or making incendiary bombs out of match-heads. When he and a friend called Weil caught scarlet fever at school, both were brought back to Tring and boarded out in isolation in the home farm, looked after by the daughter of Dr Jordan, the curator of Uncle Walter's museum. Not caring for the food, they threw it on top of a cupboard; and when it began to stink, they set fire to the furniture. Then they gave Miss Jordan the slip during a walk and roamed the town spreading germs.

Like many boys at Stanmore Park, Victor went on to Harrow, a more cosmopolitan, less aristocratic Eton. His father, the first Rothschild to leave home for a public school, looked back on his own days as a Harrovian with repugnance. More than ten years after he had left, he wrote to a friend,

> If I ever have a son he will be instructed in boxing and ju-jitsu
> before he enters school, as Jew hunts such as I experienced are
> a very one-sided amusement, and there is apt to be a lack of
> sympathy between the hunters and the hunted.

Yet bitter memories did not deter him from returning to Harrow for at least one reunion supper or from arranging that his son should follow him there in 1924. Victims of persecution some-times grow fonder of their chains than they care to admit, and time marches hand in hand with mawkish forgiveness. Charles's schoolboy friend, the historian George Macaulay Trevelyan, was another Harrovian who gave a muted account of his misery when writing his memoirs late in life.

Although Victor was coached at home in cricket, tennis and even billiards, there is no record of his having learned boxing or ju-jitsu, much less of his being required to defend himself from racial insult He probably owed his immunity to a natural talent for cricket; athletes are the aristocrats of public schools and the playing fields their fiefdoms.

He was nevertheless fortunate. Christopher Tyerman's most recent and authoritative history of Harrow records pervasive anti-Semitism throughout the schooldays of both Charles and his son. It reflected not only the prejudices of parents and preparatory schools but also, in varying degrees, of the nation. Nor were the teaching staff free from it. Tyerman notes that in correspondence with the governing body the Head Master would unthinkingly refer to 'Jewish and foreign boys': what the author calls 'a significant association'.

Sometimes it could be vicious, even under the shadow of Nazi Germany. Ten years after Victor had left Harrow, a Jewish school monitor (or prefect) took his turn reading a lesson in chapel, doubtless looking on it as a monitorial rather than a spiritual duty. A few hours later he received from the school chaplain a crude and offensive letter condemning his conduct as 'absolutely and entirely indefensible', and hoping that it would never happen again. The boy's father, incandescent with outrage and distress, was prevented with difficulty by the Head Master from making the matter public. Tyerman notes that the Head Master was scarcely less furious: 'Whatever his own opinions, a charge of anti-Semitism coming at a time when he was trying to charm Old Harrovians, including two de Rothschilds, into bailing the school out of financial ruin was more than unhelpful.'

If Victor was spared the unhappiness of his father at Harrow, he did suffer another sort of haunting experience soon after his arrival at the age of fourteen. The manner in which Charles Rothschild had died a year or so earlier had been kept from him, as it had, by some arcane influence, from the newspapers. Among family and friends, however, the truth was known and whispered abroad. So it came to pass during some schoolboy quarrel that Victor was confronted by three knowing little monsters chanting that Rothschild's father had cut his throat. The tragedy itself, and the manner in which he had learned of it, left him with a lifelong fear of both madness and suicide.

Victor does not mention that searing episode in his brief memoir of childhood and youth written fifty years later. Desiring only to entertain, he confines himself to those perennial themes of public school life: sex, work and games.

'Eleven boys were fired from my house at Harrow school in my first term,' according to Victor. 'I did not know why at the time, there having been no indoctrination on such matters either at home or at Stanmore. This lacuna in my education was, however, soon filled; just a fact or a way of life according to inclination or particular circumstances.' There is no reason to doubt that such a purge of what Tyerman called 'ferocious buggery' took place; but it was probably later than Victor's first term. In the autumn of 1924 the school was still basking in the sleepy, hedonistic regime of the Reverend Lionel Ford's headmastership. Not until the beginning of 1926 was Ford succeeded by Dr Cyril Norwood, a new broom who swept very clean indeed.

'He knew, without doubt, most of what went on in the houses,' Norwood's obituarist has written, 'for he kept his ear very close to the ground, yet never, so to speak, to the keyhole.' Whatever the Head Master's prurient contortions, immoral boys left in droves; but if Victor's light-hearted account is to be believed, many remained to carry on their traditional pursuits. Had not the author of *The School for Scandal* boarded in The Grove, the very same house as Victor, a century and a half earlier?

A boy called Whidborne minor, whom I thought particularly beautiful, behaved very badly to an older boy, Hewlett, in the Music School. Whidborne told Hewlett that he could do whatever he liked to him. Hewlett complied with alacrity and imagination, upon which Whidborne screamed and shouted, asserting that he had been indecently assaulted. Hewlett left Harrow on the 4 p.m. train to London the next day. Beautiful as he was, Whidborne minor was treated with some reserve and caution from then onwards.

Even under the aseptic regime of Dr Norwood, Victor's own Byronic good looks attracted attention (although like the Harrovian poet he had a tendency to put on weight). But when a senior boy threatened to have him beaten by the head of the house for insolence unless he agreed to a homosexual relationship with his persecutor, Victor defied schoolboy convention by complaining to his housemaster.

In Mr C. G. Pope, Victor had found both a protector and friend. That the housemaster had acquired the nickname 'Cocky' speaks for itself. Himself an Old Harrovian, he had taken a First in Classics at Cambridge and won his blue for cricket before joining the Harrow staff in 1899. As second senior housemaster and master in charge of cricket, he belonged to that oligarchy of overmighty barons (to borrow Tyerman's image) who regularly forced Head Masters to Runnymede.

Among his few defeats was a failure to thwart Norwood's plan to phase out Harrow's own distinctive brand of football (which only Harrovians, Old Harrovians and Harrow masters could understand) in favour of Rugby football; a change which would enable Harrow to play other schools and so widen its social horizons. Pope barely recognised the existence of other schools, or indeed of his own colleagues unless they happened to be Old Harrovians.

He was impressed by Victor's courage in defying sexual harassment by senior boys and pleased to have so promising a cricketer in The Grove. Chastely infatuated, he indulged his pupil in small matters of school routine, allowed him extra leave at Tring and Ashton Wold, sometimes accompanying him there. Miriam, who watched the relationship develop, noted how her brother quietly undermined Pope's sense of discipline. 'Victor was the greatest of *animateurs*,' she told the present writer, 'but also the most destructive.'

It went to his head. For although Victor shone at biology, he showed only disrespect for the Punic Wars and other traditional themes of Harrow education. At the end of one term there came a warning: 'Must do better if he wishes to stay.' Rozsika came to her son's rescue. Throughout the holidays she set him a daily essay on

Roman history, corrected it herself and sent him back to school well-equipped to stay the course.

It was but one triumph of her widowhood She was already running three houses and the Tring estate, bringing up four children, looking after a helpless Walter and an ageing Lady Rothschild: and all on an income depleted by two payments of death duties within eight years. By shrewd investment she nevertheless doubled the value of Victor's trust funds during his minority; and in defiance of old NM's injunction against female interference in the transactions of the bank, she was not infrequently consulted by her husband's successors.

Rozsika's failing was an inability to interest Victor in the running of the estate or the contents of the family houses. Nor, with five languages at her command, did she instil into her son more than a word or two of German and some Churchillian French. She devoured books and newspapers, and had a passion for Proust, but allowed Victor to remain a boisterous ruffian. Except in Latin and Greek and a little science, his education did not really begin until Cambridge.

Meanwhile he ascended the ladder of school life, acquiring privileges which less Spartan communities take for granted: a weekly hot bath, bedroom slippers, permission to close the lavatory door. In time he became a member of the Harrow cricket XI, an apotheosis scarcely ever to be matched by the triumphs of later years. It was not only a passport to popularity; he loved the game for itself and was coached by a professional at home. The veteran used to recall that when he bowled to the great Ranjitsinhji in the nets at Cambridge there was a gold watch on each stump; he never got one. Three weeks before his nineteenth birthday, Victor rang down the curtain on his Harrow career with a stylish display against Eton. George Lyttelton wrote in *The Times* of 13 July 1929,

Rothschild proceeded to play his first innings at Lord's as if it were his favourite ground and the Eton bowling his special delight. His 43 was in truth a gem of an innings. All the orthodox strokes appeared in it, played in the most orthodox manner. He never hurried; he never guessed; he took no risk. But he

32

scored off a very large proportion of the balls he received, and when he played outside an off-break of Hazlerigg's and pulled it into his wicket he had scored three-quarters of the runs without giving an inkling to the bowlers that he had a chink in his armour. At the other end Rattigan was overshadowed, as indeed all other batsmen were of either side.

There were to be few other occasions when Terence Rattigan found himself out of the limelight.

That same summer, Victor was invited to play for Northamptonshire. 'Rothschild's striped cap when he was hitting the ball through the covers', *The Times* again recorded, 'was not needed to betray the school where he learnt his cricket.' He was praised for both the skill and courage with which he despatched the body-line bowling of Larwood for Nottinghamshire and Macdonald for Lancashire: as much a deliberate attempt to terrorise a batsman as to capture his wicket – and in the days before players donned the armour of a mediaeval man at arms. Over the next three years he played fewer than a dozen matches in first-class cricket, then abandoned the game to concentrate on his academic career. It is said that he might have been awarded a Cambridge blue had he shown less truculence towards the university captain.

Both at Harrow and afterwards, his sister Miriam, herself an accomplished cricketer, undertook to be his manager. Before a school match she would arrive bearing what she called his medicine: a disguised bottle of brandy. 'Having taken a tot or two,' he confessed, 'I always felt I could make a century.' And when he went on tour with his county team, she sometimes insisted on sharing his hotel bedroom in the belief that a fellow player of her brother's had designs on him.

While Victor was achieving near deification on the cricket pitch of Lord's in the summer of 1929, nemesis overtook another mentor and guardian. 'Cocky' Pope had long thought himself immune from the conventions and courtesies of school life, displaying a particular contempt for the Head Master's edicts. As master in charge of cricket he quite properly accompanied the XI on away matches. What enraged Norwood was the hospitality he dispensed on the return journey, delivering the boys to their houses late and tipsy. Norwood warned him that he must curb his convivial instincts on pain of dismissal. Believing himself to be invulnerable, Pope persisted in his genial ways and was astounded to be dismissed at a term's notice. His appeal to the governors failed, in spite of support from boys, parents and Old Harrovians. By the end of 1929 he had gone.

Although not the oldest of Cambridge colleges, Trinity is the largest, the richest and the grandest. A young nobleman, asked in the hunting field which was his college, replied with a shrug, 'Dunno. Trinity, I suppose.' It was here that Victor spent some of his most contented years as an undergraduate and later as a Fellow. For the rest of his life, too, dignified by an honorary Fellowship, he lived almost in the shade of the college, savouring its vibrant gossip and intrigues. He was proud of the association and made several substantial benefactions, which did not always evoke as much gratitude as he would have liked.

He amused himself and his friends by choosing two teams of Trinity men to play a celestial cricket match of the intellect. The first XI consisted of Sir Isaac Newton (captain), Lord Rutherford, Bertrand Russell, Francis Bacon, Richard Porson, James Clerk Maxwell, Alfred Tennyson, Sir J. J. Thomson, Srinivasa Ramanujan, Sir Frederick Gowland Hopkins and Lord Byron. The second XI boasted Lord Macaulay (captain), John Dryden, A. E. Housman, Richard Bentley, W. M. Thackeray, Ludwig Wittgenstein, G. E. Moore, Sir James Frazer, Alfred North Whitehead, G. H. Hardy and J. E Littlewood.

No women were to be found in the courts of Trinity except for the formidable Lady Thomson, who presided over the Master's Lodge and almost up to the eve of the Second World War insisted that any undergraduate fortunate enough to dine there should wear a white tie and tailcoat.

A late developer, Victor began to realise how lazy he had been at Harrow and how in future he must train himself to use his brain, to acquire the art of concentration, to work towards a set purpose, to harness his explosive intellectual energy to a disciplined regime. He showed such promise in his early months at Cambridge, reading for the Natural Sciences Tripos, that the Professor of Zoology, Stanley Gardiner, said to him after one of his lectures, 'I imagine that what you have heard must seem very elementary to you. But you needn't take notes – just put your hands in your pockets.' That foolish incitement to idleness almost undid his clever pupil. One of the few letters Victor kept from his undergraduate days was a warning from the Dean, the Fellow of the college responsible for discipline:

> A rumour reaches me that you are giving a party today on a somewhat more ambitious scale than most are. As we are at the end of term, and consequently people are likely to be in a more than averagely lighthearted mood, and as your hospitality is likely to be worthy of the traditions of your family, I am writing just a line to say that I hope you won't overdo it in the way of pressing drinks on people who have already had enough, as I don't want to have to deal with the after-effects in the way of noisy disturbance.
>
> In other respects my best wishes for a successful party.

In time, it became clear to Victor that he might not do as well as expected in the testing ground of part one of the Tripos. He therefore asked for a special dispensation to begin the research for a doctorate without first having to take a degree. This was granted. So far, so good; let others scramble for the lesser honours. Then the university changed its regulations at short notice; Rothschild would after all have to take a degree before embarking on a pro-gramme of research. As he had been misled into neglecting the syl-labus of the Natural Sciences Tripos, he decided instead to read for an ordinary or pass degree in Physiology, French and English, and to complete it in one year before returning to the enticement of the biophysical laboratory. A pass in Physiology held no terrors for a budding zoologist. His French, albeit spoken with a Harrovian accent, was now respectable; he nevertheless enlisted the Reverend Hugh Stewart, Fellow of Trinity and an authority on Pascal, as well as a recently elected Fellow and art historian named Anthony Blunt. For a tutor in English, Victor knew just the man.

George Rylands, known to his friends as Dadie, was eight years his senior. A scholar of both Eton and King's College, Cambridge, he had taken a starred First Class in the English Tripos and been elected a Fellow of King's in 1927. He had already made his mark as an interpreter of Shakespeare and a theatrical producer of imagination and insight. As an undergraduate he had caught the eye of A. C. Benson, man of letters and Master of Magdalene College, always on the alert for good-looking, clever young men. 'Rylands,' the author of 'Land of Hope and Glory' wrote in his diary, 'a most charming, handsome, eager, unaffected boy, gracefully puritanical.' Benson paid his debts and encouraged him to write and teach rather than accept a partnership in the family cotton-broking business. (It was a cousin by marriage who in 1892 bought the magnificent library of the fifth Earl Spencer for £250,000 and presented it to the City of Manchester; later it was merged with the University Library to form the John Rylands Library.)

Virginia Woolf, who employed him for a few months in 1924 at the Hogarth Press, packing up parcels and oiling the machinery, has ensured his immortality. In *A Room of One's Own*, she describes the set in King's which he occupied for seventy-two years and the memorable luncheon party she attended in that Bloomsbury time capsule. The familiar words bear repeating. 'The lunch on this occasion', she wrote, 'began with soles, sunk in a deep dish, over which the college cook had spread a counterpane of the whitest cream, save that it was branded here and there with brown spots like the spots on the flanks of a doe...' At ninety, Dadie Rylands remained robustly unsentimental, commenting gruffly that if Virginia's description was accurate, something must have gone very wrong in the kitchen that day.

Such was the man who tutored Victor in English literature and became a lifelong friend. His methods were unconventional. After Victor had produced his first essay, Dadie said, 'Whenever I have to read an essay which begins, "Addison was born in 1672", I tear it up.' This, the culprit confessed, led him to change one set of platitudes for another. His tutor similarly proposed that one of the set books, Thackeray's *History of Henry Esmond, Esquire*, was so boring that Victor had better destroy his notes on it. This was done with fingers stained by strawberries and cream, for Dadie liked to combine tutorials with country picnics.

During one Cambridge vacation they went further afield in Victor's Bugatti, ultimate toy of the rich undergraduate, in which he established a record covering the sixty miles from Cambridge to the heart of London in forty-nine minutes. Now they motored down to Monte Carlo. Their high-minded talk of English literature was relieved at Victor's instigation by a visit to a brothel in Rheims, where their obvious nervousness prompted the madame to break them in gently with a home movie. 'Oh I can't bear it,' Dadie moaned, but Victor caught him peering at it through his fingers. Dadie had his revenge when taking him to see Somerset Maugham at Cap Ferrat. A stroll in the garden with the novelist's resident lover, Gerald Haxton, convinced an alarmed Victor that the purpose of their visit had been misunderstood.

They were accompanied to Monte Carlo by Arthur Marshall, a young schoolmaster at Oundle who shared Dadie's love of the stage and was later to spend four years as Victor's private secretary before becoming a much-acclaimed broadcaster, essayist and critic. The three friends loved pranks and wheezes, pillow fights and practical jokes. They would throw each other's clothes out of the hotel window, then haul them up with concealed strings; set fire to each other's newspapers and pour wine down each other's necks. Victor played roulette at the casino for the first time in his life and paid the bill for all three at the Hôtel de Paris with his winnings.

On returning from Monte Carlo, he settled down to fifteen hours' work a day and sailed through the papers for his ordinary degree, scoring a recorded triple First Class: results so impressive as to evoke wonder, even suspicion, in the examiners. To mark their joint triumph, Victor presented Dadie with a second-folio Shakespeare to be placed next to the first folio given to him by Maynard Keynes. A lifelong friendship was not the only by-product of those tutorials. Dadie also fired Victor with the passion for book collecting. 'In those days', Dadie later said, 'he talked of books with all the enthusiasm of a schoolboy who has suddenly discovered stamps or cigarette cards.' Ultimately he formed the best collection of eighteenth-century English books, manuscripts and bindings in private hands and presented most of it to Trinity College: a bibliomanic adventure to be described in a later chapter.

There remained one more obstacle before Victor could pursue a career of scientific research. At his mother's pleading he agreed to work at least for a trial period in N. M. Rothschild & Sons. It was a penance earlier undergone by both his uncle and his father, each a scientist rather than a banker at heart. Walter had stuck it for eighteen of his most creative years before fleeing to his natural history museum at Tring; the more dutiful Charles had remained in New Court as long as his precarious health allowed. Victor lasted only six months. He was not in the least interested, as he put it, in moving money from Point A, where it is, to Point B, where it is needed. He began, in fact, not in the counting house at New Court, but at the Royal Mint Refinery, a wholly owned subsidiary of NMR from 1852 to 1967, where gold and silver were refined for overseas governments before being made into coins at the nearby Royal Mint. Victor found it boring and depressing, although he enjoyed the annual saturnalia of burning the wooden staircases and workmen's sabots to extract the gold dust.

For gold itself he retained an atavistic respect. It was said of his grandfather that he kept £1 million of bullion in the vaults of New Court; rather than earn interest on that large sum, he preferred the quiet confidence that bullion inspired at moments of trouble or doubt. Victor collected gold objects of the finest workmanship, most of them too valuable to be displayed. He also liked an occasional gamble on the fluctuating price of gold; the index, his friends noted, could sometimes be read in his face. One day a well-informed City man told him that the time had come to buy.

'How much?' Victor asked.

'£250,000 will do,' the expert pronounced.

Victor told the bank to go ahead with the purchase on his private account.

'But it is all you have,' he was warned.

He nevertheless insisted that his instructions be carried out. The price of gold soared and he doubled his money. On the day he recounted this story, some years after it had happened, we were lunching in a private room at New Court. In the centre of the table, instead of flowers, was an ingot of gold, of an unattractive, greenish hue. 'If any of you can carry it away in one hand, you can keep it,' Victor announced. None could; for although small it was deceptively heavy. The joke had a sequel. A knowing but short-sighted guest, having heard of Victor's whim, stretched out his hand at luncheon one day and found himself clutching half a pound of butter.

The gold of the Nibelung, however, made no appeal to a young man in his early twenties and Victor was allowed to return to Cambridge. There he settled down in a basement laboratory to investigate the nature of fertilisation. One lesson in self-help he learned early. He asked his supervisor, Dr (later Sir) James Gray, if the Department of Zoology would supply him with a valve volt-meter to measure small voltages in biological material. No, he was told. If he needed a valve voltmeter he must make it himself. So he took a course in electrical engineering and produced exactly what was required with his own hands. He made another discovery. When required by Gray to examine the electrical properties of frogs' eggs, he found he knew nothing about electricity. On enquiry he was directed to the latest edition of the *Admiralty Handbook of Wireless Telegraphy*, to which Lieutenant-Commander Lord Louis Mountbatten had contributed diagrams and explanations of admirable clarity.

In 1935 Trinity elected Victor Rothschild to a Prize Fellowship for which he had submitted a dissertation (tidied up by Dadie Rylands) on the biophysics of reproduction. That was the least of the ordeal. Successful candidates had to attend a Fellowship admis-sion dinner presided over by the Master. Sir J. J. Thomson had not only discovered the electron (his first and more robust name for it was the corpuscle), but could command words of welcome that no guest ever forgot. Of Anthony Blunt, elected in 1932, he observed that it was the first time the college had given a Fellowship to someone who specialised in the history of art; he was confident it would not occur again. As for Rothschild, after a few disparaging remarks about those who pricked frogs' eggs, he went on to con-gratulate the college on making no distinction between the 'exceedingly rich', pointing at Victor, and the 'very, very poor', pointing at another successful candidate. Describing that nightmare initiation, Victor went on to relate how on the following day, walking through the Great Court of Trinity, he had met the Master who greeted him saying, 'What relation are you to the Rothschild to whom we gave a Fellowship last night?' It is a story told of other Heads of House in Oxford and Cambridge alike.

Victor's research exposed him to many glutinous jokes about the eggs of frogs, trout and sea urchins. Not even his sovereign spared him. Victor was summoned to dine in knee breeches one evening with the Liberal statesman Lord Crewe whose wife, a daughter of Lord Rosebery, was thus a Rothschild cousin. The guest of honour, King George V, had as always been well briefed. 'Ah, Rothschild,' he roared, 'don't take frogs' eggs into the bank with you.' This pleasantry the King repeated throughout the evening to his own satisfaction.

More to Victor's taste was an occasional invitation to Fort Belvedere, the country retreat of the Prince of Wales, later King Edward VIII. One weekend the guests were made to test a new sort of fire escape by hurling themselves from the roof at the end of a rope. 'I had the courage to refuse,' Victor boasted.

The most junior of Prize Fellows was not popular in his own college Some colleagues resented that a rich young Rothschild had been allowed to embark on research without first undergoing the hard slog of the Tripos examination. Even the most charitable thought that he had been elected on promise rather than achievement; they would not have grieved overmuch had he come a cropper. What few could have known is how dissatisfied Victor remained with the quality of his early research work. 'Much of what I wrote was wrong and wild,' the joint author of *Spontaneous Rhythmical Impedance Changes in the Trout's Egg* afterwards confessed. Even on his return to Trinity at the end of the war, he felt overwhelmed by the distinction of the Nobel Prizemen with whom he was expected to talk on easy terms. His refusal to dine on high table provoked a stern letter from the Vice-Master, Professor H. A. Hollond:

I remember well how keen you were, when a young man, to be successful in the Fellowship election, and it seems a great pity that having been successful you should seem now not to value that success at all. I do not see that your complete abstention from any social relations with the college can fail to produce that impression.

In his reply, Victor pleaded that in such company he suffered from shyness; but also that he knew his dissertation to have been unworthy of the college and his election a stroke of luck – a view, he felt, that others shared. Hollond wrote with kindly reassurance. He sympathised with Victor's shyness. As for the dissertation, he continued,

It is only in the case of a small percentage of men elected to Fellowship that luck does not enter into the election, because the merits are so clear. I have heard of several cases of men feeling sore after having been unlucky but never of one of a man feeling sore after having been lucky!

In case it may be of any comfort to you I may add that I have *never* heard anybody express the opinion that your election was a mistake, as one has heard it said after some elections.

With some of the senior Fellows, Victor did manage to establish friendly relations. G. M. Trevelyan, elected to succeed Sir J. J. Thomson as Master of Trinity, encouraged his book collecting. Bertrand Russell startled him as grace was being said before dinner by observing; 'Why do they continue to have this sort of rubbish nowadays?' After the war Victor persuaded him to present to Trinity the manuscript of his broadcast on the hydrogen bomb, sending the old philosopher a dozen bottles of whisky as a douceur. 'One of the few great men I have known,' was Victor's affectionate verdict on him. Then there was Peter Kapitza, who was allowed to leave the Soviet Union to work with Rutherford at the Cavendish Laboratory on magnetism at very low temperatures until recalled by Stalin in 1934. He was elected a Fellow of Trinity (as well as of the Royal Society); Victor enjoyed their rivalry at three-dimensional Peg'ity, a sophisticated version of a popular board-game.

Most willing of all to bridge the generation gap was Maynard Keynes, who by daring speculation during his Cambridge years repaired both his own finances and those of King's College. On one of several occasions when he had wrongly predicted the course of the economy, his young friend pressed him for an explanation. 'Victor,' Keynes replied, 'I made a mistake.' That marked him out as another great man.

Among his contemporaries, Victor did not readily acquire close friends. In answer to his mother's anxious enquiries a year or so after he had left school for Trinity, he was able to flourish a list of six non-Harrovians. Dick Sheepshanks was later killed as a Reuters correspondent in the Spanish Civil War and Gerald Cuthbert as an RAF pilot in 1940. Sammy (later Viscount) Hood rose high in the Diplomatic Service; Garrett Moore (later Earl of Drogheda) became a newspaper executive and chairman of the Royal Opera House, Covent Garden. The two remaining intimates were Guy Burgess, who fled to Russia with his fellow diplomat and Soviet spy Donald Maclean in 1951, and Anthony Blunt, publicly exposed as a Soviet agent in 1979. Their treachery cast a shadow over a whole generation of Cambridge men and haunted Victor to the grave.

'A clever, dissolute young man called Guy Burgess with whom my mother got on very well' was how Victor described his friend in *Meditations of a Broomstick*, published more than twenty-five years after his defection to Moscow. Too much has been made of the supposed affinity between Rozsika Rothschild and the engaging undergraduate. He is even said, on dubious evidence, to have managed her stock exchange portfolio for a fee. Not only was she exceptionally competent to look after the family fortunes; she also had at her disposal the entire establishment of N. M. Rothschild with its experience of the market and worldwide sources of intelligence. How unlikely it is that she needed Burgess's 'academic political analysis' to persuade her of the imminent rise in armament shares; or that, as Tom Driberg, journalist and Labour MP, asserted, he had inside knowledge of the nationalisation of Latin-American railways. Victor's sister Miriam, a shrewd judge of character and reliable witness, dismisses Burgess as 'charm without backbone, all bubble and squeak'. Her mother, she says, would listen indulgently to him during his visits to Tring, but would take no notice of his financial advice. She did, however, subscribe with amused scepticism to a City tipping-sheet partly written by him. And she made him a small monthly allowance, as she did to others in need of money, disguised as a retainer.

Certainly he was both clever and dissolute. Two years younger than Victor, Guy was destined to follow his father into the Royal Navy, but defective eyesight cut short his training. So he returned to Eton where he was tutored by Robert Birley, winning the coveted Rosebery prize for history and a scholarship to Trinity. Birley's regard for his pupil, however, was somewhat dimmed when he called on Burgess in his college rooms and, enthusiastic bibliophile that he was, made for the bookshelves. Alongside the Marxist textbooks he was dismayed to find an 'extraordinary array of explicit and extremely unpleasant pornographic literature'. Some may be tempted to suggest that the schoolmaster who came to be known as 'Red Robert' was responsible for Burgess's Marxist beliefs. It is a false trail. Birley was the mildest of reformers and the nickname grotesquely inappropriate. It was foisted on him as educational adviser to the Control Commission for Germany in 1947–9. A foolish Old Etonian officer who came to call on him, noticing the bearded portrait of Brahms hanging on the wall of Birley's outer office, mistook it for a likeness of Karl Marx. The gibe stuck.

But Burgess's admiration for his former history tutor owed nothing to a shared political allegiance. It is a measure of his affection that within hours of leaving England for ever in 1951, he went down to call on Birley, by now Head Master of Eton. Ostensibly the purpose of that final pilgrimage was to discuss whether he should take on the task of completing Lady Gwendolen Cecil's unfinished life of her father Lord Salisbury, the last great Conservative prime minister of the Victorian Age. Could black comedy go further? More probably it was a sentimental farewell to Eton. Throughout his life he cherished an emotional attachment to the school not uncommon among those who have spent their lotus years in that sleepy valley. Rarer today than before

the war, it owes something to the beauty of the mediaeval architecture, of meadow and river, more to those romantic friendships
that irradiate youth but inhibit maturity. For Burgess, Eton was to
remain a distant prospect; but once established by his new masters
in Moscow, he begged any of his friends contemplating a visit to
replenish his stock of Old Etonian ties.

One did not have to explore Burgess's bookshelves to discover
his sexual preferences and political creed. Goronwy Rees, whose
academic career was ultimately ruined by their friendship, first met
him in Oxford, where he was staying with Maurice Bowra:

> That evening he talked a good deal about painting and to me it
> seemed that what he said was both original and sensitive and,
> for one so young, to show an unusually wide knowledge of the
> subject. His conversation had the more charm because he was
> very good looking in a boyish, athletic, very English way; it
> seemed incongruous that almost everything he said made it quite
> clear that he was a homosexual and a communist.

Burgess was an unpromising disciple of both those pre-war conspiracies. During an undergraduate mission of goodwill to Moscow
in that same summer of 1932, he was found lying dead drunk in
the Park of Rest and Culture. As for his sexual life, Rees called it
'very active, very promiscuous and somewhat squalid'. Burgess rel-
ished pimping, too, on behalf of friends with special needs; he
spoke of such activities, Rees continues, 'with a kind of amused
candour, from which any sense of shame was entirely lacking'.
Michael Straight, another Communist sympathiser at Cambridge
who later betrayed Anthony Blunt to the British intelligence services as a Soviet spy, has painted an even grimmer portrait of
Burgess in his self-serving autobiography:

> With his curly hair, his sensual mouth, his bright blue eyes, his
> cherubic air, he seemed at first sight to embody in himself the
> ideal of male beauty that the Apostles revered. Then, on a closer
> look, you noticed the details: the black-rimmed fingernails; the
> stained forefinger in which he gripped his perpetual cigarette

stub; the dark, uneven teeth; the slouch; the open fly. If he was angelic, you sensed that he was a fallen angel.

Burgess's *dégringolade* – and there was worse to come – evoked neither disapproval nor embarrassment from Victor. He was capti-vated by Burgess's youthful sparkle, his skill in dialectic, his irrev-erence, his charm. Winston Churchill, too, found him engaging. In 1935 Burgess joined the BBC, having abandoned Cambridge without a degree after a collapse that left him unable or unwilling to face the examiners. A producer of parliamentary talks, he went down to Chartwell at the time of the Munich settlement and returned with a leather-bound volume of speeches, *Arms and the Covenant*, inscribed 'To Guy Burgess, from Winston S. Churchill, to confirm his admirable sentiments'. The young Soviet agent wrote gracefully to thank the future prime minister for the book and the inscription: 'The one unfortunately is already historic for the world, the other will be for me.'

Although wholly heterosexual in his own adult life, Victor regarded homosexual practices in others as both acceptable and amusing: perhaps just a shade too humorous at a time when they still infringed the criminal law. He devoted several Rabelaisian paragraphs of his autobiographical essay to the homosexual under-world of his schooldays at Harrow. In the same vein he wrote of Burgess's political deviations at Cambridge:

Perhaps he was a Soviet agent even then. As a matter of fact, I thought Burgess might have fascist or pro-Nazi inclinations because of his friendship with a good-looking, fair-haired under-graduate at Trinity College called Micky Burn, who was inordi-nately interested in the Hitler Youth. I now suspect that the friendship between Burgess and Burn was not political.

Victor may have meant that the friendship was not wholly politi-cal. It has since been suggested that Burgess infiltrated himself into the pre-war Anglo-German Fellowship both to conceal his contin-uing dedication to Communism and to prepare reports for the Rothschilds on the progress of British pro-Nazi associations.

On hearing of Burgess's defection to Moscow in 1951, Victor recorded neither astonishment nor sadness nor sense of betrayal. That sort of farce was only to be expected after a spate of indiscretions had brought him to the brink of dismissal from the Foreign Service, to which he had transferred from the BBC.

How different was Victor's reaction when in 1964 his former colleagues in MI5 confided to him that Anthony Blunt had confessed to having been a Soviet agent for many years. The blow, he recorded in his second volume of essays, *Random Variables* published in 1984, was 'devastating, crushing and beyond belief. I found it almost impossible to believe and childishly, felt like telephoning Blunt to ask him if this appalling news was true.' Such was Victor's epitaph on a friendship more intense, more trusting, more intellectual and ultimately more damaging than his association with Burgess.

Anthony Blunt, three years older than Victor, was a son of the chaplain of the British embassy church in Paris; one of his brothers became drawing master at Eton and an authority on botanical illustration, the other a merchant banker and noted numismatist. From Marlborough, a Victorian public school with a clerical flavour, he won a scholarship to Trinity College where he read first Mathematics, at which he failed to shine, then French and German. He tried in vain for a Fellowship at King's, Maynard Keynes having taken a dislike to him both as a Marxist and as a man. But in 1932 he was elected to a Fellowship at Trinity on the strength of a dissertation on artistic theory in Italy and France during the Renaissance and seventeenth century. With a growing reputation as an art historian he migrated to London in 1936, where he lectured at both the Warburg and the Courtauld Institutes. Let Victor himself speak of their early friendship:

I think I first got to know Blunt about a year after I went to Cambridge as an undergraduate. Like many others, I was immediately impressed by his outstanding intellectual abilities, both artistic and mathematical, and by what, for want of a better phrase, I must call his high moral or ethical principles. I knew or suspected he was a homosexual, but I saw no reason why this characteristic should conflict with the others mentioned above.

When I refer to his high moral or ethical principles, I mean that he was one of those rare persons, like Leonard Woolf, to whom I might have gone for advice when in doubt about some particular course of action.

Blunt seemed to me a somewhat cold and ascetic figure but with a sense of humour. He was an excellent conversationalist and a habitual party-goer. I don't ever remember having seen him the worse for drink though in later years I heard that he drank a great deal.

I was very ignorant about politics and ideologies in those days, being, so I thought, too busy with my scientific work, sport and social life to have much time for anything else. I remember, very vaguely, once thinking that an article about porcelain by Anthony Blunt in the *Spectator* or the *New Statesman* – I forget which – dragged in Marxism in a way I thought unnecessary and irrelevant.

In contrast to Burgess's perpetual promise of youth, Blunt passed imperceptibly from childhood to middle age. Miriam was 'stunned' by the erudition of her brother's friend. 'I remember going round an exhibition with him,' she recalled. 'He instantly noticed that two pictures by Derain had been hung in the wrong chronological order. But I never liked him. There was iced coffee in his veins.' Blunt's high moral or ethical principles do not seem to have been strained by the demands he made on his rich friend. He asked for and received more than one valuable book from the Rothschild collection. And when in 1932 he spotted for sale in Paris what he recognised as a Poussin, he touched Victor for a loan. It may have been £80 or perhaps £100; Victor could not remember fifty years later. But in those days either sum was substantial for a young man, worth between £2000 and £2500 in the currency of the late 1990s. Recalling his father's precept that lending money to a friend causes bad blood, Victor handed over the purchase price of the picture as a gift. On Blunt's death in 1983, *Eliezer and Rebecca* was inherited by a male companion, and ultimately sold for £192,500. 'Perhaps', Victor wrote in the following year, 'I shall soon see the Poussin, *for the first time*, in the Fitzwilliam Museum, Cambridge.' Those four words I have italicised imply an uncharacteristic lack of curiosity throughout the intervening half-century; or perhaps Victor, whose punctuation could be erratic, had inserted a pair of misleading commas.

There need be no reservations about another sentence from the apologia he wrote in 1984: his claim to have been 'very ignorant about politics and ideologies'. Like many young men and women of his time he was left-wing. Socialism, as he saw it, was more encouraging towards science than was Conservatism, less tinged by anti-Semitism. But he was too enthralled by biological studies, sport and a convivial social life to become a political animal. Nor is there a scrap of reliable evidence that Marxist friends – and he had others who were not Marxist – either converted him to their cause or lured him into joining a conspiracy of Soviet agents. A classic victim of guilt by association, he was exposed in later years to innuendo in the press and vilification in Parliament. That sordid tale must await another chapter.

The origin of the accusation lay in his membership of the Apostles, the oldest, most secretive and most self-conscious of Cambridge discussion groups. Blunt was elected in 1928, Burgess and Rothschild four years later. In an analysis of the twenty-six members elected to the society between 1927 and 1937, it has been estimated that twenty of them were left-wing socialists, Marxist sympathisers, Marxists or committed Communists. Four of them later confessed to being Soviet spies. That is a remarkable concentration in a student body no more than a fraction of 1 per cent Marxist. In the context of the 1930s it was understandable. The Apostles offered both a forum for uninhibited argument and a haven for beliefs that could thrive only in the shadows. In the course of the decade the growing menace of Nazi Germany and the Republican cause in the Spanish Civil War united every shade of left-wing sentiment. Goronwy Rees described the contortions of the intellectual Establishment:

To be a communist, with the declared intention of subverting and destroying the fabric of existing society, was to occupy a respectable, and respected position; the difference between a communist and a liberal was merely one of those differences of opinion which arise between the best of friends and which both find mutually stimulating. The underlying assumption was that both shared the same humane and enlightened purpose, and that only questions of method were at issue; so that when, for instance, Stephen Spender wrote a book called *Forward from Liberalism*, it was regarded as perfectly natural that the forward movement should be in the direction of communism. Indeed, the communist in certain respects commanded the admiration, and almost the envy, of the liberal, because he was willing to risk more in the cause to which the liberal was committed.

It counted for nothing in their eyes that Fascism and Communism had much in common: dictatorship, the police state, religious persecution, rigid censorship, corrupt bureaucracy, economic shortage and mass murder. There could be no friend to the right, no enemy to the left. A few fought bravely in Spain, sustained no doubt by Apostolic support from the sidelines or by Michael Straight's reports of drinking sessions in Trinity which always ended 'by our standing in a circle and singing *Arise ye Prisoners of Starvation* while poor old Housman gnashed his teeth in impotent rage in the room above'.

Victor was more fastidious. Throughout his seven years in Cambridge before the war he delivered only two papers to the Apostles, compared with Blunt's eleven. There is contemporary evidence of his antipathy to Marxism in a letter he wrote to Maynard Keynes, elected to the Apostles a whole generation earlier. Although it is undated, a reference to Victor's marriage at the end of 1933 places it in the first weeks of 1934. Victor's cousin Anthony de Rothschild had lent Palace House, Newmarket, to the young couple for their honeymoon. It was from there that he wrote to his friend and mentor,

Dear Maynard,

Barbara and I very much hope that you will come to dinner here next Sunday, with Lydia, of course, if she is in Cambridge. If not you alone, I hope.

If there is any transport difficulty, it will be perfectly simple to pick you up at King's or elsewhere and drop you back.

It seems a long time since I have seen you, though a short time since we were married.

We talk endlesssly in the Society about Communism which is rather dull. Guy, Alister and Richard Davies speak with shining eyes and sweaty forehead about this all-pervading topic, vehemently but somewhat illogically, it seems to me. (I believe I have discovered a fallacy in the whole racket; no doubt you could tell me a hundred.)

Hugh Sykes-Davies prates endlessly about Sadism and Swinburne which I believe is due to the new Italian book [The Romantic Agony, by Mario Praz]; *while Grey Walter and I content ourselves with obscure jokes about electric currents. The fact is an atmosphere of decadence is appearing and we need your presence.*

But your presence here on Sunday evening would be just as delightful.

Yours ever,

Victor R.

Not for him what Hugh Trevor-Roper called 'perhaps the only religion which can still totally paralyse the mental and moral faculties of its converts and cause them to commit any turpitude, and to suffer any indignity, for its sake'.

At heart a Rothschild, even though he played it down among his intellectual friends, Victor was not at ease in those frowsty Apostolic conclaves. The Communist party, he thought, was something of a joke and certainly beneath his dignity. Young, well-born, clever, hardworking, rich, handsome and athletic, he did not care to fritter away his golden years applying Anthony Blunt's Marxist principles to the physiology of the trout's egg, rescuing a sodden Guy Burgess from Moscow's Park of Rest and Culture or singing the 'Internationale' with Michael Straight.

Soon after I wrote these words, a paragraph in a Sunday newspaper caught my eye. Rupert Allason, at the time a Conservative

MP better known as the spy writer Nigel West, was reported to have said, 'I have absolutely incontrovertible evidence that Lord Rothschild was a member of the CP.' On my asking to examine his evidence, Allason replied,

> My source concerning Victor's membership of the CPGB [Communist Party of Great Britain] is a surprising one: my wife's maternal uncle, a distinguished paediatrician who was up at Cambridge with Victor and was also a member of the CPGB! He well remembers Victor 'going underground'. I would be delighted to introduce you or pass on a letter to him from you. He...is, perhaps understandably, slightly reticent (though not embarrassed) about his political activities in those days.

So one afternoon I called by appointment on the distinguished paediatrician, whose name I withhold at Rupert Allason's request. In his consulting rooms in Wimpole Street I found a charming, rosy-cheeked man approaching eighty, somewhat bent but alert and forthcoming. He said he had gone up to Trinity College in 1935 and joined the Communist party in the following year, having been recruited by Denis William Ewer, afterwards Professor of Zoology at the University of Ghana. (Ewer was the son of William Norman Ewer, a Communist journalist who later transferred his allegiance to Labour.)

The paediatrician remained a clandestine Communist until, like many of his contemporaries, he was repelled by the Hitler–Stalin compact of 1939 and made a clean break with the party. How well, I asked, had he known Victor, who had arrived at Trinity six years before him? He replied, 'I never met him. I only heard of him as a highly respected figure, regarded with some awe.'

'And are you sure he was a Communist?'

'Oh, no. But he was said to be supportive of Communism.'

So much for the 'incontrovertible evidence' of Victor's supposed Communism in pre-war Cambridge. In any case there were more enticing attractions in his life than political dialectic. At the age of twenty-three he married: in some Apostolic eyes a sin only a little less grave than joining the British Union of Fascists.

CHAPTER 2

Marriage

Victor Rothschild first met Barbara Hutchinson in July 1931, improbable as it may seem, at a London tea party. Thereafter they drank only champagne together. He came to call a few days later, when Barbara found him 'intriguing and odd and very intelligent and alive'. Victor dined with her on his twenty-first birthday that autumn. She gave him a cake with small candles. Four months later it was her own birthday and she received a telegram: 'A thousand good wishes you deserve them more than anybody I know best love Victor.' Barbara went to look at his lodgings in Cambridge:

> He lives in a large three-windowed room with American blue cloth curtains and large sofas covered with sacking and blue patterns. He has a large photo of a drawing of a nigger on one wall and two pictures by his sister. He has a Curtis-Moffat backgammon board and cocktail set and he has a Gaudier-Brzeska sleeping faun with long very sweet feet. He has some cigarette boxes that do odd things and a piano and some rather nice books. His bedroom is very crammed with things and he says he sleeps on the sofa.

They dined off oysters, quails and champagne. Then he took her to Tring for the first time:

> Amazing red house with plate glass windows. Indoors yellow furniture in the bedrooms, blue bows on my bed, lights over one's nose and very few bathrooms. Museum in the village.

Wonderful Lady Rothschild with a lovely witch face and Uncle Wally with spaghetti in his beard and the old house-dog way of being treated.

The Rothschild kaleidoscope turns again. Victor and Barbara picnic by the lake at Ashton Wold and he tells her of his father's suicide. In Cambridge once more he is found working in his shirtsleeves from nine in the morning until midnight, an open bottle of champagne on his desk. He has a table of his particular friends for a ball at 148 Piccadilly; nearby sits Winston Churchill, in the place of honour between the two Rothschild matriarchs, Victor's grandmother and his mother. 'Great rooms with gilt and chandeliers and plush and gold chains and huge looking glasses,' Barbara writes in her diary. 'Masses of champagne and a lovely supper and people streaming up the stairs from the hall in all their jewels and grandest dresses ... It was pure prewar perfection.'

She could bring a sharper pen than that to the London season. 'The plainness and unfreshness of all the virgins cannot be described,' she writes of a coming-out ball, 'neither can the scrubby uncouthness of the men who were cattlelike.' Lady Astor offers 'the oldest families in England and empire champagne'. Mrs Keppel, the last mistress of King Edward VII, is 'more like a dreadnought than a pleasure steamer'. Diana Cooper asks Barbara to lunch at the Ritz with 'the big buggers Eddie Gathorne-Hardy and Brian Howard'. There is another sort of hazard dining with Lady Oxford and Asquith: 'Play musical chairs with David Cecil and Osbert Sitwell. Margot then said at 10.30, "I must leave you all now" and shaking hands with her guests left for a supper party.' Randolph Churchill 'talked and drank too much'. Frank Pakenham told her she 'looked like a Catholic'. The Prince of Wales when she met him at Lady Cunard's 'did not know what to do – he was scared by everyone'. Mary Erskine, at the Café de Madrid, 'got a little tight and played the drum of the band'. Her chronicle unrolls like an early novel of Evelyn Waugh – with whom she dances at Quaglino's.

Yet Barbara was more than a Bright Young Thing. She was the only daughter of St John Hutchinson, a jovial and persuasive barrister descended from a Cromwellian regicide, who moved at ease in the world of letters and the arts. Barbara's mother Mary, a cousin of Lytton Strachey, brought her up without fear of Bloomsbury. For every dance she recorded there was Stravinsky conducting Stravinsky or a show of new paintings by Duncan Grant; Epstein sculptures competing with Walton scores, 'full of solidity and beauty'.

She was not Victor's only love. 'Pempi [Penelope] Dudley Ward passed through the room like a shooting star,' Barbara wrote of her rival, the daughter of the Prince of Wales's steadfast friend throughout the nineteen-twenties. Then there was Prudence Pelham, daughter of a cricketing Earl of Chichester, to whom Victor would send love letters composed for him by Miriam. One day he told his sister, in a phrase borrowed from the laboratory, 'I have met a sort of crystallised Pru.' It was Barbara. Yet there was scarcely a meeting that did not end in discord. 'Victor came in his new Mercedes,' she wrote in her diary. 'It is blue and narrow and exquisite and makes a relentless and loud noise – christened the Cigar. I met him at Whitehall in yellow gloves and a rage – we motored about after having a bun and I refused to go to Palace Green and we quarrelled for some hours and did not dine together.' She became moody and tearful, and Victor returned to his pursuit of Penelope Dudley Ward. By February 1933 he had turned again and was determined to marry Barbara. Their friend Jack Donaldson (later to marry King Edward VIII's biographer, become a peer and serve in a Labour government as Minister for the Arts) wrote in his diary that Victor was 'in train with all the awful business of breaking the news of his non-Jewish marriage to his grandmother who is 92 and might have a stroke'. Lady Rothschild, not yet ninety as it happened, was spared that shock when Barbara agreed to be received into the Jewish faith. They became engaged on 31 October, Victor's twenty-third birthday, and were married two months later.

The ceremony took place in the morning room at Tring rather than in a London synagogue, to spare Lady Rothschild the fatigue of the journey. The house was banked with orchids, the wedding canopy of silk brocade wreathed with white carnations. Three hours earlier, representatives of the estate workers and tenants, pensioners and tradespeople presented illuminated addresses, a silver rose bowl and other feudal tributes. The service, partly in Hebrew and partly in English, took only twenty minutes. Victor's best man was a Trinity friend, Claud Phillimore, the architect, who by Jewish tradition was required to break a glass: a symbol of the sorrow that lies concealed in rejoicing. It was not long delayed.

Barbara quite liked Anthony Blunt, whom she described as 'rather nice and limp'. But when he turned up repeatedly during their first months of married life, she asked her husband whether they need have Anthony at *every* meal. 'Darling,' Victor replied with reproach, 'you are talking of a saint.' She bore him three children: Sarah in 1934, Jacob in 1936 and Miranda in 1940.

Victor took a long lease on Merton Hall, a spacious Elizabethan house on the Cambridge Backs owned by St John's College. The most covetable private residence in the university thus became the home of a postgraduate yet to be elected a Fellow of a college and of his even younger wife. Victor liked a glass of good wine and well-cooked, simple food; otherwise his habits were abstemious, though not austere. Barbara, with a flair for interior decoration and an inspired talent for entertainment, filled their house with artists and aesthetes, writers and talkers, some drawn from local talent, more from the studios and mews of Paris and London. Her parties, separated in distance no more than half a mile from the stiff ritual feasts of high table or Master's Lodge, belonged in spirit to another age, another planet. Some took place by the river with dazzling cascades of fireworks; others were memorable for explosions of temper. For although deeply attached to each other sexually, neither of the young Rothschilds was placid or tolerant by nature.

They came, too, from contrasting backgrounds. Victor had been brought up on the Jewish tradition that a woman's place was in the home, Barbara in an altogether more liberal and liberated circle that embraced both Bloomsbury and Bohemia. There was scarcely a meal, to use Dadie's phrase, when tears were not shed with the soup. They would throw the Sèvres at each other, then be reconciled; but the patched-up peace was never more than an armed truce.

Victor did make one distinctive contribution to life at Merton Hall. He was an accomplished jazz pianist. His family in general have not been musical. When Louis Spohr arrived at New Court in 1820 with a letter of introduction to N. M. Rothschild, he politely enquired whether his host liked music. 'This is my music,' NM replied, jingling a pocketful of sovereigns. Victor was no philistine, but classical music meant little to him. Brought up on scales and arpeggios, he left Bach's Chromatic Fantasia and Fugue in D minor to his more agile sisters whom he conscripted into a jazz quartet. He also learned to play the bugle at Harrow because it was less burdensome to carry than a rifle in the Officers Training Corps.

His exemplars were those two incomparable jazz pianists Teddy Wilson and Art Tatum. Wilson's magic touch inspired Victor to seek him out in New York. He owed the meeting to his sister Nica, who had married Baron Jules de Koenigswarter, a French diplomat, and made her house a haven for distressed musicians. It is said that the owner of their favourite nightclub pleaded with Nica: 'We do not mind your friends shooting our waiters. But, please, not the chandeliers.'

Victor persuaded Teddy Wilson to give him eight lessons at $5 a time, during which the dynamic stride pianist made him play in the dark to achieve a machine-like quality in the left hand. He also paid homage to Art Tatum, whom he judged to be the greater of the two; Schnabel and Horowitz both conceded that in technique he was more than their equal. But that neurotic genius was having an off day and, although lured to the keyboard, he produced only a run or two. Nica took in Thelonious Monk during his decline. Charlie Parker also took refuge in her apartment. Taken ill one evening, he was asked by the doctor whether he drank. He replied, 'I sometimes have a glass of sherry before dinner.' Soon afterwards he died. Victor, too, confessed that like many black musicians he played much better after a slug, his optimum dose being two dry martinis.

An accident to his hand in the laboratory after the war affected his skill at the piano (and also on the tennis court and the golf links). But he continued to revere Art Tatum and, as a joke, would occasionally send a tape of the master to friends, pretending that it was his own latest recording.

Even before Victor succeeded to the family honours on the death of Uncle Walter in August 1937, he determined to be Lord Rothschild only in name. He did not relish a place in the hierarchy with all its responsibilities, an imposing London house or an estate dedicated to hunting, shooting and entertaining the neighbours. Over the past century his forebears had bought up half the county of Buckinghamshire and built a chain of country houses as socially impregnable as fortresses. But for his part he would continue his chosen career as a research scientist. That did not preclude an upholstered way of life denied most other denizens of Cambridge laboratories, much less the refined pleasures of collecting Impressionist pictures and eighteenth-century first editions. He could not, however, face the social and aesthetic implications of keeping up with the Rothschilds, of maintaining those grandiose family establishments that had scarcely changed for fifty years. Without the slightest pang of sentiment, he put 148 Piccadilly and Tring, together with most of their contents, on the market. At the private view of the London sale, the art historian Roger Hinks recalled the ball of a few years earlier that had so captivated Barbara. His journal continues,

> This afternoon the bleak April light beat unsympathetically through the plate-glass windows of the ball-room; and one saw how garish the gilt was, how false the chandeliers, and also how indifferent in quality even the famous French furniture and Dutch pictures appeared among all this shallow glory.
>
> The real significance of the house, however, lies in the bedrooms and their appurtenances: there is only one bath, and that in a cupboard without any ventilation, and the solitary W.C. is a wonderful period piece, bilious yellow varnished oak and all very willowy pattern within. But more is hardly to be expected from a house built in 1865 and virtually unaltered since. What did impress me, however, was the ugliness, the meanness, and the comfortlessness of the principal bedrooms ... No wonder Victor and Barbara Rothschild have recoiled in horror from the mere

thought of living in this nightmare and are selling the whole affair, lock, stock and barrel. How delightful to own anything so odious and so valuable, and to be free to sell it without a pang!

Others thought more highly of the Rothschild treasure trove. A picture of a Dutch courtyard by Pieter de Hooch, the friend of Vermeer, fetched a remarkable £17,000, with lesser works also in demand. But a Sèvres dinner and dessert service of 225 pieces sold for only £175, twenty-three claret glasses for £2 and thirty-nine liqueur glasses in ruby and gold for £1 10s. I cannot find a bid for one period piece: an ivory frame kept in the servants' hall for measuring the height of footmen. The entire sale brought in £85,231, more than £2 million in the currency of the late 1990s, and the fortunate vendor was reported to be 'quite elated'.

Four months later, the death of Uncle Walter spurred the new peer to rid himself of Tring. Walter had bequeathed to the British Museum his private museum and zoological collections. With Miriam's approval, Victor now offered the trustees an additional benefaction of both the family house itself and its park of 300 acres. It was a magnanimous gesture that would have enabled the British Museum to concentrate its entire natural history collection in a most attractive setting, with ideal facilities for research, only twenty-five miles from London; it would simultaneously have solved the problem of dispersal in time of war. But the unimaginative trustees, fearing that the running costs would be too high, rejected the plan. Much of the 4500-acre Tring estate was also put on the market.

Nor did the third Lord Rothschild allow himself to be burdened either by his newly inherited title or by attendance in the House of Lords. It was, in fact, nine years before he made his maiden speech. In 1938 he dined with Venetia Montagu to celebrate Winston Churchill's sixty-fourth birthday. Churchill asked him where he intended to sit. 'On the cross-benches,' he replied. Churchill despised neutrality. 'Sitting on your dividends,' he said mockingly. That was no way to speak to a young friend who, on earlier hearing from Randolph Churchill that his father had run out of his favourite Pol Roger 1921, sent his inquisitor a dozen of that fine champagne from his own dwindling stock at Merton Hall.

One hereditary duty he did not shirk. Although indifferent to both the beliefs and observances of Judaism, he did all that was required of him as head of the House of Rothschild. He had persuaded Barbara to accept conversion, at least in name, rather than outrage the sensibilities of old Lady Rothschild and other orthodox Jews. Here there was a further consideration. Had his wife remained a Gentile, the children she bore her husband would not have been accepted as Jews by the community, believing as they did that a Jewish birthright can be inherited only from a Jewish mother, whatever the faith of the father. In other ways the new Lord Rothschild took care not to offend those more scrupulous than himself. About to visit Lady Diana Cooper, he wrote asking whether he could stay over the following Monday. 'It is the Day of Atonement,' he explained, 'when all practising Jews fast and go to the Synagogue. I do not practise, but refrain from making public appearances on that day, so as not to hurt the feelings of other Jews.'

Above all, he overcame his shyness and inexperience of public speaking to plead for the relief of Jewish refugees from Nazi Germany. Little more than a generation after the first Lord Rothschild had touched many hearts and pockets on behalf of the victims of Tsarist oppression, the bearer of the same numinous title appealed for the rescue and resettlement of persecuted Jews in Germany. The occasion was a meeting in December 1938 called by the Lord Mayor of London in aid of the Earl Baldwin Fund for Refugees. After relating some of the horrors of the Nazi concentration camps, Victor continued,

I have been the unhappy recipient of so many heart-rending letters from children, of documented reports and personal accounts from observers that it is difficult for me to believe that I shall ever become again the rather care-free and happy scientist that I was before all this began.

A further passage, however, rings uneasily in modern ears. On the future of the refugees, once they had escaped from Germany, he said,

In spite of our humanitarian feelings, we probably all agree that there is something unsatisfactory in refugees encroaching on the privacy of our country, even for relatively short periods of time. That feeling in a different way is shared by the refugees themselves. To have to depart suddenly into a foreign country, with unknown customs, unknown language, with different food even, and different climatic conditions; to feel that one is deservedly unwanted, and to feel that one is dependent both morally and materially on the charity of others, is one of the most humiliating experiences that I can imagine a human being can endure...

It is for this reason that the Jews cling so tenaciously – too tenaciously, you may say – to the Palestine concept, though I think they know, as the Colonial Secretary said some days ago, that all the Jews cannot get into that tiny country; and all of them appreciate the appallingly complicated position that the British Government is in with regard to that country.

What may today seem at best apologetic, at worst heartless and self-serving, was precisely how most well-established British Jews saw the problem of Jewish refugees. They must be clothed, fed and allowed an immediate haven, but discouraged from lingering lest their alien presence provoke anti-Semitism; they must be packed off to a new life abroad, but not to the 'national home' of the Balfour Declaration if it complicated Britain's relations with the Arabs. At a meeting of the Zionist Federation in London, he delivered a speech on the same theme that could have been made by any minister of the then National government.

I am most emphatically of the opinion that it would be wise and proper for those British citizens who happen also to be Jews to support the principle of the actions decided on by Great Britain, even though this may necessitate considerable sacrifice and may imply deviations in the interpretations of previous findings, declarations or decisions.

That was how most Rothschilds felt, although there were exceptions such as James and Dorothy de Rothschild and Victor's sister,

Miriam. The family were prepared to use their chequebooks to ease the physical distress of destitute refugees, but not the moral and political influence their name commanded. By a century and a half of assiduous assimilation they had emerged from the ghetto of Frankfurt to the broad, sunlit uplands of Buckinghamshire; they were not prepared to see their security eroded by a sentimental attachment to Zionism. It was, after all, the same year in which the Prime Minister, Neville Chamberlain, referred to the Sudeten crisis as 'a quarrel in a far-away country between people of whom we know nothing'.

Of Victor's humanitarian instincts there can be no doubt. He addressed meetings in London and the provinces, raising many thousands of pounds. He presided over an office in New Court where appeals from Jews not yet able to escape from Germany received whatever help could be arranged. From the Tring collection, he gave a Reynolds conversation piece of the Braddyll family (now in the Fitzwilliam Museum) to be sold in aid of the Earl Baldwin Fund. Before the Lord Mayor of London's public meeting he asked the Catholic Archbishop of Westminster, Cardinal Hinsley, for a message from the Pope. This is what he received:

> The Holy Father, Pius XI's thoughts and feelings will be correctly interpreted by declaring that he looks with humane and Christian approval on every effort to show charity and to give effective assistance to all those who are innocent victims in these sad times of distress.

Victor responded by praising the Pope's courage and high moral principles: a fulsome tribute hardly justified by the Pontiff's cautious text that mentioned by name neither the particular plight of the Jews nor the unique barbarity of Nazi Germany. Sensing Victor's inner disappointment at the opaqueness of the papal message, Cardinal Hinsley invited him to the Archbishop's Palace and blessed him over the teacups. Victor returned the compliment by sending him a Stilton cheese for Christmas.

Five generations of assimilation failed to protect the English

Rothschilds from anti-Semitism. In those pre-Holocaust years it was a prejudice which in varying degrees infected every social class, every shade of political allegiance. Indeed, it persisted throughout Victor's lifetime, though in its milder forms.

First exposed to racial insult at his preparatory school, he had an easier passage through Harrow; skill at cricket saw to that. Nor was he at a disadvantage in the cosmopolitan research laboratories of Cambridge. But one humiliating encounter soon after his marriage was so grotesque as to reach the newspapers. With some friends he had stopped on impulse to eat at a well-known London 'road-house', a restaurant offering some of the amenities of a country club. He afterwards described the episode to an enquiring reporter from the *News Chronicle*: 'Soon after I had entered, a man whom I took to be the manager came up and said: "Excuse me, sir, are you a Jew?" My appearance is hardly Aryan. I told him that I was a Jew. He then said that he was sorry but in that case he would not serve me and I should have to leave. No explanation was offered and we left... Personally I was not in the least worried about the matter.'

When the reporter suggested that to refuse a Jew entrance to an English refreshment house was somewhat unusual, Victor replied, 'Ah, we live in an age of chains. But it does sound rather like Nazi Germany, doesn't it?' The allusion to Rousseau was applauded. But what he had in fact said, he claimed, was the milder: 'We live in an age of change.'

Even an unintentional barb could cause as much pain as the desire to wound. More than fifty years later he told me how upset he had been by a recent anti-Semitic remark let drop by a close friend, a Tory grandee of otherwise enlightened views. When the two men next met, Victor hoped to ease the tension by jocularly exclaiming, 'How can an anti-Semite like you come to the house of a Jew like me?' Expecting the reply, 'But Victor, I am not an anti-Semite,' he was doubly affronted at his friend's playful response, 'But Victor, you are different.'

The exchange continued to worry him, and in a letter to me a few days later he wrote, 'All Jews almost everywhere learn to live with the mild sort of anti-Semitism which afflicts so many people, even the liberal-minded.'

Some were nevertheless more sensitive that others. Miriam Rothschild detected prejudice in elections to the Royal Society and among the trustees of the British Museum who came to inspect her Uncle Walter's munificent bequest to Tring. And her cousin Dorothy de Rothschild, the chatelaine of Waddesdon, remarked to me how put out she had been to hear a stable lad innocently acclaim a promising racehorse as 'a real Christian'.

At least the English Rothschilds were more fortunate than their French cousins. In 1961, when Ben Gurion, the Prime Minister of Israel, was received in Paris by de Gaulle, the General asked him which nations had contributed men and money to the establishment of the State of Israel. Ben Gurion listed them: refugees from Russia, Poland, Germany and Austria, money from America and Britain.

De Gaulle: 'Any from France?'

Ben Gurion: 'There was of course Baron Edmond de Rothschild.'

De Gaulle: '*Mais il n'est pas Français.*'

There was, however, another side to the coin. When the Austrian nobleman Prince Schwarzenberg was asked why he had not invited any of the Rothschilds to a ball in Vienna, he replied, 'When the Rothschilds start inviting Jews to their houses, I will start inviting Rothschilds to mine.'

CHAPTER 3

War

Victor Rothschild's Cambridge generation grew up under the shadow of war. Some joined British intelligence, some joined Russian intelligence, a few joined both. His own response to the Nazi menace was both prompt and patriotic. Through his wife's parents, St John and Mary Hutchinson, Victor had formed a lifelong friendship with Duff and Lady Diana Cooper; he a Conservative M.P. and minister, she an outstanding beauty and actress. Victor shared their dismay at the Munich agreement of September 1938 and applauded Duff's resignation from Chamberlain's government at considerable financial sacrifice. 'You say you expect I shall receive thousands of letters,' Duff wrote to him. 'I have actually received over a thousand, and nearly as many telegrams – which show that although I was alone in the Cabinet, I am not quite alone in the country.'

At the beginning of 1939 Victor casually told his friends that he was off to the United States to seek out his paragon, the jazz pianist Teddy Wilson. It was the truth but not the whole truth. He was also received at the White House by President Roosevelt and entertained by the Secretary of State, Cordell Hull, and the Secretary of the Treasury, Henry Morgenthau. The welcome given by those busy men to a research scientist still sixteen years away from election as a Fellow of the Royal Society could be explained by the name he bore and the role he had assumed in the relief of Jewish refugees from Nazi Germany. More significant was a secret invitation from J. Edgar Hoover, the legendary head of the FBI, to a two-hour tour of his department. Major-General Walter C.

Baker, chief of the US Chemical Warfare Service, also suggested a private meeting.

Victor owed these soundings to Sir Harold Hartley, who in his last year at Harrow had examined him for a leaving scholarship to Cambridge. 'A nice old boy with a twinkling eye and a frock coat' was how the schoolboy remembered Britain's leading authority on chemical warfare; he was then just fifty. Ten years later, soon after the outbreak of war in 1939, Hartley invited Victor to become his personal assistant and had him appointed a member of a secret committee 'to originate and scrutinise new proposals for all aspects of Chemical Warfare'. By November, he was visiting the secret chemical research station at Porton Down and corresponding with Sir Henry Dale, Nobel Prizeman and a scientific adviser to the War Cabinet, about experiments 'with dry collodion membranes of measurable porosity'. Not yet thirty, he had a foot in the door to Whitehall; but it was the wrong door, for he was not a chemist and had little to contribute in that field.

He found more satisfying employment in MI5, officially known as the Security Service. It was, and remains, the organisation responsible for home security; its counterpart, MI6, the Secret Intelligence Service (or simply the Secret Service) operates largely overseas. John Masterman, the Oxford don who helped run an ingenious system of turning captured enemy agents against their own country, described MI5 as: 'A team of congenial people who worked together harmoniously and unselfishly, and among whom rank counted for little and character for much. It was a hand-picked service and a standing example of wise selection.' Sir Dick White, successively head of MI5 and MI6, and the only man to have bridged the gulf between those two rival organisations, con-fessed that both had absorbed too much of the talent available, particularly from the universities and the law: 'The demand for men of ability in other departments was enormous and we were a bit greedy.' Both he and his immediate superior, Guy Liddell, another professional who recruited Victor, showed tact and skill in creating a disciplined service out of so many prima donnas.

They first employed Rothschild on an investigation into com-mercial espionage, especially in the British machine-tool industry, which for years had been penetrated by persons of German origin or connection. The Ministry of Supply, he recommended, should seek alternative sources in the United States. In the summer of 1940 he became head of a tiny but semi-autonomous department of MI5 given the designation BI(c). Here he remained for the rest of the war: a colonel whose entire command consisted of two secretaries.

He worked from a converted cell in Wormword Scrubs prison, later moving to the more congenial atmosphere of St James's. He also had a private laboratory, maintained out of his own pocket. His business was anti-sabotage: the identification of key points to be protected against enemy saboteurs, and the discovery and dismantling of their bombs. Unlike bombs dropped from the air, they usually lay concealed in ships' cargoes and were invariably disguised as something else: detonators embedded in coathangers, raincoats made of flexible high explosive, thermos flasks containing an inch and a half of hot tea and the rest TNT, lethal sticks of shaving soap, infernal tins of frozen eggs. Most fiendish of all were small cartons of children's plasticine in various colours with instructions on how to make miniature animals; the plasticine was gelignite. There was an ingenious malevolence, too, in the booby traps resembling horse dung left on French roads in 1944 by the retreating Germans.

Reporting on the sabotage of ships bringing cargoes of fruit and vegetables from Spain via Gibraltar, Victor warned that the enemy were inevitably one jump ahead of British defences, 'especially where so benevolent an attitude is taken [by Spain] towards German secret service activities'. Most of the saboteurs were Spanish dockyard workers in German pay, a few were identified as young Spanish army officers.

The port authorities in Gibraltar were handicapped by a shortage of anti-sabotage equipment in examining ships for bombs bolted to their keels by German-hired agents in Spanish ports. 'It is somewhat ironic', Victor wrote, 'that the only diving suits made available, though most urgently needed, are ones obtained from Italian prisoners of war.'

The grim story of sabotage had its humours, too. A pair of

British-controlled agents infiltrated into the German network working under cover in Gibraltar's dockyards deceived Madrid into paying them for the fake sabotage of a petrol lighter. The Germans offered them 1500 pesetas each. This paltry sum they rejected with scorn, telling their paymasters that they could earn more than that in a week of tobacco smuggling – and without risking the death penalty. Their reward was raised to 5000 pesetas.

Victor was also amused by the instructions the Germans gave to would-be saboteurs destined for England: 'A guard dog can be lured away if a saboteur takes a bitch with him, or vice versa.'

Not all the incidents Victor investigated were the work of enemy saboteurs. Some ships' cargoes, inadequately ventilated, were destroyed by internal combustion.

He also uncovered cases of malicious damage by disgruntled servicemen. The crew of a British warship that was being refitted were late in arriving back from leave through transport difficulties beyond their control. The captain of the vessel, an unimaginative martinet, punished them severely. The following day a large steel rod was found to have put one of her engines out of action. Repairs took a further four months. Similar damage by civilian workers in British factories taught Victor the value of good industrial relations, which he later pursued as head of research in Shell.

All reports of suspected sabotage were sent to Colonel Rothschild's office in London. But he was far from desk-bound. It was also his task to take newly discovered German devices to pieces to render them harmless, find out how they were detonated and whether they had been booby-trapped to prevent their being dismantled.

Years in a Cambridge laboratory dissecting the eggs of frogs, trout and sea urchins had given him a sure touch in micro-manipulation. 'Although MI5 were scientifically sub-human and did not know the difference between sulphuric acid and a sonar wave,' he once said, 'they did recognise that I was a technical man.' His courage he bore lightly. 'When one takes a fuse to pieces,' he continued, 'there is no time to be frightened. One also becomes absorbed in its beautiful mechanism containing Swiss watches.' But he did confess that the first of the hundred or so bombs he dismantled (many of them of the same type) had made him 'rather nervous'. The only person who had previously dealt with that model of fuse was a naval officer who lost an eye and an arm when it exploded. Suspecting a booby trap and deciding that his eyes were more valuable than his hands, Rothschild took it to pieces while kneeling behind a well-padded armchair. As was customary during such operations, he had a field telephone into which he expounded, second by second, each turn of the screw; were the bomb to cost him his life, at least the truncated record would survive.

It was his examination in February 1944 of a crate of onions, part of a cargo from Spain, that brought him public recognition scarcely ever accorded to officers of the intelligence services: the award of a George Medal. Acting on a well-founded suspicion that the crate also contained a bomb timed to explode in a British port, Victor set to work on it in an open space near Northampton. The transcript of the field telephone, a dispassionate monologue some thousand words long, begins,

> It is a crate in three compartments. The right-hand compartment has onions in it. The middle compartment also appears to have onions in it. The left-hand compartment has already had most of the onions taken out but I can see right at the bottom in the left-hand corner of the left-hand compartment one characteristic block of German TNT...

So to the last moments of suspense:

> ...I have taken out the last block of TNT and I am now going to start looking at the plastic explosive.
>
> I have taken out the plastic explosive but I have not looked at it yet. It seems rather heavy.
>
> There is nothing else in the crate now and I am going to bring out the blocks of TNT and then go back to look at the plastic.
>
> I am now going to start trying to take this plastic explosive to pieces.
>
> I see a primer inside one of them. I am going to try and take that out.

I have taken the primer out and I can now see the detonator buried in the middle of the plastic.

It is a twenty-one day Mark II German time clock. I have unscrewed the electric detonator from the Mark II delay so that one is safe. I am now going back to look at the other piece of plastic.

I can just see the other Mark II delay inside the other piece of plastic.

I have taken the other primer off.

The other detonator is off.

All over, all safe now.

Victor was fortunate that his undoubted cold courage was brought to the notice of the Prime Minister. As he told Duff Cooper, MI5 liked to supply 'highly placed officials with smutty, scandalous or stimulating titbits to keep them sweet'. So it came about that his report on dismantling the crate and its lethal contents, illustrated by photographs of both bomb and onions, was sent to Sir Edward Bridges, Secretary to the Cabinet, who passed it on to the Prime Minister. Churchill was interested enough to write a minute to the director-general of MI5, Sir David Petrie, asking whether such things happened every day and whether the officer (whose name he did not yet know) was being considered for an award. Petrie was a former head of the Indian CID who, as *The Dictionary of National Biography* put it, 'always made himself perfectly clear, but was occasionally pompous and inclined to overlook the virtues of brevity and tact in his external correspondence'. His reply to Downing Street was offhand. He told the Prime Minister that exploits such as Rothschild's occurred from time to time and that the question of recognition was being taken up in appropriate quarters. It was a brush-off, or as Victor himself described it, a raspberry. The recognition, when it came, gave Colonel Rothschild the choice between a Commendation, somewhat similar to a Mention in Despatches, and Membership of the Order of the British Empire, the fifth grade of the most junior order of chivalry. His response was unenthusiastic. He told Duff Cooper,

...Though I was fully aware that captains of merchant vessels swam about for hours at a time stabbing sharks with pocket knives, or cutting off the arms of drowning men round the necks of half-drowned women, and were given the M.B.E. for their gallantry, and that my own activities did not differ much from these; an M.B.E. is almost always interpreted as meaning that you have loyally served Paddington Station in a subordinate capacity for over 30 years. I therefore asked that I should not be given it but should be allowed to have a Commendation which, as you know, is also given for acts of inconceivable heroism which, either through spite or oversight, are not given adequate reward. I must confess that I was somewhat depressed at this stage because, although I did not expect to get the George Medal (knowing the sort of thing for which people get it), I had rather hoped to be spared the indignity of being permanently stigmatised as belonging to the lowest form of Civil Service life.

What he did not know at the time was that the Prime Minister, stung by the inadequacy of Petrie's reply, angrily demanded details of the technical difficulties and dangers of taking a bomb to pieces. So Rothschild was required to write a fuller account of his onions. It was essentially an intelligence operation to investigate a new type of mechanism rather than to dispose of a single bomb. Although he joked that 'no false modesty prevented me from magnifying the episode to the largest possible proportions', he admitted he would have found it 'intolerably embarrassing had it not been that there were some independent witnesses'. In the event, Churchill insisted that he receive the far rarer and more coveted George Medal, instituted earlier in the war by King George VI and awarded largely but not entirely to civilians.

Rothschild's disparagement of the MBE, it must be said, was ill-judged. In the military division of the order, that grade is often awarded for courage in the face of the enemy. Edward Heath, whom he was later to serve when prime minister, was made MBE (mil) as an officer in the Royal Artillery during the North-West Europe campaign of 1944–5; and Tess Mayor, Victor's secretary and later assistant in counter-espionage, whom he married as his second wife in 1946, did not scorn the same recognition.

In reply to a letter from Major J. P. Hudson, Royal Engineers, who won a George Medal and Bar for bomb disposal and later became an authority on horticultural science, he wrote with modesty,

> Thank you for your congratulations. I feel very sincerely, that I have some form of apology to make to you and the other professionals, for my award. Having seen tremblers, mercury switches and other anti-withdrawal handling devices, I am fully aware that the few bombs I have dismantled in this war in no way compare with the jobs that you and your people do. To get the same sort of award, if not a higher one than some, is therefore unfortunate if not unfair and I am very conscious of this fact. This is not the traditional self-deprecation but a genuine desire to explain to an expert the feeling of uneasiness I have about the whole business.

On the day of the official announcement, Diana Cooper wrote to her husband, who three months earlier had been appointed to represent the British government in Algiers, 'Isn't it glorious. I am so madly glad. Fine for Jewry, fine for his friends. Splendid for him who has a nervous system like mine.' Shortly afterwards Victor was summoned to Buckingham Palace to receive the George Medal from the monarch who had given it his name. For once the King had been ill briefed. 'Ah, yes, Rothschild,' he said with a knowing smile. '*Oranges!*'

Newspaper reports of Victor's gallantry evoked many congratulations; but also whispers that the award had been inspired by Churchill as a symbolic gesture of his regard for the Jewish people and a recognition of the friendship that for more than half a century had united the two families. Some of these rumours may have sprung from the anti-Semitism which Victor more than once encountered in the higher ranks of Military Intelligence: an attitude, if not exactly a tradition, prevalent in the pre-war army. There was also jealousy. Senior officers of the service were decorated for their administrative talents, usually with a grade of the Order of the British Empire; in 1944 for instance, Guy Liddell was appointed a CBE and John Masterman an OBE. Although MI5 did show exceptional skill in tracking, capturing and turning every single German spy in Britain throughout the war, much of its work consisted in compiling and scrutinising office files; physical courage, when occasionally required, was taken for granted and thought undeserving of a medal for gallantry.

Nor was Rothschild popular among his colleagues. While sensitive to any suspicion of an affront, he could be careless of the feelings of others. This he recognised when light-heartedly proposing a new family motto: 'Quick to give – and to take – offence.' Not long before he received the George Medal, there was an office party to celebrate Liddell's decoration at which he almost came to blows with a former officer of the Peshawar Rifles who had charge of Camp 020, the interrogation centre for suspected German agents. After an exchange of asperities about civilians who wore uniform without ever having heard a shot fired in battle, things began to get rough. 'He kept on pointing his fingers at me,' Victor told Duff, 'as if I were one of the miserable seamen who occasionally have to go to his nursing home for an operation, so I told him to put his Palethorpes out of the way.' It was then that the director-general himself had to separate his two subordinates.

Another source of suspicion among the old guard was the friendly (though never close) relationship between the MI5 officer of thirty-three and the Prime Minister old enough to be his father. Only three days before dismantling the crate of onions and its concealed bomb, Victor had given a dinner party in a private room at the Savoy Hotel attended by Mr and Mrs Churchill. It was to mark the twenty-first birthday of Judy Montagu, whose mother Venetia was an intimate of both families. The widow of the Liberal minister Edwin Montagu (who on marriage persuaded Venetia to embrace Judaism so that his family should not disinherit him), Mrs Montagu has a more romantic place in history as the recipient of many endearments and confidences written from the Cabinet table a generation earlier by H. H. Asquith. Victor alone was the host, his marriage to Barbara having foundered. He sent this account of the party to Duff Cooper:

The evening did not start auspiciously as it was the day of the Anzio beachhead difficulties. The P.M. looked exceedingly black, and I feared a stream of 'Don't darken counsel, young man' remarks. However I had taken the precaution of bringing a little drink with me, including some Château Yquem which reminded him of the times when he used to have this at Tring, and he became slightly more mellow...The conjuror, an unvetted young man of obvious enemy origin if not of association, treated everybody including the P.M. with impunity, whipping notecases, cigarettes and watches out of their pockets. He had a particular trick of putting a small rubber ball about the size of a large cherry in the P.M.'s hand, telling him to hold it tight. Then, after making one or two passes over it, he said that on opening his hand the P.M. would find that there were two of them. Having done this two or three times, Winston said in a loud voice, 'I can feel it growing.' After this the party was a great success.

Professional duties also kept Victor close to Number 10. As head of the anti-sabotage unit of MI5 he was responsible for ensuring that the Prime Minister himself was not sabotaged. Presents of cigars, which arrived at Downing Street from all over the world, were a particular hazard. It would have been all too easy for an enemy agent to coat their rounded ends with cyanide or botulinus toxin, or to insert small explosive charges activated by the heat of a flame. So every gift box of cigars was X-rayed, after which random samples were ground up in saline and injected into mice. According to the reaction, the Prime Minister either received his cigars or he didn't. He was amused by these experiments but displeased by delay. When personally presented with a Virginia ham as he walked across Parliament Square to the House of Commons, he declared he would have it for breakfast next day. 'This war', he used to say, 'will be won by carnivores.' As there was no time for laboratory analysis, BI(c) devised a more rapid test. A very thin slice was removed by surgical instruments, leaving the ham apparently intact, then fed to the pet cat of the Medical Research Council which was kept under observation. The cat survived and Churchill had ham for breakfast. The same rule of thumb was applied when an admirer gave him a dozen bottles of old Armagnac. Victor demanded a thirteenth bottle from the donor for testing; only then was the Prime Minister allowed the original twelve.

Such windfalls did much to sustain morale. During the eighteen months that Duff Cooper spent as chairman of the security executive (thus allowing Victor privileged access to the minister responsible for intelligence), the two friends seemed better protected than most from the privations of war, though not from enemy bombs. An air raid in February 1944 dealt Victor a double blow, demolishing both his flat in St James's Street and his favourite restaurant round the corner. Duff Cooper wrote from Algiers,

> Many thanks for your letter from the Ritz Hotel, to which pigsty I suppose Hitler has been successful in reducing you. I mourn your little flat where I passed so many happy hours gazing through the window over the roofs of St James's Palace to the Surrey Hills while drinking your wines, eating your admirable omelettes and listening eagerly to your exhortations in favour of the immediate reduction of The Old 'Un [Sir David Petrie], to the ranks.

Victor had been away during the raid and arrived back in London to find the 'Daliesque sight of the cymbidia in their jug flowering peacefully but exotically among the piles of rubble'. As careless of possessions as when he disposed of 148 Piccadilly six years earlier, he did not brood over his loss. One valuable picture, however, did survive the Blitz: Cézanne's *Monsieur Choquet*, which he had lightheartedly lent Dick White to cheer up his Chelsea flat. The same raid that demolished Victor's pied-à-terre also damaged Wilton's restaurant. But its resourceful proprietor, Mr Marks, ensured that within days it had risen from the ashes and was once more dispensing, at prodigious cost, all those delectable fish and fowl exempt by their very scarcity from the rationing of baser foods. Victor relayed the good news to Duff:

Wilton's is open again. All important Second Front constructions, aircraft factories, aerodromes and other works had to stop while Mr Marks' super-priority contract was fulfilled. Right in front of Wilton's there is a vast bomb crater and the whole street is closed to everybody until the word 'Marks' is mentioned, when the barriers are lifted and one is ushered in by police and air raid wardens. On the day it opened I dined there with Bob Laycock [Major-General Robert Laycock, Chief of Combined Operations] and there were still books, pictures and corpses being rescued from nearby houses. Mr Marks himself had £300 worth of port stolen, and as usual had much to say about it; but the food was as good as ever.

Evelyn Waugh, in his novel *Unconditional Surrender*, called Wilton's 'a rare candle in a dark and naughty world' and immortalised its proprietor as Ruben. It was he who, on being asked for the secret of his wartime mayonnaise, replied, 'Quite simply, fresh eggs and olive oil.' Victor remained a lifelong customer, but declined Marks's offer to sell him the restaurant for £500. 'Bet you regret it now, m'Lord,' he would never fail to remind him.

'Oh, go away, Mr Marks,' was the invariable reply.

Another haven was Ranger's Cottage, Tring, which Victor and Miriam had retained after the sale of the big house. There they found an occasional refuge from the bombing of London for themselves and their friends (although by then Victor and Barbara were living apart). By some mysterious alchemy, their table did not seem to lack rare wartime delicacies: smoked salmon, poussins, grapes and a widow's cruse of a wine cellar. Guy Liddell lived there for long periods. Other welcome guests were Victor's assistant, and later second wife, Tess Mayor, Anthony Blunt and Diana Cooper, who vainly tried to persuade Victor to let her rent a disused folly near the cottage.

Miriam Rothschild also sought relaxation at Tring during the two years she spent at Bletchley breaking enemy ciphers before undertaking research for other wartime departments. Her admiration for colleagues such as the inspired mathematician Alan Turing did not extend to the administration of Bletchley. With a *joie de vivre* that remains undimmed into her tenth decade, she recalls how an authority on cryptogams – plants such as ferns, mosses, algae and fungi which have no true flowers or seeds – was astonished to be directed to Bletchley; he had been mistaken for a cryptographer. Nor were her occasional days in London quite like those of other civil servants. Victor offered her fresh grapefruit juice, then as rare as caviar, from a teapot. And dining at Claridge's with Professor Lindemann, Churchill's scientific adviser, was enlivened by the arrival of a former Lord Mayor of London who, determined to avoid at least one wartime peril, clutched his own lavatory seat neatly wrapped in brown paper.

Waddesdon, Baron Ferdinand's French-style chateau in Buckinghamshire, which had passed by inheritance to James de Rothschild MP, proved less welcoming when Victor invited himself over from Tring to see his cousin. He was asked to bring his own sugar and for luncheon was served an indifferent burgundy in thimble-sized glasses; these reappeared in the evening for champagne and the bottle was corked up towards the end of the meal. 'Considering that he has one of the biggest cellars in the country and that he does not drink himself at all,' Victor told Duff, 'I have decided not to visit again.' He nevertheless returned hopefully a few months later and this time was rewarded by a Margaux 1870 and a brandy a hundred years old, which the host had inherited from his father. In about 1890, Jimmy told Victor, Baron Edmond asked his butler how much of it remained. 'Monsieur le Baron,' the butler replied, 'if you gave a dinner party every night, you would have enough to last for the next five hundred years.' Victor's spirits rose as he listened to his cousin's anecdote; he thought he was about to be given at least a dozen. But like the rich man in the Gospels, he was sent empty away.

Not even MI5 was spared the lot of the common soldier: boredom relieved by spasms of fear and exhilaration. Victor made the best of it. He had gone to war in a spirit of boyish idealism, thrilled to be admitted to the arcane practices of sabotage and counter-sabotage, of agents and double agents, of codes and ciphers. A fellow scientist, Professor Solly Zuckerman, calling on him at Merton Hall in the first Christmas of the war, was amused to see that the Mercedes had been repainted in the camouflage colours of the battlefield. And when a German invasion seemed imminent a few months later, Victor acquired a poison pill in case he was arrested by the Gestapo; as the danger receded, he flushed it down a lavatory in Wormwood Scrubs.

Secretive by nature, he imposed strict security on his own tiny department and was put out when his cousin Rosebery sauntered in one day for a chat, having innocently evaded the checkpoint at the entrance. After Rosebery had gone on his way, Victor summoned the usually reliable doorkeeper to ask why he had allowed a stranger to penetrate his office. 'Oh, but his lordship is no stranger,' the man replied. 'I used to be a gatekeeper at Sandown Park racecourse.'

Victor's regard for espionage as a high-minded vocation was not shared by all his colleagues. He was much teased by an irreverent coterie of MI6 Oxonians responsible for interpreting the deciphered signals of the German Secret Service and using them to devise a web of deception: the philosophers Gilbert Ryle and Stuart Hampshire, and the historian Hugh Trevor-Roper. Warned that German agents armed with explosive teapots were plotting to blow up Anglo-Iranian oil installations at Abadan, Victor flew out under a false passport bearing the name Dr Fish. 'What a lot of trouble to take', his tormentors mocked, 'over a few snake-charmers.' And after Victor had been called in to advise on German saboteurs in Central Africa, Ryle reported that the solitary agent to have penetrated as far as Lake Chad had managed to send only one message to his masters: a request for an airdrop of Salvarsan, the popular remedy of the day for syphilis. When Ryle labelled the patient 'this unpromising evangelist', Victor resented both the irony and the ailment.

The whimsically named Operation Oatmeal also had an unexpected ending. A captured German spy who had avoided execution by agreeing to work for MI5 was ordered to send a radio message in his own distinctive rhythm to his unsuspecting controller in Germany. It asked for further supplies of money and sabotage equipment to be dropped by air at a given time and map reference in Aberdeenshire. Guided by a flashing MI5 torch, the German plane appeared punctually and dropped a canister by parachute. In case it should conceal an enemy booby-trap, Victor insisted on opening it himself. It was found to contain a new portable wireless set, £400 and much sabotage material. But when Victor examined these lethal devices he found to his amazement that they were of British manufacture and of a type used by SOE (Special Operations Executive) only once before: during a ground raid on a German heavy-water installation from the ruins of which the Germans had apparently collected some unexploded bombs. It was these which German intelligence dropped in Scotland to replenish the store of their supposed secret agent. The episode was not without humour. But there was tragedy, too, that night. For the German plane, having made its drop, went on to bomb the town of Fraserburgh, causing casualties. As MI5 had asked that there should be no RAF fighters in the area during the operation, the German plane was able to fly home unscathed.

Infernal machines were not always what they seemed. Nor were enemy agents. One of them, reported to be harbouring carrier pigeons in her lodging at Aberdovey, on the Welsh coast, was found with a suitcase full of codes and a sack of corn under her bed. It turned out to be Victor's sister Miriam, engaged on experiments in pest control for the government; no historically minded Rothschild could resist pigeons. As for the codes, they were mathematical puzzles, a taste which she shared with her brother.

To keep his brain cells polished, as he put it, Victor had early in the war consulted a Trinity colleague, G. H. Hardy, on whether he could study advanced mathematics in his spare time. After a brief oral examination, the author of *A Mathematician's Apology* told him that he had the mathematical ability of an intelligent schoolboy aged fourteen, and passed him on to Professor Hyman Levy, an authority on the numerical solution of differential equations and the calculus of finite differences. 'Ensure that you are not taught by someone too clever,' was Hardy's parting shot. So throughout the war, except for brief absences abroad, Victor received a weekly supervision, with examples to be done in between. These he found hard work. He confessed that he could manage Orthogonal Bessel

Functions, but became confused and dispirited by Poles and Residues. Eighty years earlier, as an undergraduate at Trinity, his grandfather Natty had told his parents, 'To get on one must be wedded to Mathematics and think of nothing else...I found the problems frightfully hard.'

A prisoner of his own skills in anti-sabotage, Victor was increasingly called upon to teach them to others. He told Duff,

> Life has been very dull here. We spend most of our time preparing people for the Second Front – an endless series of lectures to baboon-like Field Security non-commissioned officers. I have done it now for six weeks running and am bored to distraction.

A few weeks before his encounter with Spanish onions, irksome routine and antipathy to The Old 'Un drove him to ask Lord Woolton, who was forming a new government department called the Ministry of Reconstruction, whether he could become his scientific adviser. But Woolton, still restless and unhappy at having been moved from the Ministry of Food, was not yet ready to recruit staff.

So Victor sought other excuses for a change of scene: the interrogation of captured saboteurs on the Italian front, the discovery of 'unbelievably nasty onion marmalade' in Spain, a descent on Duff and Diana Cooper in Algiers. He rarely wore military uniform in England. But on his voyage home from the Middle East in the troopship *Orion*, he found that his obligatory badges of rank had both advantages and disadvantages. The advantages included a cabin and bathroom to himself; the disadvantages, a seat at the captain's table and nominal command of '3500 co-belligerent Italians, 500 Poles, 500 French and 50 psychopathic British officers sent home by their commanding officers'. Most of his administrative duties he delegated to an obliging psychopath; and what he had supposed to be alarming quarrels among the foreign passengers turned out to be amicable conversations in their own language.

He was also able to renew his friendly links with J. Edgar Hoover after German agents had been landed by submarine on the coast of North America, carrying bombs disguised as pieces of coal; nine of the twelve were executed by electric chair. Victor was summoned across the Atlantic to teach the FBI how to detect and defuse them. From the United States government he received the Bronze Star 'for work carried out in extreme danger'. Hoover himself gave him a characteristic token of regard: a fourteen-day time fuse. After the Allied invasion of France in June 1944, he was formally seconded to the United States army to teach American officers the arts of sabotage and counter-sabotage. The attachment brought him two more accolades. In the intelligence tests required of all recruits, he received an IQ rating of 184. His examiners wondered whether he had seen the papers before, for the only other person to do as well was their prisoner Dr Schacht, Hitler's Finance Minister. The episode left Victor sceptical of such tests when applied to persons above a fairly low level of intelligence; he recalled that the mathematician Paul Dirac had scored zero in one devised by the Psychology Laboratory at Cambridge. He also received the US Legion of Merit to add to his Bronze Star. In contrast to the brief British citation of the George Medal, 'for dangerous work in hazardous circumstances', President Truman's encomium pulled out all the stops:

As counter-sabotage officer of the British War Office, he was recognised as one of the world's greatest experts in this branch of military intelligence. He gave unstintedly of his time and energy in personally training American officers as counter-sabotage specialists. He wrote and edited many technical manuals used as textbooks by the United States Army, especially by bomb-disposal engineers and counter-intelligence personnel. He trained many sabotage teams in France which were wholeheartedly accepted by units in the field, and whose operations were marked by signal success.

The services of Colonel Lord Rothschild in the instruction of American personnel were a very valuable contribution to the success of the United Nations and an enduring achievement in the high cause of British–American co-operation.

He arrived in Paris soon after its liberation by the Allied forces and joined General Eisenhower's supreme headquarters. At first he lodged in what had been a hostel of the Young Women's Christian Association. 'How strange,' Duff said, 'since you are neither young nor a woman nor a Christian.' Family piety drove him to see what had become of the house of his cousin Baron Robert de Rothschild in the Avenue Marigny. Finding that American troops had moved in as the Germans moved out, he in turn ejected them and declared it to be the headquarters of his anti-sabotage unit and of certain other semi-detached officers who passed his own test of approval. There he was sought out by members of the family emerging from service in the Free French forces or from internment or hiding. Yvonne Cahen d'Anvers, mother-in-law of Anthony de Rothschild, a partner in New Court, was overwhelmed with joy when plucked out of her country retreat, welcomed at the Avenue Marigny by Tess Mayor, offered bed, breakfast and a hot bath, and sent on her way loaded with little luxuries.

Victor also delighted in the stratagems by which the faithful old family servants had saved the contents of Rothschild houses from damage or looting by the Germans billeted on them. One had made up the bed of a senior general each day with the finest linen sheets, removing them to be laundered the next morning; they never came back. Another, a part-time fireman, had used his fire engine to spirit away the family silver to a hiding place. A third had rescued the famous blue and white Chantilly china made for the Prince de Condé, carrying off half a dozen plates at a time on his bicycle.

Rejoicing at the liberation of Paris and the prospect of victory in Europe was stilled by the scarcely imaginable evil of the Holocaust. Seven years earlier, the tales of suffering that reached Victor from the Nazi concentration camps caused him to wonder whether he would ever again retrieve the life of a carefree young scientist. How much more indelible were the scars of the Holocaust. Among its victims were Aranka Wertheimstein, the eldest sister of Victor's mother Rozsika, an old woman beaten to death with meat hooks on a railway station outside Buchenwald; and Elisabeth, the first wife of Baron Philippe, deported from

Paris and thrown into the ovens of Ravensbrück. Others of the cousinhood suffered for their faith or took their own lives.

The Holocaust haunted Victor to the grave, as it did all Jews of his generation; annealed his consciousness of being Jewish; taught him the sobering lesson that not even the name of Rothschild had been proof against the new barbarism.

There was an odd twist to one of his missions. Among the enemy saboteurs captured in liberated Paris was a dedicated Nazi, viciously anti-Semitic yet proud to have fallen into the hands of a Rothschild. Victor took an amused satisfaction in sending him back to Germany as a double agent, first entertaining him to dinner at an expensive Paris restaurant. The 'turned' captive showed his gratitude by presenting him with a fountain pen that could fire a single lethal shot. It was a profitable exchange for both men. Acting under MI5 orders, the agent persuaded his German masters that he had sabotaged several British ships and was awarded a high grade of the Iron Cross.

The most feared German agent of all, Otto Skorzeny, a colonel in the SS, also passed through Victor's hands, although not until the end of the war. During the German counter-offensive in the Ardennes, there were rumours that the man who had so spectacularly rescued Mussolini from his Italian captors after the fall of the Fascist regime in 1943 was on his way to Paris to assassinate General Eisenhower. It proved a false alarm. When eventually he was captured, Victor interrogated him about his supposed war crimes and a particular allegation that he had supplied German saboteurs or terrorists with bullets tipped with an exceptionally lethal poison. Botulinus toxin, scientists supposed, would be burnt up by the heat of the bullet, but cyanide would not. Victor, whose German was not good enough to detect nuances of meaning or hesitations, felt handicapped by having to question him through an interpreter. Skorzeny, six foot six inches in height, with a prominent scar across his face – 'a complete thug' Victor dubbed him – bluntly denied that he had ever broken the conventions of war. Victor was not convinced, but in the absence of evidence the inquiry had to be abandoned. 'Most unsatisfactory,' he concluded. Skorzeny was charged with war crimes at the Nuremberg trials, but acquitted.

Top left: Nathan Mayer Rothschild, founder of the English branch of the family, arrived in Manchester from Frankfurt in 1798, became the paymaster of Wellington's armies and amassed a considerable fortune. When asked the secret of his success he would reply, 'To minding my own business'.

Top right: Baron Lionel de Rothschild, NM's eldest son, in 1858 became the first Jew to take his seat in the House of Commons. During his sixteen years at Westminster he never once made a speech. In 1875 he came up with four million pounds at a moment's notice to finance Disraeli's purchase of Suez Canal shares from the bankrupt Khedive of Egypt. But Queen Victoria refused to make any Jew a peer.

Left: Nathan, 1st Lord Rothschild, known as Natty, the eldest son of Baron Lionel, with his grandson Victor. In 1885 Mr Gladstone at last overcame the Queen's prejudice against bankers and Jews and Natty became a peer. The shrewdest of financiers, he attributed his success to 'selling too soon'. His prodigious philanthropy extended to scattering half-sovereigns to the village children as he drove out of the gates of Tring Park. His wife thought it vulgar.

Top left: Roszika von Wertheimstein, the Hungarian-born wife of Charles Rothschild, Natty's younger son, and mother of Victor. After Victor had been left fatherless at the age of twelve, Roszika proved a resourceful guardian, coaching him in Roman history and by astute investment doubling the value of her son's trust funds during his minority. She was rarely seen without a cigarette clinging to her lips, a habit she bequeathed to Victor.

Top right: Unlike his elder brother Walter, Charles Rothschild, Victor's father, combined the restrictive regime of the family bank with a devotion to natural history. He was a pioneer of nature reserves and even as a schoolboy published *The Lepidoptera of Harrow.* He met his wife pursuing butterflies and the flea-bearing mice of the Carpathian Mountains.

Right: Walter, 2nd Lord Rothschild, Natty's elder son and Victor's uncle, had what his niece Miriam called 'a smudge of mad genius'. Here he rides his pet tortoise from the Galapagos. He formed the largest collection of natural history specimens ever assembled by one person, literally hundreds of thousands of birds, eggs and insects. But his financial judgement was disastrous and his private life untidy. Natty disinherited his black sheep of a son.

Victor as a Wolf Cub. His cherubic countenance was deceptive. Unrestrained by an ailing father, he was a match for any governess, tutor or schoolmaster. Even his good-natured Uncle Walter was once stung by his nephew's insolence to bellow, 'Mister Victor, Mister Victor, you will be painted blue and yellow [the Rothschild racing colours] and exposed in the high street.'

Three Cambridge friends

Top left: Guy Burgess, clever and engaging, yet drunken and dissolute, was employed by the Foreign Office and in the British Embassy in Washington, where he spied for Soviet Russia. He defected to Moscow in 1951. Earlier his Eton tutor Robert Birley (afterwards Head Master of the school) was shocked on calling unexpectedly on Burgess at Cambridge to discover that much of his library was either Marxist or explicitly homosexual.

Top right: Anthony Blunt, Keeper of the Queen's Pictures and an art historian of European reputation, likewise gave his allegiance to Soviet Russia in war and peace until detected. Victor, antipathetic to Marxism and ignorant of his friends' treachery, became the innocent victim of guilt by association.

Right: 'Dadie' Rylands, uninterested in politics, was an imaginative interpreter of Shakespeare and an acclaimed theatrical producer. He tutored Victor in English literature and inspired him to form a collection of three thousand eighteenth-century first editions and manuscripts.

Left: Victor before he married Barbara Hutchinson in 1933. She found him 'intriguing and odd and very intelligent and alive'. Victor persuaded her to convert to Judaism in order not to outrage his orthodox Jewish grandmother.

Below: Victor and his eldest sister Miriam in Italy in the early 1930s. Miriam, as luminous of mind as ever in her tenth decade, loves the entire animal kingdom, not least butterflies and foxes. For her many volumes on fleas she was elected a Fellow of the Royal Society; with Victor, the only sister and brother to be so honoured. Her wit is sharp. She once described a cousin as having the brain of a flea but none of its agility.

Victor holds a council of war with Duff Cooper MP (left) in about 1936, two years before Duff courageously resigned from Neville Chamberlain's cabinet in protest at the appeasement of Nazi Germany. Politics was not the only commodity to seal their friendship. 'Two dozen of Chateau Cheval Blanc is a present to take one's breath away', Duff wrote gratefully from the Admiralty at Christmas 1937.

Victor and Barbara Rothschild in 1936, the year before he succeeded his uncle Walter as 3rd Baron. The marriage was one of intense happiness punctuated by violent quarrels. 'There was scarcely a meal,' Dadie Rylands noted, 'when tears were not shed with the soup.' After twelve years they divorced.

A rare photograph of Victor in formal morning dress, addressing a meeting at the Mansion House in December 1938 in aid of the Earl Baldwin Fund for Refugees. On Victor's left is the Archbishop of Westminster, Cardinal Hinsley, who afterwards gave Victor his blessing. Victor returned the compliment by sending him a Stilton cheese for Christmas.

Liberating Europe

Left: Colonel Lord Rothschild, head of counter-sabotage in MI5, and his assistant Tess Mayor, in France in 1944, preparing to detect and make safe lethal booby-traps planted by the retreating German army. In recognition of their hazardous duties at home and abroad, Victor was awarded the George Medal and Tess the MBE (mil). In 1946 he married her as his second wife.

Below: Victor at Berchtesgaden in 1945 with a trophy of war.

Left: Dick White (later Sir Dick White), one of Victor's closest friends, as a wartime brigadier. He rose steadily through the ranks of MI5 to become Director-General, and was then appointed head of the rival MI6 to restore efficiency and morale. Modest and self-effacing, he told the present writer, 'I have never wanted to grub about in people's lives unless there was hard evidence'.

Below: 'The best part of my life was spent in a Cambridge laboratory', Victor declared when interviewed on the radio programme *Desert Island Discs*. Some of the equipment he made himself. His contribution to gametology, the study of eggs, sperm and their interactions, bought him a Fellowship of the Royal Society.

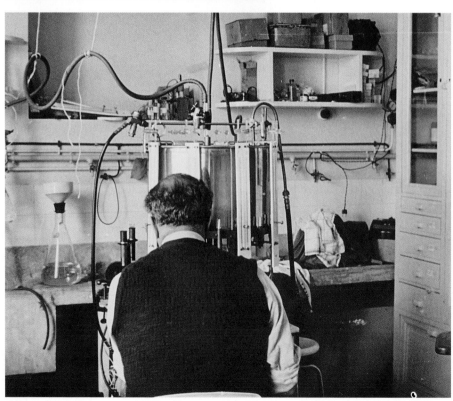

Duff Cooper's transfer from Algiers to Paris as British ambassador raised Victor's spirits. Even before Duff's arrival in September 1944, he had asked Victor to consider becoming press attaché at the embassy, though with a wider and more influential role than usual.

> You know nothing about the press but would soon pick it up and you would have an assistant with full technical knowledge. Apart from that I think you have all the qualities. We should not have to conceal that your war work has been anti-sabotage and bomb disposal. That would be quite enough to cover your past – and press attaché would be quite enough to cover your future if it were decided to make use of your experience for other purposes. Think it over.

However alluring the prospect of continuing to have a foot in the twilight world of intelligence, it is inconceivable that Victor could have accepted such a post. To be an intimate friend and fellow conspirator of the ambassador was elating; to be padlocked into a comparatively junior appointment in the diplomatic hierarchy could not fail to be restrictive, even humiliating. How insensitive, too, of Duff to suppose that Victor's ability to influence French public opinion would not be diminished by his racial background. The anguished cry of his cousin Guy de Rothschild cannot easily be erased from the pages of French history: '*Juif sous Pétain, paria sous Mitterrand.*'

Nor could Victor have been flattered to learn that Malcolm Muggeridge had already rejected the appointment. An incisive journalist with a lively sense of mischief, he had represented MI6 in Lourenço Marques before his transfer to Paris as liaison officer with the French Securité Militaire. Victor, who did not much care to be teased, was wary of him. But Muggeridge was the best of company and married to a cousin of Tess Mayor, so was invited to share the comforts of the Avenue Marigny. Nearly thirty years later, in his memoirs, *Chronicles of Wasted Time*, he repaid Victor's hospitality with a scintillating but searing portrait of his host:

For Rothschild himself, of course, the Avenue Marigny house was a home from home, but at the same time, I felt, a prison. Installed there, he was *de facto* if not *de jure* head of the family. Other Rothschilds appeared from time to time, and offered obeisance. He both liked to feel they were looking to him, and abhorred their presence; his disposition was a curious, uneasy mixture of arrogance and diffidence. Somewhere between White's Club and the Ark of the Covenant, between the Old and the New Testament, between the Kremlin and the House of Lords, he had lost his way, and been floundering about ever since. Embedded deep down in him there was something touching and vulnerable and perceptive; at times lovable even. But so overlaid with the bogus certainties of science, and the equally bogus respect, accorded and expected, on account of his wealth and famous name, that it was only rarely apparent. Once when I was going to London he asked me to take over a case of brandy, addressed in large letters to him at his English address. In the guard's van where it was put, among the porters who carried it, wherever it was seen or handled, it aroused an attitude of adoration, real or facetious, as though it had been some holy relic – the bones of a saint or a fragment of the True Cross. Even I partook of its glory, momentarily deputising for this Socialist millionaire, this Rabinical sceptic, this epicurean ascetic, this Wise Man who had followed the wrong star and found his way to the wrong manger – one complete with chef, central heating and a lift. I think of him in the Avenue Marigny dictating innumerable memoranda, as though in the hope that, if only he dictated enough of them, one would say something; on a basis of the philosophical notion that three monkeys tapping away at typewriters must infallibly, if they keep at it long enough, ultimately tap out the Bible. Rothschild, anyway, did not lack for monkeys. After the war I caught glimpses of him at Cambridge, in think-tanks, once in the Weizmann Institute in Tel Aviv, still dictating memoranda.

The subject of this caricature smiled frostily as he read it. 'I too could write an account of those days in Paris,' he told me, 'when

Muggeridge slept with a Soviet agent and returned early one morning to the Avenue Marigny, his car riddled with bullet holes.' Muggeridge's depiction of Rothschild through the distorting lens of malice sprang from a belief that his victim was soft on Russian Communism. As Moscow correspondent of the *Manchester Guardian* in 1932–3, he had witnessed the suffering caused by Stalin's enforced collectivisation of agriculture and the monstrous brutality that permeated the Soviet system. It was the attitude of the affluent, high-minded British liberals that offended him most: his own wife's aunt, for instance, Beatrice Webb. 'Old people', she wrote about her visit to starving Russia in 1932, 'often fall in love in extraordinary and ridiculous ways – with their chauffeurs, for example. Sidney and I feel it more dignified to have fallen in love with Soviet Communism.'

Victor Rothschild was innocent of such twaddle. But a furious row flared up at the Avenue Marigny one night when he declared that, in their common cause, Russia should be given access to the highest grade of Anglo-American intelligence about the German order of battle and operational plans. What he had in mind, Muggeridge later wrote, was Ultra: the most secret and valuable source of intelligence derived from the breaking of enemy ciphers at Bletchley Park. The argument grew fierce when Rothschild was supported by another guest, the MI6 officer Kim Philby, yet to be unmasked as a Soviet agent; everything should be done, he shouted, to help the Red Army to victory. But not, Muggeridge insisted, if it were to risk the security of so vital a secret as Ultra. Here the balance of argument lay against Rothschild. The Russians, although wartime Allies since 1941, habitually mistrusted all Western intelligence, not least the warnings they had received of an impending German invasion; they offered their allies nothing in return and had not hesitated to collaborate with Nazi Germany while Britain stood alone.

Muggeridge's testimony, uncorroborated and unpublished until 1973, cannot be accepted without a word of caution. The very existence of Ultra was, and remained for the next thirty years, the most closely guarded of secrets. entrusted only to those who needed to know. The fruits of Bletchley, processed and interpreted, were distributed to Allied headquarters as required; their source, never. So it is unlikely that three intelligence officers of no great seniority, each belonging to a different unit, should have known of Ultra, much less flourished the magic name over the brandy. If in 1944 Rothschild and Philby did argue for the release of military intelligence to Russia, it must have been in more general terms.

An even less convincing version of the episode appeared fifty years later in *The Perfect English Spy*, a life of Dick White by the investigative writer Tom Bower: 'White witnessed a furious argument which culminated in Rothschild grabbing a few Ultra messages, storming from the house and pushing the papers through the Soviet embassy's letter-box.' When I challenged the author, he conceded that whatever documents Victor may have had, they could never have been identified as Ultra material. But Bower insisted that the argument had indeed culminated in that bizarre manner. He added that it had been witnessed by Muggeridge, Philby, White and another MI5 officer, Christopher Harmer. By the time the book was published in 1995, Muggeridge, Philby, White and Rothschild were dead. But Harmer was alive and I wrote to him. He replied that he had not been present. 'The more I think about this story,' he added, 'the more ridiculous it becomes...Total poppycock, I would say.'

Had Muggeridge witnessed the supposed Soviet embassy incident, he would surely have included it in his account of the earlier argument in Avenue Marigny. There is no word of it. But he does relate how unwelcoming was the embassy to chance visitors: 'Every blind drawn, every door locked, every window with its iron grating, the very fire escape contained steel netting; even so, behind the doors and windows, round-the-clock guards, burglar alarms, every imaginable and unimaginable security precaution... two *flics* posted at its main entrance.' Even if Victor's rage had not evaporated in the twenty-minute walk from the Rothschild house in the Avenue Marigny to the Soviet embassy in the rue de Grenelle, is it likely that he would have found an open letter box through which to push his illicit bounty?

Muggeridge's antipathy towards Victor in the Avenue Marigny was coloured by an earlier episode at 5 Bentinck Street, three floors of which the Rothschilds had rented in the spring of 1939 as their London house. The owner of the building was *The Practitioner*, a medical journal, which retained the remaining two floors as offices but allowed Victor to turn the basement into a well-appointed air raid shelter. It was here that Muggeridge was taken one night during the Blitz by Andreas Mayor, Victor's future brother-in-law, who was also a cousin of Muggeridge's wife Kitty. Neither of the Rothschilds was there to welcome him. Barbara, who was pregnant, had returned to Merton Hall, Cambridge; Victor, who scarcely used Bentinck Street throughout the war, preferred a small flat in St James's, conveniently close to the headquarters of MI5. It was not Victor himself but its denizens who appalled Muggeridge:

There we found...John Strachey, J. D. Bernal, Anthony Blunt, Guy Burgess, a whole revolutionary Who's Who. It was the only time I ever met Burgess; and he gave me a feeling, such as I have never had from anyone else, of being morally afflicted in some way. His very physical presence was, to me, malodorous and sinister; as though he had some consuming illness...The impression fitted in well enough with his subsequent adventures; as did this millionaire's nest altogether, so well set up, providing, among other amenities, special rubber bones to bite on if the stress of the Blitz became too hard to bear. Sheltering so distinguished a company – Cabinet Minister-to-be, honoured Guru of the Extreme Left-to-be, Connoisseur Extraordinary-to-be, and other notabilities, all in a sense grouped round Burgess; Etonian mudlark and sick toast of a sick society, as beloved along Foreign Office corridors, in the quads and the clubs, as in the pubs among the pimps and ponces and street pick-ups, with their high voices and peroxide hair...There was not so much a conspiracy gathered round him as just decay and dissolution. It was the end of a class, of a way of life; something that would be written in history books, like Gibbon on Heliogabalus, with wonder and perhaps hilarity, but still tinged with sadness, as all endings are.

Muggeridge's reference to Gibbon was perhaps more apposite than he knew. For 5 Bentinck Street stood next to the site of the house where Gibbon wrote *The Decline and Fall.*

Goronwy Rees found Bentinck Street and its shifting population no less bizarre. He wrote in his autobiography, *A Chapter of Accidents,*

> This oddly assorted collection of tenants sometimes gave the flat the air of a rather high-class disorderly house, in which one could not distinguish between the staff, the management and the clients…
>
> All appeared to be employed in jobs of varying importance, some of the highest, at various ministries; some were communists or ex-communists; all were a fount of gossip about the progress of the war, and the political machine responsible for conducting it, which sometimes amused me, sometimes startled me, and sometimes convinced me that I could not possibly be fighting in the same war as themselves.

He was more explicit on the part played by Burgess in this animated scene:

> Guy brought home a series of boys, young men, soldiers, sailors, airmen, whom he had picked up among the thousands who thronged the streets of London at that time; for war, as Proust noticed, provokes an almost tropical flowering of sexual activity behind the lines which is the counterpart of the work of carnage which takes place at the front. The effect was that to spend an evening at Guy's flat was rather like watching a French farce which has been injected with all the elements of a political drama. Bedroom doors opened and shut; strange faces appeared and disappeared down the stairs where they passed some new visitor on his way up; civil servants, politicians, visitors to London, friends and colleagues of Guy's, popped in and out of bed and then continued some absorbing discussion of political intrigue, the progress of the war and the future possibilities of the peace.

The police warned Victor that they suspected his house of being used as a male brothel, but he shrugged it off as a joke. 'How easily in these darkened streets', he replied, 'the amateur can be confused with the professional.'

His responsibility was in any case limited. Since neither he nor his wife needed Bentinck Street, he generously lent it to friends in need. The first to move in was Anthony Blunt, who on being evacuated from France in the summer of 1940 as an officer in the Field Security Police – he had not yet joined MI5 – found himself homeless. He was followed by Tess Mayor and her friend Patricia Rawdon-Smith (later the wife of the architect Lord Llewellyn-Davies and Labour's chief whip in the House of Lords) after the flat they shared had been damaged in one of the first air raids on London. The Rothschilds' lease ran out at the end of 1940. Since it was too expensive for Victor's three friends to take over on their own, Blunt suggested that Guy Burgess should become the fourth tenant. The two girls, who hardly knew him, were not enthusiastic but consented when Burgess agreed to keep to his own part of the house on a separate floor: a sensible precaution given his gregariousness. So the lease passed formally from Victor to Tess, who signed it on behalf of all four. Short of assuming the role of hostel warden, an unlikely vocation for Victor, there was nothing he could have done to curb either the sexual appetites of his male tenants or the subversive ferment of their chatter. Nearly forty years later he was to pay a heavy penalty for his loyal and tolerant friendship.

The war ended, and with it Victor Rothschild's marriage to Barbara. In July 1945 he was granted a *decree nisi* in the Divorce Courts by the recently elevated Mr Justice Denning, the future Master of the Rolls and Nestor of the judicial bench. The undefended petition was on the ground of Lady Rothschild's adultery; the court exercised its discretion in favour of Lord Rothschild concerning his own. So, in the cold, unlovely language of the law, ended a partnership of twelve years that had sometimes been exhilarating, more often anguished and ultimately corroded by resentment. Garrett Drogheda, later the impresario of the Royal

Opera House, Covent Garden, saw it as a tragicomic spectacle: 'Laughter was continuous; occasional arguments, storms, disagreements, reconciliations, leading back to calm and gaiety.' Other friends took sides. Maurice Bowra compared Barbara to an atom bomb: 'Everything within five miles disintegrates.' Dadie Rylands trod delicately between the rival camps: 'She did wrong yet felt she had been wronged.'

Alan Hodgkin, the physiologist elected to a Prize Fellowship at Trinity in 1936, the year after Victor, unveiled in his memoirs the cultural and social divide that separated husband from wife; the remoteness of her exuberant Bloomsbury background from the orderly progress of a Cambridge laboratory. Until Barbara found and furnished a new home well away from Cambridge – near Oxford, as it happened – she remained alone at Merton Hall. There the recently married Hodgkins enjoyed her 'half-true gossip about people we knew or would like to know'. They also listened impassively to the tale of her light-hearted infidelities: 'I never knew that he cared. But he remembers every man – and some I'd forgotten myself.'

Hodgkin continues, 'Her society and hospitality (at Victor Rothschild's expense) were to enliven our lives for the first six months that we spent in Cambridge, but at the end of the day we were a little relieved to escape from the tangles of her private life into our own more humdrum existence.'

Humdrum indeed life must have seemed to that young scientist who, after working throughout the war on airborne radar, returned in 1945 to the servitude of a Cambridge laboratory. His contemporaries, however, recognised how sure yet imaginative were the results of his experiments in neuro-physiology: 'virtually as good today', Victor declared more than thirty years later, 'as when they were written.' Hodgkin does after all belong to what Noël Annan, in a celebrated essay, calls *The Intellectual Aristocracy*: a largely Cambridge network of relationships embracing among other families those of Macaulay, Trevelyan, Arnold, Huxley, Darwin, Keynes, Adrian, Haldane and Butler. From this sprawling dynasty sprang every Master of Trinity between 1886 and 1990. It was thus no surprise that this most modest and gentle of men, whose only capital was his brain, in time became Sir Alan Hodgkin, Nobel Laureate for Medicine, President of the Royal Society, member of the Order of Merit and Master of Trinity.

Released from the army and anxious to take up the threads of his own scientific career, Victor Rothschild found himself without a home in Cambridge. He could not continue to share Merton Hall with Barbara and hated hotel life. Alan and Marni Hodgkin offered him both shelter and companionship. For several months he had the use of the small guest room in their four-bedroom house, humbly moving to a summer house in the garden when it was required for a visitor. 'Somewhat to our surprise,' Alan wrote, 'we found him an easy person to have in the house...He took to sleeping in the summer-house with calm, and even with the appearance of enjoyment, in spite of the cold and damp. From time to time Victor invited us for a weekend in the pampering comfort of Ranger's Cottage, in Tring park – a very pleasant rest and change for all of us.' He showed his gratitude in other ways, too, offering in vain to buy the house for them. But they did accept a car, a television set, £1000 each for the children and quantities of Château Lafite; with regret they declined a consignment of ornamental pheasants because they had to be brought into the house each night. There were other kindnesses on Victor's part: the loan of laboratory apparatus and of a small Gauguin head of a Tahitian girl. Alan confessed his most lasting debt to be the influence Victor had on his life by softening the strong puritanical streak of a Quaker upbringing.

Having himself married in 1944 (and acquired in Peyton Rous an American father-in-law who was also to win a Nobel Prize for Medicine), Alan Hodgkin was overjoyed when in 1946 Victor found much happiness in his marriage to Tess Mayor: 'my old flame', as Alan called her, for they had been intimate friends for years. Yet the bruises of Victor's first marriage never quite healed. He was hurt when those he supposed to be his friends went to see Barbara at her new home. More than forty years later, shortly after her death in 1989, he told me how much it had upset him to read Paddy Leigh Fermor's affectionate memoir of her in a newspaper; it recalled her surrounded by such old friends as Peggy Ashcroft,

Dadie Rylands and Freddie Ayer, 'with feasting and talk and much laughter far into the night'.

She was married twice more; to Rex Warner, the poet, novelist and translator of Greek tragedies, and to Nico Ghika, the Greek painter, sculptor and writer. Although Victor also delighted in remarriage, his relations with the three children Barbara bore him, all of whom adored her, remained uneasy and sometimes worse.

Another casualty of the divorce was Rushbrooke Hall, near Bury St Edmunds, in Suffolk. The disposal of Tring Park, except for a cottage or two, had left the Rothschilds without an estate. Victor himself was indifferent to country life, although he took an interest in scientific farming. He did not care for trees or flowers or birds (except owls); took no pleasure in the essentially English art of landscape gardening, or in the clipped hedges, shaven lawns and massed regiments of potted plants cultivated at enormous expense by some of his French cousins ('How do you manage to have all those picturesque old leaves?' one of them asked his English host. 'Do you import them from Hungary?') But Barbara's aesthetic eye, talent for doing up houses and love of parties craved a more spacious place than Merton Hall. So in 1938 he paid £37,500 for Rushbrooke Hall, with its 300 acres of park and farmland. A red-brick moated house of tranquil beauty, it had been completed in the reign of Queen Elizabeth I and recently restored by its latest owner, Lady Islington, the widow of a governor-general of New Zealand. Its attractions included a priest hole, a dining room with Grinling Gibbons carvings, a great hall designed by William Kent and many ancient oaks. Barbara had scarcely completed her own redecoration by the outbreak of war.

Soon afterwards much of Rushbrooke was handed over to the Red Cross for use as a hospital. It emerged in 1945, much dilapidated and in need of repairs estimated at £100,000. Victor desired no monument to his failed marriage, certainly not one that consumed five tons of coal a week. Unable to sell it, he offered the house to the West Suffolk County Council for use as an agricultural college. It was accepted, but handed back some months later because no suitable farm could be acquired. Others to reject Rushbrooke included the Thingoe Rural District Council, the

British Limbless Ex-Servicemen's Association, the War Office, the Royal Society, Trinity College, the Agricultural Research Council and the National Trust (which required a substantial endowment of land or money). So it lay derelict for the next decade and more. The lead was stolen from the roof, the fabric crumbled and the palace where once Queen Elizabeth had held court became a store for farm implements and bags of fertilisers. In 1961, shortly after Rothschild had ordered the house to be demolished as unsafe, it caught fire. That was the end of Rushbrooke. Some thought it a laborious way to exorcise a ghost.

CHAPTER 4

Collector

Victor had no illusions about his ancestors. 'The first Rothschilds', he said, 'were ruthless, almost gangsters; they took risks and made money. The next generation became respectable; they bought land, built houses, gave to charity. Their children had the confidence to start collecting.' It was, he maintained, a genetic impulse that ran through every branch of the family tree. Most Rothschild collections followed the accepted pattern of the rich down the ages: pictures, sculpture, carpets, furniture, books, manuscripts, coins, enamels, gold and silver objects – not least N. M. Rothschild's sixty-four-ounce chamber-pot of 1826–7 to which a prudish descendant added a second handle. The more adventurous pursued thimbles, Derby winners, early postage stamps, death masks, irises, dog collars and a certain parasite to be found only in the tear duct of the hippopotamus.

'One always builds too small,' the French architect Gabriel-Hippolyte Destailleur warned Ferdinand de Rothschild during the construction of Waddesdon. Not every member needed such advice. Victor's Uncle Walter, the second Lord Rothschild, amassed for scientific research more than two million butterflies and moths, 300,000 bird skins, 200,000 birds' eggs, 144 giant tortoises. Across the Channel his cousin Edmond left 40,000 engravings and nearly 4000 drawings to the Louvre. Philippe, poet, proprietor and saviour of Mouton-Rothschild, boasted a private cellar of 300,000 bottles. Arthur spent prodigiously on cigars, smoked one from each box and gave away the rest; he similarly bought neckties by the hundred, wore perhaps half a dozen of them each day yet never for a second time. Most left some record of their industry. Walter identified 5000 new species and published 1500 learned papers; his niece Miriam, to whom he bequeathed 140 mother-of-pearl-handled fish knives (the forks were missing), a gold repeater watch and 500 live parakeets, produced volume after volume of a definitive and beautifully illustrated work on fleas.

Victor seemed at first to be immune to the collector's gene. On succeeding to the family honours in 1937 he disembarrassed himself of Tring and 148 Piccadilly together with their plethoric contents. He cared little for old masters or ornate furniture, but retained some rare Hilliard portraits, larger than the artist's better-known miniatures; and Gainsborough's *The Morning Walk*, bought by the first Lord Rothschild for £10,000 in 1884 and sold by his grandson to the National Gallery for £30,000 in 1954. He found more pleasure in Braque and Modigliani, most of all in Cézanne's *Arlequin*, which he bought for £11,000 in the 1930s and gave to his son Jacob. He regretted letting slip Cézanne's *Boy in the Red Waistcoat*, put on the market by a German collector because Hitler thought the artist decadent.

With expert advice, particularly from John Lumley, he formed one dazzling collection of English silver and another of gold objects, including four eighteenth-century racing cups. At the time of their sale at Christie's in 2001, the ten pieces he had formerly owned represented about one-seventh of all known pre-1800 English gold objects. They fetched a total of £1.44 million. A few years before his death he sold for £1 million the fifty-eight gold boxes that his Rothschild grandmother Emma had inherited from her father, a Rothschild of the Frankfurt branch of the family.

Any rich man could have done as well. Victor Rothschild's early fame as a collector rests neither on pictures nor silver nor gold but on the library of some 3000 eighteenth-century printed books, manuscripts and bindings he acquired in scarcely more than a dozen years. He began to collect in 1932 under the inspiration of his English literature tutor at Cambridge, Dadie Rylands. The syllabus included Joseph Addison, which prompted Victor to pick up an eighteenth-century edition of his *Works* on David's bookstall in the marketplace, that lucky dip for discerning but impecunious bibliophiles. His next purchase was a first edition of *A Sentimental Journey* from another Cambridge bookshop, Heffer. Then came raids on the London dealers under the guidance of Rylands. Half a century later I listened to the tutor teasing his old pupil with affectionate malice. 'Everything I know of English literature I learned from George Lyttelton at Eton,' Dadie proclaimed, 'and everything you know of English literature you learned from me.'

Victor became a trusting customer of the Robinson brothers, whose premises in Pall Mall more resembled a country house than a shop. Their suave yet scrupulously fair business methods enabled them to make private purchases from almost eighty peerage families during those years of economic depression and retrenchment, and Victor was a beneficiary. Among the earliest treasures they flourished before him was a first issue of *Gulliver's Travels*, the nucleus of his celebrated collection of Swift books and manuscripts. He established a similar rapport with the formidable New York bookseller Dr A. S. W. Rosenbach, who in the guise of gentleman-collector and scholar snared the young patrician with guile and flattery. The Doctor assured Rothschild that although he had been extravagant in forming his own collection, he was always careful in protecting the interests of his customers. But Rothschild caught him out after buying a supposed presentation copy of Swift's *Memoirs of Sir William Temple*; the inscription was not in the author's hand but in that of the publisher. Rosenbach tore up Rothschild's cheque and insisted that he should keep the volume as a gesture of reparation and repentance. Rothschild was impressed; he found nothing wrong with the finest known copy of Gray's *Elegy*, for which he willingly paid Rosenbach $33,000, or with Horace Walpole's copy of the Strawberry Hill Press *Odes*.

A month after Rothschild's twenty-fourth birthday, the saleroom correspondent of the *Daily Telegraph* wrote of him as 'one of the keenest private collectors of 18th-century books', when he bid for part of Edward Gibbon's library. Three years later, in 1937, the bibliographer John Hayward, whose caustic tongue was much feared, saluted Rothschild as the man who had restored confidence in the London book trade and so revived its fortunes. Another friend and bibliographer, John Carter, later wrote of the inspired timing of his collection,

> Lord Rothschild was able to take advantage of that violent reaction of the majority against eighteenth-century books which followed the boom of the twenties. For some years at any rate competition would be limited; a keen buyer in a temporarily unfashionable department would get the offers; and a reasonable beginning might secure foundations which ten years later would need twenty years of patient laying.

As in so many of his undertakings, Rothschild sought the best professional advice; but the determination and flair were his. And although he was driven to collect by the thrill of the chase, he did not scorn value for money: the itch of the family gold bug which he dignified by the name of chrysogene. In 1981 he amused himself by calculating whether his expensive pastime had also proved a profitable investment compared with buying the shares of a large established company such as Royal Dutch. He selected ten volumes acquired between 1933 and 1948. Allowing for inflation, or the fall in the purchasing power of sterling, five turned out to have appreciated well, two had fallen a little, three had proved very bad bargains. By 1981 the books were worth £52,500; the equivalent number of Royal Dutch shares purchased during the same period, £140,000. And of course the books, while bringing their owner pride and pleasure, had paid no monetary dividend.

Wartime service in military intelligence left him little opportunity of adding to his library. In 1942, however, the discovery that he had earlier been swindled provoked him into suing one of the leading book dealers of New York, Gabriel Wells. The story begins in 1937, when Wells arrived in London bearing among other works for sale what purported to be the finest known copy of Fielding's novel *Tom Jones*, published in 1749 in six volumes. It had been acquired in about 1924 by the songwriter Jerome Kern, whose library was sold at auction in 1929. Victor Rothschild's friend Dr Rosenbach bought it at the Kern sale for the astonishingly high sum of $29,000: equivalent at the time to £6000, or not less than

£120,000 in the currency of the late 1990s. Shortly afterwards, Rosenbach sold it to the American steel magnate Owen D. Young at a profit of 10 per cent. In 1937, about to retire as president of General Electric and wanting to dispose of his collection on leaving New York, Young allowed the dealer Gabriel Wells to take certain works to England to test the market.

Rothschild was introduced to Wells by Lionel Robinson, a partner in the book dealers W. H. Robinson. Wells offered him two works: the celebrated Kern copy of *Tom Jones* and an autograph manuscript of the first three books of Pope's *Essay on Man*, which had also been knocked down to Rosenbach for $29,000 at the Kern sale and subsequently sold to Owen D. Young. Wells told Rothschild he could have the pair for a total of £5000. Rothschild was attracted by *Tom Jones*, a beautiful copy with uncut leaves in its original binding, but not by the Pope manuscript; the only manuscripts he collected were those of Swift. He also considered £5000, although less than half what Rosenbach had paid for the pair in 1929, too high a price for 1937. Nor would Wells sell him *Tom Jones* alone. Rothschild rejected the transaction. But as he later wrote,

> Wells pestered me so much, however, that in the end, almost in desperation, I decided to make him what I considered was an unnecessarily low offer in the hope that he would become sick of trying to sell them to me and take them back with him to America. I remember ringing him up from 19 Royal Mint Street in the City and saying 'I'll offer you £3,500 for the pair.' Wells said he would have to consult Mr Young in New York and subsequently I was very surprised and not altogether pleased to hear that the offer had been accepted. I sent Wells a cheque for £3,500.

In fact, such was the wealth of young Lord Rothschild (he had succeeded to his uncle's title one month earlier) that he carelessly sent Wells two identical cheques for £3500 within the space of a few days. Wells obligingly returned the second cheque.

Victor now had an incomparable copy of *Tom Jones* and placed it on his shelves at Merton Hall, Cambridge. There it remained until the outbreak of war in 1939 when he moved his valuable library for greater safety to his country house, Rushbrooke Hall, Suffolk. Nothing more might have been heard of it except as a coveted collector's piece had not Victor, with characteristic charity, invited a physically disabled friend to spend the wartime years at Cambridge as his guest and so escape the danger of air raids on London. He was John Hayward, the scholar and bibliophile, 'my faithful and patient mentor', as Victor described him, already the victim of an incurable muscular ailment that allowed him to move only with difficulty. In the new year of 1940 he accompanied Victor to a weekend party at Rushbrooke. There, one wet Sunday morning, he took down the Jerome Kern copy of *Tom Jones* in order to solve a small technical problem for John Carter. Hayward later wrote,

> While I was casually turning over the leaves of one of the volumes I was suddenly aware of a slight difference in the feel (between thumb and forefinger) and (to an eye familiar with the type and paper of books of that period) the appearance of one of the leaves. A doubt immediately entered my mind as to the authenticity of the leaf in question and consequently of the whole set of volumes.

He therefore made a careful examination of each volume, which convinced him that the Kern *Tom Jones* was not an authentic first edition but a doctored copy containing leaves either reprinted or inserted from later editions. This opinion was endorsed by Lionel Robinson who had innocently engineered the sale by bringing Wells and Rothschild together. On the strength of this double testimony by expert bibliographers, Rothschild asked Wells to take back both *Tom Jones* and the Pope manuscript, and to return the £3500 he had paid for them. When Wells refused, Rothschild sued him for fraudulent misrepresentation. Although at the time of purchase he had thought £1750 'a knock-down price' for the finest known copy of *Tom Jones*, its value as a fake could be little more than £100. He therefore demanded the sum of £1650 ($8151), together with interest and costs.

The action was heard in the United States District Court, Southern District of New York, in 1942, although the British parties to the case were allowed to testify in London. Both sides hired counsel of the highest calibre. Rothschild was represented by Gerald Gardiner, who twenty-two years later became Lord Chancellor in the first Labour government of Harold Wilson; Wells and Young (as the owner of the book for whom Wells had acted) by E. Holroyd Pearce, who as Lord Pearce was elevated in 1962 to be a Lord of Appeal in Ordinary. Kenneth Diplock, a young English barrister who was called as an expert witness on the law of sale, also went to the House of Lords six years after Pearce. Rothschild had no experience of the courts, but having been coached in giving evidence by his father-in-law, St John Hutchinson KC, was thought to have acquitted himself well.

Both Wells and Young denied any knowledge of *Tom Jones* having been doctored; so too did Rosenbach, from whom Young had bought it. All pleaded that they had accepted it as genuine on the strength of the catalogue entry at the Jerome Kern sale, without troubling to subject it to more than a cursory inspection. Nor, of course, had Rothschild appraised the book with an expert eye; indeed, he admitted in court that he did not have the necessary skill to do so. As John Carter wrote, 'Seldom has so publicised a book passed through such a succession of diligent hands, to be accused of such glaring imperfections at the end.' Rather than risk a damaging judgement, the defendants settled out of court for $14,000; terms which Rothschild described as 'entirely satisfactory'. Rosenbach, although not formally joined in the action, agreed to pay a share to avoid further involvement, as did the bookseller who had originally sold *Tom Jones* to Kern.

As part of the settlement, Rosenbach received back from Rothschild the doctored volumes, which by then had no more than a curiosity value, and later sold them to a Chicago collector. Rothschild, however, retained the genuine but unwanted Pope manuscript for which he had unwillingly paid Wells £1750. In October 1942 he gave it to be auctioned at a sale he organised in aid of the wartime Red Cross and St John Fund. There the *Essay on Man* fetched a disappointing £1300 compared with the

£6000 Rosenbach had paid for it at the Kern sale thirteen years earlier.

Who was responsible for the cosmetic surgery on *Tom Jones*? In the account of the case which he later wrote, Victor Rothschild pointed accusingly to what few had earlier noticed in the catalogue of the Kern sale of 1929: that immediately following lot 511, the *Tom Jones* bought by Rosenbach for $29,000, was lot 512, a second edition of the same novel which Rosenbach also bought for a mere $1700. An associate of Rosenbach's, Victor believed, having examined the Doctor's expensive purchase, realised that it lacked a dozen pages. So he dismembered both copies, removed from lot 512 the pages required to complete lot 511, inserted them into lot 511, then sewed up both copies. The top edge of the pages of lot 512, however, had been gilded. Why did this adornment not show on certain pages of the doctored lot 511? Because, according to what a Rosenbach mole told Victor in 1982, the culprit had used a razor blade to cut a very thin slice off the top gilt edge of every page needed to make good the master copy; and as a perfectionist in his shady business, the bibliosurgeon had deliberately made his hand shake so that the new edges were as serrated as those of lot 511. If Owen Young did not get a pristine first edition of *Tom Jones* for his $29,000 plus 10 per cent, at least he acquired a dazzling example of the forger's art.

There are, it must be confessed, other plausible versions of when and how the deception took place. One is that the insertion of the missing leaves went back to the early or mid 1920s, before Kern had acquired his *Tom Jones*, and before the future lot 512 had been rebound with gilt edges. A more picturesque tale is that the first person to notice the incomplete state of lot 511 after the Kern sale was Young's female librarian, who indignantly returned *Tom Jones* to Rosenbach. The book was sent back to her a week or two later, its pages complete and the whole enfolded in a mink coat – 'because we have run out of wrapping paper'.

The cast of this delectable drama continued to gather fame. John Hayward, whose erudition and sensitive fingers enabled Rothschild to pierce the defences of the American book dealers, remained in the former nursery of Merton Hall until the end of the war, when he returned to London to share a flat in Chelsea with T. S. Eliot. His lasting friendship with the Rothschild family also embraced their cook Mabel, who would apostrophise the bibliographer in letters that began 'Dear Sir and Pie-fancier'.

The learned antagonists Gerald Gardiner and Holroyd Pearce both rose to the top of their profession, as we have seen. But Gardiner disappointed Rothschild when they met again nearly twenty years later by apparently having no recollection of the contest. 'I feel very ashamed', he wrote, 'at not having had the case more clearly in mind when you spoke to me about it. As you may have discovered, barristers have very bad memories. I think that this is because we have to acquire the art of learning a large number of new facts very quickly and would probably be unable to do so if we could not forget those of previous cases.'

As for Pearce, it may be that *Tom Jones* had sharpened his eye for an aesthetic bargain. On his death in 1990 in his ninetieth year, even close friends were astounded to learn that he had left a fortune of £5.5 million; for he had neither inherited a large sum nor could he possibly have earned it at the Bar. It emerged that Pearce, who liked to dabble in works of art, had in 1951 bought a three-foot-high bronze of a dancing boy for £7, as a garden ornament. In the last year of his life he put it up for sale anonymously at Sotheby's, where it was identified as a rare Adriaen de Vries of about 1610 and bought by a London dealer for £6.82 million. It is now in the Getty Museum, Malibu.

Well satisfied with his victory, Victor prepared a verbatim account of the lawsuit, had it privately printed in an edition of 150 and sent it to his friends; a truncated version of it later appeared in a volume of his essays, *Random Variables*. He confessed to having learned two lessons from the case. First, that if you are a collector and people like John Hayward or John Carter are your friends, you are bound to have some unpleasant surprises when they have 'had a look' at your library. Secondly, 'that the law is very complicated and if you try to understand it, you will never again buy a barrel of glue, a stallion or a valuable old book.' Hence the epigraph which he gave his collector's piece: *Caveat emptor*. The full title of Fielding's novel was *The History of Tom Jones, a Foundling*.

Victor called his book about the case *The History of Tom Jones, a Changeling*.

'I am starting to reinterest myself in my books,' Victor wrote to Duff Cooper in the spring of 1946, 'and have the idea of producing a catalogue of my library.' It was to be on a spacious scale He sent to nineteen of the country's leading bibliographers a copy of his 'Proposals', a printed eight-page flysheet, for their comments. No man was more persuasive in enlisting the skills and knowledge of others, however busy their lives. They included John Carter, R. W. Chapman, Sir Walter Greg, John Hayward, Sir Geoffrey Keynes, P. H. Muir, A. N. L. Munby, George Rylands and John Sparrow. The heaviest burden fell on Miss N. M. Shawyer, who worked on the catalogue for six years.

The sumptuous two-volume work that emerged from the Cambridge University Press in 1954 is called *The Rothschild Library. A Catalogue of the Collection of Eighteenth-century Printed Books and Manuscripts formed by Lord Rothschild*. It is both an accolade and a monument. 'Had he done nothing else,' William Waldegrave said at his memorial service, 'his name would be known to bibliophiles as long as Rothschild numbers, like Köchel numbers for Mozart, are used to classify eighteenth-century books.' One reviewer dwelt on Rothschild's fondness for uncut copies in original wrappers or boards, 'transcendent specimens that have a sort of uncanny luxuriance about them, like giant vegetables at the village flower show'. The future Librarian of the House of Commons, David Holland, also praised Rothschild's skill in linking his authors through their libraries. Gibbon leads to Walpole, Walpole to Gray, Gray to Pope, Pope to Young; or from Johnson to Boswell to Goldsmith to Burke to Reynolds to Garrick. Thus does the compiler lay bare the sinews of literary history.

Most of his spoils had been taken by storm in the saleroom or by discreet negotiation with the dealers of two continents. A few were presents. His mother gave him Boswell's first important work, *An Account of Corsica*; Geoffrey Keynes, brother of Victor's much closer friend Maynard, a volume of Swift's *Miscellanies*; John Hayward, a dozen books that whimsically included an anonymous *Discourse of*

Free Thinking for the Use of the Poor; Judy Montagu, a Sheridan given by H. H. Asquith to her mother, the prime minister's inamorata.

He gave more than he received. That helps to explain why William Blake is represented in the catalogue by only a single work, *Poetical Sketches*. While still a boy, Victor had inherited a copy of Blake's *Songs of Innocence and Experience*, bought originally by his grandfather to give to his mistress, Lady Gosford. For some reason it never reached her, passing instead to Victor. As a Cambridge undergraduate, before he had begun his collection, he showed it to Anthony Blunt who admired it. In the same open-handed spirit that also moved Victor to give his friend £80 to buy a Poussin, he allowed Blunt to walk off with Blake's exceptionally beautiful illustrated work. Later he realised the value of what he had relinquished and Blunt was persuaded to return it, not to Victor but to a ten-year-old daughter for whom it was kept in trust. 'No doubt', Victor said when telling me the story many years later, 'his conscience was pricking him about the Poussin.' He presented another old friend, Dadie Rylands, with a first edition of Johnson's *Rasselas*; the recipient was more amused than affronted when asked to leave it back to Victor in his Will.

Victor was not a clubbable man. He disliked large parties, company not of his choice, formal clothes and late nights. He nevertheless allowed himself to be elected to that select gathering of bibliophiles, the Roxburghe Club. It had been founded on 17 June 1812 to commemorate the sale by the Duke of Roxburghe of Valdarfer's 1471 edition of Boccaccio's *Decameron* to Lord Blandford. The book fetched £2260, the highest price yet paid for a single volume and not to be eclipsed until 1884. On or near the anniversary, the club dines year by year in London or the country, usually at the house of a member, who lays out his treasures for inspection. It was and remains both aristocratic and learned. The roll of members, printed in strict order of social precedence, included in 1964, the year that Victor was host, three dukes, a marquess, four earls, four lesser peers and several substantial landowners. Collectors, curators of great libraries and academics brought a more professional flavour to the evening.

Each member in turn, if he is so minded, produces a finely

printed and bound edition of a previously unpublished manuscript to be distributed throughout the club. When it came to Victor's turn, he proposed *The History of Tom Jones, a Changeling.* The club turned it down as defamatory without having read the book. He next suggested *The Rothschild Library.* This too was rejected unseen as not being of sufficient interest. Well might Victor have echoed the judgement of his cousin by marriage Lord Rosebery, a former president of the club, that 'the great mass of the Roxburghe publications are twaddle – mere bibliomaniac reprints of dry superannuated husks, of no savour to man or beast'. Victor's third and ultimately successful choice was a sumptuous edition of Baron Ferdinand de Rothschild's *Livre d'Or,* published in 1957 with an illuminating commentary by James Pope-Hennessy. It is the apotheosis of the boarding-house visitors' book; the children's autograph album writ large. It reflects an era when guests invited to Waddesdon or similar establishments would as soon leave behind their gun cases and billiard cues as their private hoard of aphorisms and epigrams: sentiments for all seasons to be inscribed personally on the thick creamy pages of a richly bound album. Queen Victoria exactly caught the spirit of the *livre d'or* when in 1886 she wrote out a couplet by the obscure Scottish poet William Maccall:

> *Noble names no nobleness can give*
> *If within no nobleness there live.*

Poets and painters, composers and historians, novelists and men of action escort their sovereign through her reign. Politicians abound. Gladstone is sententious: 'The principle of Conservatism is mistrust of the people, qualified by fear: the principle of Liberalism is trust in the people qualified by prudence.' Disraeli writes with practised eloquence, 'The defects of great men are the consolation of dunces.' The last entry of all in Baron Ferdinand's *Livre d'Or* before his death in 1898 belongs to a skeleton at the feast, a raven on the castle wall: Sir William Harcourt, who as Chancellor of the Exchequer had just introduced the death duties that were to cripple his own family twice in a single year. That was not

something members of the Roxburghe Club could read without
interest.

Within a dozen or so years of making his first find as a Cambridge
undergraduate, Rothschild's collection approached completion. He
possessed first editions and many association copies of all the most
famous books printed in eighteenth-century England; the best collection of Swift first editions and original manuscripts outside the
British Museum; some of the most covetable English eighteenth-
century bindings, particularly those of Roger Payne. All were in
splendid condition and so very valuable. Only a few gaps remained.

Repletion turned his thoughts to the ultimate disposal of his
library. One of the last of his important purchases was twenty-eight
pages of the original manuscript of Swift's *Directions to Servants*,
published posthumously in 1745 and found among the papers of
the first Earl of Normanton: an ambitious parson who died in 1809
as Archbishop of Dublin with a clutch of acquired peerages and a
fortune of £400,000 made on the Stock Exchange. Thinking that
both the manuscript and its provenance might appeal to G. M.
Trevelyan, Victor asked the Master of Trinity round to Merton
Hall. 'Trevelyan was deeply moved by it,' he wrote. 'His hand
shook so violently with emotion as he turned the pages over that I
became greatly frightened that he might tear a page.' Then our
most celebrated social historian began to read it, and once again the
frail leaves were in danger as he shouted with laughter. It was the
emotion and pleasure evoked by Swift's satire that largely
prompted Victor to give his collection to Trinity College, where it
occupies a bay of the Wren Library. The handing-over of the benefaction was protracted. Although the initial offer was made in
October 1948, it was not until January 1952 that Victor wrote to
Trevelyan,

> This afternoon is rather an important one for me, as I am taking
> the first book out of my library to Trinity Library. The episode
> will pass unnoticed except by the under-librarian, but as you
> may imagine it is quite something for me. I expect there will be
> an anti-climax and the book, a rather large copy of Pope's

translation of the Iliad, will not fit in to the shelves. I have become quite devoted to my bay, as I call it to myself.

The last items reached Trinity in October 1969, and Victor rejoiced that his cherished collection had found a second home in the college 'within whose shadow I have spent all my life since I was a schoolboy and for which I have such a great respect and affection'.

His euphoria did not last. In April 1975 he told me how bitterly he regretted parting with his library to Trinity. Ten years later he sent me a copy of his privately printed *Open Letter to the Master of Trinity College Cambridge from Lord Rothschild*. It reproduced among other documents his informal offer to Trevelyan of 1948 and his formal declaration of trust of 1951. In the first he emphasised the necessary care of the books, 'although this is neither a difficult nor arduous task'. In the second he was more explicit: 'The said Library shall be maintained in good condition in accordance with a Memorandum on the preservation and treatment of valuable books compiled by me and included in the said Library.' In scalding terms he now reproached the college for its seeming neglect of his collection. The Master, Sir Andrew Huxley, having been elected into office less than a year before, could scarcely be culpable. He was nevertheless obliged to face the Rothschild onslaught:

Alan Hodgkin and Peter Medawar (both Nobel Prizewinners and holders of the Order of Merit) cleaned their glassware in their laboratories. They, and you if you did the same, were not too important to undertake a menial task. The same cannot be said about the Librarian, his deputy or his staff who have not seen fit to clean or grease the bindings over a period of sixteen years.

The Swift manuscripts, moreover, had been confined 'in what can only be described as a small, locked airing cupboard... The effect, not unnaturally, was to distort the special cases... to such an extent that it is now difficult to extract the manuscripts. A sharp instrument, perhaps a chisel, has clearly been used to open one of the cases.' His open letter went on to remind the Master of the many other treasures in the Trinity library which had been allowed to accumulate dirt and dust, from Isaac Barrow's copy of *Euclid's Elements* which he gave to Newton, to the original manuscript of Milton's *Lycidas*. As for 'the so-called catalogue', it was no more than 'an incomplete card index'. There was a reference to the 'scandalous neglect and violation of the Declaration of Trust' and much more in the same vein.

Trinity College may well have had an adequate defence to charges they considered exaggerated; Victor Rothschild was not a man to waste a good grievance, and certainly his library appears to have suffered no permanent damage. In sending copies of the *Open Letter* to his friends, the aggrieved collector followed the practice of Winston Churchill's *War Memoirs*; he published the rebuke but not the riposte.

There remained one consolation. Victor told me of it in a letter about three months before his death:

> When my detestable great-aunt Theresa decided to leave Paris in a hurry during its bombardment, she left on foot with a Gladstone bag in one hand and a Benvenuto Cellini in the other.
>
> When I decided to give my beloved library of 18th-century first editions, bindings and Swift manuscripts to Trinity College Library, by analogy with my great-aunt Theresa I wondered – and then decided – what few items I would *not* give Trinity because I cherished them so much. At the same time I realised that when withholding a few items, I must not interfere with runs or the general significance of my collection. I therefore held back the following books and one relatively unimportant manuscript.

His list of thirty-five items would without any addition have entitled their owner to be considered a discerning and well-endowed collector. It began with first editions of Frances Burney's *Evelina* and of Robert Burns's *Poems, chiefly in the Scottish Dialect*; it ended with one leaf from the Gutenberg Bible 1450–5, another from Caxton's *Chronicles of England* 1480 and a presentation copy of the third edition of Newton's *Principia*. Between them could be found a first edition of Gray's *Elegy*, half a dozen Swifts and as many bindings by Roger Payne.

'Then I felt', Victor's letter to me continued, 'that these few books and the Swift manuscript would remind me too much of my beloved Library and, in 1960, I gave them to my daughter Emma who at that time was an infant prodigy – she got a scholarship to Oxford when she was fifteen. So Emma probably has the finest micro-collection of books plus one manuscript in the world.'

Institutions are ambivalent towards their benefactors; they welcome the benefaction but do not care to be told in too much detail how it should be spent. So Rothschild invited another rebuff from those proud and prickly Fellows when he suggested to Trinity that the college should publish and that he should subsidise what he called 'a swell book' about the riches of its library. On the recto of each page would be reproduced a leaf of a manuscript or the title page of a book; on the verso facing it, a short essay on both the work and its author. And who better to engrave the diamond than Dadie Rylands, now well into his ninth decade but as inspired in style as he was elastic of step. As his pupil and patron said of him on his eighty-fifth birthday, 'he is one of those who hears the music of the spheres but who far too rarely records what he hears.' Dadie began the series with Shakespeare's *Venus and Adonis*, of which Trinity possessed one of the very few remaining copies. It is an elegant and allusive piece, as exquisite as an Elizabethan miniature. But the library committee of the college, having at first welcomed Rothschild's plan, then appointed the inevitable sub-committee. 'I will recount some of the headaches,' Victor wrote to Dadie. 'It is difficult to appreciate infinity, but when I think about the headaches, I get an idea of what infinity is.'

Negotiations foundered, so Rothschild persuaded his friend to produce half a dozen or so more essays, from Edmund Spenser to A. E. Housman ('that hock-loving epicene,' as Victor labelled the poet and classicist). Together with one or two other Dadiana and an essay on the music of the spheres by Victor's youngest daughter Victoria, he had them beautifully printed and bound by James

Stourton in a limited edition of 200. At a small luncheon given by Victor in Cambridge on his eighty-sixth birthday, Dadie found a copy of *Rylands* on his plate. We drank his health in a double magnum of Château Lafite 1870 that like the guest of honour was full of years but robust and spirited.

CHAPTER 5

Post-war World

'I congratulate you most heartily on your marriage,' Duff Cooper wrote to Victor in August 1946. 'Tess has my deepest sympathy. Give her my love and assure her that when you begin to neglect her I shall always be there.' He dated his letter Feast of the Purification of the Blessed Virgin.

Teresa Mayor, known to her family and friends as Tess, and to one or two others as Red Tess, came of an intellectual dynasty. Her father, Robert John Grote Mayor, had been a King's Scholar at Eton and a Fellow of King's College, Cambridge, as well as an Apostle. He retired early from a senior civil service post in the Board of Education to pursue a life of philosophic speculation. Among those to be found in his family tree are George Grote, historian of Greece, banker and MP; his brother John Grote, Knightbridge Professor of Moral Philosophy at Cambridge; and J. E. B. Mayor, classical scholar and Professor of Latin in the university. Tess's mother Beatrice was a daughter of the banker Daniel Meinertzhagen, whose marriage to the fourth of the nine Potter sisters brought the Mayors into the orbit of a huge high-minded cousinage that embraced, among others, the Webb, Cripps, Courtney, Holt and Hobhouse families. Tess's brother, Andreas Mayor, like his father a KS at Eton and an Apostle at Cambridge, joined the staff of the British Museum, became a member of the wartime Bletchley élite and translated the last volume of Proust.

Five years younger than her future husband, Tess was sent first to a school near Wendover run by Roger Fry's sister Isabel. The curriculum included a thorough grounding in grammar, learning poetry by heart, guided tours of the library and reading at least one serious book a term. Even the dining room was hung with chronological tables, farming took the place of games and there was a ban on lipstick and silk stockings. It all proved too puritanical for Mrs Mayor, who withdrew her fourteen-year-old daughter and sent her to Bedales. There Tess encountered those perennial hallmarks of a progressive education: non-denominational services and the discouragement of competition.

One nearby diversion was Passfield Corner, the home of the Webbs; on reluctantly accepting a peerage, Sidney had become Lord Passfield but his wife insisted on remaining Mrs Webb. Tess recalls how her great-aunt once asked a sporting visitor what he thought of the Poor Law, on which she was an authority. 'Polo?' he replied. 'Used to play quite a lot of it.' Malcolm Muggeridge also lowered the tone by inciting Sidney to flop down on the nearest haystack for an illicit snooze when ordered out by his wife for a three-mile walk.

'A student of unearthly beauty came to Cambridge in my second year,' Michael Straight wrote in his memoirs. 'Her name was Teresa Mayor. She had the gaunt nobility of Yeats's beloved, Maude Gonne, and some of Maud Gonne's cold fire.' Tess, too, was a talented actress who as a child had taken part in a charity show with the legendary Ellen Terry. She shone in every production of the Marlowe Society; in her first year as Portia, in her second as Castiza in *The Revenger's Tragedy*, in her third as Goneril. Straight takes the credit for having diverted her from membership of the Communist party. She herself has described how another Trinity friend, Brian Simon, gravely informed her: 'We have discussed whether you should become a member of the Party. But no, you are not dedicated enough.' She showed suitable contrition for her frivolity but was secretly much relieved by the verdict of the future Professor of Education at Leicester University.

With so many distractions, Tess Mayor did well to take a II.2 in English. But the advice she received from Newnham College was discouraging: 'Your degree precludes you from the civil service. You don't want to teach. You are obviously no good at business. I believe there is a drama school. Good morning.' Instead she took a secretarial course with another friend of the Left, Patricia Rawdon-Smith. Tess went to work for the publisher Jonathan Cape, her friend for Philip Noel-Baker, Olympic athlete, Labour politician, champion of the League of Nations and winner of the Nobel Prize for Peace. Soon after the outbreak of war, Victor Rothschild tried to recruit Pat to MI5 as his secretary. Unwilling to desert Noel-Baker, she recommended Tess, with whom she was sharing a flat in Gower Street before both girls moved to the shelter of Bentinck Street. So Tess reported to Wormwood Scrubs and remained with Victor for the rest of the war, first as his secretary then with commissioned rank as his assistant. In Paris after the Allied occupation she searched for concealed German bombs and booby traps: what the citation of her MBE called 'dangerous work in hazardous circumstances'.

At the end of the war she returned to England and demobilisation. Her services to the Crown, however, were not quite over. While Pat was having a baby – she had married Richard Llewellyn-Davies in 1943 – Tess took her place as a private secretary to Noel-Baker at the Foreign Office; meanwhile she lodged with Pat and Richard in their London house. It was thus as 'a thirty-year-old civil servant living in one room' that the newspapers described her when on 14 August 1946 she was married to Victor at the City of London Registrar's Office: a 'rags-to-riches romance' scarcely justified by the facts.

It was a true marriage of minds, for in November 1945 Victor had joined the Labour party. That a Rothschild should declare such an allegiance was not unprecedented; his father had in youth described himself as a radical-socialist tinged with conservative-individualistic views. What diminished respect for Victor's conversion was the speed with which he had allied himself to Labour little more than three months after its sweeping victory in the general election. 'If you had asked my advice at the time,' Duff later told him, 'I should have counselled delay, as the appearance of rushing to the assistance of the winners is always apt to arouse criticism.' But none doubted the sincerity of his belief in Labour, by no means confined in 1945 to the traditional supporters of the party. As much may be inferred from personal correspondence in which he wrote with satisfaction of the socialism he shared with Tess. In an interview with *Reynold's News*, the paper of the Co-operative Movement, he spoke its language correctly but with the stiffness only to be expected of a pupil who had learned it by heart from an approved textbook.

> We have had Conservative Governments for a long while in England. We have come to associate with Conservative rule the following conditions: unemployment, under-nourishment, unpre-paredness, unpopularity abroad, unequal pay, education and opportunities, undeveloped resources, and lack of opposition to Fascism.
>
> Someone with more experience could no doubt double this list without difficulty. The only time when some of these wrongs were put right was during the war, when conditions and the Labour members of the Cabinet forced the State Control of basic industries and commodities on the Government...

He went on to declare that 'the privilege of serving one's country in time of war is never questioned; the privilege of serving one's country in time of peace is a Socialist idea'. That is a baffling judge-ment from a man who had sold the Tring estate because he was not willing to take on the unpaid responsibilities of the country landowner: local government, the magistracy, the Territorial Army and all those charitable and sporting institutions that are woven into the social fabric of the nation. Could he really believe that vol-untary workers were to be found only in the ranks of Labour?' Lord Rothschild's eccentric creed may perhaps be traced to the two friends, both members of the new government, whom he acknow-ledged to be his most influential mentors: John Strachey, Under-Secretary for Air, and Lord Jowitt, the Lord Chancellor. Neither, as it happened, inspired wholehearted confidence, even among their party colleagues.

Strachey's political progress, in the words of his biographer Professor Hugh Thomas, had been 'indecisive and perhaps evasive'. From the Labour party he switched to Oswald Mosley's New party, then to approval (though never overt membership) of the Communist party, and so back to Labour. Victor, who in youth had read *The Coming Struggle for Power*, asked its author whether he thought a Rothschild could join the Labour party. Strachey assured him that as there were no class distinctions in its ranks, he would be welcome. Thus was the third Baron Rothschild ushered into the egalitarian society by the heir presumptive to the Strachey baronetcy; thus did Eton point the way of salvation to Harrow.

His other sponsor, William Jowitt, had also reached the New Jerusalem by a circuitous route. Having been elected to the House of Commons as a Liberal in the general election of 1929, he abruptly abandoned his colleagues a day or two later to take office as Attorney-General in the new Labour government. None questioned his ability as a Law Officer, and later as Lord Chancellor; but that act of opportunism remained a topic of recrimination and ribaldry to the end of his days. As intimates of St John and Mary Hutchinson, the Jowitts became friends of Victor; collecting modern pictures was one of several shared interests. After the war they took a lease from him on a house near Rushbrooke. So it was natural enough for Victor to put the same question to the new Lord Chancellor as he had to Strachey: 'Is there a place in the Labour party for a Rothschild?' Jowitt replied obliquely that it was more scientific and more modern than any other in England; others might have described Labour as the party of monolithic trade unionism, of xenophobia, of ancient grievances and antique remedies. But the assurance satisfied Victor, who took the plunge.

Membership of the Labour party did not much change his life. He had no relish for the manoeuvres and intrigue of party politics, even less for the prospect of office that would further delay his return to scientific research. In April 1946 he devoted his maiden speech to a plea for the compulsory pasteurisation of milk. 'It is an alarming experience to speak in the House of Lords,' he later wrote. 'Not only are there rows of amplifiers attached to the old gentlemen, some of which oscillated audibly during my speech; but also I found it disconcerting to have people coming in and going out while one is talking. It is so unlike lecturing at Cambridge, or to troops about bombs.' Milk contaminated by the bovine tuberculosis germ, he explained, caused thousands of deaths: as if every member of the House were killed twice every year. Their Lordships took the news calmly. So too did Duff Cooper, to whom Victor sent a copy of the speech. 'The subject of pasteurisation of milk', he replied, 'is not one of palpitating interest to me.'

His adherence to Labour sent occasional tremors through his social life. In January 1945 he had been put up for membership of White's, the club in St James's frequented by the rich, the rakish, the well-born and the merely ambitious. His cousin Lord Rosebery, son of the prime minister and wartime Regional Commissioner for Scotland, proposed him; his seconder was Duff Cooper. There followed the usual months of waiting while other members added their signatures to his page in the candidates' book or privately expressed misgivings to the committee. In October 1946 his candidature was 'postponed at the request of his proposer': a tactfully worded withdrawal to avert the humiliation of being blackballed by the election committee. Duff, always the most loyal of friends, protested that he had never heard such nonsense in his life; that White's was not and never had been a political club; and that he could agree neither to withdraw the candidate's name nor even to consult him. Rosebery, however, overruled Duff. It is of interest but scarcely relevant that Victor never cared for the camaraderie of club life. His membership of the Labour party appears to have been but one factor in a disagreeable episode. He may also have been the victim of an anti-Semitic sentiment sharpened by a recent speech in the House of Lords: a courageous but embarrassed attempt on his part to explain the historical background to the Palestine conflict and the murder of British soldiers by the Stern Gang.

In lighter vein he complained to Duff that in common with other Labour supporters invited to the wedding of Miss Mary Churchill to Captain Christopher Soames, he had been placed where he could see nothing except the back of a Conservative minister's neck. Evelyn Waugh dined with him one night at the Savoy: 'Girls pretty and well dressed, the men shabby and celebrated. The host, whom I only knew as a bumptious, exuberant fellow, paralysed with shyness and shame.'

Crumbs of government patronage mitigated these vexations, including a seat on the board of the British Overseas Airways Corporation under the chairmanship of Victor's old friend and mentor, Sir Harold Hartley. The most controversial was a non-executive directorship of the Overseas Food Corporation. Here was his chance to demonstrate on a vast scale what he had blithely asserted on joining the Labour party: that a nationalised industry is more efficient than private enterprise. The primary task of the corporation was to grow groundnuts in Tanganyika: a well-meaning project designed to relieve a worldwide shortage of natural oil, lop at least £10 million a year off Britain's food bill and bring the benefits of economic development to East Africa. John Strachey, by now Minister of Food, was impatient to score a political success. In his haste he omitted to take even the most elementary precautions before plunging into the unknown or to exercise a prudent control over expenditure.

There was no pilot scheme that would have detected some of the difficulties of growing groundnuts on unfamiliar territory. There were inadequate studies of rainfall records, of soil analysis, of the mechanics of clearing virgin scrub. Workers were engaged before they could be housed; sawmills erected without reference to sources of timber; pipelines and railways begun without a thought of where they were to end. Mechanical diggers failed to arrive until the ground had set firm at the end of the rainy season; tractors and converted wartime tanks broke down through age and excessive wear and inadequate maintenance. 'Give us the job and we will finish the tools' was a popular variant on Churchill's wartime exhortation to President Roosevelt. Witch doctors proved troublesome when baobab trees, said to house the rain gods, were pulled down. Personal feuds in the administration were matched by discontent among the labourers; but here at least London showed its initiative by despatching experienced trade union officials to teach them how to strike in the traditional British manner.

Much obloquy, some of it unfair, fell on Strachey and on the chairman of the Overseas Food Corporation, Leslie Plummer (a director of Express Newspapers who, like many of Lord Beaverbrook's employees, professed socialist sympathies). Rothschild went largely unscathed. Recruited to the board as a scientific adviser, he could not be blamed for its erratic strategy or incompetent management. He nevertheless felt obliged to defend his colleagues, though in terms that lacked conviction:

> Scientists have done and are doing a magnificent job of work under conditions which might easily have disheartened if not discouraged them altogether. How many scientists in England like myself would have been able to carry on when the microscope or a simple chemical like hydrochloric acid was unavailable?

He went on to concede that the forecasts had been too optimistic, but declared his confidence in the ultimate success of groundnuts. It was not to be. The second year's harvest yielded no more than 2000 tons, half the amount of the original seed order. By the time the scheme had been wound up at the insistence of Labour's austere Chancellor of the Exchequer, Stafford Cripps, the loss approached £40 million. Victor thought he could do rather better on his own. 'I have bought a little fruit farm,' he wrote in May 1949. 'It only produces apples and an occasional early strawberry. I bought it mainly as an investment. Most people think I am crazy, but I have a rather non-Party predilection for private ownership of the means of production, particularly when it concerns myself.'

The English Rothschilds put down roots in every sense. Less than half a century after the arrival of Nathan Mayer in Manchester they were busy with their farms and their studs. It was a love of the land that went deeper than social advancement or sport. They did not scorn to become high sheriffs and deputy lieutenants, racehorse owners and masters of staghounds. But they also displayed the arcane, almost instinctive arts of animal husbandry as well as the more scientific skills of agricultural improvement.

Baron Mayer, the youngest of old NM's sons, nicknamed 'Muffy' or 'Tup' , bred both the Derby winner Favorius and a scarcely less famous Jersey bull which he named Mentmore after the estate he had bought and enlarged in 1842. With his genial countenance, generous nature and love of the chase, he might have stepped out of a novel by Surtees. *Hillingdon Hall*, published in 1834, is less well known than its companion volume, *Handley Cross*. It has a place in Rothschild family history, however, by paying Baron Mayer's father a compliment of a sort. Surtees immortalises Mr Jorrocks, the cockney grocer and dedicated master of fox-hounds, as the man 'who had once got to the windward of Rothschild in a deal, and who was reckoned the second-best judge of treacle in the trade'. I like to think that Muff would have chuckled as loudly over Jorrocks's improbable coup on 'Change as over his discourse on such newfangled aids to agriculture as soluble draining tiles, guano and 'sober o'nitrate'.

Muff's nephew Natty, the first Lord Rothschild, was recognised as one of the most knowledgeable breeders of pure stock in Europe; visitors from every corner of the world came to see the Jersey herd and shire-horses at Tring. His fellow landowner the seventeenth Earl of Derby, with a net annual income of £100,000, used to confess that his farm always made a profit until he did the accounts. Rothschild, applying the methods of New Court to the Tring estate, came to the same conclusion, at least on his kitchen garden. Each plate of spinach, he calculated, cost thirty shillings: almost twice the weekly wage of an agricultural labourer before the First World War. But at least he satisfied himself that there was no waste. In 1906, for instance, 200 head of cattle produced precisely 33,404.20 gallons of milk, with only 44 gallons lost in handling.

Such statistical control was dear to his grandson's heart when he too became a farmer. He displayed every quality required of the calling except patience. 'You will see,' Victor wrote to me one summer from Rushbrooke, 'I am what is called "buried" in the country, but a more apposite description would be interfering in the farm operations.' He liked to recall his cousin Baron Maurice, the brother of James de Rothschild MP, who on being elected to the French National Assembly to represent the Hautes-Pyrénées, paid his first official visit to Lourdes. How many miracles had there been in the past few years, he asked the bishop. Only two, he was told. '*On va changer tout ça*,' the new deputy exclaimed. So with Farmer Rothschild, for whom the seasons revolved too slowly. He looked on his farm as a laboratory, but the laboratory of a rich man who could afford to experiment boldly. He liked the unexpected: magicians and conjurors at his parties, wheezes and short cuts in his fields and pastures. He injected hormones into certain breeds of ewe, both to double the number of lambs and to arrange the time of their birth to suit the convenience of the farm. He experimented with quick-growing conifers. He force-fed cockerels with milk through tubes to whiten their flesh.

From his orchards at Risley, also in Suffolk, he was proud to sell apples to Marks & Spencer; but not even his close friendship with Marcus Sieff, the chairman, could persuade the firm to lower its exacting standards of quality and uniformity. He produced on too small a scale to ensure a steady market for his fruit, yet declined to go into partnership with other growers. When he could not sell what he grew, he turned the rejected apples into juice; but in those years before organic farming became all the rage, it proved too cloudy for the fastidious customer.

Another disappointment was to let slip the chance of owning one of the half-dozen most famous vineyards of Bordeaux. Two of them were already in Rothschild hands. Baron Elie, with a few other members of the family, was co-owner of Château Lafite; and Baron Philippe owned Château Mouton-Rothschild. Soon after the war Elie told Victor that Château Margaux was on the market at what in retrospect was a bargain price. 'Buy it,' Elie urged him, 'and I will run it for you.' Victor was enthusiastic, as well he might have been. For Elie, having taken over the management of Lafite in 1946, had within two years seen it pay a dividend for the first time since its purchase by Baron James in 1868. The Treasury, however, refused to release the necessary foreign currency. Looking back on the lost opportunity, Victor regretted he had not bought it on Rothschild credit, repaying the loan whenever it became legal to do so.

In 1949 the Labour government appointed Victor to be chairman of the Agricultural Research Council, a part-time post which he held for the next ten years. Founded as recently as 1931, it was a poor relation of the Medical Research Council with a restricted degree of independence. The Ministry of Agriculture, which controlled its budget, insisted that its role should be no more than advisory. Victor, who had hoped to plan the long-term agricultural needs of the nation, found himself forbidden even to express an opinion on those broad themes. Whitehall confined him to supervising research into important but more limited projects. They included selective weedkillers, bacteria in cheese, lamb dysentery, artificial insemination, the use of nitrogenous fertilisers to improve yields of grass, and in turn milk production.

One typical experiment that caught the chairman's eye was to feed double rations to pigs on Saturday morning, then nothing again until Monday morning. Did the pig suffer any metabolic deficiency or stress at the expense of the economic and social advantages of a free weekend for the pigman? His wartime experience of the unexpected also served him well. During a periodic survey of the agricultural scene, he remarked to his colleagues that the turkey alone seemed to have absolutely no problems to engage the aspiring researcher. Very soon afterwards the industry was struck by a mysterious disease known as Turkey Syndrome 65. An emergency programme of research by the ARC, with help from other agencies, revealed that the birds were being poisoned by Aflatoxin, derived from mouldy peanuts in their food.

Impatient at being denied a wider stage by the Ministry of Agriculture, Victor was thought by his ARC colleagues to interfere too much on matters of scientific detail and personnel best left to the experts, usually men and women of experience and judgement. Sir Solly Zuckerman, the anatomist and wartime scientific adviser who as Lord Zuckerman OM ultimately became Chief Scientific Adviser to the government, was a member of the ARC from 1949 to to 1959. He wrote:

Victor Rothschild was an assiduous but autocratic chairman, who never disguised his dislikes, which were not always shared. On one occasion they focused on the highly respected director of one of the ARC's institutes. A concerted effort had to be made to frustrate Victor in his manoeuvres to remove the man from his post. Victor was also so diligent in seeing that the Council discharged its duties that we sometimes found ourselves cutting across those of Bill Slater, who had joined the Council as Secretary when he retired from his post as Chief Scientific Adviser to the Ministry of Agriculture.

It was during such internal dissensions, Zuckerman later told me in his droll way, that 'Victor would withhold his embassy from me'. There are other witnesses to the rough time the chairman gave the respected Sir William Slater. Victor himself thought the tensions had been exaggerated: 'Slater and I worked harmoniously together for nearly ten years. He used to say he did not like cold water but that when I pushed him in, he was a strong swimmer.' Together the two men did much to improve the scientific standards of the ARC and in turn win more financial independence from Whitehall, as eventually guaranteed by the Agricultural Research Act of 1956.

Another valued member (and Slater's successor as secretary) was Sir Gordon Cox FRS, who had worked amicably with Victor during the war as his opposite number in SOE. Not even that bond of counter-sabotage protected him from written rebukes so robustly worded that they had to be kept off the office files. 'My main object', Victor once wrote to him, 'is to make you admit that you deliberately distorted the facts and that you are ashamed of having done so.' The next paragraph of the chairman's letter implied ignorance as well as duplicity: 'I presume that you know all about sucrose and eel-worms?' Cox was too big a man to let such breezes ruffle his temper. Sometimes they evoked admiration at the ease with which his boss could arrive at the solution of a complex problem, as intellectually impregnable as it was imaginative; sometimes sadness at how little account those solutions took of the hopes and fears, the prejudices and ambitions of the people whom they would affect; sometimes compassion at Victor's ill-disguised need for reassurance. Thus it was that another superior person, the Marquess Curzon of Kedleston, had inspired awe, affection and pity in his bruised subordinates; thus it was that Victor, too, sought to make amends by devising little treats or presents that restored morale.

Scarcely any of the ARC scientists were cast into permanent

outer darkness. But Victor did write in exasperation of one who refused to toe the Rothschild line:

> My experience of —— is that tact, firmness, pleasantness, brandy, or even letting him go to Ceylon to see his girl friends, in the end do not help. He has a congenital chip on his shoulder which cannot be erased, except by putting him in charge of things which he would either destroy or harm.

But the acuteness of observation that provoked censure also led him to intervene on behalf of those in trouble. Noticing Sir Gordon Cox's low spirits after the death of his first wife, Victor contrived to give him a complete change of scene under guise of needing his advice on some agricultural experiments in Italy.

It cannot have helped his relationship with the recalcitrant when, in a lecture at an ARC station, he divided scientific research workers (though not by name) into four groups: the very good, the good, the competent and 'shall we say, the not-so-good'. He wondered whether this last group, 'who often are conscientious and careful workers but without much inspiration or drive, should be allowed to scan a list of scientific subjects soon after graduation and almost at random select one to work on, for nobody's benefit and for an indefinite period'. Rather would he see them 'influenced' – a euphemism perhaps for 'directed' – into more profitable, practical fields. If scientists of such distinction as his friend Alan Hodgkin (he continued) could in wartime turn from such recondite questions as the properties of the membranes of single nerve fibres to work on unfamiliar subjects such as radar, why should not lesser men turn from the morphology of fossil fish to helping the nation's efficient production of food in peacetime?

Although Victor had been appointed to the ARC by Labour, he felt himself increasingly alienated from that essentially urban movement. 'I am on holiday,' he wrote to me from Rushbrooke one August, 'watching the harvest go wrong – contrary to the views of so many members of the Labour party that farmers regularly make a killing.' Ten years' experience of the ARC, buttressed by pride in his own acres, led him to champion the farming community whenever he encountered prejudice: the resentment of the townsman at the rural way of life or hostility to the supposed feather-bedding of agricultural at the expense of manufacturing industry. One example that angered him was a paper produced in 1974 by the Trade Union Research Unit of Ruskin College, Oxford, calling for a curb on the excessive rewards of farming. Replying to it in *The Times*, he accused its authors of having deliberately chosen to begin their survey in 1968, a year of notoriously bad harvests and diminished income, in order to accentuate the rise in income throughout the following five years; and then of having omitted all factors that vitiated their case. Their report, he pointed out, failed to mention that agriculture was 80 per cent financed by individual farmers and landowners who ploughed back much of their profits; that a large part of the apparent increase in farm income came from increases in valuation; that inflation magnified the apparent size of farm incomes, though not in real terms; that other sectors of the economy showed similar increases, not least as the result of government support.

When a lecturer at Trinity later wrote to *The Times* demanding an increase in the capital transfer tax levied on farms, Victor allowed his reply to verge on the discourteous: 'His ideological prejudices shine forth like ill-fitting false teeth ... To coin a phrase: God rid us of these academic economists.' Like his antagonist, Victor, too, gave as his address Trinity College, Cambridge: a band of brothers only in name.

'The best part of my life was spent in a Cambridge laboratory,' Victor told an audience of millions when interviewed on the radio programme, *Desert Island Discs*. Scientific research was for him an enclosed world in which neither his name nor his money, wartime exploits nor government patronage, could pave the way to the top. Some of these attributes, indeed, proved to be obstacles. He was convinced that no scientist called Rothschild would ever find it easy to be taken seriously; and that if he was to use his money to further the cause of science, it must be done by proverbial stealth.

That is why, having rejoined the department of zoology at Cambridge soon after the war, he kept secret a generous plan he confided only to Sir James Gray, the Professor of Zoology. It was to support no fewer than four assistant directors of research out of his own pocket, without the beneficiaries suspecting that they owed their places to a munificent colleague rather than to their own undisputed talents. Three of the four, Victor told me with satisfaction forty years later, were in time elected Fellows of the Royal Society. And although by then he had moved to the right of the Labour party, he commended the legislation of Hugh Dalton, Labour's Chancellor of the Exchequer, by which a donation from a person paying a high rate of tax enabled a recognised charity such as a university to benefit disproportionately. As a further stimulus to research, Victor followed it in 1948 with an anonymous contribution of £2000 – perhaps £30,000 in today's currency – to reduce the time elapsing between the receipt of a manuscript by the *Journal of Experimental Biology* and its publication.

In his volume of essays, *Meditations of a Broomstick*, he acknowledges the compression of twenty-five years of intensive research into two paragraphs and a snippet. 'I owe it to the layman to spare him a long chapter in my life that can only be written in technical language. How captivated, I wonder, would the common reader be by a discourse on the Rheotaxis of Spermatozoa?' That disclaimer did not deter him from adorning his Christmas card of 1956 with an electron micrograph, magnification 30,000, of the surface of a sea urchin's egg three minutes after fertilisation. The result of overcoming immense technical difficulties, it captured for the first time on film the one-in-two-thousand chance of slicing a just-fertilised egg in such a way that the whole length of the sperm head could be seen inside it.

Here the reader will receive only a marginally more expansive account of Victor Rothschild's contribution to gametology, the study of eggs, sperm and their interactions. Unlike his earlier experiments with the eggs of frogs and trout, his later research was into the eggs of the sea urchin, which displays the same general features of fertilisation as in human reproduction. Sea urchins' eggs also have two exceptional advantages that make them the classic material in this field. They are transparent and they can be gathered in huge quantities. If all the spermatozoa produced in one breeding season by a single British sea urchin were put end to end (Victor wrote), they would stretch for 24,000 miles, or almost round the world.

Here lay the root of his experiments. Although each egg is bombarded by many thousands of sperm, only one succeeds in penetrating it and so starting the process of fertilisation. What, he determined to discover, keeps out the others? How are the doors shut behind the successful spermatozoon? Each year, usually at Easter, he would spend a week or two at the Millport marine biological station on the Isle of Great Cumbrae, in the river Clyde, a prolific breeding ground of the sea urchin (though he could never be persuaded to eat what others considered a delicacy). There he worked with fellow Cambridge scientists, notably Michael (later Lord) Swann, an authority on the mechanics of mitosis, or cell division.

He was generous to the resident staff of the station, establishing a discretionary fund that enabled the director to travel in pursuit of research. 'Only enough for a good weekend in Paris,' Victor said. In fact it yields about £2000 a year. In return he exercised a sort of *droit de seigneur* by poaching both an excellent technician and secretary, later Mr and Mrs Michael Thompson, who went to work for him in Cambridge.

It emerged from their experiments that when a sperm does attach itself to an egg, it initiates a structural change in the proteins of the cell wall which is propagated over the entire surface of the egg in a few seconds, preventing any others from entering. An account of his researches which he sent to Duff Cooper in 1952 evoked a whimsical poem entitled 'The Lay of the Spermatozoon: a Love Story'. Here it is in full:

THE LAY OF THE SPERMATOZOON
A Love Story
dedicated
to
The Lord Rothschild, G.M., Sc.D

———

An ill shapen egg, less oval than cube,
Lay snugly ensconced in a Fallopian tube.
In her follicle cells she was feeling pathetic
Dreaming of agents parthenogenetic.

'We mammals' she sighed 'had much better have been
Invertebrates of the species marine,
For British sea-urchins can give at one birth
Enough spermatozoa to go round the earth.

Would that one could come here, without moratorium,
Equipped with an adequate perforatorium
For the last that I met was regrettably flaccid.
Can it be that I'm lacking in L-malic acid?

But I cannot see how this family can go on
Unless I discover a spermatozoon.'
At that very moment some movement outside
Shot a fat little fellow right in on the tide.

The egg gave a cheer. 'You bet I can know a
Nut from a nance among spermatozoa!
How gladly for him would my surface divide,
But the question is will he, or won't he collide?'

Gently impelled by his vibratile tail
(Used by spermatozoa in place of a sail)
He approached her and – whether by manly decision
Or just by a fluke – there occurred the collision.

His tail he stuck out in a radical direction,
Which was, so the egg thought, a wasted erection
Impatient she cried, 'Rotate, if you please
As much as a hundred and eighty degrees,

But kindly remember that while you're rotating
You're keeping my poor little nucleus waiting,
So let us get on with the work of creation
And hope for a fortunate fertilization.'

Victor did not welcome Duff's ribald verses with the enthusiasm they deserved. 'I am not quite clear why the egg is cubical?' he enquired.

The poet replied, 'I could find no other rhyme for tube except jujube – which I rejected.'

The study of sperm and eggs led Victor to investigate the metabolism, heat production and hydrodynamic properties of sperm; its biology, biochemistry and biophysics; and that pivotal substance of which its head is almost wholly composed: DNA, or deoxyribonucleic acid, the self-replicating material present in nearly all living organisms which is the carrier of genetic information. As always, he was attracted by the unusual and wrote a paper on the unorthodox methods of sperm transfer to be found in the sponge, the bedbug, the spider and the leech. Another diversion sprang from his studies of sperm. He was occasionally frustrated by not knowing to which animals his scientific colleagues were referring in their published work. Could they not give the English as opposed to the Latin name? But there were difficulties:

> I found that the animal in which I was interested and whose ovaries you may sometimes have eaten when holidaying in the Mediterranean, was sometimes called a sea hedgehog, sometimes an egg urchin, or a sea egg, or an egg fish, a button-fish, a needle shell, a chestnut, a burr, a spike, a zart, a sea borer, a porcupine and, from time to time, a whore's egg.

He decided that the best way of learning names he did not know, both Latin and English, was to write a book about them. So he produced *A Classification of Living Animals*, which was published in 1961 and sold well.

'Looking back on my scientific career,' he wrote in later years, 'I believe I had one original idea which is now of no consequence, and investigated a few, but only a few, subjects which in retrospect do not seem pedestrian.' That is a modest assessment. Even to the layman, his single 'original idea' is striking. It was prompted by a footnote to an article in the scientific journal *Nature* by the astrophysicist and Fellow of Trinity, Subrahmanyan Chandrasekhar. He had written that if you looked out of the window and at regular intervals counted the number of pedestrians walking along a particular, known length of pavement, you could deduce from the counts the average speed at which they were walking. Like other scientists, Victor had long wondered how to measure the speed at which sperm swim. By translating Chandrasekhar's one-dimensional problem into two dimensions with the aid of his wartime supervisions in mathematics, he solved the problem.

Victor's diffidence about his own scientific achievements was not shared by the Royal Society, which in 1953 elected him a Fellow at the age of forty-three. As five of those years had been occupied by war work, it was an unusually early age for any scientist other than a precocious mathematician or theoretical physicist. He had moreover been elected only two years after being proposed; so short a wait was also rare. To belong to a company of scientists more than 600 strong may not seem to be the most coveted of distinctions; but the society had received its charter from King Charles II in 1662 and was held in respect throughout the academic world. As J. B. S. Haldane told Victor: 'It is not much fun to be in, but hell to be out.'

The election of the third Lord Rothschild could be seen to redeem a family injustice, too. His Uncle Walter, it will be remembered, had been elected FRS in 1911, but as a distinguished patron of zoology, a rich amateur, rather than as the scientist he had proved himself to be. It rankled. Responsibility for the slight was thought to lie with Sir Ray Lankester, the leading British authority in zoology, elected to the Royal Society more than thirty-five years earlier. He had long held Walter Rothschild in exasperated contempt, failing to recognise what his niece Miriam called a 'smudge of mad genius'. Walter's brother Charles, Victor's father, was asked a few years later whether he would care to be put up for the Royal Society. Although well qualified by his work on fleas and butterflies, he declined, still smarting from the treatment of his brother. Victor's election closed that unhappy chapter.

In 1985, Miriam Rothschild was elected for her studies on fleas: the first time that a brother and sister had become FRS. Like her uncle, she had not always followed the path of convention and was made to wait fifteen years for admittance. 'There were four reasons for the delay,' she told me tongue in cheek, or almost so. 'I am a woman. I am rich. I am Jewish. I am Victor's sister.' Her brother had escaped lightly. She once described a cousin as having the brain of a flea without its agility.

The new Fellow did not often attend meetings at the Royal Society premises where learned papers were read and discussed. Behind the scenes, however, he occasionally intervened in the intrigues and cabals that preceded the election of new Fellows. Hearing that the brilliant but supposedly erratic molecular biologist Francis Crick was likely to be blackballed, Victor warned his opponents that he was a contender for the Nobel Prize and that the Royal Society would look very foolish if they turned him down. So Crick was elected, three years before being awarded the Nobel Prize for Medicine.

Otherwise he took pride in putting the letters FRS after his name, and gently reproached the fifth Marquess of Salisbury, a former minister responsible for science, for omitting them in the printed list of members of the Roxburghe Club. Salisbury replied gracefully:

I accept your rebuke about not having put FRS after my name in the Roxburghe Club productions. The reason is – and I expect the answer is the same in the case of Hughie Northumberland – that though I am extremely proud of being a Fellow of the Society, I am painfully conscious of my unworthiness for that position. As you will I expect know, I was only appointed a Fellow because I did a service which the Society thought justified this. It did not in any way indicate that any scientific eminence qualified me for election.

Victor once told me that he felt unworthy when elected FRS in the same list as John Cornforth, future winner of a Nobel Prize for Chemistry, who had overcome the handicap of being deaf since boyhood. He was similarly moved when the newly ennobled Lord Adrian, president both of Trinity and the Royal Society, invited him to be one of his sponsors when introduced into the House of Lords in 1955.

'I had one success which eludes many scientists,' Victor wrote of his career in retrospect, 'to know when to stop.' Not long after his election to the Royal Society he began to feel that his research, although competent, had lost something of its former vigour. His resolve to retire from the laboratory bench was sharpened by an accident. A glass tube broke as he was pushing it into a cork, severing a nerve in one of his fingers and impairing the dexterity that had served him well over the years: dismantling wartime bombs, biological dissection, the piano, tennis and golf. So he said goodbye to the department of zoology at Cambridge, but not to the world of science or to the frissons of academic intrigue.

One of the many episodes in which Victor failed to mind his own business was the election of a new Provost of King's College Cambridge, in 1956. When Dadie Rylands declined to stand, the next most promising candidate was Noël Annan. Although he was not yet forty, his intellectual strength and sparkle, his reforming zeal and affinity with the undergraduates – a King's tradition – seemed to assure him of success. Shortly before the election, however, Victor appeared at Annan's house one evening, urging him to withdraw in favour of Sir James Gray, the Professor of Zoology and Victor's early mentor in the laboratory.

That clumsy incursion by Victor into the affairs of a college with which he had no connection was despite Gray's own declaration that at sixty-five he would be reluctant to stand, and then only if the college failed to agree on a single candidate. Words were exchanged, Annan later told me, that made the survival of their friendship improbable. But after Noël had been duly elected, none was warmer in his congratulations than Victor. Their friendship was instantly repaired and grew with the years.

CHAPTER 6

Well-ordered Life

Victor liked a well-ordered life and with Tess he found it. On moving back to Merton Hall with her after the war he unpacked his books, assembled a domestic and secretarial staff and settled down to the regime of a research scientist punctuated by part-time public duties and holidays abroad. Tess bore and raised a second brood of Rothschilds (although unlike Barbara she did not embrace Judaism), became a magistrate, worked on one book about David Garrick and another about his leading lady, George Anne Bellamy. There was entertainment but it was less frenetic than in pre-war years. Victor was a better host than guest. He accepted invitations, whenever possible on his own terms: few fellow guests, informal clothes, an early departure. Roy Jenkins has described a New Year's Eve party in 1977 that could have taken place at any time in the past thirty years: 'Victor, in some ways in obstreperous form, but very typically insisting on leaving at about seven minutes to twelve, thereby avoiding any midnight celebrations.'

The linchpin of the household was Sweeney, the butler, whom Victor first encountered in 1944 when staying with Duff and Diana in Algiers. 'On no account unpack his Lordship's bag,' Duff warned him, 'it's full of bombs.' Formerly with Lord Gretton, the brewer, he had come to the Coopers as Rifleman Sweeney. On demobilisation he preferred to live with his wife in England rather than accompany the Coopers to Paris, so found employment with the Rothschilds, whom he served with affectionate loyalty until his own death nearly forty years later. Although Victor was an exacting master, Sweeney found Cambridge more tranquil than Diana

132

Cooper's theatre of the unexpected: 'goats in the dining room, meals in the garden'. He was accepted as an arbiter of social convention. 'Whatever would Sweeney think?' Victor exclaimed on hearing of some indecorous episode in the family. Sweeney believed in an old-fashioned hierarchical society. William Waldegrave liked to think that when dining with the Rothschilds his wineglass was refilled more frequently than those of other guests: a tribute neither to his palate nor to the closeness of his friendship with the family, but because he was the son – albeit the second son – of an earl.

Sometimes he would travel with Victor. 'We shall very much look forward to seeing Sweeney in your suite,' Duff wrote from Paris soon after Labour's defeat at the general election of 1951. 'I am glad to think that under the Conservative administration your standard of living has already gone up sufficiently to enable you to travel with a manservant.'

The other pillar of the Cambridge household was Mrs Prentice, the cook, always known as Mrs P. Born Ena Mary Huxley, she had started work aged fifteen as a scullery maid to Victor's mother in Palace Green, Kensington. In 1953 she joined the staff at Merton Hall where she married Victor's chauffeur, Wally Prentice, and retired in 1986 after sixty-four years of service with the Rothschild family. She died three years later, sitting peacefully in her chair while her meals-on-wheels delivery remained untasted. Late in life, Victor made a list of dishes headed 'What Mrs Prentice does better than anyone else in the world'. As a birthday present in 1989, his daughter Sarah Daniel expanded it into an elegant little volume entitled *Lord Rothschild's Favourite Recipes*. The cover bears patterns for decorating pastry designed by Carême, the celebrated chef of Baron James de Rothschild who had earlier abandoned the kitchens of the Prince Regent because he did not like 'that bourgeois ménage'. Attractive in themselves, they belie the contents of the book. Victor clung to the homely cooking of the nursery which those of mature age may still find in the peers' dining room of the House of Lords.

Only a very few of Mrs Prentice's recipes are rich and elaborate. There is a crab soufflé borrowed from Bruno, the chef at New Court (where presumably the Jewish dietary laws were not allowed to intrude between a banker and his sustenance); a saddle of lamb sprouting clusters of kidneys; hare steaks as cooked by M. Tissot, chef to Mrs James de Rothschild, (doubly non-kosher, since the sauce contains cream); chocolate soufflés and puddings about which the compiler reminds us that 'a penchant for chocolate is as efficient a way of identifying a Rothschild as genetic finger-printing'. The dish which Victor most esteemed was *Gigot de sept heures*, leg of lamb spiked with garlic and slowly braised with vegetables for seven hours, then eaten with a spoon. Mrs Prentice, accompanied by her husband, was sent to Paris to learn about this curiosity of the kitchen from Baron Alain de Rothschild's chef (where they fitted in a visit to the Folies Bergères). Wally called it '*Gigolo de sept heures*'.

But Mrs P was most at home with good plain cooking, including a variety of egg dishes, haddock, meat balls and curry. Nor, her recipe book discloses, did she scorn such conveniences unknown to Carême as bottled sauces and chutneys, Marmite and tinned foie gras. Tales of privation in post-war England prompted Liliane de Rothschild, the generous-hearted wife of Baron Elie, to cross the Channel bearing joints of scarce red meat. They reached neither Cambridge nor New Court. The customs at Dover declared them a forbidden import and they were confiscated. 'What are you going to do with them?' the outraged Baroness enquired.

'Burn them,' she was told.

'Oh,' she said, 'like Joan of Arc?'

If Victor's everyday tastes were modest, and shared by Tess, both could rise to a great occasion: the birthday of an old friend or the dinner Victor gave to his fellow members of the Roxburghe Club in the candlelit Wren Library at Trinity. In order not to disrupt the college kitchens, *Gigot de sept heures* was cooked in a field kitchen set up specially in Nevile's Court; it was buttressed by double magnums of Château Lafite 1864. At the other end of the gastronomic scale, he was proud to have had a humble potato dish named after him and to have been the first person – or perhaps the second – to taste edible protein made from North Sea gas.

Victor used to tell the story of the ageing and dyspeptic Baron Lionel de Rothschild who could no longer do justice to the skill of his chef. So while he himself dined off a rusk and a glass of milk, he would seat a younger Rothschild by his side, charged with describing to him the fragrance of each ambrosial dish. Victor too loved talking about food and found a ready ally in Queen Elizabeth the Queen Mother when placed next to her at a dinner in London University, of which she was Chancellor. They talked throughout of their favourite dishes, an exchange made all the more piquant by the institutional fare set before them. On the following day Victor sent her a Rothschild recipe for champagne water ice, to which Her Majesty responded with one of her own for *Sole Murat*.

I recall another such talk at a dinner party given by William and Caroline Waldegrave at which the guests included Victor and Tess, and Harold Macmillan. The conversation turned to asparagus. One of us liked it with hollandaise sauce, another with scrambled egg, a third sprinkled with Parmesan cheese and put under the grill. Mr Macmillan's plaintive voice broke through our discussion. 'How greedy you all are,' he said. 'Now *I* came here for high-minded conversation.' Abashed, we waited for him to embark on a more elevating topic. 'What a pity it is', he said, 'that the golden sovereign has given way to paper money. One never knows what to give one's loader.'

Although Victor was proud of the great vineyards of Lafite and Mouton owned by his French cousins, he himself preferred to drink *blanc de blancs*, a still champagne made only from white grapes. But he loved to flourish the noble vintages of Bordeaux when entertaining his friends or delighting them with surprises from his cellar. Duff Cooper wrote from the Admiralty at Christmas 1937 to acknowledge one of a long succession of benefactions:

Two dozen of Cheval Blanc 1906 is a present to take one's breath away. I can only say that I sleep happier every night for the knowledge that it is quietly reposing in the cellar and recovering during its short and fashionable journey from the bottom of St. James's St through Pall Mall. And all the time it is improving! If only one could be equally sure that a similar process was taking place in one's own body or mind.

Some of Victor's friends would assert that for a man who did not mind serving Château Lafite with curry and who rarely dined without having drunk a large dry martini or two, he attached too much importance to the care and presentation of wine. Some were amused, others irritated (but not for long) at the inclusion of type-written instructions on how the present was to be stored, decanted and served. Without such guidance, he seemed to imply, his bounty might be drunk straight from the bottle, shaken up till it foamed or even boiled in a saucepan. One sentence of the decree, however, was both wise and welcome: 'The absolute maximum number of people allowed to drink a bottle of Lafite 1945 at a meal is two.' If the present were dessert wine, each bottle had first to be chilled for several hours, then placed in a deep freezer for thirty minutes or so. Between these two operations, the cork was to be withdrawn, then lightly but firmly reinserted; otherwise it could not be extracted when the bottle was removed from the freezer. 'The law $PV = RT$', he added helpfully, 'tells one about the contraction of air at the top of the bottle.'

Such attention to detail in his frenetic, many-sided life required more than one secretary at Merton Hall. In 1954 Victor invited Arthur Marshall to join the team, installing him in a cottage near the main house. Since the pre-war days when he had light-heartedly driven down to Monte Carlo and back with Victor and Dadie, Artie had joined the army, been attached to Combined Operations as a staff officer and risen to the rank of lieutenant-colonel at Supreme Allied Headquarters. His intelligence duties had not precluded a study of girls' school fiction that inspired him to refer to the best-known of field marshals as Brenda Montgomery. Returning to run a boys' house and teach at Oundle, he had grown weary of school routine and eagerly accepted Victor's offer of employment. He described it as a world of bells, buzzers and telephones, with no fewer than a thousand files of correspondence to be kept in order.

Victor enjoyed his humour and found him competent in all domestic matters except those of finance. 'If I ask Artie to handle money,' he said, 'he bursts into tears.' There were other reasons why the working relationship did not last. According to Dadie, Victor maintained too close a watch on Artie to make sure he did not dawdle in working hours; he also seemed to resent Artie's many invitations to dinner parties, where his monologues were much in demand. They parted without rancour and remained friends throughout Artie's flourishing career as an essayist and television performer.

A routine as unbending as that of Merton Hall governed the weeks which Victor and Tess spent each year until the 1970s in Barbados. Yeoman's Point, St James's was designed as much as a place of work as a refuge from an English winter. Guests with expert knowledge were summoned from Europe or the United States to help solve the current scientific or administrative problem. There was congenial company, too, in that affluent enclave. At Heron Bay were the most welcoming of neighbours, Ronald and Marietta Tree. He, an heir to the Marshall Field fortune of Chicago, was a former anti-appeasement Conservative MP and wartime host to Churchill at Ditchley Park as an alternative to Chequers on weekends of a full moon; his wife combined a trusted role in the US Democratic party with enviable social skills. Sidney Bernstein, the television tycoon, was also close at hand.

In 1962 the Rothschilds moved from Merton Hall to a large new house, 11 Herschel Road, with seven acres of land on the rural fringes of the town: reputedly the most expensive to be built in Cambridgeshire since the war. Their chosen architect, it was said, had made his name designing council houses. The sensitive found its white façade austere, even intimidating, its proportions unpleasing. But Impressionist pictures showed to advantage on uncluttered walls; and the drawing room, with its long expanse of plate glass from floor to ceiling, commanded a fine prospect of garden and trees. It was just such a house to be expected from a rich scientist who shunned ostentation and found adornment distracting. One essential fixture was the largest size of television set. Guests soon learned that it was as much a solecism to chatter during the evening news as to sit in Victor's armchair facing the screen; it bore the needlework injunction 'GET OUT'.

As his work came to centre increasingly on London, he used the Cambridge house as a weekend retreat where he could think, write, maintain his links with the academic world and entertain his friends. During these years he was fortunate in finding a no less secluded eyrie in the very centre of London. The recently widowed Mrs James de Rothschild offered Tess and Victor the third floor of her ample but unobtrusive Edwardian house overlooking Buckingham Palace and Green Park. 'I hesitated no longer than a micro-second,' Victor told me, 'before saying yes.' Until his death more than thirty years later, 23 St James's Place remained his London home.

James de Rothschild, named after his grandfather, the founder of the French branch of the family, was born and brought up in Paris, spent three years at Cambridge and went round the world with an undergraduate friend, the future Earl of Bessborough (at Lord Curzon's Coronation Durbar of 1903, the Viceroy character-istically gave his French guest an honorific 'Hon.'). Jimmy, as he was known in circles far beyond family and friends, joined the French Army as a *poilu* in 1914, was seconded to the British Third Corps as an interpreter and decorated with the Distinguished Conduct Medal, the highest award except the Victoria Cross open to those of non-commissioned rank. Later he received a commis-sion in the British Army and raised a Jewish battalion in Palestine for service under General Allenby. Three of his recruits were named Ben Zvi, Ben Gurion and Sprinzak; one became President of Israel, another Prime Minister, a third Speaker of the Israeli Parliament. Like his father, James was one of the few Rothschilds to become a passionate Zionist. As long ago as 1882 Baron Edmond had begun to colonise Palestine as a haven for Russian Jews living under the terror of the pogrom. A generation later, as Dorothy wrote in a memoir of her husband,

> Some of the innumerable difficulties of establishing preponder-antly intellectual Jews in an uncultivated desert, or in malarial swamps infested by mosquitoes, had been overcome. Jimmy was captivated by the courage, persistence and ingenuity which had created the existing settlements, with their orchards, oranges, grape-fruit and vines in the midst of a desert landscape and vowed then to do all he could to help his father continue his

work; and to further the Zionist cause which he saw as the one
hope of his tortured co-religionists in Eastern Europe

Having become a naturalised British subject in 1919, he was
elected to the House of Commons ten years later as Liberal MP
for the Isle of Ely. It was a speech in 1942 on the sufferings of the
Jews in Nazi Germany that brought the whole House to its feet in
a spontaneous and unprecedented gesture of sympathy. But to end
any account of his parliamentary career on that poignant note
would be misleading. Meeting Jimmy on a railway platform in
London, a friend asked why he looked so depressed. 'I am on my
way to my constituency,' he replied. 'And what is more, I shall
have to go there again next year.'

His unexpected inheritance in 1922 of Waddesdon from Miss
Alice de Rothschild, the sister of its first owner, Baron Ferdinand,
fired his love of English country pursuits to the exclusion of all
except Zionism. One handicap he endured with stoicism: the
gradual loss of sight that left him almost blind by the end of his
life. Having survived the battlefields of Flanders, he lost an eye on
the golf course at Deauville from a ball sliced by his cousin the
Duc de Gramont. Thereafter he surveyed his grandiose French
chateau built on Buckinghamshire acres through a single eyeglass.
It became as famous on the racecourse as did those of Joseph and
Austen Chamberlain at Westminster. Another misfortune was to
have backed the winner of the Derby at odds of 100 to 1 at the
first race meeting he ever attended. It lured him into becoming a
prodigious and largely unsuccessful racehorse owner, breeder and
gambler. 'Others back outsiders,' Lord Rosebery said of him.
'Jimmy alone tries to breed from them.'

After occasional visits to Waddesdon during the war, Victor had
grumbled at his cousin's frugal hospitality. Those thimble-sized
and rarely refilled wineglasses he thought unworthy of the
Rothschild tradition. But on Jimmy's death in 1957 – he left an
estate of £11 million – his widow redeemed all. Victor and Tess
acquired not only a covetable, rent-free flat for life but a resident
landlady of unusual distinction.

Dorothy Pinto was married to James de Rothschild when scarcely out of the schoolroom; she was seventeen, he thirty-four. Her father, Eugene Pinto, came of a family of Sephardic Jews who left Spain first for Egypt, then France and finally England. His fluctuating fortunes on the London Stock Exchange enabled him at their peak to send Dorothy's only brother Richard to Eton, then into the Coldstream Guards, from which he retired after the First World War with the rank of major and a Military Cross. Eugene could also afford to take a lease from 1913 to 1919 on Number 1 Carlton Gardens, a large, handsome house overlooking St James's Park. Among its other tenants have been the future Emperor Napoleon III while in exile; Viscount Goderich, prime minister in 1827–8; Northcliffe, founder of the *Daily Mail,* and Lord Bearsted of Shell. Since 1945 it has been the official residence of the foreign secretary. Through her father's own marriage, Dorothy was also brought into the orbit of two other clever and successful families of Ashkenazic Jews: the Cohens who founded the 'Liberal' synagogue, and the Woolfs, including Virginia's husband Leonard. A less intellectual link was forged between Eugene Pinto and Rufus Isaacs, who as Lord Reading became Lord Chief Justice and Viceroy of India; as young men in the City, they took up boxing together as a pastime.

Sir Isaiah Berlin spoke for many in his tribute to Dorothy de Rothschild on her death in 1988 at the age of ninety-three:

> What was most remarkable about her was the extent and depth of the love and admiration by which she was surrounded on the part of virtually everyone who had known her, or even met her. She combined an unsullied innocence, purity of heart, the sweetest of natures and, indeed, a saintliness of character, with overwhelming charm, great dignity, a very lively sense of humour, pleasure in the oddities of life, an unconquerable vitality and a kind of eternal youth and an eager responsiveness to all that passed – which lasted to her dying day.

Victor revered his cousin with both affection and awe. But he could not wholly share either of the causes that dominated her life:

a failing that cast a shadow between them. One was Zionism, the other the preservation of Waddesdon and its collections. She had been converted to Zionism by her husband, whose death served only to renew her dedication and to reveal in her an unsuspected strength of character. From the vast charitable foundation established by Baron Edmond, his son James presented a new Knesset, or parliament building, to the State of Israel; it shocked even a Rothschild to learn that the assembly had been obliged to meet in a converted bank. Towards the end of her life, his widow drew on the same fund to build a new Supreme Court in Jerusalem. (Proposing to visit the site, she had difficulty in renewing her expired passport; the computer choked over someone born as long ago as 1895).

Such stately benefactions, symbolising the twin pillars of democracy and the law, earned her the reverence of all Israelis and the respect of the Jewish people worldwide. She asked that neither building should bear a plaque commemorating the donors; but she was touched when Teddy Kollek, the Mayor of Jerusalem, came to St James's Place with a street sign that in English, Hebrew and Arabic proclaimed 'Rehov James de Rothschild'.

Victor, as we have seen, was not unsympathetic towards Zionism and subsequently towards the State of Israel. But he reserved the right to deplore, even condemn, political measures he thought excessive and destabilising to peace in the Middle East. Dorothy, by contrast, tolerant of almost any caprice of conduct or belief and as irregular as Victor in her religious observances, reacted to the least criticism of Israel with distress and anger. She enjoyed Victor's lively mind and sardonic gossip; but when called to her councils of war in defence of Israel's reputation, he was found wanting in her own fiery fanaticism.

Nor could he overcome an aversion to the ornate profusion of Waddesdon. For Dollie, the care of its fabric and contents was the most enduring aesthetic experience of her long life. Even after handing over Waddesdon to the National Trust with a substantial endowment, she retained control in firm hands. It would have pained her to learn that her benefaction worth so many millions of pounds had not been accepted unanimously; Lord Esher and

Harold Nicolson were two members of the committee who felt that Waddesdon did not qualify as a place of either 'historic interest' or 'natural beauty'. It was she who encouraged the Trust to publish a comprehensive catalogue of its contents in many volumes under the editorship of Anthony Blunt, and who herself wrote an evocative history of the house and its quirky owners. In contrast to the exuberance of Waddesdon that spilt over into Dollie's rooms in St James's Place, the third floor became the workshop of a don.

Although Victor lived rent-free for more than thirty years, he did have a duty to perform: as a trustee for some of Dorothy's money. It was not a complicated trust, consisting almost entirely of huge holdings in only two stocks, Royal Dutch and De Beers. Mrs de Rothschild was as authoritarian in its management as in the restoration of Waddesdon. After conferring with the trustees at their periodic meetings, she would ring for her butler and command him to 'show up the brokers'. At which two senior City figures would rise to their feet from the wooden bench in the entrance hall where they had been waiting. Once there was an unusual delay. They sent in a message through the butler, hoping that the meeting could begin soon as they had an appointment with the Governor of the Bank. Dollie de Rothschild was a very splendid *grande dame*, uncorrupted by wealth and indifferent to her own occasional misfortune. She did, however, believe in a settled order of things. To this day there are two brass bellpushes outside 23 St James's Place. One reads 'Visitors', the other 'Servants'.

Victor used to say that for every Rothschild who made money, there were a dozen who spent it; and he was not ashamed to include himself in the profligate majority. He had plenty to spend. He was the only grandson in the male line of the first Lord Rothschild, who left £2.5 million at his death in 1915: not less than £125 million in our present currency; considerably more when the marked disparity between rich and poor at that time is taken into account. Although Victor's inheritance was depleted twice in eight years by death duties on the estates of his grandfather and father, his widowed mother more than made good the deficit by shrewd investment during his minority.

The Great Crash of 1929, followed by a decade of economic depression, took its toll of the Rothschilds. *'Même Edouard est touché,'* it was whispered in the Bourse; and he was the richest of the French cousins. Yet in 1932, aged only twenty-one, Victor began to form his very valuable collection of eighteenth-century books and manuscripts. In the following year he married Barbara Hutchinson, sharing with her a style of living matched by no other young Cambridge graduate, or indeed by scarcely any senior member of the university. The sale in 1937 of 148 Piccadilly, followed by that of Tring, further embellished his fortune.

Wealth sat uneasily on his conscience. He liked to present himself as a meritocrat whose record of scientific research and public service owed little to his name, even less to his money. He avoided wherever possible the signature of 'Rothschild', preferring 'R' or 'VR' or 'Victor'. He was furiously resentful when a scientist at a research establishment introduced him to a party of Japanese visitors with the flourish: 'And here we have Lord Rothschild, one of the richest men in the world.' It was, he insisted, both inaccurate and vulgar.

He loathed ostentation, or what the economists call conspicuous consumption (except behind the discreet wooden partitions of Wilton's restaurant). Both the Piccadilly mansion and Rushbrooke Hall he parted with in turn because they were psychological as well as financial burdens.

He was at his happiest after the war, living modestly with Tess either on the top floor of St James's Place or in the suburbs of Cambridge. He stabled neither racehorses nor Rolls-Royces, possessed an exiguous wardrobe and wore his pyjamas until they were in ribbons. Dying in his eightieth year, he left a net estate of £270,410: near penury on the Rothschild scale. But the figure was misleading.

Baron Elie affected to believe that his English cousin lacked the family instinct for high finance. One weekend we were fellow guests of Sybil Cholmondeley (whose mother was a French Rothschild) at Houghton, her great Norfolk palace built for Sir Robert Walpole. Over the breakfast coffee and kidneys he embroidered his theme with light-hearted malice: 'There are three ways of losing money. One can order a kilo of caviare at Maxim's and eat only a teaspoon of it. One can rebuild Versailles. Or, like Victor, one can timidly invest small sums in the best companies.'

Elie omitted to mention a fourth and more spectacular way of losing money, for it lay in the future. The sum was £100 million and the victim was himself. After President Mitterrand had nationalised the Banque Rothschild in Paris, Elie riposted by setting up a new Rothschild bank in Zurich. But it suffered gigantic misfortune and fraud, and had to be rescued by the staider practices of N. M. Rothschild of New Court.

In leaving so small an estate the butt of Elie's breakfast-table wit had of course shown skill rather than incompetence. There is a family legend that when James de Rothschild so mismanaged his affairs as to burden his heirs with death duties of £7.5 million on an estate of £11 million, a cousin was heard to sigh: 'It could happen to anyone.' Victor had long determined that it should not happen to him. Over the years, with the guidance of bankers, lawyers and accountants, he had distributed his fortune to individuals and institutions without incurring an unnecessary penny of transfer tax.

At his house in Cambridge I once witnessed this attention to detail. He gave me a fine volume from his library which he knew I did not possess, and inscribed it with my name and his own. Having thanked him warmly, I asked whether he would not add the date. 'I have omitted it', he said, 'for fiscal reasons.'

The scientist James Lovelock records in his memoirs this conversation with Victor: 'Lovelock, do you pay income tax?'

'Yes, of course I do. Why do you ask?'

'How unfortunate for you. You know, I have never paid tax. It is quite simple. You see, I have no income.'

He was, it seems, referring to a legal device by which capital was deemed to generate not income but more capital. With the introduction of a capital gains tax in 1962 – what the then prime minister Harold Macmillan wanted to call a tax on short-term speculative profits – the investor found it far less atractive.

So what did happen to his millions? He spent profusely on his collections, a large part of which he gave away or sold to further other pursuits. He poured money almost literally down the drain at his experimental farms at Rushbrooke, which he retained after the big house itself had been abandoned. (Less obviously in character, he enjoyed shooting partridges there with a few friends such as Lord Jowitt and Professor Sir James Gray, though he never accepted invitations to shoot elsewhere.)

He made settlements on Tess and on the children of both marriages: trust funds, houses and works of art. An indication of the scale of these family benefactions is to be found in two published Wills. Tess, who died in May 1996, left a net estate of £4.5 million; their younger son Amschel, who took his life six weeks later aged forty-one, left £18.5 million. The daughters were less well provided for.

Philanthropy was the emollient of Victor's life. He used to say, 'I have always been a strong opponent of the proposition that the kind thought is as acceptable as the gift.' The pages of this book are punctuated by both. Many others may never be known.

The motives of generosity are never easy to identify and separate. Victor liked to savour the pride and pleasure of Maecenas, not excluding the flamboyant and the picturesque. Sometimes he gave to attract or fortify friendship, for behind the bravado there lurked insecurity. Often, in both his private and professional lives, it was to reward those with specialist skills whom he had cajoled or bullied into forced labour. Mostly his open-handedness concealed only warmth of heart.

Even as his marriage to Barbara was crumbling, he gave a generous sum to her recently widowed mother, Mary Hutchinson. Part of it was to protect her son Jeremy, then serving as a naval officer, from the uncertainties of a career at the Bar after the war. (Hutchinson repaid Victor's quixotry by becoming an astute advocate, a Queen's Counsel and in 1978 a Labour peer.) Mary Hutchinson wrote to her son-in-law, 'I can never forget the *grand chic* of the way you took me out to lunch and with the lightest stroke of the pen wrote those few figures which undid the past and made the future.'

Duff Cooper was another grateful recipient, this time of a rare edition of Racine's *Esther*. 'I shall never again', he told Victor, 'dare to mention in your presence the name of a book I want for fear of finding it on my table a few days later – perhaps I shall, though.'

Clever children from poor homes were found places in appropriate schools. Research scientists both in Britain and Israel received bursaries, often anonymously. Overwrought civil servants were whisked away to recuperate at Victor's villa in Barbados. There was champagne for a least three prime ministers, Churchill, Wilson and Heath; an early TV set for the immobile John Hayward ('it produces only sheet lightning on its screen,' Victor warned him); a cigar for the geneticist J. B. S. Haldane, who defiantly smoked it in his pipe; a Strasbourg pie for Aldous and Maria Huxley, who unfortunately disapproved of foie gras.

Perhaps I should declare my own interest in this bounty: several beautiful volumes of the Roxburghe Club, a *magnolia grandiflora* for my London garden, a case of the legendary Château Lafite 1945 after a particularly arduous literary task on Victor's behalf. It was a challenge to return the kindness of a man without material needs, but he seemed pleased by my own tokens of gratitude: a large magnifying glass, a long-handled shoehorn and an eighteenth-century French cookbook.

As is the way of the world, the more generous the proposal, the less grateful the response. A previous chapter records the cavalier manner in which Trinity College treated his gift of an immensely valuable collection of eighteenth-century books and manuscripts. Victor was similarly thwarted when the most grandiose of his benefactions was rejected out of hand. Scandalised to hear that the Queen's Flight was still using only propeller-driven Andover aircraft – safe enough but slow and easily affected by turbulence – he offered to raise several million pounds for the purchase of the latest jet, which would then be presented anonymously for Her Majesty's use. At Buckingham Palace, however, a senior official of the Royal Household was at his most obstructive. 'By the way,' he languidly enquired, 'whom do you represent?'

'Myself,' Victor replied, and left.

Among those closest to him was the future Cabinet minister William Waldegrave. Devoted to his much older friend and mentor, he nevertheless felt overwhelmed by Victor's relentless

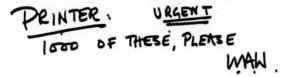

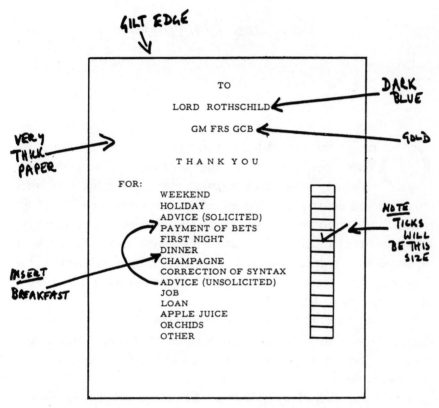

generosity. He tried to curb it by drafting this spoof instruction to a printer, a copy of which found its way, as intended, to Victor's desk.

CHAPTER 7

Sons and Daughters

O nly in the material sense did charity begin at home, for Victor could be an exacting husband and an oppressive father. If Tess's eyes revealed pride in her husband, they also betrayed anxiety. He appointed her the guardian both of his privacy and of a domestic routine devised to meet his every whim. It did not take much in the home to evoke a frown or a rebuke delivered in a menacing drawl: an unwelcome experiment in the kitchen, perhaps, a mislaid paperknife or the intrusion of 'a person on business from Porlock'.

Tess's responsibilities went far beyond those of other wives. He once told me that his doctor had put him on a severe diet to lose weight. 'Then surely', I said, 'you should not be drinking that sweet vermouth.'

'Yes,' he replied, 'I wish Tess would get me off it.' Her friends noticed that the slight facial twinge that had afflicted her for some years disappeared within a few months of her husband's death. Nevertheless he loved and respected his wife, shared his triumphs and anxieties with her, deferred to her judgement.

His children had a less easy passage. There were six of them, a son and two daughters by each of his wives. Barbara bore Sarah (1934), Jacob (1936) and Miranda (1940); Tess's brood were Emma (1948), Victoria (1953) and Amschel (1955).

Victor followed their intellectual progress with obsessive concern. If the second trio had the best of their father's affection and encouragement, it requires little psychological insight to discern the reason. Sarah, Jacob and Miranda recalled a paradise lost; Emma, Victoria

148

and Amschel a paradise regained. His first marriage, punctuated by storms and faithlessness (on both sides), by humiliation and resentment, ended in divorce. It left him with a wound that never quite healed and three young children whom he was obliged to deliver over to Barbara for half of each school holidays. How could their presence, and even more their absence, fail to remind him of an unhappiness that not even marriage to Tess wholly erased?

Before that shadow fell across their lives the three children of Barbara and Victor were carefree enough, although there was a limited appeal in being taught the square root of minus one at the age of three and the physiology of reproduction a year or two later. But there were less alarming treats, too: country treks in a horse-drawn gypsy caravan and visits to their Aunt Miriam at Ashton Wold. 'Welcome to Liberty Hall,' she would greet them. They responded with enthusiasm to an idyll shared with bird and beast, to as much grown-up food as they could eat and no rules about bedtime. 'It will take six months of beating and starving to undo the harm,' Victor told his sister after their return. That *was* a joke, for he never beat his children. He did, however, subject them to relentless cross-examination with the skill of what one victim called 'a psychological gangster'. Jacob, aged five, was once summoned to a drawing room full of disconcerted visitors and asked by his father whether he believed in God – and if not, why not.

Not until they went away to school were religious values woven into their education. Barbara's conversion to a formal Judaism ensured that they should be Jewish by birth though not by affinity. Nor was Victor moved to introduce them to Jewish observances or ritual to which he himself was indifferent. The children enjoyed the story of their father, a guest at a formal dinner, instructing the waiter, 'I am Lord Rothschild. I do not eat pork. Bring me a ham sandwich.'

But he looked on religious belief with the confident agnosticism of a Victorian freethinker, a Huxleyan rationalist. The biologist who eagerly embraced every advance in physical science remained an incurious stranger to the mysteries of the spirit. One of his children asserts that she never saw, much less read, a Bible in the home except for a rare edition or two in her father's eighteenth-century library. The phenomenon was not unknown in the upbringing of other well-born intellectual families. A Trevelyan child once excitedly announced, 'I have found an old book in the attic called *Holly Bibble*, and it is *most* improper.'

On hearing that the eleven-year-old Jacob Rothschild had contracted infantile paralysis, or polio, Diana Cooper wrote in agonised sympathy to the boy's father, 'I never had such a shock of horror as when I heard – the words are like a knell.' Victor's reply was reassuring but matter of fact:

> Jacob has just returned to Cambridge to convalesce. It was a nerve-racking moment when he first got out of bed. Not only was there the possibility of him being paralysed, which of course he realised in spite of the evasive stupidities of the doctors in telling him that they did not know what was the matter with him (he reads the papers every day and had a paralysed boy in the same room with him for three weeks); but also being nervous himself, he did not want to stand up in case he might fall down. However, he can stand up and walk in a rather wobbly way. The doctors assure me that this will get all right in a month or so. He was rather pathetic about his cricket, at which he is a rather good bowler. He said to me that he had thought of taking up bowling left-handed. I asked him why, and he said he thought a good left-armed bowler was better than a good right-arm one. Of course the reason in fact was that his right arm is weak, and he thought that he would never be able to bowl again. However, I have disabused him of this fancy.

Victor spent much of his life disabusing others of their fancies. But could he not have brought himself to write a shade less objectively about an apprehensive schoolboy who happened to be his son?

A year or so later Jacob became the first Rothschild to go to Eton after his father, his grandfather and several cousins had endured varying degrees of anti-Semitism and other unhappy experiences at Harrow. It did not work out well. Winston Churchill, the grandson of the prime minister, who fagged for Jacob, detested the cult of conformity that made life difficult for any boy who appeared in any way different from the herd, whether as a Rothschild or a Churchill, a scholarship boy from the suburbs or a foreigner. Beating and bullying were the order of the day.

Jacob afterwards admitted to being 'an awkward and difficult boy' who played cricket moderately well but failed to shine academically or to achieve Eton's ultimate social accolade, election to Pop. He did, however, make his mark when, with an opulent gesture worthy of any Rothschild, he gave the library, or house prefects, a television set, then a rarity at Eton.

His housemaster, Tom Brocklebank, was an international rowing man and Everest mountaineer, as well as an amateur of the arts. But another boy in his house, Tam Dalyell MP, wrote that Brocklebank 'could be very cutting and sarcastic, and he was moody, sometimes malicious'. Jacob, to whom he offered neither moral support nor encouragement, came to believe that he was the victim of his housemaster's infatuation for Tess. He suspected Brocklebank of engineering emotional crises in which he falsely accused Jacob of some serious school misdemeanour, smoking for instance, threatening to have him removed from his boys' house, and relenting only if Tess were prepared to hurry down to Eton to plead for leniency. That *mise en scène* in an English public school was not as bizarre as it may seem, for Brocklebank and Tess knew each other well, both being friends of Anthony Blunt.

Nor was Jacob free from bullying in the school holidays. A cousin recalls a family party at the villa of Cecile de Rothschild, Elie's sister, in the south of France, ruined by Victor's unkindness. On an island picnic he suddenly decided that he needed some sea urchins for an experiment, so ordered Jacob and his cousin, both aged about fifteen, down to the rocks. The cousin refused but Jacob obeyed, returned with swollen bleeding hands and fell ill. 'Victor was a brusque and dismissive tyrant,' the cousin says, 'seeking revenge for his failed first marriage by humiliating his son.'

Between Eton and the university, Jacob spent his statutory two years of National Service in The Life Guards, an aristocratic, devil-may-care regiment with the lingering flavour of Lord Cardigan's army. The father of a would-be officer was required by convention to introduce his son and to commend his virtues in a letter to the colonel of the regiment. Victor wrote that he could not imagine Jacob ever making an officer. It was an untimely and insensitive quip that very nearly proved prophetic. For Jacob, having endured much bullying in the ranks at the Guards Depot, a hell-hole at the best of times, twice failed his War Office selection board and had to spend some weeks as a waiter in the officers' mess at Windsor. What ultimately brought him a commission was his success and determination as a cross-country runner. That restored some of his self-confidence. But even as an officer he was dejected not to sail with the regiment in the Suez expedition of 1956. He need not have worried. In an evocation of the Crimean tradition, The Life Guards succeeded in landing only one of its vehicles before the ceasefire: the truck containing the officers' mess silver and other comforts.

On release from the army, this shy, rather battered and uneasy young man found a haven at Christ Church, Oxford, a college admired for its architectural magnificence and stylish ways. Victor wanted him to follow in his footsteps as a scientist, a career for which Jacob felt ill-suited. It happened that an Eton contemporary at Mr Brocklebank's house was Graham Greene, nephew and namesake of the novelist, and a future chairman of the trustees of the British Museum. A knowledgeable bibliophile even as a school-boy, he had been asked by Victor to do some research on his behalf in the celebrated Eton College library (his contribution is acknowledged in the two-volume catalogue of the Rothschild Library). While talking to Victor, Greene urged him to let Jacob switch from Science to History; and Victor, who respected the opinions of other people's children more than his own, agreed.

Jacob at last found fulfilment at Oxford. He was encouraged by the sage Isaiah Berlin, more a friend of Barbara Rothschild than of Victor. And he had the further good fortune to be tutored by Hugh Trevor-Roper (later Lord Dacre). On being appointed Regius Professor of Modern History at Oxford in 1957, he broke with tradition by continuing to give individual tuition to a few undergraduates, mostly the sons of friends, including 'the diffident and gentle Jacob Rothschild'. Fired by the Regius Professor's lightly borne erudition and quicksilver mind, Jacob took First Class honours in Modern History. A surprised father, though no doubt rejoicing in his heart at any family success, did not exactly overwhelm his son with congratulations. And Trevor-Roper thought Victor's letter of thanks lacking in warmth.

In 1961 Jacob married Serena, a granddaughter of Sir James Dunn, a successful Canadian financier. They have one son and three daughters.

After an apprenticeship with a range of leading firms in the City of London, Jacob joined the family bank of N. M. Rothschild & Sons in 1963. It brought an infusion of young Rothschild blood to an ageing, ailing institution but aroused no pride in Victor, who had rejected such a vocation thirty years before. His only influence on Jacob's choice of career had been to share his children's addiction to the board game of Monopoly in the nursery.

Like a quiescent volcano, their antipathy smouldered gently for the next decade or two. What caused it suddenly to erupt into a spectacular semi-public feud will be related in its place.

Victor's four daughters were endowed with beauty, brains and money. Both as an ambitious father and an exponent of genetic farming he hoped that they would find well-matched husbands and produce yet another generation of talented Rothschilds. To his dismay, Sarah and Miranda embarked on relationships of which he disapproved; and Emma and Tory postponed marriage until after his death, too late for either to bear children.

How far was their father to blame? At the heart of his heavy-handed concern lay paradoxes. By no means puritanical in his own private life, he clung to the role of a Victorian papa, the arbiter of what was or what was not acceptable in a grown-up daughter. However audaciously he assailed scientific, technical and administrative problems, he remained the most conventional guardian of family morals and demeanour. And having rejected the doctrines of Judaism, he retained an outdated Jewish mistrust of the emancipation of women.

He had an exaggerated respect, too, for that nebulous entity the

Establishment to which he belonged both by birth and achievement (though rarely for individual members of it unless they were self-made men, leavened perhaps by a duke or two). He minded what others thought, said or wrote about him. Like most public men he disliked personal publicity except on his own terms. Speculative gossip about the family caused him immoderate annoyance and he was as sensitive to mockery as to anti-Semitism. That, I think, is why he preferred to eat at home or at Wilton's rather than in the clubs of St James's. He could scarcely ever be persuaded to brave the convivial and sometimes ribald talk of Pratt's, the dining club of which he was made an honorary member by the proprietor, the Duke of Devonshire.

As in other authoritarian regimes, the young Rothschilds were more unsettled by the arbitrary and the unexpected than by severity. Victor's friend Stuart Hampshire observed how he would flirt happily with his daughters, then discard them if they responded too demonstratively; how he feared evoking the affection of others as much as revealing his own. No doubt he could have benefited from a session with the well-known woman psychologist to whom he sent his children for analysis. For them it was a huge joke. One day they left a message for their father: 'Please telephone Miss Alcock IMMEDIATELY.'

He could be imaginative in educating his daughters. As a birthday treat he took Sarah to New York for ten days, where she met Greta Garbo, the friend of his French cousin Cécile de Rothschild (David Pryce-Jones, another cousin, memorably described Garbo and Cécile walking together down Bond Street like two Pomeranian grenadiers). Sarah pressed in her diary the alarmingly short stub of a cigarette Garbo had smoked; she and her father then went out to dine and spent the entire meal discussing Garbo's elusive magic. Visiting the Rothschilds in Cambridge, she caught a tender moment when Victor 'took one little girl's head in his hands and she looked up so still, just like a little *catt*'.

Both Sarah and Miranda led busy, fruitful lives on leaving the nest. From a convent school, Sarah went up to St Hilda's College, Oxford, and attracted many admirers. Her articles in the undergraduate magazine *Cherwell* caught the eye of the *Evening Standard*.

Abandoning Oxford at the end of her second year, she went to work for the paper in London as a feature writer. She took a course in Comparative Religion with the Open University and had several exhibitions of her pictures made from artfully arranged seaweeds.

With a compelling interest in child welfare, she bought an old manse in Scotland, which she lent and ultimately sold cheaply to the local authority as a centre for children, many thousands of whom enjoyed the benefaction. That was characteristic of her generosity, for although not at all rich by Rothschild standards, she endearingly behaved as if she were, mostly on behalf of good causes. A valuable brooch bequeathed to her by cousin Dollie soon raised some £15,000 for distressed Romanians.

Only occasionally did she spend on herself. At a wine sale she bid on the spur of the moment for a single bottle of Château Lafite, which she secured for the then high price of £90. Having allowed it to rest for three months, she decanted it. The wine turned out to be undrinkable. 'Serve you right', Tess said, 'for buying something you could not afford.' There spoke the great-niece of Beatrice Webb.

Sarah lived for some years on the island of Islay, in Scotland, then bought a small house in Cambridge. But relations with her father remained cool. As a gesture of appeasement on his seventy-ninth birthday, she compiled the beautifully printed little volume *Lord Rothschild's Favourite Recipes* (see page 133). Even that withered on the bough. Victor, having decided to buy more than one hundred copies to distribute as a Christmas present, changed his mind. Instead, he sent out a pamphlet of the letters he had exchanged with another daughter on the anguish of giving up smoking. Sarah had to be content with seventeen words of type-written congratulations: 'Just a line to say that I have received a number of appreciative letters about your booklet.'

When I embarked upon this book, Sarah offered me, among other family papers, a file of letters he had written to her during the last decade of his life. All of them typed, except for the signature, they were mostly about houses and money and ill health. On returning them to Sarah, I asked, 'Did he never send you affectionate letters?'

'Those', she said, 'are the affectionate ones.'

Sarah's younger sister Miranda was not yet eighteen when she broke away from the family circle to work in a kibbutz in Israel – prelude to a restless, colourful and sometimes tragic life. In 1962 she married Boudjemaa Boumaza, a Berber political activist whom she had met at an exhibition of Egyptian antiquities in Amsterdam. He was murdered in Tunis two years later after she had borne him a daughter, Da'ad. She lived in Greece, in Paris and at the houses in England of her divorced mother Barbara.

A poet, graphologist, painter and art dealer, she belonged to a coterie that included the Hellenic scholars and travel writers Patrick Leigh Fermor and Peter Levi. It was Levi, the one-time Jesuit priest, who arranged a marriage of convenience with his best friend Iain Watson so that Da'ad could acquire a passport.

Through Levi, too, Miranda became part of the Bruce Chatwin legend. 'He looked gorgeous, thin, a wheaty, bronzy colour and cold blue eyes,' she said of the author of *The Songlines*, 'he was every Jewish girl's dream.' Less conventionally, Bruce was mesmerised by Miranda's extraordinary resemblance to a boy. She confided to Chatwin's biographer, Nicholas Shakespeare, how they had performed an act of lovemaking of great speed and savagery: 'I was lacerated as if by a Bengal tiger.' It was the beginning and the end of the affair. A far cry, too, from the proprieties of 11 Herschel Road, Cambridge.

From her earliest years Victor believed that he had a child prodigy in Emma, the elder of his two daughters by Tess. It is not every little girl who has been instructed in eighteenth-century bookbinding or the theory of artificial insemination when scarcely out of her pram. At twelve he endowed her with a valuable library of antiquarian books, thirty-five of the choicest items kept back from the huge collection which over the years he presented to Trinity College (see page 105 *et seq.*).

At Cranborne Chase, a fashionable boarding school, she was allowed to forge ahead of her contemporaries, winning a scholarship to Somerville College, Oxford at fifteen. There followed a

Kennedy scholarship in Economics at the Massachusetts Institute of Technology, where she subsequently held associate professorships of Science, Technology and Society. At twenty-five she published her tour de force, *Paradise Lost: the Decline of the Auto-Industrial Age*.

Close friendship with Olof Palme, the Social Democrat Prime Minister of Sweden, assassinated in 1986 without known cause, brought her a seat on the governing body of the Stockholm International Peace Research Institute and other Swedish bodies with a radical flavour.

What filled Victor and Tess with renewed pride was her election in 1988 to a Fellowship at King's College, Cambridge. Victor asked whether they could be given inconspicuous seats in college chapel to witness her induction.

Emma sat on the Royal Commission on Environmental Pollution, 1986–94. All in all, Victor boasted, she had inherited the genes of both the Rothschild and Mayor intellectual dynasties.

But it was not until 1991, the year after her father's death, that she married. Her husband, the distinguished economist and Nobel Prizewinner Amartya Kumar Sen, was later elected Master of Trinity, Victor's own college.

Through the eyes of Victor's youngest daughter, he seemed more like a grandfather than a father. He was indeed into his fifties as Tory played in the nursery; but the gulf was not one of years alone. The children of Barbara and Tess alike were exposed to the same curt interrogation as a forgetful servant or a captured enemy agent. Forty years on, Tory would still wonder why he needed to crush as well as to instruct the young. 'I withstood it', she told me, 'by absenting myself emotionally or in person. I pleaded the Fifth Amendment.'

Even before she sat for her A levels, he wrongly concluded that Tory would not be clever enough to pursue an academic career like Emma. Instead she received a message from her father's secretary that, without consulting her, he had arranged for her to be interviewed by Marcus Sieff at Marks & Spencer with a view to being employed there. She refused. Steeling herself against discouragement, she went from Cranborne Chase to London University, where she took a First Class in English and was appointed a lecturer in Mediaeval Literature.

Jacob owed his success at Oxford to Hugh Trevor-Roper. At London his half-sister was similarly inspired by Anne Barton, an authority on Renaissance drama and later Professor of English at Cambridge. Tory published a work of textual criticism of Chaucer, shared with her mother an interest in the eighteenth-century stage and wrote poetry.

In spite of the belated pride Victor took in Tory's achievements, he would not allow that she was free to accept or reject the suitors that all his daughters attracted. There were traumatic episodes culminating in her considered rejection of one brilliant young man whom her father urged her to marry with self-defeating persistence. That will be mentioned in its place. It was not until after Victor's death that she at last married. Her husband is the playwright Simon Gray.

Amschel, the youngest of Victor's children, was in youth tortured by a shyness he never quite overcame. Taller than most Rothschilds, very pale and with the finely drawn features of a thoroughbred as well as its uncertain temper, he would slide obliquely into the drawing room at Herschel Road, exchange perfunctory greetings, then bolt – I suspect to the security of Sweeney's pantry. But the embodiment of Disraeli's 'transient and embarrassed phantom' already revealed a sweetness of nature and a core of physical courage that persisted to the end of his comparatively short life.

It is doubtful if he would have been happy at any public school. As it was, he survived a year or two at The Leys, Cambridge, a non-sectarian, cosmopolitan school that still bore the imprint of its Methodist founders. He was spared anti-Semitism, he later told me, but the spectre of untold wealth evoked by his family name incited his schoolfellows to ribaldry.

Victor, as it happened, did deploy his wealth to secure one attribute for the boy. Although he had no dogmatic belief in Judaism, he though it seemly that his sons, in common with all other Jewish boys of thirteen, should experience the initiation ceremony of bar mitzvah. To his consternation he discovered that no English rabbi would preside over the service. For a Jewish birthright, in its strict sense, emanates from the mother, not from the father; and whereas Barbara had converted to Judaism on marriage, so ensuring that Jacob would be indisputably Jewish by birth, Tess had not done so. By the letter of the law, Amschel was not a Jew.

That was just the sort of obstacle that Victor delighted in evading. And evade it he did by persuading an American rabbi to overlook what to Victor was no more than a bureaucratic quibble. Amschel duly underwent bar mitzvah in a New York synagogue. He later became an active trustee of Hanadiv, the Rothschild foundation that supported many good works in Israel.

However crushed he seemed by the weight of his father's personality, Amschel had an easier upbringing than did most of his siblings. In the year of his bar mitzvah he was allowed to compete in motorcycle scrambling. He graduated to motor racing, in which he scored well-publicised successes at Silverstone and elsewhere, driving historic models from his own stable of cars. He also qualified for a private pilot's licence. His father denied him none of these expensive pastimes.

Victor accepted without reproach his son's failure to gain a place at Oxford or Cambridge. Amschel did, however, read Economics, History and Archaeology with credit at the City University, London, then worked for some years as circulation manager of *New Review*, a literary magazine. But his heart lay in farming at Rushbrooke, which his father later made over to him, and in the shooting, cricket and hospitality that went with it. Other bounty included a house in London, a farm in New Hampshire (bought with money from the sale of the house in Barbados) and Victor's collection of Hilliard portraits. In 1981 he married Anita, a daughter of James Guinness, of the banking branch of the family, who bore him a son and two daughters.

His career took an unexpected turn in 1987 when at the age of thirty-two he was found a place in N. M. Rothschild. In time, it was thought, he might well succeed to the chairmanship then held by his cousin Evelyn de Rothschild. Although Amschel had no previous experience of banking, Victor assured his critics that the new recruit was doubly qualified, having inherited the financial genes both of the Rothschilds and of the Grotes and Meinertzhagens in Tess's family tree.

Evelyn seemed to share his optimism when he cut short Amschel's laborious apprenticeship and installed him in the chairman's office as his personal assistant. In January 1990 Amschel was appointed chief executive of Rothschild Asset Management, an important subsidiary of NMR, and its chairman three years later. Victor, dying in March 1990, lived to enjoy the exhilaration of his son's meteoric promotion but was spared its ultimate tragedy. In July 1996, after a day of talks with colleagues in Paris, he was found hanged in an hotel room.

I spoke to Amschel for the last time a week before he died, at the gathering in Herschel Road which followed a memorial tribute to Tess in Newnham College. He showed no sign of strain, and the next day I wrote to tell him how moved we had all been, not least by his own charm, dignity and sense of occasion.

Six hundred mourners attended his own funeral exactly two weeks later. It was an epitaph that would have astonished him.

'My father never grew up,' one of Victor's daughter recalls. 'He was shy and insecure, and he hid his lack of confidence behind banter.' Miriam called it a family failing, a tiresome and unattractive habit which spared neither friend nor foe.

Greta Garbo, who lacked a skin or two of her own, found him brutally tactless when they were fellow guests of Cecil Beaton in New York. 'Why did you go on Onassis's yacht?' he challenged her. 'What do you get out of it?' Beaton's diary continues,

> She is generally witty and quick of answer but the bull-like Victor was too strong a breath of air for her ... I wondered why Greta left so early. Immediately after the Rothschilds had left to catch the elevator Greta telephoned. 'Don't let them know who you're speaking to – if they're still there – But what happened? I didn't enjoy myself. The Lord never even looked at me. He paid

no attention to me whatsoever. It wasn't at all a nice atmosphere and I was numb and I've come home very depressed.' I
told her that all Rothschilds are coarse. 'Well when you're as
sensitive as I am it isn't very pleasant.'

There was humiliation too for his friend and mentor Stuart
Hampshire, Grote Professor of Mind and Logic, when Victor
overheard one of the Rothschild children asking, 'What is philosophy?' Hampshire's long, elaborate reply left nothing to chance. But
Victor had no time for those gossamer subtleties. In scalding terms
he lampooned the futility of a philosopher who could not expound
his craft more lucidly. Retribution, however, awaited Victor when
he sent Christopher Peacocke, the future Waynflete Professor of
Metaphysical Philosophy, a bold logical insight that would change
its whole concept. Peacocke replied on a postcard: 'The same
thought sometimes occurs to my first-year undergraduates.' Victor
delighted in telling this story against himself.

On such a level of donnish insult, not far distant from that of
the nursery, the Titans amused themselves. The Duke of
Devonshire has described him 'radiating malice'. Victor and a few
intimates also clung to the idiom of Billy Bunter that entertained
generations of schoolboys who knew not television. Cries of
'Don't fib' and 'What a whopper' flashed across the dinner table.
He would introduce the racehorse owner Jakie Aster as a German
pork butcher; the victim would respond by naming him Lord
Spoiltchild. And to an opponent on the golf course who had
paused before making his stroke: 'I hope you are not attempting to
think.'

He was addicted to the harmless pranks and wheezes of his
youth, such as spoof telegrams from the prime minister. When
unable to sleep, he would telephone the head office of Marks &
Spencer at four in the morning, express astonishment to the
watchman that Lord Sieff had not yet arrived and leave a message
for the chairman to return his call. Once he accompanied Harry
Rosebery to Ruthven Castle for a weight-losing regime. There they
found the patrician Lord Derby, who had arrived with a case of
very old brandy. Rosebery told him that his cousin Victor, an

eminent scientist, had declared that nothing could be more harmful to a man in Derby's condition that old brandy. So disturbed was Derby by this expert opinion that he gave the case to Rosebery as a present. The two younger men shared it. They also broke out of the castle every now and then, as Rosebery put it, 'to have a pat of butter each'.

CHAPTER 8

Shell

From 1958 to 1970, Victor Rothschild's life and fortunes were tied to those of Shell, first as a consultant, then as a member and later chairman of the board of Shell Research Ltd, ultimately research director of the entire Royal Dutch Shell Group. This huge multinational company had been formed half a century earlier by the merging of two oil companies. One was Sir Henry Deterding's Royal Dutch Petroleum Company; the other Shell Transport and Trading Company, founded by Sir Marcus Samuel (later Viscount Bearsted) and named after his first business venture, importing painted shells from the East. Victor, having spent more than twenty-five years in a Cambridge laboratory studying the sex life of the all but invisible spermatozoa, now found himself supervising a worldwide programme of industrial research with an annual budget of some £500 million.

He gave his loyalty as much to Shell as to the military and academic institutions with which he had been associated and took pride in the company's international standing and influence. Sir William Armstrong, a permanent secretary to the Treasury, once said to him that Shell ought to have a seat at the United Nations. 'I wish we did,' he replied, 'instead of some of the baboons who have that distinction.' He boasted too that no fewer than five Fellows of the Royal Society were simultaneously working for Shell: Sir John Cornforth, Professor George Popják, Sir Robert Robinson OM, T. M. Sugden and himself. He thought it old-fashioned and snobbish of other research scientists to hold aloof from the marketplace of applied science. 'How much *useless* research do we do?' a member of the group board asked him during his early days with Shell. It prompted him to formulate and put into practice what came to be known as the customer-contractor principle: 'The customer says what he wants; the contractor does it (if he can); the customer pays.' The customers were Shell operating companies throughout the world; the contractor was the director of research who sub-contracted each desired project to the appropriate laboratory in his network. Yet Shell's programme of research had to be flexible enough to finance schemes that did not necessarily pay for themselves: perhaps 10 per cent of the budget. Victor liked to quote the example of his predecessor who thought that a certain gadget should be studied and developed. Although no businessmen were interested in it, he persisted. It happened to be a very early computer.

As chairman of the Agricultural Research Council Victor was thought by some of his colleagues to have interfered too much on matters of detail, a habit that delayed urgent decisions and frayed the tempers of subordinates. At Shell he similarly insisted on making himself familiar not only with every stage of the extraction and refining of crude oil but also with a multitude of industrial processes that either depend on or contain its chemical derivatives. Among the experiments to catch his imagination were ways of inhibiting the growth of seaweed on the hulls of tankers and so of increasing their speed; the transport of coal along pipelines by grinding it to dust, then suspending it in water or oil; the conversion of the otherwise valueless Brazilian water hyacinth into methane.

Much of his task was in deciding priorities. The simplest decision was to say, 'They are interesting experiments, but commercially they can lead nowhere. They must cease.' It was more difficult to judge whether experiments that in time would undoubtedly produce a better lubricating oil than any yet available were worth continuing in terms of time and cost. Scientists are always reluctant to abandon a piece of research and his closing or amalgamating of Shell laboratories was resented by those who worked there. At least one senior member of the board felt that some of the resulting friction could have been avoided by a more tactful or sympathetic touch. At the same time Victor did protect his teams of scientists from what he called 'the ravages of administration' : red tape, unnecessary paperwork, petty restrictions, a burdensome system of communication. Even he felt himself to be the victim of bureaucracy when required to present and defend his budget to the board annually; he failed to convince his inquisitors that it was difficult to plan research on less than a three-year basis. He would also compare research in Shell with exploration: 'If you find oil or make a discovery, the reaction is, "about time". If you don't, the reaction is, "why not"?'

Jonkheer John Loudon, the much-respected president and later chairman of Royal Dutch Shell, appreciated Victor's questing mind but from time to time warned him not to tread on too many toes. The director of research accepted these friendly rebukes in good part but never came to terms with Willen Starrenburg, the managing director responsible for overseeing his programme. Every Tuesday evening the two men would meet at Grosvenor House, in Park Lane, where the Dutch managing directors had suites. Their encounters usually ended in tears. After one virulent exchange, Victor burst out, 'You are a bastard.'

Starrenburg replied plaintively, 'No one has said that to me since I became a managing director.'

'Then cube it,' was Victor's inelegant riposte, after which they patched up some sort of truce. During another skirmish, Victor enquired, 'Wim, is that an order?'

'No,' he replied, 'it is binding advice.'

Telling me the story years later, Victor conceded, 'Quite good for a Dutchman.'

By the 1960s he had shed almost all his Labour beliefs. But he was shocked by the failure of Shell's management to establish a trusting relationship with either local trade union leaders or the workforce they represented: an attitude he found as monolithic as the Shell Centre on the South Bank. He began his campaign to improve matters at one of the company's biggest laboratories, Thornton Research Centre, close to the Shell refinery at Stanlow, near Chester. Among the staff of nearly a thousand, many of them engaged in testing engine lubricants, were a hundred or so hourly-paid workers considered to be of an inferior status, who belonged to a sub-group of the main trade union at Stanlow. Having heard murmurs of their discontent, he telephoned the director of Thornton, asking him to summon the shop stewards to a meeting on a certain morning, coffee and sandwiches to be provided. The director was horrified, but Victor insisted. 'We met', he wrote, 'in an atmosphere of some suspicion. The director was not present at my request. I explained that the object was to exchange views on Thornton, on Shell Centre and on other Shell undertakings. It was not a meeting at which complaints would be ventilated; but if it was generally thought to be useful, we would meet once a quarter.' So they talked to each other about Shell and its problems great and small.

At the second meeting, grievances emerged which Victor thought justified but did not say so. One was that the workers had to queue in the open for their pay, whatever the weather; another, the filthy state of the lavatories allotted to them. Afterwards, Victor saw the director and told him to see that a covered way of glass or perspex be built, and that the lavatories were in future to be kept absolutely clean. What not even he could change was the system, of which he disapproved, that each category of worker in the Shell hierarchy had its own separate lavatories. (I well remember, when doing research in the Rothschild archives housed in an extension to New Court, being entrusted with a press-button code number that alone could open the door to a sumptuous lavatory for senior executives. To deter the unlettered, the buttons were marked in Roman numerals.)

By the third meeting the atmosphere had grown friendlier and Victor received unsought assurances that in the event of union-imposed strikes, sudden stoppages or working-to-rule, these restrictions would be ignored at Thornton. When in 1970 Victor retired from Shell, the shop stewards' committee presented him with an inscribed beer mug. He called it 'my most treasured possession'.

Victor welcomed the occasional diversion further afield. One such call came from his cousin Baron Elie de Rothschild, who on behalf of his co-owners of Château Lafite complained about the insensitive behaviour of Shell Française in Bordeaux. First they had put up two tall chimneys which ruined the view. Much worse than that, however, the company had erected a very tall flare to burn off waste gases from the adjacent refinery. It illuminated the landscape at night, made a noise that disturbed the sleep of the inhabitants over a wide area and emitted unpleasant gases. In an age before governments and local authorities had become alert to the pollution of the environment, protests from the Rothschilds and other wine growers had been ignored.

Never too dedicated to combine business with pleasure, Victor suggested to a senior colleague that they should fly to Bordeaux with their wives in one of Shell's fleet of aircraft to investigate the nuisance. And of course Baron and Baroness Elie were delighted to welcome them to their chateau and its cellar of memorable vintages. As a result of the report produced by the two directors, the chimneys were painted green to help them blend into the landscape and much of the offensive plant of the refinery was either modified or placed underground at considerable expense. Victor blamed the local Shell management for not having foreseen the effect of intrusive noise, light, smell and possible pollution on one of the most famous and valuable wine-growing districts of the world. Baron Elie was so grateful that he sent Victor several cases of Château Lafite 1961 – *vins exceptionnels*, as the proprietors' cellar book describes them. His neighbour Baron Philippe, proprietor of Château Mouton Rothschild, with the fickleness of the poet he was, omitted to send even his thanks. But then the enmity between the two French cousins was legendary and each played his part with relish. When Philippe gave a luncheon at Mouton to celebrate the upgrading of this magnificent wine to join Lafite among the first-growths of the original 1855 classification, he invited Elie to share his triumph.

As Elie lifted a glass of Mouton to his nose he enquired, 'Tell me, Philippe, it is several years since I was last here. Where exactly does your vineyard begin?'

'About fifty metres away, on the other side of that wall.'

'What a pity your beautiful wine does not travel.'

In 1970, his last year as research director of Royal Dutch Shell, Victor was drawn into the affairs of Iran. The board of the group decided on political grounds that a company which removed so much of the country's natural resources in the form of oil should be seen to put something back. Victor was therefore despatched to Tehran to set up a business unconnected with oil or petrochemicals that would benefit local industry and employment. Having considered building modern hotels, of which there were few, and a stock exchange, that proved impracticable, his choice fell on agriculture. As always, he drew on the experience of others. The British ambassador, Sir Denis Wright, told him to consult Sir Arthur Gaitskell, brother of the former leader of the Labour party, who had successfully managed the Gezira cotton development in the Sudan. Gaitskell in turn recommended Kenneth Dick, a director of the trading firm Mitchell Cotts and pioneer of similar schemes in Ethiopia. The initial cost was to be borne by a joint company known as ShellCott, which would grow cotton at Dez, in the south-west of Iran, where a new hydroelectric dam ensured an abundance of water for irrigation. ShellCott was prepared to make every concession to national pride and custom. It renounced the use of mechanical picking, for instance, in favour of a local labour force. The Iranian government nevertheless imposed unreasonable restrictions that other developing countries would readily have waived; these included the instant payment of water rates rather than an extension of credit until the cotton crop had been harvested. From the very beginning, the Dez project was being smothered by an obstructive and paralysing bureaucracy that had scarcely changed for centuries.

One man alone had both the power and the will to change these supine attitudes: the ruler whose subjects were forbidden to refer to him except by his full style, His Imperial Majesty Mohammed Reza Shah Pahlavi, Shahanshah of Iran. It was a resounding panoply designed to confirm him as the heir of those legendary Persian heroes Cyrus and Darius, a myth in which he himself came to believe. In 1971, amid the ruins of Persepolis, the ancient capital, he gave a party of bizarre extravagance to celebrate the 2500th anniversary of the empire founded by Cyrus the Great. He invited the crowned heads and rulers of the world, and many of them came (though not, to his annoyance, Queen Elizabeth II). Housed in a tented city of silken walls and modern plumbing, gorged, dazzled and bemused, they witnessed an unfolding pageant that by implication linked the earliest Persian empire to that of their host: a supposedly seamless saga of valour and enlightenment.

The truth was less romantic. The Shah's own imperial line had been founded as recently as 1926. His father, a colonel risen from the ranks, had overthrown the Qajar dynasty, crowned himself Reza Shah Pahlavi, changed the name of the country from Persia to Iran and ruled until deposed by the invading Allied armies in 1941 for his pro-Nazi sympathies. The son, who thus succeeded to the Peacock Throne on the eve of his twenty-second birthday, reigned under supervision until the end of the war brought his country independence. He had been educated at Le Rosey, the fashionable Swiss school for the international rich. Although scarcely a nursery of democracy, it did open a window on to Europe that inspired the young Shah to embark on his 'White Revolution'. The daunting task he set himself was to hustle a sleepy Islamic community into the semblance of a modern, indus-trialised, literate state; to barter oil for the technology and weapons of the West; to force such enterprises as the Dez development on his intransigent and xenophobic subjects.

However eagerly the Shah sought a role on the world stage, he was reclusive by temperament, an autocrat who could be reached only through a handful of confidants. One was Assadollah Alam, Prime Minister and later Minister of the Court, perhaps the only member of his master's entourage able to pierce the miasma of sycophancy with which the Shah surrounded himself. The other was Shapoor Reporter, the son of a Bombay Parsi who had arrived in Tehran in 1893 and found employment at the British legation. It was Ardeshirji Reporter who in 1920 commended Reza Khan to the commander of the British troops in Persia, General Sir Edmund (later Lord) Ironside, who in turn encouraged the future Shah to seize power. Reza Khan's son never forgot this service. Known to have the Shah's ear, Shapoor Reporter became the most experienced and trusted middleman in all commercial negotiations between Britain and Iran, not least in the purchase of arms. In 1969 Britain's Labour government awarded him the OBE; three years later, on the recommendation of Lord Carrington, Conservative Minister of Defence, he was advanced to KBE as Sir Shapoor Reporter.

In seeking ultimate approval for the Dez project, Victor Rothschild would have found it only too easy to ask the British ambassador in Tehran for an introduction to Reporter. As always, he preferred a more oblique approach, this time through his friend Marcus Sieff, the joint managing director and future chairman of Marks & Spencer. A nephew and acolyte of Lord Marks, the joint founder of the firm, Sieff had already realised the commercial possibilities of importing fruit from Iran and even of setting up a pilot scheme for a store in Tehran. To lubricate both plans he agreed to lend the Shah some of his best managers. That both Rothschild and Sieff were Jews was no handicap in the only Middle East country which supplied Israel with oil and in return received technical and military advice. Reporter, when I met him at the Naval and Military Club in Piccadilly (of which he is a member) quoted some words of the Shah on this: 'If one of my tanks breaks down, the Americans will tell me to get a new engine. The Israelis will mend it.' And although the Shah never overcame his dislike of Britain, the country that had driven his father into humiliating exile, he could be charmed into a semblance of friendship. Victor, his path smoothed by Reporter, was received amiably. With him he brought a dossier of technical information and a hugely expensive toy train for the nine-year-old Crown Prince. He received in return the letter reproduced on page 171.

The Dez agreement was subsequently signed by the Shah and by Kenneth Dick, the chairman of ShellCott. Victor remained in London, but with a touch of oriental flamboyance sent out two gold pens for the ceremony. They failed to reach the signatories.

Nor did the development prosper, in spite of a visit to the site by the Shah himself. There is no short cut to growing cotton. ShellCott technicians had first to move vast amounts of earth to achieve the correct gradients for irrigation, then construct a

LE MINISTRE DE LA COUR

14th January, 1970.

Dear Lord Rothschild,

I have the honour to inform you that the recommendations which you sent to Mr. Shapoor Reporter as regards the improvement of Iran's pesticide procedures were duly laid before His Imperial Majesty The Shahanshah Aryamehr.

My August Sovereign has commanded that the Ministry of Water and Power co-operate with your firm in the implementation of your proposed scheme for the Dez Irrigation Project.

With best wishes and warm regards,

Yours sincerely,

Assadollah Alam
Minister of the Imperial Court.

The Honourable Lord Rothschild,
Shell Centre,
London , S. E. 1.

network of canals and locks. Only by trial and error, too, could the team discover the cotton crop cycle for that part of the world, as opposed to the known cycles for the Sudan or Ethiopia. They were on their way to ultimate success when the Shah was driven from his throne at the beginning of 1979. With him fell the Dez project, at considerable loss to its financial backers.

Victor retired from Shell Research at the end of 1970 on reaching his sixtieth birthday, so played no further part in the rise and fall of ShellCott's fortunes. But his interest in Iran and his easy access to the Shah continued during his years as head of the government Think Tank, from 1971 to 1974, and proved of some service to his country.

For Victor, even the Dez scheme had its humours. His Imperial Majesty's entourage, he once told me, were not alone in practising the arts of flattery and deceit. After the Shah had expressed a wish for Dez to produce strawberries as well as cotton, the company discovered an old lady who grew some fine fruit nearby. 'Every now and then,' Victor said, 'we bought a basket of her strawberries and presented them to the Shah who, it seems, drew the right conclusion.'

CHAPTER 9

Think Tank

Returning to his office after a farewell luncheon with his colleagues at Shell in October 1970, Victor found a cryptic message on his desk: 'Please telephone Mr Trend, who says he is a secretary.' The caller turned out to be Sir Burke Trend, Secretary of the Cabinet, who on the instructions of the Prime Minister, Edward Heath, invited Victor to be the first head of the government's Central Policy Review Staff, or Think Tank as it became known outside Whitehall. Thus was he rescued from an unwilling retirement at sixty to embark on four of the most exhilarating years of his life.

From the moment Heath led the Conservative party to an unexpected victory in the general election of June 1970, he began to tinker with the machinery of government. Most prime ministers do. They are daunted by the number and complexity of problems that demand instant action and inhibit long-term planning; by the conflicting claims of individual departments that invite compromise or even paralysis. So a new prime minister will juggle portfolios; create, abolish or merge ministries; recruit outsiders from finance, commerce and industry to reinforce the established civil service.

Heath embraced all these remedies, few of which either served or survived. The most striking was the creation of an independent department at the very heart of Whitehall, a task force of lively minds free from bureaucratic restraints. Its role was to advise not the Prime Minister alone, but the entire Cabinet. By appointing a Rothschild to be its first head, Heath also ensured that it would capture the public imagination.

In retrospect it was an inspired choice. But at the time it seemed somewhat daring to pluck a Labour peer (however inactive) from the obscurity of a laboratory to teach ministers and mandarins their business. Rothschild was in fact only fourth on the Cabinet Secretary's list of candidates. Trend had initially selected Professor Hugh Ford, who held the chair of Mechanical Engineering at Imperial College, London. After some hesitation he declined, as did Christopher McMahon, executive director at the Bank of England. Professor Richard Ross, an academic economist, was prepared to accept; but he was turned down by Lord Jellicoe, Minister for the Civil Service, as too indecisive. Only then did the prize fall to Victor, under whom Ross loyally agreed to serve.

He recorded his first, unpromising encounter with the Prime Minister at Number 10. Heath was accompanied by Trend and Sir William Armstrong, head of the civil service. ('Not until I came to Whitehall', Victor later recalled, 'did I learn that the country was run by two men, neither of whom I had ever heard of.')

Mr Heath: 'It's funny we have never met before.' Then there was a sort of row of dots. I could not think what to say; after a while I said, rather desperately: 'Prime Minister, do you not think it would be better to have an economist in charge of this Unit?'
Mr Heath: 'I did economics at Oxford.' Another row of dots. Again after a while, I said rather desperately: 'Prime Minister, could you give me an example of the type of problem you want the Unit to tackle?'
Mr Heath: 'Concorde.' At that moment I thought, perhaps wrongly, that I detected some anguished vibrations emanating from Sir Burke Trend and Sir William Armstrong, as they then were, who were hovering in the background. There was some justification for their anguish, if I did not imagine it, because an hour beforehand they had told me it was precisely things like Concorde that the Government Think Tank would *not* be expected to study.
While I was still feeling the vibes, a secretary came in and handed the Prime Minister a piece of paper which he read with

some signs of displeasure, and said, 'Oh well, I had better see him.' Turning to me, he concluded the interview by saying, 'Let me know if there are any other points.'

In a less distracted moment, Heath set the Think Tank two tasks. The first was to take a long-term view of national prospects and government policies: 'to rub ministers' noses in the future,' according to Douglas Hurd, Heath's political secretary and later Mrs Thatcher's foreign secretary. Secondly, it was to analyse the differences that arose between departments; to refine and set out the options open to ministers, and so enable the Cabinet to take decisions with greater ease and effectiveness.

The Prime Minister was later to observe that the Think Tank achieved considerable success in its first task, but encountered difficulty in its second, trespassing as it did on the preserves of a long-established civil service.

Victor was not in the least awed by the challenge. Although a rich man, he negotiated for himself a substantial salary of £14,000, precisely that of the Prime Minister and only £1000 less than that of Sir Burke Trend, to uphold his prestige in the Whitehall jungle. Then he insisted on several weeks' holiday at his house in Barbados before taking up his post as director-general on 1 February 1971.

With very few exceptions he was allowed to recruit his own team, limiting it to the number who could sit round a table: never fewer than thirteen or more than twenty. Most came from the civil service, a few from the professions, universities and industry. Almost all were male but far from misogynous. Their average age was thirty-five.

Civil service seniority counted for little within the Think Tank. But there did exist an inner ring of those from whom Victor, secretive by nature, least excluded his confidences. They were young, clever, presentable, mostly educated at the older public schools and the ancient universities. He drove them on the light rein with which a worldly housemaster would handle his precocious prefects. In the seclusion of the Think Tank offices he encouraged debate, flights of fancy, mockery. He defended his acolytes against accusations from other government departments of disrespect or disruption or breaking bounds.

If ever they found themselves in serious trouble, he would protect them from the wrath of the headmaster, as it were, a role in which the Think Tank gleefully cast Burke Trend. A valued young member one evening took home a briefcase of confidential documents to read overnight. It was stolen from the entrance hall of his house, and he was obliged to confess his double breach of security. Thirty years after serving in MI5, Victor remained obsessive about the need for official secrecy (except when he considered an inspired leak to be in the public interest). On this occasion he protected the culprit from penalties that would have damaged if not ended his career.

One of the first to take the Rothschild shilling was, at twenty-four, the youngest. William Waldegrave had swept the board at Eton, taken an exceptional First Class in Classics at Oxford and within months was to be elected to a prize Fellowship of All Souls. The son of a twelfth earl, he had inherited social graces and patrician self-confidence. Victor loved him as a son and at one moment seemed destined to become his father-in-law. But Tory Rothschild did not share the political ambitions that within eight years would carry her fiancé into the House of Commons and eventually to a seat in the Cabinet. The engagement was broken off without reproach or bitterness.

Waldegrave later liked to recall the trials and humours of working successively for the three most difficult men in England. They were Victor Rothschild, in the Think Tank; Edward Heath, at 10 Downing Street; and Arnold Weinstock, in GEC. He places his trio of taskmasters in no particular order. Victor wrote to Weinstock, 'You have a better bargain in Waldegrave than you think. And he is not as rich as you think.' Lord Waldegrave was grateful to Victor on his son's behalf. He gave a new plant the name Rothschild. It was a *Phlomis fruticosa*, or Jerusalem Sage.

Another early recruit was Robin Butler, a thirty-three-year-old Treasury official who had been secretary to the Budget Committee. It was no disadvantage to this man of outstanding ability and easy charm that he had been to school at Harrow, Victor's Alma Mater, or that his father-in-law had worked in Shell Research. Butler afterwards rose effortlessly through the civil service hierarchy until he sat in the chair of Burke Trend himself as Cabinet Secretary.

From the diplomatic service, though by no means concerned only with foreign policy, came Robert Wade-Gery. Educated at those twin foundations of William of Wykeham that bear the motto 'Manners Makyth Man', Winchester and New College, Oxford, he displayed a formidable intellect and elaborate courtesy that did not entirely conceal a playful sense of humour. He too was a Fellow of All Souls College, Oxford.

Rothschild's early inner circle was completed by the forty-seven-year-old Peter Carey, under-secretary in the Ministry of Technology, who became one of the two deputy directors of the Think Tank. He brought the ballast of age and experience to what Waldegrave called 'this private sloop weaving her way among the stately departmental three-deckers'. After little more than a year he was recalled to more conventional duties and eventually promoted to be permanent secretary of the Department of Industry.

It must not be assumed that the Think Tank was wholly a band of brothers. Two members had been wished on Victor by Burke Trend without consultation, which alone damned them in his eyes.

John Mayne, a promising official in the Ministry of Defence, had drafted part of Edward Heath's White Paper on 'The Reorganisation of Central Government', published in October 1970. He had subsequently been chosen to brief Rothschild on the purpose of the CPRS and to join the team. But he was wedded to the habits of civil service thought and language, and excluded from the Think Tank's more adventurous enterprises.

Trend had likewise appointed Professor Ross, the unsuccessful candidate for the directorship, to be joint deputy director with Carey. Ross assumed the subordinate post with dignity and good-will. He proved a match for the wiliest of Treasury negotiators and a brilliant draftsman. Victor, however, could not warm to any man thrust on him from above. But Ross's place in the CPRS was secure and he survived Victor's retirement in 1974 by four years.

Victor affected to believe that Mayne and Ross were the Cabinet Secretary's moles who reported to him the unorthodoxies of Think

Tank thought. 'It never passed our minds', Victor wrote with elabo-rate irony, 'that they had been planted for Byzantine or Smileyesque reasons. Had that been the case, some of us knew a bit about turning people round *and* round.'

Burke Trend's moles took their place in a whole lexicon of Think Tank jokes: the excessive length of William Waldegrave's hair, the sharpness of John Guinness's suits, the fatigued state in which the economist Adam Ridley would return from a shooting weekend. The victims took it in good part. But others were un-comfortable at the systematic undermining, even humiliation, of their two conventional colleagues.

By encouraging irreverence, Victor ensured that the morale of the Think Tank remained high. At its first full meeting he set the tone by asking, 'What the bloody hell do we do now?' The answers were euphoric.

'We must clamour for attention,' said Robin Butler.

'We must sabotage the smooth-functioning of the machinery of government,' said Robert Wade-Gery.

'We must create a legend,' said William Waldegrave.

And Victor added a threat of his own: 'We must not get the reputation of being good losers.' Douglas Hurd later wrote,

> Lord Rothschild roamed like a condottiere through Whitehall, laying an ambush here, there breaching some crumbling fortress which had outlived its usefulness. He wrote in short sharp sen-tences; he made jokes; he respected persons occasionally but rarely policies. He had the independence of position and person-ality which was needed to make the CPRS a success from the start.

Government by epigram was exhilarating, but it did not deflect Rothschild's team from a twofold intellectual grind: to appraise long-term policy and to analyse and report on current problems as they arose, each buttressed by a firm conclusion.

These reports were designed to enlighten not the Prime Minister alone but all members of the Cabinet with whom he shared collec-tive responsibility. Indeed, Victor particularly had in mind ministers who were not directly concerned with the subject under discussion. He had extracted from Burke Trend reluctant permission for himself or his deputy to attend and speak at Cabinet committees, though not at meetings of the full Cabinet. At one Cabinet committee, sitting next to a minister, he had allowed his eyes to stray to the brief prepared for his neighbour by the permanent secretary of his department. Against one item of the agenda was written, 'This is of no interest to you.' It shocked Victor that collective responsibility was thus being abrogated.

CPRS collective briefs offered an alternative, even contradictory, source of advice, encouraging ministers to ask questions, to resist where necessary Whitehall's departmental loyalties and traditional fudges.

That is why Victor insisted that each collective brief should carry an unambiguous conclusion, however intractable the problem. He recalled asking an eminent economic planner whether or not Britain should go into the Common Market. 'Victor,' the wise man replied, 'we can't go in and we can't stay out.' Or as he himself used to say: 'I am aware of the beatification accorded to compromise, but you cannot have half a Channel tunnel.'

The value of the Think Tank, as Douglas Hurd observed from Heath's private office at Number 10, was its opportunity to say: 'There is a case for spending nothing on a project. There is a case for spending £500 million on it. There is no case for spending £250 million. The compromise would give you the worst of both worlds.'

It may be asked what the Young Turks of the Think Tank could contribute to solving intractable problems after only a few weeks of study when civil servants had been labouring over them for twenty years. Robin Butler's answer is that those who have been doing something for twenty years are so certain they are right that they become impervious to doubt or self-criticism. Whitehall wisdom acquires a momentum of its own. The Think Tank claimed a licence to challenge departmental conventions, to scrutinise cosy deals negotiated by civil servants behind the backs of their ministers, to reopen debate at Cabinet level.

Its reports were ruthless in analysis, bold in presentation. They

seized the attention of busy ministers by brevity and a brisk, epi-
grammatic style: a deliberate affront to the smoothly flowing,
scrupulously balanced antitheses of the mandarins. And to ensure
that, when placed in a minister's despatch box, Think Tank reports
did not sink beneath a sea of flotsam, each was elegantly laid out
by the Foreign Office printing department (with whom Victor had
some private arrangement) and bound in thick scarlet paper. How
could even an exhausted minister ignore so tempting a *bonne
bouche*?

The first Think Tank report exploded under the noses of a
scandalised Cabinet in June 1971. 'Concorde is a commercial disaster,' it proclaimed, 'it should never have been started.' Then,
having hooked the reader, it went on to argue with conviction that
the Anglo-French project must be preserved, speedily completed
and aggressively marketed. In its way, the report was as much a
classic of design as Concorde itself. It was a model, too, of a collective brief; it deployed on a single sheet of paper the interests of
every government department concerned, concluding with a firm
recommendation.

No head of department other than Victor would have dared
follow up the report by commissioning Marks & Spencer to
produce a Concorde tie for each member of the Cabinet, with a
Concorde scarf for Margaret Thatcher the Education Secretary. No
other head of department could have afforded to extract the cost
of Concorde at the French end of the operation by plying a
French general with Château Lafite from his private cellar.

But for the intervention of the Prime Minister, the impact of the
Think Tank on Cabinet thinking would have been blunted from the
very start. For Burke Trend had exercised his right as Cabinet
Secretary to intercept the Concorde report on its way to Number
10. Affronted by its strident style, he rewrote it in the more emollient language of the established civil service before sending it to
the Prime Minister. The report was accompanied by a minute
admitting that it had been 'improved' by his experienced hand.
Heath asked to see the original text, declared that it was 'infinitely
more effective' than Trend's and ordered it to be circulated to the
Cabinet.

Trend took a characteristic revenge. He would not allow the Think Tank to say that it was *investigating* a subject; only that it was *taking an interest*. The euphemism deceived nobody. Among other topics in which the CPRS 'took an interest' during Victor's four years at the helm were computers, coal, the construction industry, energy, miners' wages, nationalised industries, Northern Ireland, nuclear reactor safety, oil and race relations. Most were thrust on him by the Prime Minister or the Cabinet, often at short notice. But he himself suggested a study of nuclear waste: a little-regarded problem that was to become acutely sensitive in later years.

Victor was at heart an impresario. He would spend days planning a birthday party for a friend, an appearance on television or a memorial address. The Think Tank brought him a new arena. He persuaded the Prime Minister to let him organise unprecedented six-monthly reviews of government strategy that offered ministers a wider perspective than could be gleaned from their day-to-day business.

These presentations were usually held at Chequers and lasted a whole day. The Cabinet sat round a table to hear a series of short papers by members of the Think Tank, followed by a general discussion. The agenda was threefold: objectives the government had set itself, progress achieved and any necessary changes to be made. Charts and even cartoons were used to enliven the spoken word. The presentation would be repeated a day or two later for middle-grade ministers and again for under-secretaries and whips.

Although the head of the Think Tank would intervene in discussion, he preferred to leave the presentation to the more presentable members of his team. As Waldegrave wrote, 'No one other than Victor could have entrusted to a 24-year-old, with hair then much too long, part of a presentation on the failings of their strategy to an astounded Cabinet.'

Robin Butler – 'rather a good-looking, well-scrubbed young man,' as Victor described him – was another *jeune premier* to tread the boards at Chequers. Robert Wade-Gery's polished performance owed something to elocution lessons from the mellifluous Dadie Rylands. Dick Ross put into practice his own mot: 'Think the unthinkable, but wear a dark suit when presenting the results.'

Senior civil servants (who were not invited) disapproved of the circus; and some ministers, according to the Prime Minister's private secretary, Robert Armstrong, felt 'uncomfortable'. Even Edward Heath, without whose protection and encouragement the Think Tank could not have displayed such braggadocio, did sometimes think its behaviour self-indulgent and its conclusions doubtful.

For the CPRS dwelt in something of a vacuum, without responsibility for the political consequences of its recommendations. Victor himself was reminded of this when a senior civil servant, noticing that the head of the Think Tank had no pictures on his office walls, went on, 'It does not matter. If you want your masters to take notice of you, the only picture you will need is a map of Britain with the marginal seats coloured in red.'

From his twelve years with Shell, Victor brought to the Think Tank specialist knowledge in two fields. There was his application of the customer-contractor principle to scientific research; and there was his experience of the oil industry, strengthened by the personal links he had established with the Shah of Iran and his entourage. Both interests were put to effective use in Whitehall.

Even before his appointment as head of the CPRS, he had been asked to write a report on government research and development (known as R & D), eventually published under his name as a green paper, or discussion document, in November 1971.

Most Think Tank reports were drafted by a small team and subsequently enlivened by a Rothschild firework or two. R & D was largely his own work. Although toned down by the fluent Whitehall hand of John Mayne, it embroiled its author in virulent conflict with his fellow scientists.

The study embodied the principle he had evolved at Shell: that the customer says what he wants; the contractor does it (if he can); the customer pays. But what was widely acceptable in the world of commerce affronted the scientific Establishment, including a majority of Fellows of the Royal Society. The autonomous Science, Social Science, Medical, Agricultural and Natural Environment Research Councils resented his recommendation that Whitehall should have more control over both the direction and cost of their research programmes. Victor demanded value for money, his antagonists scientific freedom. It was a battle between irreconcilables.

Stung by taunts of betrayal, he included in the text of a speech he was about to make to one of the research councils a reference to 'the squeals of anger uttered with Gadarene-like intensity by the older members of the scientific establishment'. Fortunately for his friendship with Alan Hodgkin, by now President of the Royal Society, he was persuaded to remove the offensive passage before delivery. Miriam, dining with another learned society, held up a card as she sat down: 'I am not my brother's keeper.'

The report also cast a shadow over his fitful friendship of thirty years with Solly Zuckerman, chief scientific adviser to the government. To borrow the compliment paid by one Edwardian statesman to another, they pursued each other with malignant fidelity. Neither Judaism nor shared scientific endeavour struck a common note of cordiality. Victor thought the zoologist from South Africa devious and self-serving, a scientific adviser whose advice was more political than scientific. Zuckerman conceded that the head of the house of Rothschild had a brain, but regretted that his well-upholstered upbringing had deprived him of originality, confined him to too narrow a field, left him dependent on his name, his money and his social prestige.

Each made jokes about the other. Victor liked to describe an alarming experience when, as newly appointed head of the CPRS, he came to see a Cabinet minister on business:

As the minister began to talk, before I could say why I had come, I started to have a very curious feeling, somewhat akin, I fancy, to that experienced by people who have taken LSD. I felt I was floating upside down... Gradually it dawned on me that the minister was under the impression I was Solly Zuckerman. Overwhelmed as I was by this unexpected and undeserved compliment, it made communication on the subject I had in mind rather difficult. Nor was I capable of reproducing Solly's Svengali-like power to manipulate ministers to his way of thinking: no Sollycisms came to mind. Not even a Sollypsism.

Soon after the announcement that Zuckerman was to be made a peer on retirement from government service, the two men met in Downing Street. Victor incautiously asked, 'What are you going to call yourself?'

Solly: 'Why, Lord Rothschild, of course.'

Victor's proposals for R & D were largely accepted by the government, though not before he had been given a hard time in a two-day debate in the House of Lords. As a civil servant, albeit of an unusual kind, he felt inhibited from defending himself from the floor of the House; he had in any case applied for leave of absence from legislative duties. Zuckerman, in his memoirs, shed crocodile tears over Victor's discomfiture:

> I participated with what I hoped would, in the circumstances, be regarded as a well-balanced speech. But I had not reckoned with Victor's sensitivity to criticism. He was much bruised by the way the debate had gone. I can see him sitting in the 'box' – the little enclosure for civil servants – with his head down on his arms on the ledge. He had tried before the debate to explain his proposals in the scientific press but, inevitably, in trying to obviate possible criticism, he had equivocated at the expense of clarity. Whether it was my pointing this out that irked him, I never knew, but for some time after, our relations remained cool.

Younger members of the Think Tank cheered on the contestants. At their first anniversary dinner at the Mirabelle a telegram was handed to Victor: 'My unbounded admiration for a wonderful first year. Who else could have succeeded in uniting the whole scientific establishment, something beyond even me? Solly.'

Later there was a letter for Victor from 10 Downing Street: 'I much enjoyed my visit to the CPRS first birthday party. I also enjoyed the champagne – it really was glorious stuff.'

But that, unlike Solly Zuckerman's barb, was genuine.

The Prime Minister had cause to be grateful to Rothschild for another reason. The former head of Shell Research gave the government early warning of an approaching oil crisis and the need to recast Britain's energy resources.

Soon after arriving at the Think Tank he had recruited Dr Anthony Fish, a senior executive of Shell; and when Fish's six-month secondment expired, others were lured from the big oil companies. He also depended on the advice of Dr Walter Levy, a leading American oil consultant. Early in 1972 he launched a long-term inquiry into energy policy: not only oil but also coal, electricity and ultimately nuclear fuel. The report was presented to the Cabinet in the summer of 1973.

It was not so much the drastic recommendations which alarmed ministers, many of them designed to lessen Britain's dependence on oil, as the scarcely credible forecasts on which they were based. The price of oil in 1972 was $1.90 a barrel. By 1985 it was unlikely to be less than $3.75, could reach $6, or even a crisis level of $9. The trend was correct but not the steepness of the rise. Far from exaggerating the leap in oil prices, the report had seriously underestimated them. The Arab–Israeli war of October 1973 caused the price to soar to $11. The pessimism of the Think Tank had been vindicated and its reputation enhanced.

Since retiring from Shell, Victor had kept his friendship with Sir Shapoor Reporter in good repair. He wrote an introduction to Reporter's *Dictionary of Persian–English Idioms*, had him to dine at the Mirabelle after he was invested a KBE by the Queen, and urged the BBC (according to Reporter) to moderate its hostility to the Shah and his regime. As the oil-producing countries put pressure on the West by restricting supplies and raising prices, Victor asked Reporter to pave his way to an audience with the Shah. This was granted, at a time when the autocratic ruler of Iran would receive no member of the British embassy. But Victor pleaded in vain with him not to allow his ambitions to precipitate a world crisis.

During a tour of government departments to discover how best his team could help ministers, Victor was asked by the Foreign Secretary, Sir Alec Douglas-Home, whether the amount of paper he was expected to read could be reduced. The minister had already found a partial solution. In his box one day there appeared a report on Icelandic fisheries two inches thick, to which his private secretary had appended a note: 'The Secretary of State may care to read this during the weekend.'

Sir Alec minuted, 'A kindly thought, but erroneous.'

Victor himself would recall having 'a rather good dinner' with Lord Jellicoe. At about ten o'clock the Minister for the Civil Service gave a frightful groan and said he had to rush home to look through four boxes of Cabinet papers before the morning meeting. His host afterwards exploded:

> 'That's not a sensible way to live. Why the hell had he got four boxes of papers? Why hadn't they been properly digested in the office and condensed into four pages? Were not ministers already fully stretched and more by the competing claims of the department, the Commons and the constituency?'

He suspected that the problem was insoluble as long as civil servants, for their own convenience, deliberately stifled ministerial initiative beneath a mountain of paper or between the pages of a burdensome engagement book; and that even if an obstinate minister were to insist on challenging established practices, his civil servants would courteously delay their response, report on it at paralysing length, pare it down and ultimately 'refine' it, a euphemism for tearing its heart out.

Only a radical reform of the machinery of government could ease ministerial strain; and by the Prime Minister's own orders the subject was excluded from the Think Tank. The best Victor could do for overworked ministers was to recommend an intelligence test devised by the Medical Research Council. This enabled them to discover whether they were capable of logical thought after a bout of 'flu, dining well ('two large martinis, at least half a bottle of claret and two large brandies') or arriving ashen-faced for an important meeting with the prime minister after flying non-stop from Nairobi, then by helicopter to Chequers.

Although, as he explained, only the person taking the three-minute test would know the result, it proved so unpopular with permanent secretaries that he did not feel able to ask ministers to become guinea pigs. But Field Marshal Lord Carver, the Chief of Defence Staff, sportingly agreed to do so 'after a long trip and a couple of martinis on the aeroplane', and scored 97 out of 100.

The machinery of government was not the only forbidden topic. Another was defence, the Secretary of State, Lord Carrington, having been heard to say that whenever he heard the words Think Tank, he reached for his anti-tank gun. So too was foreign policy, except obliquely: as when Concorde, 'a commercial disaster', was saved from cancellation to preserve Anglo–French amity. Investigation of the intelligence services, in which Victor had continued to take an obsessive and ultimately damaging interest since his wartime years in MI5, was likewise denied to the Think Tank.

Nor was he allowed to see, much less tamper with, the government's closely guarded 'List of the Great and the Good', from which most appointments to public offices and committees are made. Victor affected to believe that all its members were aged fifty-three, lived in the South-East, had the right accent and belonged to the Reform Club. But he was left in no doubt that patronage was too valuable a commodity to be exposed to the irreverent.

Soon after Victor Rothschild's arrival in Whitehall he began to invite small groups of permanent secretaries to lunch informally in his office. He gave them lobster sandwiches and cider cup heavily laced with brandy: fare designed first to induce, then to allay, intimations of social insecurity. A Think Tank colleague afterwards asked how he had found his first two guests. 'One was intelligent,' he replied, 'the other was sober.'

From their desultory gossip he would learn what they were up to behind the backs of their ministers, just how far they were mining and sapping government intentions in order to pursue trusted policies of their own. Victor would then thwart their designs by well-directed collective briefs. He enjoyed sticking pins into bureaucrats: what he called 'acupuncture at the request of the Cabinet'. Sometimes he got things wrong, as when he heard that Burke Trend had ordered new curtains and other furnishings for the office of the Cabinet Secretary only a few weeks before he retired. Victor called it 'paranoia out of control'. It did not occur to him that the refurbishment was to welcome his successor, Sir John Hunt.

There was, however, one senior official of whom he invariably spoke with almost awed respect. When the puzzled Think Tank asked him why, Victor answered, 'A most unusual civil servant. He is extremely rich.'

When in later years he heard that another mandarin had described him as court jester to the Prime Minister and Cabinet, Victor did not wholly dissent:

> If, exceptionally, the CPRS through its oral or written work evoked an appreciative smile, it was doing something, however little, to relieve the atmosphere of somnolent ossification that pervades some parts of the bureaucracy.

That note of self-justification was echoed even in Whitehall, notably by Sir Patrick Nairne, a wise and imaginative permanent secretary. 'Victor's brooding presence', he told the present writer, 'was an invaluable threat to our defensive and sometimes complacent ritual – that we in our department knew our business best.'

'I regarded the CPRS as one of the best innovations of my years at No. 10.' Edward Heath wrote in his memoirs, published in 1998. There was generous praise for Victor Rothschild, too. Yet the awkwardness of their first encounter in Downing Street was never wholly overcome. Both were prickly by nature, uneasy in the presence of all but a few intimates. They shared no interests other than the nation's business and rarely met, even in Whitehall. When Victor asked an embarrassed Prime Minister to inscribe a photograph of himself, it was eventually returned from Number 10 bearing the greeting 'To Victor Rothschild from Edward Heath'.

The Prime Minister continued to protect the Think Tank against the civil servants and some of his ministers. But as the going got rough, with soaring inflation, unemployment and labour unrest, he came to look on Victor as a dilettante, a dabbler in high policy tiresomely remote from the pressures and consequences of party politics.

One source of friction was their contrasting approach to the militant miners and the future of the coal industry. Victor regarded coal mining as hard, dangerous and dirty, conditions which should be reflected in a doubled pay packet; he was outraged to learn that some miners had to buy their own safety equipment. On economic grounds, too, he preached the need for a well-paid, strike-free coal industry to counterbalance rising oil prices.

For Heath the problem was not primarily one of economics but of parliamentary democracy: who was to govern Britain, the elected government or a miners' union holding the nation to ransom by mob rule?

Even so, Heath's protégés were allowed to think the unthinkable, however facile, and to circulate their briefs, however barbed, within the confines of Whitehall and Chequers. But on 24 September 1973 the taut fabric of trust between them was ripped to shreds. Victor Rothschild went public.

As a former chairman of the Agricultural Research Council he had been invited to open a new seminar room at one of its laboratories near Wantage, in Berkshire. Directing the Think Tank for the past two and a half years as a near-autonomous fiefdom had led him to forget – if he ever did remember – that he was a civil servant, forbidden to speak publicly on political issues except with the permission of the Cabinet Secretary. So he neglected either to submit a draft of his speech or to ensure that it was not reported. Its publication by a news agency, and subsequently in the national press, provoked the most humiliating rebuke of his career.

His theme, based on a CPRS Cabinet presentation, was that Britain must cease to think of itself as one of the wealthiest and most influential countries in the world, as in the reign of Queen Victoria. Unless there were a severe reduction of public expenditure, he warned, Britain would in twelve years' time have an economic weight half that of France or Germany, and about equal to that of Italy.

He went on to compare the dangers facing the country with those of the Second World War and to advocate drastic remedies, however unpalatable:

It is not easy to scrap Concorde and put about 25,000 men out of work...It is not easy to scrap a new form of surface transport. It is not easy to stop thinking it quite reasonable to have four different sorts of nuclear reactors on the go at the same time.

Geoffrey Howe, Minister of Trade, had by chance just made a similar speech, predicting that within twenty years Britain would be overtaken in prosperity by Spain and Portugal. But then he was a politician, not a civil servant. Rothschild's indiscretion was aggravated by an unfortunate coincidence. On the very day of the Wantage speech, the Prime Minister was complacently extolling Britain's rising standard of living as measured by the sale of colour television sets.

Victor was astounded, and temporarily shattered, by the effect of his speech, which he had thought to consist of statesmanlike musings remote from the asperities of party politics. Most prime ministers, however nettled by the lapse of a subordinate, would have rebuked the culprit in private but defended him in public. That was not the way of Edward Heath. Number 10 announced that Rothschild had been reminded by the head of the civil service of the rules he had infringed and, more ominously, that he had had a thirty-minute meeting with the Prime Minister.

The press took the hint. The headline in the *Daily Telegraph*, 'HEATH PUTS ROTHSCHILD ON CARPET', was echoed by every other newspaper. Nor was that the end of his chastisement. When Parliament reassembled in October, the Prime Minister announced in answer to a question, 'Lord Rothschild has undertaken in future to abide by the rules governing public speeches by civil servants, and I have told him that I regard the episode as closed.'

A few days after what Victor called 'a rather unpleasant dressing-down', I spent an evening with him in St James's Place. He was dishevelled and distressed; comforted by a huge mailbag of support from friends and sympathisers, but disproportionately cast down by a few that were anti-Semitic. He conceded that he should have cleared his speech with the Cabinet Secretary, even though he had neither sought nor expected publicity at what he assumed would be a private meeting of fellow scientists.

Heath's impetuous reaction had astonished him. 'It was', Victor explained, 'because the Prime Minister had not had a summer holiday; and the reason for that was Burke Trend's foolishness in having fixed the date of the Ottawa conference of Commonwealth leaders for August.'

At Number 10, Victor continued, a still enraged Heath had taunted him with the loss to the government of the next by-election. The forecast was only partly true. On 8 November the Conservatives lost Berwick to the Liberals by fifty-seven votes, but held on to two other seats with reduced majorities.

Victor's crystal ball, by contrast, proved startlingly reliable. Britain did not have to wait until 1985 for the full impact of economic decline. Between 1973 and 1976, industrial production dropped by 7 per cent, unemployment climbed by 120 per cent and public-sector borrowing increased by 144 per cent.

Always prepared to squeeze a drop of mordant humour out of misfortune, he told me how, dining with Dollie Rothschild after the storm had broken at Number 10, he had been called to the telephone. It was Solly Zuckerman, offering to help in any way he could.

I too came to Victor's defence with a column from the *Sunday Telegraph* that mischievously tilted the scales in his favour:

The Prime Minister is fortunate still to have Lord Rothschild as head of the Think Tank.

Away from London when the explosion took place, I was astonished that a man both exceptionally sensitive to censure and in no need of a government salary of £15,000 should have swallowed a near-public reprimand.

There are, I believe, three reasons which led him to behave with such restraint. The first is the genuine regard which Rothschild and Heath have for each other – temporarily forgotten by the Prime Minister but not by the head of the Think Tank.

Secondly, the Civil Service hierarchy would be only too pleased to see Rothschild's departure from Whitehall in the wake of the businessmen whom the Prime Minister similarly recruited against official advice. But the intended victim determined to stay.

Thirdly, Rothschild has contrived to grow another skin since assuming his present post three years ago.

He once suggested to me that he ought to change his family motto. Instead of 'Concordia, Integritas, Industria', he preferred 'Quick to Give and to Take Offence'.

I think the original will suffice – although he may now be tempted to drop the word 'Concordia'.

For the director-general of the Think Tank it was 'never glad confident morning again'. The episode robbed him of any influence he might have exerted on Heath to settle with the striking miners and to avert a three-day working week: a national humiliation that provoked the Prime Minister to call the general election of February 1974 in which the Conservatives were narrowly defeated by Labour. In any case, Victor was on leave during much of that critical period, sick at heart in every sense. Without him, the Think Tank drifted rudderless.

The CPRS had feared that the new Prime Minister, Harold Wilson, would find no place for it in his remodelled machinery of government, having set up his own Downing Street Policy Unit. But it was allowed to continue. 'How do you like the change at Number 10?' I asked Victor.

He replied, 'I don't know which sort of prime minister one ought to prefer: the fitfully disagreeable or the falsely friendly.' Victor was back on form. He also liked to quote the reply of the gnarled old civil servant when asked what differences he saw between the two parties: 'Conservative ministers grunt, Labour ministers give us out-of-date lectures on economics.'

One Labour minister with whom Victor established a working relationship was Tony Benn, Secretary of State for Industry. An entry in Benn's diary for 2 June 1974 reflects both Victor's continuing suspicion of the List of the Great and the Good and his relish for backstairs intrigue:

Lord Rothschild rang to say he was interested in my ideas to get public appointments made more open and asked if he could send me a private letter at my home address. I feel I get on well with him. Also I have supported some of the papers prepared by his Central Policy Review Staff and suggested they should be published; Rothschild is a great believer in open government and has upset Whitehall which, of course, doesn't like it. He supported me a bit on Meriden [a motorcycle workers' co-operative], which I appreciate, so I think he is quite a useful ally to have. Certainly he would be a dangerous enemy.

Less obligingly, Benn noted, 'Rothschild was rather creepy-crawly. Considering he had served three and a half years under Heath, he might have been a bit more loyal.'

Victor slowly patched up his quarrel with Heath who in spite of preoccupations with the deepening economic and political crisis had visited him after Victor had suffered a heart attack in December 1973, and later asked him to dine at the Athenaeum. In 1977 Victor sent him a copy of his newly published essays, *Meditations of a Broomstick*. 'I shall always recall', the former prime minister replied with elephantine jocosity, 'what an honour it was to serve in your administration.'

'We have quite a few of your sort through here,' a civil servant in the Cabinet Office airily assured Victor. 'They come and they go.' In September 1974 he went. He had worked easily enough with Harold Wilson, but confessed to being worn out and too personally involved in the questions of the day to think clearly about them. He also wished to devote some time to his private affairs, neglected for the past three years.

He left in a haze of goodwill. It had been his habit to give each departing member of the Think Tank an engraved and dated glass tankard. This time the team presented him with an identical gift bearing the single additional word 'Chieftain'. The Foreign Office printers, although on strike at the time, offered a leather-bound album containing their signatures. Other tributes came from the draftsmen of the Central Statistical Office and the Ministry of

Defence, who had, to his meticulous instructions, prepared material for Cabinet presentations.

After years of sulky resentment, the Whitehall mandarins gave the interloper a dinner in the Reform Club, albeit on an evening pointedly close to the Day of Atonement. Mr Wilson recommended to the Queen that he should be appointed a Knight Grand Cross of the Order of the British Empire; his friends thought that like Solly Zuckerman (and later Alan Hodgkin) he ought to have had the Order of Merit.

In a farewell letter to the Prime Minister he struck a more sombre note:

> I leave the arena troubled, anxious and not too hopeful; but praying for understanding, cohesion and a new sense of national unity to defeat the most formidable enemies this country has so far encountered: inflation and social division.

So what memorial was there to his tenure of the CPRS other than the 'Three Cs' mockingly flaunted by his colleagues: Concorde, Coal, Chaos? Certainly those whom Victor had recruited paid no penalty for 'going native', as the mandarins put it. All rose to positions of dignity, trust and emolument in the public service, politics or the City; it would have been a reckless subordinate of *theirs* who dared to think the unthinkable, much less to sabotage the smooth functioning of *their* authority.

Of all the epitaphs on the Rothschild era of the Think Tank – which was ultimately abolished by Margaret Thatcher in 1983 – two stand out. Burke Trend said, 'They made a lot of extra work for very busy people.' And a minister told Victor, 'You made us think.'

Both are true.

CHAPTER 10

Chairman of NMR

In the spring of 1975 the editorial staff of the *Daily Telegraph*, and perhaps of other newspapers too, received a request from the new chairman of N. M. Rothschild & Sons Ltd. He wished in future to be described not as a banker but as scientist and former head of the government's Think Tank. The supplicant was Lord Rothschild, who at the age of sixty-four had been persuaded to join a profession for which he had neither vocation nor respect. His interest in money extended no further than the perpetual dew of his own bank balance. As Cousin Elie put it, 'Victor was made to be a banker like I was made to be a cardinal.'

So how had this elderly novice come to be appointed chairman of the most famous of all banks? The four Rothschilds at New Court, three cousins and his own son Jacob, had formed a delegation begging him to act as their arbiter. He was to bring his experience and wisdom to bear on internal disputes that threatened to leave NMR divided and indecisive in the face of ruthless competition from newer City banks and from Wall Street.

For a century and a half, the name Rothschild had been synonymous with flair and fortune; it was envied but respected, the subject of a thousand anecdotes and as many myths. The First World War tolled the end of its ascendancy. In 1913 the capital of NMR was £8 million. A generation later it had fallen to £1.5 million in a currency that had since lost 40 per cent of its purchasing power.

High taxation, an embargo on business with Germany, the Russian Revolution: these were not the only reasons for decline. Baron Lionel's three sons, all partners in NMR, died during the

First World War: Natty, Lord Rothschild in 1915, Leo in 1917, Alfred in 1918. Alfred alienated much of his estate of £1.5 million from New Court by leaving it to his mistress's child Almina, who had already received a dowry of £500,000 from him on marrying the Earl of Carnarvon as well as another £150,000 to settle her debts. The premature death in 1923 of Charles Rothschild, Victor's father and the more reliable of Natty's two sons, further weakened the dynasty.

The direction of the bank was thus left in the hands of only two partners, the sons of Leo: Anthony (1887–1961) and Lionel (1882–1942). A third brother, Evelyn, died of wounds received in action in 1917. An historian of NMR has referred to the 'genteel inactivity' of the inter-war years. There was nothing so vulgar as an aggressive search for new clients. 'They know where we live,' Anthony would say. 'If they want to do business with us let them come and talk to us.' That supine attitude pervaded New Court from top to bottom. 'This is the best club in Europe,' a senior employee boasted. 'We really ought to be paying a subscription instead of receiving a salary.' One man was taken on the payroll for his knowledge of Italian. He was required to display it only once in his long years of service, when sent to Victoria Station to meet a new Italian maid for Mrs Lionel.

There was a sterling quality about both the brothers who between the wars kept NMR alive on heavily depleted capital. Lionel, however, was profligate in his personal expenditure to a degree he would never have tolerated even in the happy-go-lucky regime of New Court. Having inherited Halton from his bachelor Uncle Alfred in 1918, he sold it to the recently established Royal Air Force as a technical training centre. With the proceeds he bought the 2600-acre estate of Exbury, on the Beaulieu river in Hampshire. There he spent prodigiously, laying out his now celebrated arboretum and gardens of rhododendrons, azaleas and camellias, a task that occupied 150 men for ten years, in addition to a regular staff of seventy-five gardeners. He also employed 200 builders to construct twenty-six miles of paths wide enough to take his Armstrong Siddeley (there were Rolls-Royces for longer journeys), to rebuild the house and to double the size of Exbury village.

Lionel's name will always be associated with his whimsical advice to the City Horticultural Society: 'No garden, however small, should contain less than two acres of rough woodland.' Not so well remembered is that on his death in 1942 he burdened his family with debts of £500,000 and a demand for £200,000 in estate duty.

Anthony, who succeeded him as senior partner, was described by a long-serving manager of NMR as 'formidable, aloof and slow to smile, often impatient and irritable'. He had gained a First Class in both parts of the History Tripos at Cambridge, fought at Gallipoli and been mentioned in dispatches. Some of his tastes were expensive – racehorses, porcelain and fine claret – but his collars were frayed and when he returned to Ascott, in Buckinghamshire, he would take the Tube from the Bank to Euston. He gave a Van Dyck to the National Gallery and other old masters, together with his country house, to the National Trust.

Each brother also ensured that the Rothschild dynasty would continue at New Court. Of Lionel's two sons, Edmund joined in 1946 and Leo in 1956. Anthony's only son Evelyn followed them in 1957.

Victor's aversion to banking had left the senior branch of the family unrepresented at New Court since his father's death in 1923. The hiatus lasted forty years, until in 1963 the twenty-seven-year-old Jacob asked to join his cousins at NMR. Victor was predictably discouraging. 'Jacob thinks a lot about money,' he warned his son's future colleagues, 'perhaps too much.'

An antipathy soon began to develop between Evelyn and Jacob, as much a matter of temperament as of policy. In gladiatorial terms, Evelyn could be seen as secure and authoritative, determined to retain the bank's independence, its conservative traditions, its control by family shareholders. By contrast Jacob emerges as energetic and ambitious, his self-confidence restored, alert to every opportunity for expansion and enrichment.

Both portraits contain an element of caricature. It was Evelyn who suggested that the Dickensian offices of NMR should be demolished in 1962 and replaced by the present marble palace. It was with his encouragement that Jacob founded a successful corporate finance division, offering advice on loans, mergers and takeover bids. It is under Evelyn's long chairmanship that NMR has prospered, without scare or scandal.

Jacob, for his part, resented being called a buccaneer. 'The first fifteen years of my working life', he says, 'were wholly dedicated to the rebuilding of NMR. There wasn't too much there before.' He could boast an acute financial brain, an ability to judge risk and – like his father – a readiness to think the unthinkable. He was particularly proud of his chairmanship of Rothschild Investment Trust, which within two years had soared in value from £5 million to £80 million, dwarfing its less daring parent, NMR itself.

Throughout that period of strain at New Court, the senior partner (or chairman as he became after the bank's incorporation as a limited company in 1970) was Edmund de Rothschild, Lionel's elder son. He was proud to sit at the same desk from which his great-grandfather Baron Lionel had negotiated the Suez Canal loan of 1875; but osmosis failed to inspire Edmund with the same ruthlessness of purpose. Genial and easygoing, he made no attempt to impose his will on the partnership as had Natty and, a generation later, Anthony. In his good-natured memoirs, Edmund describes how, signing a pile of documents with Anthony, he would from time to time say, 'I'm afraid I don't understand this.'

Invariably Anthony would reply, 'No, you wouldn't.'

Frequent absences from New Court also eroded his authority. Having been round the world in youth and seen much service abroad as a wartime gunnery officer, he had an itch to travel. In pursuit of a grandiose hydroelectric scheme for Newfoundland and Labrador (from which NMR were ultimately squeezed out by Canadian national pride) he made 400 flights across the Atlantic. He was a frequent visitor to Japan, too. This provoked the Governor of the Bank of England, in his supervisory role, to suggest to the peripatetic senior partner that he should spend more time in his counting house.

In any case, by 1975 Edmund was in his sixtieth year and the time had come to seek a stronger chairman. The contest seemed to lie between Evelyn and Jacob, although Leo, Edmund's younger brother and senior in age and experience to both, could not be discounted as a compromise candidate. But who was to make the choice? It was then that the four Rothschild directors agreed to invite Victor to become chairman in succession to Edmund, who would receive the honorific office of president. The recently retired head of the Think Tank, already bored by inactivity, accepted.

Jacob and Evelyn each had reason for optimism in courting Victor's favour: Jacob because he could not believe that a father would fail to support his son, Evelyn because he held more voting shares in NMR than did all the other directors combined. Each of these propositions demands closer scrutiny.

Since joining NMR, Jacob had built up a pivotal position as an enterprising creator of wealth. Whatever differences there had been with his father in youth, he knew that Victor admired those who made money, as opposed to those who had merely inherited it. He nevertheless cannot have forgotten an ominous little episode that had occurred two or three years before. At a press conference on the Think Tank, as public an occasion as could be imagined, a journalist asked Victor, 'How does it come about that your son is so good at finance while you are said to be so bad?'

He replied, 'Jacob is so brilliant at finance and I so much the reverse that some people think it casts doubt on his legitimacy.' He later conceded that his unsmiling jocularity was misplaced, but repeated the witticism in an after-dinner speech to the Press Club of London even after becoming chairman of the bank. Jacob had been warned. His father could sometimes appear to have buried the hatchet; but he always knew where to find the handle.

It was, however, a mere pinprick compared with a blunder on Victor's part that cast a shadow over Jacob's years at New Court and led ultimately to his departure. As the first Lord Rothschild's only grandson in the male line, Victor had inherited a majority of the ordinary (or voting) shares in NMR, which by family practice Jacob had reason to look on as his birthright. Had those shares been made over to Jacob when he joined NMR, his influence there would have been paramount, his position impregnable. But during an earlier restructuring of the bank's capital, Victor had agreed to exchange some of those voting shares for cumulative preference shares that carried no vote. The transaction left Anthony with 60 per cent of the ordinary shares as against Victor's 20 per cent: a shift in the balance of power within the bank from Victor to Anthony, and in turn to Evelyn after his father's death.

There are conflicting explanations for Victor's lack of fore-thought: ignorance, indifference, inadvertence. The most plausible is that Victor or his advisers, lacking confidence in the recovery of NMR from its long decline, preferred to hold cumulative prefer-ence shares with guaranteed fixed interest rather than ordinary shares exposed to volatile markets. As it turned out, the ordinary shares soared in value from decade to decade while the cumulative preference lagged far behind. Victor had lost both his ducats and his son.

Even had he supported Jacob's claims to the chairmanship from ties of family loyalty, he could not have prevailed against Evelyn's superior shareholding. As Disraeli wrote in *Tancred*, 'A majority is always the best repartee.' On the merits of the case, too, the other directors favoured Evelyn. They contrasted his restrained style of banking with that of Jacob: an inspired wheeler-dealer impatient of both tradition and regulation. Even Jacob himself confessed to a colleague that he loved doing deals but hated clearing up afterwards. The coveted chairmanship went to Evelyn.

Jacob deeply resented this betrayal at his father's hands. 'Since then,' Victor told me nearly ten years later, 'we have never spoken, except politely on public occasions.' It would have been under-standable had Jacob at once cut his ties with NMR and sought his fortune elsewhere. But he remained, hoping to persuade his col-leagues of the need to expand in a competitive world. One bold plan was to merge with the younger and more aggressive merchant bank S. G. Warburg; another to merge NMR with Jacob's flourish-ing Rothschild Investment Trust. Both, however, would have ended family control of NMR; both were duly vetoed by Evelyn and other members of the board, including Victor.

By 1980 Jacob had had enough. He sold his minority sharehold-ing in NMR for £6.6 million and resigned as a director. It was agreed that he should continue to manage Rothschild Investment

Trust, whose assets were by now in sight of £100 million; but so that there should be no confusion between the two institutions each bearing the name Rothschild, it would be known only by its acronym RIT. He enshrined his departure from New Court by changing his entry in the next annual volume of *Who's Who*. He deleted 'Director, N M Rothschild & Sons Ltd since 1963' and substituted 'Chairman RIT Ltd (formerly Rothschild Investment Trust Ltd) since 1971'.

While NMR continued its unspectacular but steady growth under Evelyn, Jacob pursued a more erratic path, trading under his evocatively named companies, J. Rothschild Holdings and Five Arrows Ltd. Some deals were successful, some were not. What caught the public eye was the failure of his bid of £15 billion for the tobacco company BAT in partnership with James Goldsmith and Kerry Packer. His justification for an operation that ultimately lost him £13 million was ingenious. He touched on nothing so vulgar as the desire of three very rich men to make themselves richer, but rather a mission to turn 'the impurity of BAT's architecture into clean, classical lines'.

Few other corporate raiders would have chosen to clothe an act of plunder in the language of aesthetics. But then few other corporate raiders are qualified to become chairman of the trustees of the National Gallery or of the National Heritage Memorial Fund, appointments which Jacob held in turn with flair and success. He attracted and put to imaginative use benefactions of £50 million from J. Paul Getty and of £30 million from the Sainsbury family. He gave powerful support to the architect Paul Venturi whose Trafalgar Square extension happily replaced earlier plans for a 'monstrous carbuncle on the face of a much-loved and elegant friend', as the Prince of Wales called it. And as a farewell gift on retirement from the National Gallery he paid for the restoration of its opulent central hall, surmounted by a frieze any Roman emperor might have envied: *'Jacobi Rothschild Munificenta Integrum Restituta'* ('Restored to its former state by the generosity of Jacob Rothschild'). In 2002 he was appointed to the Order of Merit.

He also supervised and financed the costly renovation of two great houses. One was Waddesdon, the sprawling Victorian pile of

James and Dorothy de Rothschild, made over to the National Trust but a virtual fiefdom of Jacob, Dorothy's heir. The other was Spencer House, overlooking Green Park. The home of Diana Princess of Wales's family since the eighteenth century, it had been much neglected for a generation. Having taken a long lease on it through J. Rothschild Holdings, Jacob restored both house and contents to near perfection. This labour of love he has chosen to commemorate not by a brazen Latin inscription but by a little brass plate rescued from the debris and let into the desk of his office a few yards away in St James's Place. 'Spencer House: Tradesmen's Entrance', it reads: a reminder of how much beauty has its origin in the sordid craft of money management.

Victor had never intended to act as chairman of NMR for more than a year or two. After fifteen months of trauma, adjudicating between Jacob and Evelyn, he had endured enough. 'The pace is too hot for someone of my age,' he wrote in June 1976. But he was content to remain at New Court for the next twelve years in a less demanding role, as chairman of Rothschilds Continuation Ltd, a holding company of which NMR was a wholly owned subsidiary. It had been formed by Anthony in 1941 as a partner in its own right, a device to ensure the survival of the bank should either he or the only other partner, Lionel, be killed during the bombing of London.

To be chairman of Rothschilds Continuation in 1976 was less important than it sounded. The power house remained NMR, of which Victor was but one of a score of directors. He accepted his diminished powers reluctantly. When his friend Leonard Hoffmann QC asked for and received some trifling favour from the bank, he added a postscript to his letter of thanks: 'I hope you have not acted outside your authority.'

Victor replied, 'It is impossible for me to act outside my authority because it is infinite.'

Although kept informed of current business, he was not encouraged to intervene. He had never studied economics, except in the broadest terms required of the Think Tank, and his judgements on people lacked psychological insight. He was proud to be a

Rothschild but neither understood nor appreciated banking as an art. The scientist in him strove for certainties. 'Is this right or wrong?' he would ask Evelyn, and was dissatisfied with the answer: 'It is a grey area between the two.' He found New Court too small a stage, its problems too ephemeral to stretch his mind. As at the Think Tank, however, he was diverted by inside politics and manoeuvres, and he took to pumping quite junior executives for gossip.

In time he came to appreciate that banking was not merely a matter of shifting money from point A to point B. Indeed, he was engrossed at one moment by a proposed deal between NMR and four other principals: a New England gas company, the Marxist regimes of Algeria and Russia, and the Republic of Brazil (whose independence NMR had financed in 1825). A colleague suggested that it merited another of Victor's historical pamphlets, to be called 'You Have It, Comrade'.

Where he came into his own was in fulfilling Baron Elie's unkind description of him as *'un petit fonctionnaire'*, a species of administrator feared and admired across the Channel with equal passion. 'What exactly do you do at New Court?' I asked Victor soon after his arrival.

He replied, 'I turn over stones and see what lies beneath.' It was an unhappy phrase. As a close colleague said of him, 'He could be warm, generous and stimulating. He could also leap to conclusions and suspect dishonesty where none existed.' Nor was his banter always understood. A memorandum from Leo to Victor was returned to its author covered with the red-ink corrections of a pedantic schoolmaster. When Leo protested, Victor laughed. 'I thought it would amuse you,' he said.

Yet even his humiliated colleagues conceded that his examination of age-old practices at NMR, however insensitive, was a spur to reform. One discovery was the right of employees to take out bank overdrafts from NMR. In future, he told them, they must go to the high street like everyone else. Nor would he permit the use of NMR writing paper for appeals on behalf of a charity, however deserving. He insisted on meticulous procedures. No memorandum was to be accepted as authentic, he ruled, unless it bore a signature. When NMR won the right to privatise British Gas and similar enterprises, he scrutinised each document word by word.

His obsession with detail could be farcical. After complaints that the steps of New Court became slippery in wet weather, he designed some rubber mats in the shape of footprints. There was a rebellion and they were replaced by plain square ones.

As the doyen of the Rothschilds, Victor supervised the entertainment of distinguished guests. Before the arrival for tea of Teddy Kollek, the Mayor of Jerusalem, he rejected the sandwiches for a thinner variety and insisted that the rich chocolate cake he had personally ordered should be cut not by the commonplace cutlery of New Court but by a superior knife. This he selected himself but charged to NMR.

Margaret Thatcher came to lunch in 1975 after winning the first round of her election as leader of the Conservative party. But nobody gave much for her chances of ultimate success and her welcome was perfunctory. As prime minister, however, she returned several times through the next decade and Victor surpassed himself. It was alleged that the programme he devised for her reception and entertainment covered three sheets of typescript to get her from her car to the lift. He was also said to have ordered flowers of exquisite beauty and fragrance so that even her visit to the lavatory should be a memorable experience. Needless to say, the Iron Lady's personal arrangements had been attended to before she left 10 Downing Street.

From such delectable, such delicate duties he would return to the counting house, literally so, as chairman of the remuneration committee of NMR. Its decisions could exert a profound influence on morale and demanded both his mathematical skills and his obsessive concern with secrecy. When a fellow director and member of the committee mislaid a draft report on salaries, Victor did not hesitate to send the bank security staff into the culprit's office: the sort of overreaction to which New Court became accustomed.

He was equally sensitive about the name Rothschild and the dangers of kidnapping or political assassination to which it might expose him. During the war he had sheltered behind the alias Dr

Fish. On his travels from New Court he borrowed the name of the directors' butler and became Mr Reynolds.

The alias held until he revisited Monte Carlo for a short holiday. On being ushered into his hotel suite, booked in the name of Mr Reynolds, he found a bottle of champagne with a card that read 'Welcome, Lord Rothschild'.

As at the Think Tank, Victor liked to exercise patronage. Among the friends he recruited to NMR was Marcus Sieff, by then chairman of Marks & Spencer, and in 1980 created Lord Sieff of Brimpton. In spite of the earlier failure of their joint enterprises in Iran (see pages 168–171), each admired the commercial astuteness of the other. On Victor's advice, Sieff had replaced the innumerable electric light bulbs in all Marks & Spencer stores by some 200 miles of fluorescent tubes that gave the same intensity of light with the saving of £50 million over twelve years. Victor hoped that Sieff would repay him in the boardroom by suggesting administrative reforms as bold as those which had in those pre-computer days cut the group's paperwork by 26 million forms and documents a year.

Sieff began to earn his keep on the first day he turned up at New Court. He was told that as a director he could buy several cases of Château Lafite each year 'at a special price, by courtesy of our French cousins'. A telephone call by Sieff to his London wine merchant established that the price of the cousins' superlative claret in New Court was indeed special: rather more than its retail price in fashionable St James's Street. Thereafter the tariff was brought down to bargain basement levels.

Another partner of Victor's in the ill-fated Iran venture, Kenneth Dick, joined the bank in 1978. He too received a robust welcome from the chairman: 'When you attend your first meeting of the board of NMR and you think you have made a mistake and gone into a lunatic asylum, just relax.'

The research scientist in Victor Rothschild never died. The accumulated experience of a Cambridge laboratory, of his own experimental farms, of Shell and of Whitehall inspired him in 1981 to found Biotechnology Investments Ltd, a venture capital company under the umbrella of Rothschild Asset Management.

Biotechnology, in simple language, is the application of biological organisms, systems or processes to manufacturing and service industries. The best known of these organisms is yeast, essential to most forms of baking and brewing. What revolutionised biotechnology in Victor's day were advances in the understanding of DNA: the genetic material carrying hereditary instructions for the development and function of every living cell. Biotechnology, it seemed to the far-sighted, would before long embrace and enhance almost every aspect of material civilisation: food and animal feed production, alternative energy sources, waste recycling, pollution control, medical and veterinary health care.

Victor was attracted by the commercial exploitation of these discoveries: potentially a very profitable though highly specialised long-term investment. As in the parallel field of information technology, the risk of failure was high.

Since most of the investment opportunities would be found in the United States, the shares of BIL were quoted in dollars. That, as it turned out, was an additional hazard. One year Victor took a view on the movement of sterling–dollars rates, was proved correct and made a useful profit for the company in its currency transactions. The following year he decided that sterling would appreciate and sold a large dollar holding. But sterling fell, Victor obstinately clung to his position and BIL lost £1.5 million. Some of the responsibility must rest with his professional advisers in the NMR foreign currency department for not, as a colleague put it, 'shouting louder and earlier'.

In 1988, on retirement from the chairmanship of Rothschilds Continuation, Victor handed over the chairmanship of BIL to Robert Armstrong, the former Cabinet Secretary recently ennobled as Lord Armstrong of Ilminster. Victor's stewardship had been strenuous but not unrewarding for the investor. In the first decade of the company, the success of its initial investments was reflected in the rise of the net asset value of each share from US$1 to US$3.35.

Against that, however, the share price remained throughout at a considerable discount to its net asset value: a chronic ailment that afflicts many such speculative investments. Another adverse factor was the growing public hostility to genetic engineering. There were also management problems, leading ultimately to the winding up of BIL in 2000.

Yet it is something for any man of Victor's age to have displayed the vision and resilience of a pioneer in unexplored territory.

Victor's most enduring achievement at NMR was the rescue, preservation and cataloguing of its archives. Until 1979 they lay in an outhouse at Exbury, the home of Edmund de Rothschild. The building was damp and insecure, the catalogue brief and makeshift, the contents inaccessible. 'My life has been a series of obsessions,' Victor once confided to me. Among them was the meticulous care and condition he demanded for his unrivalled collection of eighteenth-century first editions, bindings and manuscripts (as the Master and Fellows of Trinity discovered when Victor learned of their neglect of his benefaction to the college library). This obsession also engulfed NMR's endangered archives.

Although indifferent to the practice of banking, he was as proud as any man of his family origins. On assuming chairmanship of Rothschilds Continuation he set about rescuing the manuscript history of his forebears from the mists of the Solent. The correspondence and accounts of more than a century were brought to London, placed in the care of a professional archivist, removed from their worn wrappings and stored in acid-free boxes. Damp-stained documents and the dry, flaking leather bindings of old ledgers received the best known treatment. The entire archive was then housed in rooms equipped with spacious shelves, air-conditioning and humidity control. In 1983 a new card-index catalogue was superseded by computerisation.

The most valuable material to emerge consisted of 135 boxes of 'private letters', as they were called: correspondence between the partners in London, Frankfurt, Paris, Vienna and Naples from 1812 to 1898. Niall Ferguson included no few than 5000 extracts from them in the 1330-page history of the house of Rothschild entitled *The World's Banker* (1998) written to mark the bicentenary of Nathan Mayer Rothschild's arrival in England. 'Mingling political news, financial information, business enquiries and answers with family gossip and personal grumblings,' the author writes, 'they were, it might be said, the telephone calls of the 19th century in that they contain the kind of information businessmen today rarely commit to paper.'

One deterrent to their previous use by historians is that to ensure secrecy the partners corresponded with each other in *Judendeutsch*, German written in Hebrew characters. For years now Mordechai Zucker has been systematically translating them for the archives of New Court. But Victor, too, deserves a share of the credit.

He himself was one of the first to use the treasures he had freed from their long exile. His duties at New Court left him leisure enough to produce two monographs of family history. In 1980 he published *You Have It, Madam*, the story of the purchase of Suez Canal Shares in 1875 by Disraeli and Baron Lionel. Two years later came *The Shadow of a Great Man*, an affectionate sketch of Nathan Mayer Rothschild, founder of the English branch of the dynasty (see pages 6–8 and 2–4).

Victor loved words as long as there were not too many of them. His one-line minutes could pierce like a shaft of steel, his two-paragraph letters contained multitudes. But he did not care for sustained composition; and there were few books, non-scientific articles, reports or speeches bearing his name which did not owe something to the labour of others. Their help he would generously acknowledge in public and sometimes reward in private. His monograph of sixty-two pages on the Suez Canal shares expresses gratitude to three institutions and eighteen named persons, including the Queen, the Governor of the Bank of England and the First Permanent Secretary to the Treasury. An inner circle earned the accolade of 'my mentors'. Among them were Professor Richard Davis, Sir Stuart Hampshire, Leonard Hoffmann, Professor J. R. Vincent, William Waldegrave and the present writer. Others recruited in Whitehall remained anonymous.

Victor took as much pride in these literary excursions as in his scientific publications. Fifteen years before the novelist C. P. Snow coined his phrase 'The Two Cultures', Rothschild insisted that it was as uncouth for a student of the humanities to be ignorant of science as for a scientist to neglect the arts. He wrote to Duff Cooper in 1944,

> As I have often said over a glass of Meursault, a cultured English gentleman need never have heard of Faraday nor read Freud. But every scientist is a Barbarian or even a Yahoo if he has not done his Herrick.

He was not, in fact, a well-read man. He devoured scientific papers, government reports, works on mathematics and thrillers. But both his conversation and his letters were almost bare of literary allusion. Since his tutorials with Dadie Rylands he had taken little interest in English or foreign literature unless in manuscript or printed on uncut pages between original boards. He was seemingly proud of T. S. Eliot's admonition: 'Victor, you only like the rumtity-tumtity of poetry.' The nine pages of commonplace book with which he filled out *Random Variables* (1984), the second volume of his miscellaneous writings, includes nothing from his eighteenth-century library of 3000 items except a sentence of Swift and another of Johnson. The rest read mostly as if they had been lifted from the 'wit and wisdom' column of any middlebrow magazine.

It was from Swift that Victor borrowed the title of his first book of essays, *Meditations of a Broomstick* (1977): a passage in which the satirist likens himself to a beautiful sapling in youth that becomes a broomstick in old age. Swift was his exemplar. 'I want more daggers,' he demanded as we went through his draft manuscripts, paring and polishing, here adding a touch of caustic, there removing a pleonasm (one of his favourite words).

But ultimately he was his own man. Before a charity dinner at which Margaret Thatcher would be present, I failed to dissuade him from a coarse attack on her political opponents. I doubted in 1985, and I doubt still, whether she was the sort of prime minister who would enjoy his description of the Labour benches as 'a maniacal rabble'.

He delighted in the nuances of English usage, 'Do you know if the word "agenda" is singular? Sounds plural to me.' Another day: 'I find that on the 5th of February 1833, N. M. Rothschild's wife Hannah wrote to him a letter from Brighton starting "dear Rothschild". I should be very surprised if Tess started a letter to me like that. But was it normal at that time?' Soon after Robert Armstrong had gone to work at New Court, I asked Victor what exactly he did. Victor handed me the former cabinet secretary's erudite reply to his query on the etymology of the word 'antediluvian'.

Nothing was left to chance when in 1978 the BBC invited him to deliver the televised Dimbleby Lecture on the theme of 'Risk'. He took as much trouble with his performance as with his text, spending his substantial fee on flying to the United States to be coached by Bill Paley, of CBS. He also insisted on discussing with the BBC every detail of such technical matters as microphones, lighting and graphics. There was even to be a producer at the back of the lecture hall clutching two placards, either of which could be raised to catch the lecturer's eye. One read, 'Faster, my Lord', the other, 'Slower, my Lord'. The inquisition continued. 'Thank you for your five letters dated between 15th and 20th June,' an exasperated BBC official replied.

Victor's career as a research scientist had given him an exaggerated regard for numbered footnotes and source references. While discussing the lecture, I suggested lightly that there was a risk even in a blameless life. Did not the Chinese have a proverb: 'The couple who go to bed early to save candles end up with twins'? 'Let us include it,' Victor said. A few days later he wrote to ask if I had a source reference.

CHAPTER 11

Employed on Commission

E ven as the overworked chairman of N. M. Rothschild, Victor agreed in February 1976 to preside over a new Royal Commission on Gambling. Having scarcely ever been to a race meeting or a casino, and never to a betting shop, he brought no Dostoevskian inhibitions to his task. Yet what urgent need was there for him and his nine fellow commissioners to spend more than two years covering much the same ground as the Royal Commission on Gambling which had reported twenty-five years earlier?

It was the response of Roy Jenkins, a liberal-minded Home Secretary in Harold Wilson's government, to the growth of the permissive society. Side by side with public impatience at literary censorship – epitomised by the case of *Lady Chatterley's Lover* in 1959 – a nation of gamblers resented restrictions on their less cerebral forms of relaxation: flutters on racehorses and dogs, on bingo and the pools, on one-armed bandits, lotteries and gaming tables. How far, Rothschild's Royal Commission had to decide, could these restraints be relaxed without exposing the punter to the fraud and crime inseparable from any industry with an annual turnover of £7 billion?

That three of its ten members were lawyers reflected concerns about the licensing, taxation and financial manipulation of gambling. The least known at the time, but subsequently the most eminent, was Leonard Hoffmann, South African by origin and a close friend of Rothschild. In spite of never having been on a racecourse or backed a horse, he was the sole author of the long, lucid and masterly section of the Royal Commission report devoted to horseracing (a subject on which it received more evidence than on everything else about gambling put together). He was appointed a judge of the High Court in 1985, a Lord Justice of Appeal in 1992 and a Lord of Appeal in Ordinary in 1995.

The six remaining commissioners were William Blair (trade unionist), Thomas Carbery (specialist in office administration), David Coleman (sports commentator), John Disley (Olympic medallist), Marjorie Proops (journalist) and Bernard Williams (philosopher).

Between 1976 and 1978 they met formally on twenty-nine occasions, took oral evidence from thirty-eight people and institutions, and written evidence from 141 more. In small groups they visited forty casinos, twenty-four greyhound tracks, ten bingo clubs, eleven racecourses and eight football clubs. They fanned out across Europe, from Paris to Stockholm and from Basle to Munster, to inspect comparable institutions.

All the commissioners carried out their allotted tasks without remuneration or leave of absence from their jobs. Victor, in his obsessive way, spent some five hours a day co-ordinating their efforts. It almost proved too much for him. Halfway through the ordeal he wrote to me, 'I am all the keener to get out of my present arduous and somewhat boring duties.' But he enjoyed its lighter moments. When an apprehensive owner of a casino asked him whether it would be improper to offer him a dry martini, he replied, 'It takes more than that to bribe a Rothschild.'

From the outset, the Royal Commission refused to condemn gambling on puritanical grounds:

> The objection that punters are wasting their time is a moral or possibly an aesthetic judgement. As it happens, none of us is attracted by the idea of spending an afternoon in a betting office. But the people who frequent betting offices have chosen to enjoy themselves in their own way and we think that in a free society it would be wrong to prevent them from doing so merely because others think that they would be better employed in digging the garden, reading to their children or playing healthy outdoor sports.

Some members believed they had a duty to protect gamblers and their families from overspending. Others maintained that such a degree of paternalism negated the virtues of self-control. All, however, agreed 'that gamblers should invariably be made aware of what they were letting themselves in for – in other words what they may lose (gamblers usually know, or think they know, what they may win)'.

The report therefore included elaborate tables on the percentage return to the punter not only from betting shops and racecourse wagers, but also from slot machines ('one-armed bandits'), bingo, roulette and almost every known card game. It also drew a distinction between games of pure chance, such as roulette, and those of skill, such as blackjack: a characteristic spark from Rothschild's analytical mind.

Presumably for the protection of the compulsive or desperate gambler, it was recommended that the closing time for all casinos should be 4 a.m.: not, it may be thought, an exceptionally onerous restriction. There was some small comfort, too, for the British racehorse owner. In 1976, Leonard Hoffmann's researches disclosed, 40 per cent of horses racing on the flat and 63 per cent over jumps won £100 or less. These discouraging figures prompted a recommendation that Value Added Tax should be abolished on the purchase of foals and yearlings.

Bookmakers received less sympathy. 'As Jane Austen might have said, it is a truth universally acknowledged that bookmakers make too much money. In fact one might say that this opinion is held by everybody except bookmakers.' The proliferation of lotteries run by one of the largest firms evoked a disapproving sniff from the Royal Commission. 'Some of the names are a little surprising, for example the Retired Greyhound Trust and St. Catherine's College, Oxford, alone in the field of general education.'

There was concern over the alleged 'milking' of one-armed bandits by the managers of the 29,000 machines in 17,000 clubs and institutions, and a demand for accurate records to be kept by law. Nor was the comfort of the betting-shop punter forgotten. 'Some of the rules governing the facilities are mere pin-pricks, causing irritation to the majority of punters without being likely to have even a marginal effect on the incidence of compulsive gambling which these rules were supposed to inhibit.' Among the suggested amenities to be allowed for the first time were vending machines for non-alcoholic drinks and lavatories.

In recommending the establishment of a National Lottery for Good Causes, the Royal Commission invoked precedents of surprising antiquity. The first recorded lottery of its kind in England, it discovered, took place in 1569, to raise money for the repair of the Cinque Ports that guarded the Channel against invasion. During the next century there were others, to support English plantations in Virginia, to bring fresh water to London, to ransom English slaves in Tunis and to house poor and maimed soldiers of the Civil War.

The Royal Commission confidently laid down how the proceeds of a National Lottery were to be divided 300 years later. Prizes and good causes were each to receive 37.5 per cent, the operators 15 per cent and the tax man 10 per cent. Twenty-five years were to elapse before the National Lottery Act of 1993 set up such an enterprise, with a mere 27 per cent of proceeds to be divided among five 'good causes': the arts, charities, the heritage, sport and the millennium fund, a white elephant of monumental proportions.

In July 1978, the report of the Royal Commission on Gambling was laid before an appreciative Home Secretary and an indifferent nation. 'I do not believe', Roy Jenkins wrote to Rothschild, 'that I have ever seen any Royal Commission subject so accurately researched, so penetratingly and constructively analysed, and so succinctly presented.' It ran to 581 closely printed pages containing evidence, deliberations, appendices, annexes, statistical tables and 303 recommendations. The printing and administrative costs of the Royal Commission amounted to £589,312.

Few of its recommendations were implemented and those that were – the National Lottery, for instance – suffered such long delay as to deny the Royal Commission any causal connection. Victor referred sarcastically in print to the 'great honour of a debate in the House of Commons lasting no less than six hours', and wondered 'whether the sweat and cost were worthwhile'.

The Treasury certainly did not think so. As well as travelling expenses, the chairman could claim £27 for each day's work and other members £23. They spurned these honoraria. Victor also received the traditional reward of a Royal Commission chairman: a modern reproduction of the elegant silver inkstand used by the prime minister as First Lord of the Treasury. Again by custom, each commissioner was given a leather-covered despatch box bearing the royal cipher, similar to those in which ministers keep confidential papers. That was all.

With mingled amusement and contempt, Victor told me in 1978 of his discovery that members of future Royal Commissions would be denied even so modest a token unless they paid £78 for each box. Otherwise each would receive a standard black civil service briefcase that cost the Treasury £30 less.

As it turned out, there was no need for this shabby little economy until 1993, when Lord Runciman was appointed chairman of a Royal Commission on Criminal Justice. Margaret Thatcher, prime minister from 1979 to 1990, decided that elaborate inquiries by laymen were a waste of time. Victor agreed.

That two-year study of betting shops and gaming tables brought Victor a more elevated reward. It revived his life-long flirtation with higher mathematics. As soon as he was free of the Royal Commission he began private tutorials on probability and statistics from Dr Pat Altham, a Fellow of Newnham College, Cambridge. He proved a diligent, courteous and grateful pupil. His written work was meticulous, his questions searching. By 1984 he had covered as much ground as a third-year undergraduate. Then his interest drifted towards number theory, a more abstract branch of mathematics.

He enjoyed a teasing relationship with Dr Altham. 'Do you think I'm a senile schoolboy?' he asked her.

'Not exactly,' she replied, 'but let's get on with the work.'

Relishing academic gossip, he asked her one day the name of the newly elected principal of her college. 'Somebody told me ...' he persisted.

'Oh no they didn't,' she replied, 'we have all been sworn to secrecy.' For tea he would offer tiny sandwiches of different fillings, then note how many and of which kind she ate.

In 1986 he was confident enough to bring out *The Distribution of English Dictionary Word Lengths*: an investigation into the relative frequency of words of different lengths to see if they followed a statistical pattern that could contribute to the format of a dictionary. In the same prolific year he was co-author with N. Logothetis of a booklet entitled *Probability Distributions*. Having long proclaimed that most mathematicians were spent forces after the age of thirty, he was proud of writing these papers in his seventy-sixth year.

Certainly it was more of a triumph than that of an Austrian cousin, Baron Eugene de Rothschild, who thought he had detected a miscalculation in the works of Einstein and wrote to tell him so. Yes, the great man replied politely, it was a printer's error.

Mathematics coloured his life in unexpected ways. He persuaded the mathematical astronomer Subrahmanyan Chandrasekhar, Nobel Prizewinner and former Fellow of Trinity, to give the college his manuscripts predicting 'black holes' in the heavens. And the owner of the finest eighteenth-century library in England, asked on the radio programme *Desert Island Discs* what single book he would have with him, chose neither Boswell, Gibbon nor Swift but a 700-page volume on pure mathematics, with examples. It was the ultimate aesthetic experience of his life.

After his death, NMR established a trust fund at the Isaac Newton Institute of Mathematical Sciences in Cambridge. Its purposes were to commemorate his name, to encourage the study of mathematics in schools and to continue his mission of paying for the education of especially gifted children from poor backgrounds.

Although it is the boast of pure mathematicians that their pursuit has no practical value, Victor found one. About to undergo an operation for the relief of a partially blocked right carotid artery, he asked whether the anaesthetic or the operation itself was likely to cause a stroke or even death. The risk, he learned, was very low. He nevertheless decided to carry out his own test for a stroke the moment he regained consciousness after the operation by reciting the prime numbers 2, 3, 5, 7, 11, 13, 17, 19, 23 ... The medical staff thought he must be demented; but Tess, hovering in the background, explained the phenomenon, adding anxiously,

'But he did get one wrong.' More conventional tests confirmed that the patient had indeed escaped a stroke.

In December 1989, a few months before his death, Victor told me of his dismay that the Prime Minister, Margaret Thatcher, had been heard to speak of him among intimates as the author of the poll tax. His embarrassment was understandable. The poll tax, or community charge as it was sometimes called, was already widely recognised as the greatest blunder of her regime. During its passage through the Commons it had provoked resentment and fear among Conservative backbenchers; in the months to come it would cut deeply into her parliamentary majority, cost her party several seats at by-elections and ultimately help to eject her from Number 10 in November 1990.

Yet it was precisely the pockets of Conservative voters she had had in mind when superseding local government rates by a poll tax. She had long disliked the established system which required householders to pay rates in proportion to the value of their property. 'Essentially a tax on improving one's home,' she called it, 'manifestly unfair and un-Conservative.' She was also concerned that soaring local authority expenditure and excessive rate increases were driving businesses into bankruptcy and alienating yet another class of Conservative voter. By contrast, only a small proportion of Labour voters were having to pay for the profligacy of Labour councils and the services they provided.

As long ago as 1974, when Edward Heath appointed Margaret Thatcher to be shadow Environment Secretary after the Conservative defeat in February, she had promised to abolish rates in favour of new taxes 'more broadly based and related to people's ability to pay'. But urgent political and economic problems delayed the fulfilment of her pledge until five years after she had become Prime Minister.

In 1984 she instructed the Department of the Environment to find an alternative form of local government finance that was simple, fair, efficient, understandable by the taxpayer and as far as possible requiring no support from the Treasury. The task fell to Kenneth Baker, Minister of State at the DoE, who delegated the detailed investigation to William Waldegrave, the Parliamentary Under-Secretary. And Waldegrave in turn called on his friend and former boss from the Think Tank, Victor Rothschild, to be an outside, unpaid adviser.

It is true that Rothschild had no expert knowledge of local government finance. But he was held in high esteem by the Prime Minister and he welcomed a return, however temporary, to the corridors of power. As in his Think Tank years he delighted in bringing an uncluttered mind to an intractable problem, in thinking the unthinkable, in engaging the attention of the Cabinet with a well-presented and sometimes startling solution.

He made only one condition: that he should be allowed to recruit to the list of Waldegrave's consultants Leonard Hoffmann QC, the most indispensable of his colleagues on the Royal Commission on Gambling. 'Co-operation in our case', Rothschild wrote to him, 'is more or less a solo effort by you, because I always agree with what you say and particularly how you write it.'

Waldegrave's team approached the problem of finding a substitute for rates through a process of elimination. By February 1985 a poll tax had begun to emerge as the solution with the fewest drawbacks and the distinct advantage of being intelligible and accountable. But it was not to be a poll tax alone; rather a supplementary tax based on the electoral register, precisely and publicly declared each year, alongside a modified property tax.

A month later Waldegrave's wise men had reverted to the idea of a poll tax alone. They were driven to the complete abolition of rates by political pressure from Scotland, where a statutory rating revaluation had borne heavily on Conservative pockets and encouraged local authorities to even more reckless spending.

But the team was not unanimous. Shortly before the Chequers meeting on 31 March at which the Prime Minister and her senior colleagues were to make their final choice, Hoffmann issued an eight-page document of dissent. Although it bore only Hoffmann's name, Rothschild's involvement could be inferred from its format. It exactly resembled those reports to the Cabinet which he had produced a decade earlier in the Think Tank: a finely printed text, spaciously set and bound in an arresting shade of red. Here indeed was one ratepayer who had not been beggared by local government exactions.

'Although domestic rates are not an ideal form of local taxation,' the Hoffmann tract declared, 'there is no other which is not open to more serious objections.' As for Waldegrave's preference for a uniform poll tax on all adult residents, Hoffmann commented,

> This will require wholly new administrative machinery and will undoubtedly be more difficult to collect than rates. Its principal advantage is that it will be paid by rich and poor alike, thereby increasing accountability. On the other hand, this advantage will be bought at the cost of greater administrative costs and the unpopularity bound to be caused by the introduction of an overtly regressive tax.

Where did Victor stand? The absence of his name from the title page of the document implied that he did not share Hoffmann's scepticism about the poll tax. He also referred to 'your piece' when writing to tell Hoffmann that the Prime Minister had praised 'its marvellous lucidity'. Yet the format of the pamphlet in the unmistakable red livery of the Rothschild Think Tank silently proclaimed the contrary. How are the two positions to be reconciled?

Victor later told me that he and Hoffmann were as one in rejecting the proposed poll tax. To that extent he felt justified in financing Hoffmann's paper and giving it the format of a Think Tank report. Thereafter the two men differed. Hoffmann wanted to retain rates, though with certain improvements. Victor pleaded instead for a local income tax capped by central government to curb expenditure. He therefore decided that it would be misleading to add his name to Hoffmann's closely argued thesis.

These variants, however, are of only academic interest. Neither was acceptable to Waldegrave or ultimately to Thatcher.

It is doubtful whether Victor enjoyed his brief return to Whitehall. He was not in robust health. He had been given no clear role, had no prior knowledge of local government finance, was ill at ease and unusually silent throughout the deliberations of his fellow advisers. Above all, he hesitated to challenge the political experience and instincts of ministers, least of all the formidable omniscience of Margaret Thatcher. His humiliation by Heath in 1973 on just such a sensitive political issue had left a scar. Now he was hedging his bets.

On 31 March 1985, however, shortly after the distribution of Hoffmann's paper, Victor once more came into his own. Putting aside his personal doubts, he accepted Waldegrave's invitation to mastermind one of those elaborate presentations with which he had mesmerised Edward Heath's Cabinet a decade earlier; only this time he was selling not Concorde but the poll tax. So rejuvenated was he by the task, so dedicated to the arts of persuasion, that he insisted on two full-dress rehearsals, one before the Secretary of State for the Environment, the other before the Cabinet Secretary.

Michael Crick, an historian of the poll tax, compared Rothschild with 'a barrister defending his client to the best of his abilities even though he was convinced of his guilt'. The five-hour pantomime was performed at Chequers that afternoon before the Prime Minister, half the Cabinet and a constellation of senior civil servants and party officials. The script was Victor's but the peroration Waldegrave's own: 'And so, Prime Minister, by means of the poll tax you will have fulfilled your longstanding promise to abolish the rates.' Margaret Thatcher fell for it. Who could have resisted?

With hindsight the historian can discern the flaws of the poll tax: too swiftly implemented and too rigid, requiring too many people to pay too much. But the Prime Minister did not forget the euphoria of that afternoon at Chequers in March 1985. Confusing image with reality, the impresario with the playwright, she came to look upon Victor as the author of the most unpopular measure in living memory.

Although unpaid for his services, Victor did not leave the DoE empty-handed. The head of Waldegrave's research team was Anthony Mayer, a high-flying civil servant not yet forty. Recalling the intellectual excitement of his days in the Think Tank a decade earlier, he jumped at Victor's offer of a well-remunerated job in NMR. Waldegrave was dismayed by this blatant poaching of his brightest DoE official but unwilling to quarrel with the poacher. Caroline Waldegrave showed no such delicacy on her husband's behalf. Bearding Victor in his office at New Court, she gave him a roasting such as he had never experienced before. His response was to write Caroline a letter saying that she did not understand such things. That was as near an apology as could ever be expected from Victor Rothschild.

CHAPTER 12

Spies and Spycatchers

It was the tragedy of Victor Rothschild's life that two close friends of Cambridge days spied for Soviet Russia. That Guy Burgess and Anthony Blunt, like others of his generation, were driven by youthful idealism to embrace Communism was understandable. But that they would willingly betray their fellow countrymen to Soviet Russia, a regime as cruel and callous as that of Nazi Germany, defied reason as well as trust.

Their conduct was at its most repugnant from the outbreak of war in 1939 until 1941. During those two years, Soviet Russia and Nazi Germany were locked into a non-aggression pact. Intelligence about Britain's military and industrial capacity, leaked to Moscow by Communist spies, was readily made available to the German High Command. If not technically treason – defined by the still prevalent statute of 1351 as adhering to the king's enemies, giving them aid and comfort – it was no less infamous. In 1941 Germany broke the pact to invade Russia, which overnight aligned herself with Britain. Thereafter the Cambridge spies were able to pursue their dirty trade with a clearer conscience.

Remote from the constraints of Communist dialectic, ignorant of his friends' contortions, Victor spent five years in MI5. He displayed courage and dedication, ingenuity and good humour; he saved his country from countless acts of sabotage. But his record of service failed to protect him from bizarre rumours while he lived, vile slanders since his death. How fanciful it was to suppose that a man of his temperament and interests should have given his allegiance to Communism; how grotesque that he was reported to have compromised Ultra, a weapon beyond price, in a drunken gesture of support for the Red Army; how contemptible that he was named under the cloak of privilege in the House of Commons as having spied for Soviet Russia.

Not a shred of viable evidence has ever emerged to sustain the last and gravest of those smears. There has been nothing from his colleagues in MI5 responsible for vetting him each time he assumed a new appointment in Whitehall; nothing from the ever-suspicious agents of the FBI in Washington; nothing in the confessions of the so-called 'Ring of Five' who did spy for Soviet Russia – Burgess, Blunt, Maclean, Philby and Cairncross; nothing from their KGB controller, Yuri Modin, who has published his memoirs in Britain under the title *My Five Cambridge Spies*; nothing from KGB officers defecting to the West, in particular Oleg Gordievsky and Vasili Mitrokhin (who over ten years smuggled more than 300,000 documents out of KGB headquarters); nothing from any of the British historians who in recent years have been allowed access to the Moscow archives. Sleuths, professional and amateur, have coveted the scalp of a Rothschild. They have laboured in vain.

Victor, it can be argued, was a victim of guilt by association, of class-conscious envy, of anti-Semitism. Yet there were awkward circumstances, too, in his close relationship with Burgess and Blunt that incited ill will. One, damaging in retrospect, was their presence under his roof for much of the war, albeit in the guise of fellow officers of the security services. Another was Burgess's scandalous behaviour – drunken, dirty and dissolute – culminating in his flight to Russia in 1951 with another Soviet agent, Donald Maclean. A third was the exposure of Blunt as a spy and allegations that it was Victor who had originally recruited him into MI5 in 1940. A fourth was Victor's ill-judged efforts to clear himself from any taint of treason: clandestine manoeuvres that invited prosecution under the Official Secrets Act and darkened the last decade of his life.

Victor's friendship for Burgess waned in the course of the war. What he had found engaging in the shared euphoria of Cambridge had began to embarrass the MI5 officer who directed counter-sabotage at the highest level, had been decorated at the personal insistence of the prime minister, was an intimate of Duff Cooper, the minister responsible for the security services.

Burgess, however, had other patrons in high places. By charm, guile and an original and stimulating mind, this licensed scallywag insinuated himself into the very heart of the Establishment. From the BBC he was recruited in turn by MI6, by Special Operations Executive, by MI5 as a part-time agent. In 1944 he was taken on by the Foreign Office as an assistant to the minister of state, in whose private safe Burgess kept his personal copy of Professor Alfred Kinsey's *Sexual Behaviour of the Human Male*, a covetable work unavailable in England at that time. As a member of a sub-committee of the United Nations General Assembly in Paris in 1948, he was at the heart of policy in the Balkans. Then he was moved to the Far Eastern department of the Foreign Office where he helped influence the decision to recognise Mao Tse-tung's Communist takeover of China.

In August 1950 Burgess was posted as a second secretary to the British embassy in Washington, which within eight months was to prove the graveyard of his diplomatic career. His ability was not in doubt. As liaison officer to the State Department he reported to his British and his Soviet masters with equal fluency on the international tensions of the Korean War; and trips to the UN Far East Commission in New York gave him both an insight into Japanese psychology and the opportunity to exchange confidences with his Soviet control. It was noticed by his seniors in the embassy chancery that he had an appetite for classified papers that did not strictly concern him and would carelessly leave them lying about on his desk.

Colleagues found his personal habits offensive. When one of them complained that his homosexual and drunken antics, his stained appearance and virulent anti-American sentiments were degrading Britain's reputation abroad, a Foreign Office mandarin replied that the service traditionally tolerated 'innocent eccentricity'. Would that it had been innocent. Perhaps he realised that his outrageous conduct blinded the authorities to any suspicion of disloyalty. However could Moscow, it was afterwards surmised, have employed so conspicuously unreliable an agent?

Burgess had an accomplice in his trade of treachery: Harold Philby, Washington representative of MI6, the service responsible for intelligence-gathering and espionage, mainly abroad. Better known as 'Kim' (an irony savoured by readers of Kipling), he was the son of St John Philby, member of the Indian civil service, explorer and orientalist, which ensured him a measure of guarded respect in the Establishment world. Recruited at Cambridge as one of the 'Ring of Five', he concealed but did not abandon his Communist allegiance. He reported on the Spanish Civil War for *The Times* as if through the eyes of General Franco, who rewarded his lack of objectivity with the Red Cross of Military Merit.

Philby joined MI6 in 1940 with the help of his friend Burgess, became head of its anti-Soviet operations in 1944, was posted in 1949 to Washington and seemed in line for promotion to director-general. He and his wife took in the dubiously house-trained Burgess as their lodger, an act as much of faith as of charity.

As MI6 liaison officer to the FBI, Philby set out to dispel the traditional mistrust of US intelligence agencies for their British counterparts. His friendliness persuaded the FBI to let him monitor progress on their long, slow, painstaking decipherment of Venona, the codename for a huge archive of recorded wartime signal traffic between the Soviet Union and other countries, particularly the USA. In the autumn of 1949 he was shown a partly deciphered message from a Soviet agent in New York to the Moscow centre. It turned out to be a résumé of two telegrams sent by Winston Churchill to President Truman in June 1945, urging him to be robust in negotiations with the Russians about the precarious future of Poland and to reject Stalin's spurious compromise. That insight into Anglo-American foreign policy must have been welcome to the Kremlin on the eve of the Potsdam conference.

The problem faced by the FBI four years later was to discover the origin of the leak. Could it be the White House; or the State Department; or perhaps the British embassy in Washington to which messages between the prime minister and the president would routinely have been repeated?

An alert FBI codebreaker at work on Venona strengthened earlier suspicions. It was the KGB practice to transmit all stolen documents to Moscow by radio from New York, where the Russians maintained a large mission protected by diplomatic immunity. The traffic was in a cipher that gave no clue to the source of the material. But on this single occasion in 1945 a negligent radio operator had included an obtrusive group: what the FBI recognised as an internal Foreign Office code number for the British embassy in Washington. In theory the identification of the Soviet mole would prove difficult. For the staff of the embassy, no more than 200 in 1939, had by 1945 grown to some 9000, including its military and civil missions. In practice, however, only a small fraction of that number could have seen the Churchill–Truman telegrams.

Philby congratulated the FBI and promised that he would help to uncover the culprit by a swift process of elimination. His joy was feigned, his intention false. For he had long known the identify of the embassy mole responsible for the leak of the telegrams in 1945 and of much else since. It was his old friend Donald Maclean, first secretary of the embassy in 1945 and now head of the American department of the Foreign Office in London.

Burgess lurched unsteadily down the corridors of power. Maclean was born to tread them with confidence. The son of a Liberal party Cabinet minister, Sir Donald Maclean, he took a First Class in his final examinations at Trinity Hall, Cambridge (not to be confused with the grander but less ancient Trinity College, Alma Mater of the other four members of the 'Ring of Five'). In 1935 he sat for the Diplomatic Service but encountered a momentary check when the interviewer asked whether he had not been a Communist as an undergraduate. 'I did have such views,' he admitted, 'and have not entirely shaken them off.' That honest, manly reply impressed the board, and Sir Donald's boy sailed through in the top half-dozen.

By 1944 he was installed at the Washington embassy. As UK representative on the combined policy committee on atomic research he had access to such prized secrets as strategic reserves of uranium; from 1947, as secretary of the committee, he was allowed to visit the Atomic Energy Commission's headquarters at all hours and unescorted. Those privileges enabled Maclean to pilfer documents later linked to Russia's spectacular progress in manufacturing her own atomic bomb as early as 1949.

The strain on him was too much. On promotion to be counsellor of the British embassy in Cairo – the youngest officer in the diplomatic service to hold the rank – his behaviour deteriorated. He took to the bottle, smashed the flat of an American friend, broke a colleague's leg in a brawl. The Foreign Office hushed up the scandal, as is its way, and allowed him six months' sick leave in England during which he received psychiatric treatment for alcoholism and homosexuality (although he had married while in Washington and had two children).

Apparently cured, he was then appointed head of the American department of the Foreign Office. In spite of intense Anglo-American consultations on the Korean War, the post was less important than it sounded, for the big decisions were taken elsewhere. It is quaint to find Maclean in London and Burgess in Washington solemnly corresponding on the upsurge of anti-British sentiment provoked by President Truman's dismissal of General MacArthur, allegedly under pressure from Britain's Labour government. Little could American public opinion guess what else those two drunken homosexual Brits had been up to.

Kim Philby knew only too well. Within a matter of weeks, he surmised, Maclean's name would be revealed by eliminating all others who had served in the British embassy between 1944 and 1948. He doubted whether Maclean was either physically or psychologically robust enough after his recent breakdown to withstand interrogation without blurting out the secrets of the Soviet spy ring. He must flee to Russia before MI5 pounced. Burgess, too, although not yet known to be suspected by either the FBI or MI5, must accompany him or risk investigation the moment his friend Maclean was found to be missing from his desk at the Foreign Office. Philby realised that this defection would also place him in jeopardy, but he hoped to brazen it out. Aware of the risk of warning Maclean in London by telephone or telegraph, he sent him a brief message through the KGB in New York, then set about planning Burgess's journey to London.

Fortune smiled on the conspirators. They were allowed all the time they needed and more to ensure that Burgess sailed to England without arousing any suspicion of panic. Because the Foreign Office could not face up to the shame of exposing a spy in its senior ranks, its security department dragged its feet in preparing a list of suspects. MI5, too, anticipating the damage to its own reputation once the existence of the embassy spy had been made public, was reluctant to co-operate with a near hostile FBI. Instead of the process of elimination reaching a successful climax within weeks, it took rather more than a year. Even after Maclean had been identified as the most likely suspect, he was not challenged but merely kept under fitful surveillance.

The ambassador played an unwitting role in reuniting Burgess and Maclean. Almost from the day Burgess arrived in Washington as a second secretary he had been riding for a fall. In March 1951 he fell. His final outrage enlivened an official goodwill visit to a military academy at Charleston, South Carolina to lecture on 'Britain: a Partner for Peace'. He travelled the 500 miles in his cherished 12-cylinder white Lincoln convertible, as instantly recognisable as the ambassador's Rolls-Royce. During the journey he picked up three tickets for reckless speeding and a hitch-hiker whom he installed at the wheel by day and in his bed at night. He spent much of the conference drinking and fell asleep during the banquet. Sir Oliver Franks, disenchanted with his subordinate's sloth and unpleasant habits, asked London for his recall, with a recommendation that he be dismissed from the service. Burgess sailed for England in the *Queen Mary* on 1 May, acquiring a new boyfriend on board to while away the voyage.

FBI files and Yuri Modin's memoirs both assert that the Charleston spree had been contrived to provoke his premature return. That postscript to Burgess's odyssey was only to be expected from two sources revelling in Britain's humiliation. It may or may not be true; but his last rampage was not so very different from his everyday routine while serving as second secretary of His Britannic Majesty's embassy in Washington.

MI5, meanwhile, was at last ready to confront Maclean and to question him about the secret documents that had passed through his hands in Washington and his coincidental journeys to New York to meet his KGB control. On the morning of Friday, 25 May, the Foreign Secretary, Herbert Morrison, gave his formal consent for the interrogation. But instead of instantly summoning Maclean from his office within the building, the MI5 officials decided to wait until he turned up for work on the Monday. Even in MI5 the English weekend was sacrosanct. That same Friday, just before midnight, Maclean and Burgess slipped away by ferry from Southampton to St Malo. By Sunday night they were in Russia. On Monday morning the MI5 interrogators found that the birds had flown.

The exculpatory statement later issued by the Foreign Office was a classic whitewash, crammed with untrue or misleading assertions, mostly designed to conceal procrastination and incompetence. Teasing questions remained. Was Maclean warned by a mole in or close to MI5 that he was about to be interrogated? Had Burgess hoped to return to his louche London ways after delivering Maclean to the KGB in Prague? As it was, he accompanied Maclean all the way to Moscow. Burgess died in lonely exile twelve years later, consoled by alcohol and cigarettes, the *New Statesman* and *Autocar*, an occasional pick-up in a public lavatory and his Old Etonian tie.

Maclean by contrast settled down well in Moscow. He was at heart an apparatchik, content to meet the wishes of any current employer. Before leaving the Foreign Office for ever on that Friday afternoon he had punctiliously written up the minutes of a meeting with a counsellor of the Argentine embassy about a trade agreement. Treason could be excused; a lapse in office procedure never.

His flight to Moscow was welcomed by the Kremlin. Had he not by his treachery accelerated the development of Russia's nuclear bomb and dealt a catastrophic blow to Anglo-American trust? Whether in London or in Moscow, few could match the clarity of his memoranda.

Maclean's marriage ran a less tranquil course. In 1953 his wife joined him, but did not care for the drab Moscow life. She later sought diversion in the arms of Kim Philby, who had defected in

1963 and died in 1988. Maclean died in Moscow in 1983. His coffin, covered with a red flag, bore the inscription 'Bon voyage, Donald Donaldovich'. He was Sir Donald's boy to the end.

Like so many others after the defection of Burgess and Maclean, Victor was questioned repeatedly and intensively by MI5, not so much to test his own loyalty as to discover whether he could recall the names of others who might have gone underground. As it happened, he could. He drew the attention of MI5 to a former undergraduate at King's College called Alister Watson; a fellow scientist, a close friend of Burgess, an undoubted Communist and a member of the Apostles who had delivered no fewer than nineteen papers, seventeen more than Victor.

That first warning by Victor was ignored. But some years later, when working at an Admiralty research laboratory on anti-submarine devices, Watson was seen talking to KGB agents in London and discovered to have concealed his Communist past in his positive vetting papers. He was spared prosecution but moved to non-secret work at the Oceanic Institute. Victor would one day be pleased to have this patriotic gesture chalked up to his credit.

Victor also earned the gratitude of the security services when he reported a chance conversation at the Weizmann Institute, in Israel. A fellow English guest was Flora Solomon, who among other interests developed the celebrated welfare department of Marks & Spencer, and had been the mistress of Alexander Kerensky, a leader of the Russian revolution, later deposed by the Bolsheviks. She told him how much she resented the anti-Israeli articles written by Kim Philby for the *Observer* after his enforced resignation from MI6 in the wake of the Burgess–Maclean scandal. In her excitable way she went on to tell Victor that she knew Philby to have been a Soviet agent since the 1930s and that he had tried to recruit her. With difficulty Victor persuaded her to tell her story to MI5. Although her evidence was confirmed by other sources, it was too circumstantial to sustain a prosecution. A few months later Philby did confess to a senior MI6 officer in Beirut; but before a case could be prepared against him, KGB agents had whisked him off to safety in Moscow. It became difficult to walk down Gorky Street without bumping into a fugitive British spy.

Some commentators have belittled Victor's role as a private sleuth, insisting that the guilt of Watson, Philby and others had long been suspected by the authorities. A former head of MI5 took a contrary view. Too often, Dick White said, their acquaintances were unwilling to volunteer information, inhibited by an English schoolboy's code of honour that forbade sneaking; by a fear of unsympathetic MI5 interrogators; or by a belief that the authorities were already in the know. Only if public-spirited women and men like Victor were prepared to do their duty, White continued, could MI5 turn a plausible case against a suspect into a convincing case. To that extent he condoned Victor's unofficial role.

Amid those battered Cambridge reputations, Anthony Blunt seemed to move on an altogether higher plane. Earlier chapters have recorded Victor's admiration and awe of Blunt's 'outstanding intellectual abilities, both artistic and mathematical...the high moral or ethical principles', and other saintly attributes. We must now briefly rejoin the paragon of those pre-war years. From his Fellowship at Cambridge he moved to the Warburg Institute of Art at London University and in 1939 became deputy director of the Courtauld Institute. In the spirit of Rupert Brooke, or perhaps on the instructions of the KGB, he volunteered for the army and, with fluent French and German, was accepted for the Intelligence Corps. But he had hardly begun training for the field security service when his posting was cancelled; a War Office file disclosed that at Cambridge he had written articles for a Communist magazine and visited Moscow. Having explained away those youthful aberrations, he was reinstated, commissioned and despatched to the British Expeditionary Force in France. During the retreat from Dunkirk he was reported to have behaved coolly under enemy fire. He returned to England, shed his boring duties as an army policeman and was recruited to MI5.

Raking over the ashes of his career, amateur sleuths have alleged that it was Victor who recommended him. Blunt seemed to confirm the assumption when interviewed by selected journalists after his exposure as a Russian spy in 1979, almost forty years later.

Q   How did you join?
A   Someone who was in MI5 recommended me.
Q   The old boy network?
A   Yes.
Q   Is he clean?
A   Perfectly.
Q   Presumably the old boy who recruited you to MI5 would
    have been aware of your open past convictions?
A   Yes.

Victor admitted that he fitted the description and that he had helped to recruit Blunt; but he denied having written a letter of recommendation. What he had done, he later said, was to have introduced Blunt to Liddell, the deputy director of MI5, at an informal meeting in St James's Place. The two men took to each other and Blunt's formal recruitment followed.

Sir Dick White, director-general in 1940, in old age gave me another version, different from Victor's but consistent with it. He said that Blunt, when applying to join MI5, had given Victor's name as a referee but that this had not been followed up. That would explain why Victor denied so vehemently that he had written a letter of recommendation.

The differences between the three versions were wafer-thin, an experience familiar to any historian writing sixty years after an event. In any case, why should not Victor have helped a trusted friend to put his analytical brain at the disposal of MI5, a service rapidly expanding in size and intellectual muscle?

Blunt would never have confided to a non-Communist friend, least of all one already entrenched in MI5, that his own Communist beliefs were not dead but dormant. The War Office had already brushed aside evidence of his own Marxist articles and visit to Moscow. It was not for Victor to reopen the inquiry. That was the responsibility of Blunt's new employers and they took him on trust.

Like Donald Maclean he was nevertheless fortunate to escape more rigorous vetting. In June 1939, MI5 had a card index of 900,000 possible suspects across the political spectrum. By the summer of 1940 the register had grown to 4.5 million: nearly 10 per cent of the population. It is little wonder, in that pre-computerised age, that MI5 could not keep track of every Marxist don.

Victor was always evasive about Blunt's duties. Late in life, after the death of his disgraced friend, he wrote,

> Blunt joined the Security Service [the official name for MI5] during World War II some time after me, and our paths rarely crossed because I was concerned with bombs whereas he, after a brief incubation period, became involved in a highly secret work, so secret that the weeders will see that it is not disclosed even after thirty years.

The weeders have not relented. But Robert Cecil, a member of the Diplomatic Service who succeeded Donald Maclean as head of the American department. has given a plausible version of the 'highly secret work'. One of Blunt's roles was to supervise a team trained to steal mailbags of Allied governments in exile (including those of Denmark, the Netherlands and Poland) and of neutral countries with diplomatic missions in London (such as Spain, Sweden and Switzerland). Abstracted in transit, the mailbags were expertly cut open, their contents swiftly memorised or photographed, then restitched with seals intact before being sent on their way. Blunt found exhilaration in flirting with danger, outwitting guards and couriers, and reaping the fruits of serving two masters. How eagerly, it may be surmised, did the KGB acquire from him the identities of Allied agents and Soviet dissidents mentioned in the stolen correspondence. 'Without the slightest risk of exaggeration,' Modin wrote after the war, 'he supplied us with literally thousands of documents.' At least one such transaction is said to have left Blunt with blood on his hands.

By the end of the war even that cold, calculating personality seems to have been under strain. At a chance meeting with Colonel T. A. Robertson, architect of the MI5 'double-cross' system which turned round captured German spies against the *Abwehr*, Blunt boasted, 'It has given me great pleasure to have been able to pass the names of every MI5 officer to the Russians.' Perhaps it was a joke, perhaps a taunt. Certainly it was out of character.

During his years in MI5 Blunt found time to pursue his career as an art historian of growing reputation. He was often at Windsor, working on the incomparable collection of drawings in the royal library for a series of catalogues, erudite and graceful, that was to appear over the years. He also became a friend of Sir Owen Morshead, the King's librarian and of Sir Gerald Kelly, who lingered at the castle throughout the war painting state portraits of the King and Queen.

James Lees-Milne, the architectural historian, heard Blunt lecture at the Courtauld in 1944 on Baldassare Castiglione, the friend of Raphael, without a note of any kind. 'K. Clark looked benignly approving,' the diarist wrote, 'which is the greatest compliment a man can receive.' Few in the audience could have suspected that Blunt's celebrated photographic memory was simultaneously being used for swift scrutiny of purloined diplomatic correspondence.

Sir Kenneth Clark's benign approval bore fruit. In 1945 Blunt was appointed to succeed him as Surveyor of the King's Pictures; a post that carried a small honorarium but immense prestige. Two years later he was promoted by London University to be Professor of the History of Art and director of the Courtauld Institute. Barely forty, he had already reached the summit of his profession.

His successor as Surveyor, Sir Oliver Millar, saluted 'the age of enlightenment that Anthony Blunt's appointment ushered in'. Almost at once he scored a triumph by putting on display at the Royal Academy 500 of the King's pictures and writing a short history of them for the catalogue. The instant success of the exhibition prompted Duff Cooper to write to Victor from the British embassy in Paris, asking whether he could persuade Blunt to ship it across the Channel. Blunt replied that it would be useless for him to put the request before the King; Duff's best course would be to approach the Queen personally. Blunt well knew how sensitive the King was to the care of his collection and how reluctant he would be to send it on its travels so soon after its release from wartime incarceration. The exhibition never reached Paris.

'You must admit I'm a very good actor,' Blunt remarked to a brother towards the end of his life. Perhaps he exaggerated his skill, for he was a conceited man. From a royal source I heard how in 1948 a young ex-officer, Philip Hay, came to Buckingham Palace to be interviewed for the post of private secretary to the widowed Princess Marina, Duchess of Kent. As he walked down a passage with Sir Alan Lascelles, the King's private secretary, they passed Blunt. When he was out of earshot, Lascelles said in a matter-of-fact-way, 'That's our Russian spy.' Hay never forgot those ominous words. Other members of the royal household, I learned, also purported to know of Blunt's hidden past.

Having been denounced as a Soviet spy thirty years later, Blunt denied that he had worked for Russia after his demobilisation from MI5 at the end of the war. Here is another extract from his interrogation by journalists in 1979:

Q What did you do for the Russians between 1945 and 1951?
A Nothing.
Q Absolutely nothing?
A ...I was in no position to give them any information of interest.

Blunt was lying. Modin has written about those post-war years: 'Blunt, in effect, served as Burgess's permanent liaison with me. I would also seek him out whenever I needed information about MI5, where he still had plenty of friends. Sometimes I even asked him to procure up-to-date data on individual agents in the British counter-espionage service...I was to continue seeing Blunt on a regular basis until 1951.' Blunt was an indispensable link between the KGB and his friends Burgess and Maclean in their flight to Russia. After they had fled, he asked Burgess's boyfriend for the keys to his flat, which Blunt searched for compromising letters and documents. Having destroyed them, he handed over the keys to a grateful MI5 so that they could begin their own more leisurely trawl.

But even so astute an operator as Blunt tripped up when questioned by the press years later. After clearing up after Burgess in

1951, he boasted, 'I had orders to go to Russia and I refused.' An alert journalist saw the flaw: 'You use the term *orders*. In what sense? Because you had not worked for the Russians after the war.' Blunt floundered. 'Well, I had not formally broken,' was his lame excuse.

The events of 1951 sealed his ultimate fate. MI5, probably the source of suspicions at Buckingham Palace in 1948, were by now certain of his involvement in the Burgess–Maclean fiasco. In spite of repeated interrogations, however, MI5 could not extract a confession or evidence to sustain a criminal prosecution. So for the next thirteen years, having finally broken with the KGB, he cultivated his career as an eminent art historian, respected head of the Courtauld and Surveyor of the King's Pictures. Confirmed in the appointment on the accession of Elizabeth II in 1952, he was four years later made a Knight Commander of the Royal Victorian Order, a distinction in the Queen's personal gift that transmogrified the traitor into Sir Anthony Blunt.

He might have taken the secret of his espionage to the grave but for the intervention of a vengeful ghost from his Cambridge years. Michael Straight, born into a prosperous Long Island family, would have preferred to remain in England (as did his brother Whitney Straight, racing motorist, aviator and industrialist). But Blunt instructed him to return to New York, become a banker and uncover Wall Street's plans to dominate the world economy. Crushed and blackmailed by Blunt into obedience, Straight unwillingly sailed for the States in 1937, carrying in his baggage the fashionable left-wing virus of the Apostles.

Straight was employed in minor posts by the State Department and passed classified documents to a Soviet agent. In 1941 he resigned to become Washington editor of the *New Republic* and involved himself in left-wing causes. He accepted in 1963 the chairmanship of an advisory council on the Arts in President Kennedy's administration. But on being told that he must submit to a routine FBI check, he refused the appointment and confessed his Communist past. The trail led back to Blunt, who did not attempt to deny Straight's evidence.

MI5, delighted that their long-held suspicions had been

confirmed, nevertheless moved with caution. Straight's testimony of the 1930s might not prove strong enough to secure a criminal conviction. MI5 were also anxious to avoid the obloquy and derision which paradoxically greeted each new triumph of detection.

So in 1964 Blunt was offered a secret deal. In return for revealing to MI5 all he had learned about Soviet penetration of British security services over the years, he would be spared public exposure and disgrace, and be allowed to remain as director of the Courtauld Institute and Surveyor of the Queen's Pictures.

Under the gentle, almost apologetic questioning of MI5, Blunt proved amnesic, evasive and self-serving. He had the best of the bargain. Meanwhile he continued without a break the life of an industrious and admired art historian and a particular authority on Poussin. Dollie de Rothschild, in her history of Waddesdon, commended his 'persuasive powers and remarkable capacity for work' as general editor of the catalogues of its contents.

He also served his sovereign with devotion and imagination, at least in the picture galleries of Buckingham Palace, Windsor Castle and Hampton Court. The Queen, the most punctilious of constitutional monarchs, agreed without enthusiasm to harbour a traitor under her roof for reasons of state. But it was discreetly arranged that he should never come face to face with her. Only those familiar with the arcane structure of orders and decorations noticed that on reaching the retiring age of sixty-five in 1972 he did not receive the expected promotion in the Royal Victorian Order from Knight Commander to Knight Grand Cross.

Within days of Blunt's secret confession of 1964, Victor heard of it from his friends in MI5, whom he had never ceased to cultivate. But it was not until twenty years later that he recorded his emotional shock as 'devastating, crushing and beyond belief'. Those anguished words, already quoted in an earlier chapter on Cambridge, (pages 46 *et seq.*) are taken from a short essay published by Victor, with other pieces, in 1984. A *cri de coeur* should perhaps be spared carping scrutiny. Yet it contains anomalies which invite comment.

Devastating, crushing and beyond belief. Victor knew in 1964 that

Blunt had long been suspected by MI5 of working for the KGB and of close involvement with Burgess.

Blunt joined the security service [MI5] *during World War II some time after me, and our paths rarely crossed.* For much of the war Blunt shared a flat with Burgess at 5 Bentinck Street, of which Victor held the lease. In another flat lived Tess Mayor, Victor's MI5 assistant and future wife. Victor did not live there himself but was a frequent visitor.

Blunt inevitably came into contact with a close friend of mine at the top of the security service, G. M. Liddell. Victor omits to say in the essay (though he later confided to me) that it was he who brought Blunt and Liddell together so that Liddell could vet Blunt as a candidate for MI5.

Many years before [i.e. before 1964] *I had been a close friend of Blunt, though we drifted apart in about 1950.* The close friendship lasted longer than that. Victor's youngest daughter, Victoria, was brought up to regard Blunt as her godfather, though not in a religious sense. She was born in 1953.

You never get over a blow of this sort. That was for Victor to say. But he and Tess continued to see Blunt with what outwardly gave every appearance of friendship. Could it have been part of the deception at which even the Queen was obliged to connive? Roy Jenkins describes in his memoirs, *A Life at the Centre*, dining with Noël Annan and his wife in Cambridge in 1966, a few months after being appointed Home Secretary in the Labour government. The other guests were Ann Fleming, wife of the creator of James Bond, and Tess and Victor. With them the Rothschilds brought their own house guest, Anthony Blunt. It was as well that Jenkins had not yet been told by his officials of Blunt's confession two years earlier.

No apology should be necessary for subjecting Victor's essay on Blunt to this exegesis. After all, he gave it the title '*The File is never closed*'. The overwhelming inference to be drawn from the available evidence is that neither Victor nor Tess Rothschild was at any time a Soviet spy. In the circumstances, the innocent no less than the guilty may be forgiven for nudging aside awkward facts.

Nor does it damage Tess's integrity. However rooted her beliefs in the left, her friendship with Blunt was not primarily political; it more resembled the uncritical attachment of a lover. In his company she found intellectual solace from a preoccupied and sometimes censorious husband, a shared world of art and ideas, a gentler understanding. As her sister-in-law Miriam put it, 'Anthony was a sort of girl-friend.'

I never heard Victor condone Blunt's treachery. But in casual conversation he did once muse that Blunt had done some brave and valuable things for his country.

'What?' I asked.

'I cannot tell you,' Victor replied, 'because of the Official Secrets Act.'

Blunt showed no such generosity to Victor. Sir John ('Jakie') Astor, agriculturist and racehorse owner, drove Blunt home one night after both had dined with the Rothschilds. Blunt said, 'I had forgotten how ghastly the whole act of Victor's was.' Astor was shocked by Blunt's disloyalty to the man who had once been his best friend.

Victor could not keep his paws off intelligence. Long after he had retired from MI5 in 1945, he continued to take an obsessive interest in its structure, personalities and operations. The infatuation lasted for the rest of his life, almost half a century, as he moved from one demanding post to another. Whether running the Agricultural Research Council, Shell Research, Edward Heath's Think Tank or N. M. Rothschild & Sons, there were always Reds under the bed and time enough to ferret them out. He contrived to remain at the centre of the security service, to collect intelligence as he had once collected gold boxes and eighteenth-century first editions. He provoked the irritation and impatience of the professionals, occasionally their gratitude.

Those who have never dwelt in that hall of mirrors may wonder how an outsider, and a former suspect at that, achieved so influential a role. He laid a trail to this Soviet agent and that, meddled in the appointment of a new director-general of MI5, bid boldly but without success to become the supremo of Britain's intelligence services.

Throughout his life he was a master of the Establishment network. He would cultivate those in high places, befriend them, entertain them, put them in his debt, pump them, use them. At the heart of MI5 there were three private moles on whose knowledge and skills he depended. They were Guy Liddell, Dick White and Peter Wright.

Victor wrote of Liddell as 'a close friend of mine at the top of the Security Service, a brilliant, sensitive and delightful man whose image, I am sorry to say, has become somewhat tarnished with no justification'. Descended from a line of baronets created in 1642 and ennobled with the Barony of Ravensworth in 1821, he was something of a dandy. He played the cello, had been decorated in First World War and married the glamorous Calypso Baring, a granddaughter of Lord Revelstoke, King George V's banker. He recruited Victor to MI5 (and later Blunt), and was a long-standing guest at Merton Hall, Rushbrooke and Tring. Malicious voices impugned his patriotism, his sexual tastes and his competence, but Victor was right to give him the benefit of every doubt. The rumours caused Liddell to be passed over as head of MI5 in 1946. Disillusioned, he retired from the service in 1953 and died in 1958.

Dick White, the second of Victor's intimates in MI5, came from a humbler background. The son of a Tonbridge ironmonger who fell on hard times through drink and gambling, he was educated at Bishop's Stortford College, a modest establishment for the sons of Methodist parents. Among his mentors was Brendan Bracken, a future colleague and crony of Winston Churchill. White was awarded an exhibition at Christ Church, Oxford, as much on athletics as on academic promise. He fulfilled both, just missing a First Class in History and ensuring his Blue by running the Iffley Road mile in the then record time of 4 minutes 27.4 seconds.

After a year or two as a schoolmaster, he joined MI5 as Guy Liddell's assistant, the first graduate to be enrolled. He displayed every quality required by the service: intelligence, industry, insight, loyalty. Rising steadily and unchallenged, he became director-general in 1953. Three years later he was switched to become head of the rival MI6 to restore its efficiency and morale after a series of setbacks that included the disappearance of Philby to Russia at the moment he had promised to confess. From 1968 until his retirement in 1972 White was co-ordinator of intelligence to the Cabinet.

His self-effacing manner belonged more to the shy academic than to the braggadocio spycatcher of fiction. It was reflected in a philosophy uncommon elsewhere in MI5. He told me in old age,

> Perhaps I was in the wrong service. My nature is inclined to openness. I have never wanted to grub about in people's lives unless there was hard evidence against them. That is what we mean by the freedom of the individual – and it is worth preserving. The alternative is the police state.

Dick White was indeed the *verray, parfit gentil knight* of Britain's security.

'I liked Victor from the first,' White's confidences continued. 'In spite of birth and money he wanted to be judged as a man of action.' Victor reciprocated his regard; one does not lightly lend a Cézanne to any chance acquaintance during the wartime Blitz on London. Yet if ever there were a flaw, Victor was the man to spot it. He wrote to Duff Cooper in 1944, 'I sent a letter to you with Dick White. I am afraid that he will not exactly ring a bell with you if you see him in Algiers as he suffers from a social and intellectual inferiority complex.'

Wartime MI5 was never a band of brothers. There were the senior officers of peacetime, often from the Indian Army, whose pretensions were social rather than intellectual. There were the academics and lawyers who laughed at the colonels and were more impressed by brains than birth. And there were the policemen, tough and sometimes rough fellows who were patronised by the dons and scorned by the well-born.

Here is a vignette of what MI5 executives called the 'afternoon tea club' in the canteen. Present were Percy Sillitoe, successively chief constable of Sheffield and Glasgow, and since 1946 director-general of MI5; his future successors, Dick White and Roger Hollis; and Guy Liddell, Sillitoe's deputy. The narrator is Sillitoe's son.

Suddenly, Hollis half-turned his back on my father and switched into Latin, a language he was well aware my father did not understand. I knew enough to know they were talking in epigrams. I thought it was some joke but they carried on and on and it was evident they were simply snubbing the man. My father called his chauffeur and stormed out of the building. When we got in the car, I said, 'What was all that about?' He said, 'One word – Bastards!'

Old school ties cast no such malign spell over Victor Rothschild; Harrow had seen to that. Nor were they as welcome as of old among the post-war recruits who came increasingly from the grammar schools and state schools. Where, after all, had the treacherous Ring of Five been educated? Burgess at Eton, Blunt at Marlborough, Philby at Rugby, Maclean at Gresham's School, Holt (also the Alma Mater of W. H. Auden). Alone of the five, Cairncross made his way to Cambridge from a working-class background.

Peter Wright, the third of the MI5 officers whom Victor cultivated, endured an early struggle similar to Dick White's. His father, an engineer at Marconi, lost his job in the pre-war slump and found consolation in drink. But enough money was scraped together to send the boy to Bishop's Stortford College, White's old school, then on to St Peter's, Oxford, founded as recently as 1929. He spent fifteen years in the Admiralty Research Laboratory and the Services Electronics Research Laboratory until lured away by MI5 in 1955 as a scientific adviser. From technical duties, in which he showed a high degree of ingenuity, he acquired a near impregnable role in tracking suspected spies.

Victor and Wright were brought together in about 1960 at the suggestion of Dick White and with the encouragement of Roger Hollis, then head of MI5. They took to each other at once. 'I doubt I have ever met a man who impressed me as much as Victor Rothschild,' Wright wrote. 'He has been much much more than a scientist. His contacts in politics, in intelligence, in banking, in the civil service and abroad are legendary.' Wright was awed by Victor's ability to put a whole range of Shell laboratories at the

The three children of Victor by his second marriage: Amschel, Emma and Tory, at the Rothschild villa in Barbados. Through Tory's eyes, Victor seemed more like a grandfather than a father. She found it a bruising experience to be taught the square root of minus one when scarcely out of the pram.

Victor amid the clutter of his study at Merton Hall, Cambridge. Artfully displayed in the bottom right-hand corner is his first scientific book *Fertilisation* (1956). Behind is a photograph of his daughter Emma and other family memorabilia. For the rest there is gadgetry and gold. Out of sight is surely lurking his favourite piece of office equipment, the shredder. In the wall cabinet is some of the gold for which he had an atavistic regard. He owned one-seventh of all known pre-1800 English gold objects.

Above: James de Rothschild, Liberal MP and racehorse owner. Victor thought him unduly mean in dispensing the contents of his enormous cellar. Having backed the winner of the Derby at odds of 100 to 1 at the first race meeting he ever attended, he was lured into a largely unsuccessful career on the turf. 'Others back outsiders', Lord Rosebery said of him, 'Jimmy alone tries to breed from them'.

Left: Dorothy ('Dollie') de Rothschild, the wife of James. She was the proud chatelaine of Waddesdon Manor, Buckinghamshire, which she did much to adorn. She bequeathed its care and restoration to her cousin by marriage, Victor's son Jacob, the 4th Baron, together with a fortune of ninety million pounds. In widowhood she also allowed Victor and Tess to live rent-free on the top floor of her house in St James's Place, London.

'Well, you're going to stay in there, Rothschild,
till you come up with the same answer as me!'

Above: Victor Rothschild with his Central Policy Review Staff in October 1972, popularly known as the Think Tank, a score or so of lively-minded men and women who gave independent advice to the Cabinet. Their average age was thirty-five. They were much resented by the established civil service.

Back row (left to right): Chris Saunders, Peter Bocock, John Rosenfeld, Richard Crum, Madeleine Aston, Anthony Fish, William Waldegrave, Robin Butler
Front row (left to right): John Mayne, Hector Hawkins, Robert Wade-Gery, Dick Ross, Victor Rothschild, Peter Carey, William Plowden, Brian Reading, Adam Ridley

Left: How the cartoonist JAK saw the public dispute in 1973 between the Prime Minister, Edward Heath, and the head of his Think Tank, who had made an unauthorised public speech forecasting Britain's economic doom.

Rivals for the chairmanship of N.
Rothschild & Sons Ltd, 1975.

Above: Jacob (later 4th Baron)
Rothschild, Victor's elder son.

Left: Evelyn (later Sir Evelyn) de
Rothschild, a cousin.

Each hoped for the support of
Victor, about to resign as chairma
Jacob because he could not believ
that a father would fail to choose
son, Evelyn because he held an
overwhelming majority of voting
shares.
The prize went to Evelyn.

Two more Rothschild smokers

Victor with his favourite French cousin, Baron Henri. In youth, Henri was rationed by his formidable mother to one cigarette a day, with an injunction not to drop ash out of the window in case he set fire to the garden. This inveterate smoker later became a much esteemed children's doctor.

 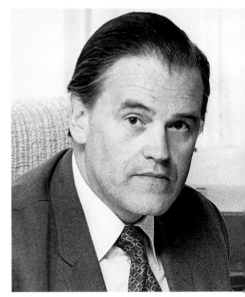

The Spycatcher trial in the Supreme Court of New South Wales, 1986.

Top left: Peter Wright, the disgruntled former officer of MI5, whose memoirs infringed the Official Secrets Act and so could not be published in Britain. Margaret Thatcher's government also tried to suppress them in Australia by appealing to the Supreme Court of New South Wales. *Top right:* Malcolm Turnbull, Wright's bright young Australian lawyer, who conducted a brilliant but unscrupulous defence both inside and outside the court room. He enlisted Labour MPs at Westminster to ask embarrasing questions of the Thatcher government during which Victor Rothschild, Wright's onetime friend, was persistently vilified. *Bottom left:* Justice Philip Powell, who heard the case in Sydney, was a clever, conscientious and genial judge. Yet there were moments when he and Turnbull seemed to be acting in collusion to tweak the tail of the British Establishment. *Bottom right:* Sir Robert Armstrong, the Cabinet Secretary and principal witness for the British Government. His confession in the box that, in order to protect a confidential source of intelligence, he had been 'economical with the truth', exposed this honourable public servant to undeserved ridicule and contempt. He was in fact quoting a phrase used by Thomas Burke two centuries earlier.

disposal of MI5 for solving technical problems. One valuable
success was the development of a grease that protected equipment
buried underground for long periods. Another was the range of
sophisticated devices for surveillance and other arcane practices
developed by the scientist James Lovelock. With that flair for
recognising hidden or neglected talent, Victor had recruited him as
a Shell consultant after the US security services had shown indifference to his discoveries. Lovelock went on to achieve worldwide
fame in his study of environmental problems, sharpening Victor's
interest in them at Shell and later.

Wright was also dazzled, as was no doubt intended, by Victor's
social life. 'He knew everyone. I met more distinguished people at
his house in Cambridge or in his flat in London than anywhere
else.' But a later reference to Victor as head of the Think Tank
does not ring true:

> I was in Victor's room in the Cabinet Office when Ted Heath
> put his head around the door.
> 'Prime Minister,' said Victor, 'I think you should meet Peter
> Wright, he is one of the strangest phenomena in Whitehall.'
> Heath looked humourlessly over in my direction, and asked
> me where I worked.
> 'The Security Service, sir,' I replied.
> He grunted.

The grunt was authentic, but prime ministers do not put their
heads round the doors of civil servants; they send for them. To
reach Victor's office on the second floor of the Cabinet Office
overlooking Whitehall would have required Heath to walk a long
way down labyrinthine passages from 10 Downing Street, then to
go up in a poky lift. Nor would Victor have addressed any prime
minister in such jaunty terms. He dismissed Wright's account as
'complete fiction'.

Another passage in Wright's memoirs is also suspect. He pur-
ports to describe Victor's intervention in the choice of a new
director-general of MI5 on the retirement of Sir Martin Furnival
Jones in 1972. The committee of Whitehall mandarins that advised

the Home Secretary (and through him the Prime Minister) put forward one of their own, Michael Waddell: the traditional safe pair of hands that could be expected to curb the bizarre witch-hunts that were destroying service morale. These obsessions, none of which Victor shared, included Wright's pursuit of the former head of MI5, Sir Roger Hollis, as a Soviet mole: and his near certain belief that Harold Wilson, Heath's predecessor at Number 10, had close private links with Russia.

MI5, however, anxious to remain independent of Whitehall, hoped for an internal appointment: the promotion of Michael Hanley, the deputy director-general. White's decision to back him prevailed although taken with characteristic hesitance. 'On balance,' he told me years later, 'I preferred Hanley, but I did not think him all that good.'

Wright's memoirs exaggerate the weight given by the Prime Minister and the Home Secretary to both his own and Victor's views. Dick White, modest and fair-minded, mentioned neither of them when he gave me his own account of how Hanley came to be preferred to Waddell. In 1972 he alone of serving intelligence officers carried the guns to challenge the Whitehall mandarins. Wright was too unbalanced to be trusted, too junior in the hierarchy for his voice to be heard – styled in MI5 parlance an assistant director, he was no more than a section head under a departmental chief.

Nor was there any reason why Heath should have heeded Victor on such a matter. It is improbable, as Wright asserts, that Victor had taken the Prime Minister for a walk in the gardens at Chequers, 'to bend his ear'. (From middle age, as it happened, Victor had detested both walking and gardens.) It was nearly thirty years since he had served in MI5. And although he had been running the Think Tank since 1971, the Prime Minister had excluded security from its agenda. Victor in fact insisted to me that Heath never consulted him on matters of security, in the garden at Chequers or elsewhere. Victor no doubt discussed with White and Wright how best to secure Hanley's promotion, and he certainly welcomed the result. But he played no effective part in the coup.

Michael Hanley's appointment in 1972 as head of MI5 set in motion a chain of events that proved disastrous for Victor. Peter Wright, who had hoped for an extension of his licence to hunt down Soviet moles, found himself increasingly restrained by the new regime. Driven towards early retirement in 1976, Wright described his last four years in MI5 as 'an extended farewell'. He was nevertheless allowed to fly 370,000 kilometres during that period in his fruitless quest.

His departure was curdled by resentment. On transferring to MI5 in 1955 he had been obliged to renounce the fifteen years of pension rights acquired while working for the Admiralty; the depleted pension, he was assured, would be adjusted at his final retirement. In 1972, however, he was told that the undertaking would be dishonoured. As no rules had been broken and no special circumstances had been recorded in writing, the injustice could not be remedied. The award to him of a CBE (Commander of the Order of the British Empire) soothed his pride but not his pocket.

Victor did what he could for Wright. He was moved not only by indignation, but also by obligation to the man who after repeated interrogation of Victor and his wife declared that there was no evidence pointing to either having been a Soviet agent – as near as it is possible in the world of espionage to prove a negative.

He offered Wright employment as a part-time consultant to N. M. Rothschild & Sons for four days a week. It was at a time of terrorist attacks on Jews, including the all but fatal shooting of Edward Sieff, Marcus's uncle, on the doorstep of his London house. Wright's duties would have been to advise the bank on personal protection and on impending terrorist plans; information presumably to be gleaned under cover from his former colleagues. Wright preferred to emigrate to Tasmania and to fulfil a long-held ambition to run a stud farm. While he was awaiting a retirement gratuity of £5000 that could not be paid until his birthday later in the year, Victor lent him the sum. It was punctiliously repaid as promised.

Wright continued to nurse a grievance about his pension. He was short of working capital, suffered ill health and drank heavily. In November 1976 he wrote to Victor from Tasmania,

[Blunt] shall have a special place in my memoirs. I've still got my notes of my talks with him. Although I found him a likeable chap to talk to, I find it still incredible to look back on some of his admissions to me. His story is a book in itself – perhaps I ought to write it.

That veiled threat alarmed Victor. The revelation by a disgruntled ex-MI5 officer of Blunt's confession and immunity from prosecution would outrage public opinion at home and provoke deep mistrust in the United States, eagerly alert to the failings of British intelligence. It would also deal a devastating blow to the reputations of Blunt's innocent friends the Rothschilds.

Victor at once wrote to Michael Hanley, warning him of the danger. Hanley replied nonchalantly. So Victor wrote again, stressing the additional risk of failing to placate a would-be author living 12,000 miles beyond the reach of the Official Secrets Act. This time Hanley reacted by asking for a special inquiry into Wright's pension by a senior civil servant, Sir John Wilson. Once more the verdict went against him. Writing to Victor in April 1977, Hanley hoped that he would persuade Wright to put his resentment behind him. Accordingly, Victor wrote to Wright in May, 'I do not think that Michael could have done more than get an independent and fair-minded person such as John Wilson to examine the case.'

In retrospect, however, Victor thought that Hanley could and should have arranged an ex-gratia payment to Wright out of secret service funds not accountable to Parliament. His efforts on behalf of his protégé failed to stifle Wright's literary ambitions. He wrote to Victor in July 1977, 'I'm also thinking of writing a paper on the Russian threat.' It then occurred to Victor that perhaps he could limit the damage both to MI5 and to himself by purporting to act as a friendly censor of Wright's recollections. Tess accordingly wrote to Wright, 'V says he hopes you will write something, but don't post it. He'll be in touch.'

There was another reason why the Rothschilds remained apprehensive. Tess, whose affection for Blunt had survived his confession, wrote in the same letter to Wright, 'I saw Anthony the other day. He is a bit nervous as I gather there is a good deal of journal-istic gossip going on with names being freely mentioned. Also a projected book by an ex-BBC man called Andrew Boyle.'

For some years the BBC reporter and biographer had been fol-lowing up clues to Blunt's involvement with Soviet Russia as whis-pers of his treason spread here and there through the Establishment. Some of these deliberate leaks sprang from the resentment of officers in MI5 and MI6 at the gentle treatment given to a Soviet spy who had caused far more harm to his country than had lesser agents further down the social scale. Blunt continued to be held in esteem at the Courtauld Institute, the British Academy and Buckingham Palace; John Vassall, a clerk in the British embassy in Moscow who spied for Russia, was sentenced to eighteen years in prison.

Others to help Boyle in writing *The Climate of Treason* were Goronwy Rees, the one-time confidant of Burgess; James Angleton, the CIA agent even more obsessed by phantom spies than was Wright; and the retired Dick White, usually the epitome of discretion, who reluctantly and with many circumlocutions, all but confirmed Blunt's guilt. Victor was approached by Boyle, but confined himself to disowning any interest in Soviet Communism, least of all in his Apostolic years at Cambridge.

Tess again wrote to Wright in October 1979, 'Boyle's book will have appeared by the time you read this and it is causing a good deal of anxiety to A. But neither V nor I know what it's going to say. Nor does A.' Victor escaped quite lightly when the book was published in the following month, although annoyed to see his photograph as an undergraduate printed below a group that included Blunt and Watson, and opposite one of Maclean.

Blunt fared less well. He was not named as a spy. Instead the author created a *doppelgänger* artfully cast in Blunt's likeness. He called him Maurice, after the hero of E. M. Forster's homosexual novel of the same name, thus nudging the reader to recall Forster's much-quoted but false antithesis: that if he had to choose between betraying his country or betraying his friend, he hoped he would have the guts to betray his country.

Within days, *Private Eye* had identified Boyle's Maurice with

Blunt and the floodgates of the press had opened. On 15 November the Prime Minister, Margaret Thatcher, denounced him in the House of Commons as a Soviet spy. She had inherited the decision of the Attorney-General in 1964 to grant him immunity from prosecution in return for his private confession; but she saw no reason why she should protect him from public exposure. He was at once deprived of his knighthood and reverted to the style of professor. His press conference under the auspices of *The Times* served only to reveal unattractive qualities of deceit and evasiveness. 'Suave, condescending deviousness,' Sir Roy Strong, a fellow historian of art, noted, 'no single word of regret, no expression of sorrow for having conceivably exposed the Queen to any embarrassment.'

Blunt died in 1983 in obscurity and disgrace but comforted by the kindness and hospitality of two old friends, an Eton master and his wife who had retired to Dorset. It was as well that the newspapers never discovered the Good Samaritan to be Tom Brocklebank, Jacob Rothschild's former housemaster. Given the hysteria of the time, that coincidence could have enmeshed Victor in the most tortuous and misleading of conspiracy theories.

Victor allowed himself little repose during those dark days. He scrupulously carried out his duties as a director of the bank, where the conflict between Jacob and the rest of the board added to the strain. He planned the launch of his brainchild, Biotechnology Investments Ltd. He completed his two-volume report of the Royal Commission on Gambling. He wrote his Dimbleby lecture, 'Risk', and a monograph on the acquisition of the Suez Canal shares. It was occupation enough for any man approaching his seventieth birthday.

Even his relaxations were punishing. Roy Jenkins, staying with the Rothschilds in Cambridge during the last days of 1979, wrote, 'Victor never goes out, sits in his shirtsleeves the whole time, and just shouts at Sweeney for dry martinis or Buck's Fizz – a most incredible unhealthy life.' He also chain-smoked heavy Turkish cigarettes. The regime took its toll, both physically and in nervous fatigue. 'I have only just come out of hospital after a long period of irritating examinations,' he had written to me earlier that year, 'but "they" seem to think I am all right.'

'They' were mistaken. From February to April 1980 he was again in hospital for cardiac surgery, followed by bacterial endocarditis and a severe ailment affecting his sight.

Convalescence was clouded by the publication of a revised second edition of Boyle's *The Climate of Treason*. The author could now give Blunt his real name without risk of legal action. But he did not yet dare to be as explicit in referring to Victor's links with him. At the launch of the revised edition, however, Boyle told his audience that after the defection of Burgess and Maclean in 1951, two members of the House of Lords were questioned as possible accomplices but that no conclusive evidence had been found against them. Boyle refused to identify them beyond saying that one was an hereditary peer, the other elevated to the peerage; and that one had served in the intelligence services in the Second World War.

Ermine was scarce in MI5, and it required little research to identify Victor as the hereditary peer. The other exonerated suspect could also be no other than Richard Llewellyn-Davies, a fellow Apostle with Marxist views who became an authority on town planning and was created a life peer by Harold Wilson in 1964. Victor later commissioned him to design a new model village at Rushbrooke. There was another link between the two families, a left-wing *Debrett* from the heady days of socialism. Llewellyn-Davies married Patricia Rawdon-Smith, Tess Rothschild's friend and wartime flatmate in Bentinck Street. A champion of many radical causes, she too was made a life peer by Wilson and held minor office in successive governments. Neither husband nor wife plays any further part in our story.

In answer to a sympathetic enquiry from Peter Wright in Tasmania, Victor replied, 'Things are starting to get rough.' That was untrue; Victor had panicked. The only mention of him in the press after Boyle's second edition was a mischievous article in the *Spectator* by the satirist Auberon Waugh entitled 'Lord Rothschild is innocent'. Victor consulted the fashionable solicitor Lord Goodman, who dissuaded him from bringing an action for libel.

What could he do to reclaim his reputation? Friends advised him to do nothing; but then Victor could never do nothing. Agitated and in poor health, he exaggerated the harm done to him by Boyle's innuendos. Would death not evoke crueller doubts about his patriotism to haunt his family and his name beyond the grave? The dead have no protection against libel. Justice must be done in his lifetime.

The plan he evolved was daring to a degree: nothing less than to ask Margaret Thatcher, who had been Prime Minister for little more than a year, to make him her adviser on security and curator of the skeletons that still lurked in the cupboards of MI5 and MI6. The appointment would draw a line under the Blunt affair; announce to the nation that he was once more at the very heart of government; assuage his thirst for gossip and the details of other people's business. Dick White spelled out to me another attraction. It would enable a jealous Victor to emulate Solly Zuckerman by acquiring a near permanent office and secretary in the Cabinet offices.

Margaret Thatcher had come to know Victor well when they worked together during Heath's government, she as Secretary of State for Science and Education, he as head of the Think Tank. In her memoirs she wrote of her high regard for him.

Had Victor sought a formal interview with the Prime Minister to put his case for becoming her adviser on security, her civil servants at Number 10 would have been obliged to keep a record of his request. From his Think Tank years he knew with what unobtrusive skill the Whitehall mandarins would have smothered the plan. (There are no fingerprints on *his* dagger, Harold Wilson said of Burke Trend.)

Victor preferred to seize his chance at a private party to meet the Prime Minister in July 1980. Although he was put next to Mrs Thatcher at dinner, the hostess, Lady Avon, widow of Anthony Eden, had not arranged the evening to further Victor's ambitions, of which she was unaware; and as the thirty or so other guests included such energetic talkers as Isaiah Berlin, Arnold Goodman and Hugh Trevor-Roper, he could not have had time to exchange many confidences with the Prime Minister. But Margaret Thatcher is agile at picking up a point and said she would consider his request. Her answer was dismissive.

It could not have been otherwise. As Dick White put it, 'The moment any such irregular proposal is made to the Establishment, it packs itself into a solid phalanx of hostility.' Nor was it Victor's only aim. He also coveted the appointment of director-general of MI6, a bigger and more exciting organisation than MI5. That too was preposterous. He had not served officially in either of the two security services since 1945. Suspicions about his friendship with Blunt hung on the air. And the antagonism between the two services would have made a former MI5 officer unwelcome as head of MI6, as White had discovered in 1956.

'Victor should never have put his nose back into intelligence,' White complained. 'He was too close to Peter Wright. I told Victor that if this continued, Wright might ask him to do things that went too far and put him in danger. He resented my warnings and ceased to consult me.' Their parting of the ways was a tragedy. For Victor was about to embark on an enterprise that required, as never before, sober advice and a restraining hand.

Fearing that his plan to become security adviser to the Prime Minister would fail, as indeed it did, Victor had another grand design in mind. A few weeks before Lady Avon's dinner party, Peter Wright had written to him from Australia with two disconcerting reports. The stud farm, in desperate need of capital, was driving him to the brink of bankruptcy; and he was at work on a book about the Soviet penetration of British society with the provisional title, 'The Cancer in Our Midst'. Three years earlier Victor had warned Michael Hanley, the director-general of MI5, against failing to satisfy Wright's claim to a full pension; now the threat of a damaging book drew nearer. Never before had a long-serving officer of MI5 proposed to reveal its secrets and the author could expect to receive substantial royalties. But Wright's motives were not only revenge and solvency; he was also driven by a patriotic urge to warn his country against the enemies within the gates.

Wright was aware of the risks involved. His letter to Victor of June 1980 continued,

It is not the Official Secrets Act that concerns me. With all the books written it would be very difficult to make it stick. But I was made to sign a document when I retired, never to disclose anything I knew as a result of my employment, whether classified or not. I can avoid action against me by staying in Australia and never returning to my beloved England.

Without encouraging the would-be author to publish his dangerous recollections of MI5, Victor saw an opportunity of turning them to his own advantage. He replied to Wright,

I cannot see that it would be a breach of the Official Secrets Act for you to put on a piece of paper but not to send to anyone, a detailed account of your relationship with me, including all details, and let me have it by a method which I shall let you know in due course. There is certainly a need to know and you would only be telling someone something that, memory lapses apart, he could put down himself. I think it might be a good idea for you to come over to this country for a few days if you could bear it, but I shall think about it.

He would have preferred an authoritative exoneration from the director-general of MI5. But it was the invariable practice of both security services – whose very existence was in those days never publicly acknowledged – to work behind a wall of silence. He did not even trouble to ask for a line of commendation for his past services, knowing how unhelpful their answer would be. Instead he turned to Peter Wright whose interrogation of the Russian defector Oleg Gordievsky had elicited a detailed analysis of the spy network operating from the Soviet embassy in London. That Gordievsky had made no mention of Victor was itself convincing proof of his innocence. And of course Wright had questioned Victor many times, declared him innocent and had become his friend. In spite of his flaws of temperament and irrational obsessions, he was Victor's best bet.

In August 1980, his mind made up, Victor sent Wright a return air ticket from Hobart, Tasmania to London. There was later a dispute about whether it was for a first-class or an economy seat. That was the least anomaly of a journey that changed the fortunes of both men in bizarre, unpredictable ways: public humiliation for Victor, untold wealth for Wright.

Several years later I asked Victor whether I could read the three-page testimonial. He told me that he had destroyed his only copy after Wright had betrayed him by publicly revealing his secret mission to London. That was unlikely but may have been true; he did sometimes panic under pressure. From hints let drop by Peter Wright's associates, it seems to have consisted largely of the services of Victor to MI5 already mentioned in these pages, including examples of technical and scientific help, and leads that pointed to the unmasking of Alister Watson and Kim Philby.

The reported conclusion of Wright's testimonial was all that the Rothschilds could have desired: 'I do not believe it is conceivable that either Victor Rothschild or Tess Rothschild have ever been Soviet agents...I am willing to testify to that effect in any way deemed suitable.'

A cartoon by Max Beerbohm depicts Benjamin Jowett, Master of Balliol College, Oxford, watching Rossetti at work on his murals of the Search for the Holy Grail in the Oxford Union. 'And what were they to do with the Grail when they had found it, Mr Rossetti?' he enquires. Victor now had his Holy Grail. What was he to do with it? 'I thought it would be a good idea,' he wrote to me, 'if only for posterity.'

Posterity seemed the only possible recipient. He did not need to show it to the Cabinet or to the Whitehall mandarins or to all those other members of the Establishment with whom he had worked and played for the past half-century. None of them doubted his integrity. Nor could he silence his enemies in the press by flourishing his part in the secret history of MI5 or use it as evidence in an action for defamation. Even had those remedies been open to him, how could he have justified to the world his self-appointed roles since 1951 as guardian of national security and honorary sleuth extraordinary? As long as he lived it remained unpublishable.

To be read privately by succeeding generations of his family was another matter. At least, he must have surmised, they would be able to learn of his services to the state and to take pride in his patriotism. I hope that a copy lies in the vaults of N. M. Rothschild & Sons Ltd. His grandfather found comfort there in contemplating a ton of gold. Victor has left a flimsier talisman: three sheets of paper, in their day as potent and as dangerous as enriched uranium.

Having secured his long service and good conduct certificate from Wright, Victor had some unfinished business before his guest returned to Tasmania. The lurid revelations of the ten chapters of 'The Cancer in Our Midst' which Wright had brought with him alarmed Victor: their publication, he surmised, could cause a crisis of confidence at home and in the United States. The exposure of Blunt's treachery by Margaret Thatcher had been shocking enough. How much more angrily would the nation react to Wright's allegations that Roger Hollis, director-general of MI5 for nine years, had also spied for Russia? Or that Prime Minister Harold Wilson had been under surveillance as a Soviet agent? Or that MI5 had bugged and burgled its way across London in pursuit of phantom spies and the secrets of even 'friendly' diplomatic missions?

Victor had a protective, almost romantic reverence for the security services. Twice he had warned MI5 about the damage Wright's book could inflict. Now he determined as a patriotic duty to draw its sting while ensuring that neither the author's pride nor his pocket should suffer. His plan was to induce Wright to co-operate with a professional writer who knew his way about the world of intelligence yet did not belong to it. Wright would disgorge twenty years of MI5 secrets; the writer, whose name alone would appear on the title page, would make a somewhat sanitised book out of them; and the two men would share the net royalties of what promised to be a best-seller.

The man Victor had in mind as Wright's ghostwriter was Chapman Pincher, as much admired by the public as he was feared in Whitehall for his informed articles on defence and intelligence. His convivial manner, combined with a love of shooting and fishing, disarmed the suspicions of those who most felt themselves at risk from journalists; law officers of the Crown, senior commanders of the armed forces, even heads of the security services.

Victor's plan to enlist him seems to have been a last-minute decision. The two friends had not been in touch for several weeks when Victor telephoned Pincher at his house in Berkshire one September afternoon in 1980. Victor said that he had a visitor from overseas staying with him in Cambridge who would like to meet Pincher to discuss interests they had in common. But as the visitor had to leave on the following morning, Victor proposed sending a car and chauffeur to drive Pincher the hundred or so miles to Cambridge, where he could spend the night and be driven home the next day. Pincher, scenting excitement and intrigue, agreed to make the journey. Had Victor telephoned only five minutes later, Pincher would have left for the local river to fish for trout and an adventure that changed the lives of Victor, Wright and Pincher himself would have eluded him.

Reaching Cambridge before 8 p.m. Pincher was introduced to Wright as 'Philip'; obfuscation was Victor's stock-in-trade. Pincher was not impressed. He afterwards described Victor and Wright as 'two old spooks playing silly buggers'. Victor had apparently briefed Wright but not Pincher. He left them alone to reach agreement on the terms of their enterprise.

The plan that emerged satisfied both conspirators. Pincher expected to have no difficulty in securing generous terms from his publisher. 'I had been looking for someone like Wright for 40 years,' Pincher wrote, 'as had my rivals in Fleet Street.' Wright was relieved that his partner would be the sole author of the book, for he was in poor health and lacked fluency as a writer; as a 'consultant' he would nevertheless receive a coveted £5,000 on signature of the contract, followed by a half-share of the royalties. The book was no longer to be called 'The Cancer in Our Midst' but *Their Trade Is Treachery*.

What at first sight seemed ingenious was to prove a foolhardy scheme over which Victor would have no ultimate control. Having brought together a disaffected MI5 officer and a calculating journalist to thwart both the Official Secrets Act and Wright's pledge of confidentiality, he thought it was protection enough for him to withdraw to the shadows. So he did not sit in on the discussions in his house at Cambridge, enquire the terms of their agreement or ask to read the proofs of the book before publication. If that most cautious of men did have misgivings, they were stilled by the conviction that he was acting on a noble impulse: to protect the security services from public vilification in London, mistrust and contempt in Washington, triumph and derision in Moscow. For whereas the exposure of an incompetent and spy-ridden MI5 by a journalist could be dismissed as wild speculation, a similar account by a named ex-MI5 officer would seem both authentic and treacherous. So little guilt did Victor feel in procuring that colossal breach of security that he continued to address letters to *The Times* deploring the steady leakage of classified documents to the press.

Victor never again saw or corresponded with Peter Wright; nor did he ever receive a line of gratitude for having saved him from degrading poverty. There for the moment we may leave him, brooding and inscrutable, while we briefly pursue the fortunes of *Their Trade Is Treachery*.

The collaboration took longer than expected. Wright was anxious to begin work with Pincher at the earliest moment so that he could lay hands on his own share of the royalties. But he had told none of his former MI5 colleagues of his return to London and feared their enquiries if he were spotted. Pincher therefore had to follow him out to Tasmania for a prolonged briefing, working a ten-hour day for more than a week.

The 12,000-mile journey and the discomfort in which Wright lived eventually paid immense dividends. Pincher wrote,

> I was astonished by the depth of Wright's knowledge and his involvement in so many interesting cases which had provided evidence of Soviet penetration...I was even more surprised by his willingness to tell me secrets for publication on a scale which I knew to be unprecedented in the entire history of the secret services and, almost certainly, in British history as a whole.

Pincher returned to England with his illicit treasure trove; extracted more secrets from Wright in a copious correspondence using coded names and accommodation addresses; completed his text. One hurdle remained. How would the authorities react when they heard of the Tasmanian time bomb about to explode in London? Would they not seek an injunction to ban the book and prosecute its author for breach of the Official Secrets Act?

Wright was safe enough, his comprehensive breach of trust not yet known to MI5. In any case, he was immune from prosecution as long as he remained in Australia, where British subjects suspected of infringing the Official Secrets Act cannot be extradited. As for Pincher, the ease with which he used his contacts in high places to evade the scrutiny of the law suggests a privileged position, perhaps even a government-inspired conspiracy. From the moment that Victor summoned Pincher to meet Wright in Cambridge, could he have been taking part in a deniable operation, a charade masterminded by the authorities? These suspicions will be examined as the tale unfolds.

Preceded by serialisation in the *Daily Mail* and a flurry of sensational news stories, *Their Trade Is Treachery* was published in March 1981. Its principal revelation was that Sir Roger Hollis, director-general of MI5 from 1956 to 1965, had been interrogated as a suspected Soviet spy. There were allegations that he had discouraged the investigation of Blunt, warned Philby of his imminent arrest, thwarted inquiries about other suspected Russian agents in the security services. But the evidence against Hollis was circumstantial and no Cabinet secretary or head of MI5 or MI6 doubted his integrity. The flimsy case against him can be traced to James Angleton, the Joe McCarthy of US intelligence, who tipped off Jonathan Aitken MP, who in turn enlisted Chapman Pincher, whose suspicions were reinforced by Peter Wright.

Victor Rothschild, who had similarly been pursued by rumour, was so convinced of Hollis's innocence that he wrote to Pincher in July 1980, warning him against 'a small number of people who have got the subject on the brain to the extent of paranoia...To make a poor pun, I am inclined to think that one should let the dogs lie without comment.'

Ignoring Victor's advice, Pincher made his case against Hollis the core argument of *Their Trade Is Treachery*. It would have carried more weight with his readers had he not blundered in reporting the conclusions of Sir Burke, now Lord, Trend, the former secretary of the Cabinet, who in 1974 reviewed all previous investigations into Hollis's conduct. Mrs Thatcher was at her most formidable when she spoke to the Commons on the day of publication:

> Mr Pincher's account of Lord Trend's conclusions is wrong. The book asserts that Lord Trend 'concluded that there was a strong prima facie case that MI5 had been deeply penetrated over many years by someone who was not Blunt', and that he 'named Hollis as the likely suspect'.
>
> Lord Trend said neither of these things and nothing resembling them. He reviewed the investigation of the case and found that it had been carried out exhaustively and objectively. He was satisfied that nothing had been covered up. He agreed that none of the relevant leads identified Sir Roger Hollis as an agent of the Russian intelligence service … [and] concluded that Sir Roger Hollis had not been an agent of the Russian intelligence service.

Initial sales of the book had been promising, but fell away under the Prime Minister's onslaught, and the publisher, Sidgwick & Jackson, was left with 11,000 copies to be remaindered.

The Cambridge plot had nevertheless worked out well. Concerns about Hollis's supposed links with Russia had been brought out into the open and magisterially refuted by the Prime Minister. Public opinion had been persuaded to focus on the blunder of a journalist rather than on his source, an ex-MI5 dissident. Wright had been saved from bankruptcy by some £30,000 of royalties from *Their Trade Is Treachery*. Pincher had received a similar sum for a tactful pen that made no mention of Victor's post-war flirtation with the security services.

Yet Wright remained unsatisfied. He thought on reflection that he should have sold the stolen secrets of MI5 for more than the thirty pieces of silver he had received from his publisher.

Encouraged by Pincher, he determined to try again. For a year or two more they corresponded across 12,000 miles, hoping to apply the same formula to another book provisionally called 'The Atlantic Connection': the story of security co-operation between Britain, the United States and Canada. But *Their Trade Is Treachery* had exhausted Wright's publishable recollections: from motives of patriotism he would record nothing of British intelligence operations in Northern Ireland. Nor could Pincher hold out any prospect of a second lucrative contract from a publisher. Early in 1983 the two men ceased to write to each other.

Wright then acquired a new ghostwriter. He was Paul Greengrass, a television producer who persuaded Wright to be filmed in Tasmania for a documentary about MI5, shown on British television in 1984. They then collaborated in the writing of Wright's memoirs that ultimately appeared under the title *Spycatcher*. This time the government showed none of the indulgence given to *Their Trade Is Treachery*. The London publisher, Heinemann, threatened with an injunction in England, transferred the book to their Australian subsidiary, hoping that they would one day be allowed to reimport it.

In 1986, however, the government began an action to suppress publication in Australia: HM Attorney-General v. Heinemann (Australia) and Peter Wright. It was to last several years, embroil no fewer than eleven judges of the Australian judicial system and cost the British Treasury more than £3 million. It would also hugely enrich Peter Wright and embroil Victor Rothschild in persecution more humiliating than any he had earlier endured.

The British case rested on the declaration signed by Wright in 1955 that he was aware of the provisions of the Official Secrets Act prohibiting the revelation of any 'official' information. Wright's defence was that almost everything in *Spycatcher* had been published before, particularly in *Their Trade Is Treachery* and in another book by Pincher, *Too Secret Too Long*; that much of it was twenty or thirty years out of date and so irrelevant to current MI5 operations; and that if the government agreed to indicate which 'objectionable' passages it would like removed, publisher and author were willing to negotiate in good faith. At least that would have allowed Wright to deploy once more his case against Hollis and other suspected spies, and to plead for a rigorous government inquiry.

The authorities refused to co-operate. They wanted to establish that any officer of MI5, past or present, had an obligation not to publish anything about the service, regardless of whether the information was common knowledge, out of date, trivial or evidence of illegal conduct. It was in short a blanket ban designed to deter other members of the service from writing their memoirs.

Having failed to act against earlier books about the security services by Chapman Pincher and Nigel West (among others) the British government had surrendered any moral right to censorship. Its rigidity in an Australian courtroom seemed at best inconsistent, at worst hypocritical; and insofar as it sought to impose English law on a Commonwealth country suffused with republican sentiment, patronisingly insular.

The British government also blundered in failing to send to Australia an expert witness, preferably a law officer of the Crown, to unravel the manoeuvres preceding the publication of *Their Trade Is Treachery*. The Prime Minister, however, decided that the Attorney-General could not be spared from his duties in London. Instead, Sir Robert Armstrong, the Cabinet Secretary, was despatched to Sydney. An able civil servant and Mrs Thatcher's principal adviser on security, he had nevertheless not been fully consulted about *Their Trade Is Treachery* at the time or adequately briefed before his departure for Australia. He fell easy victim to the rhetoric and stratagems of Wright's defence team.

The British case seemed to be doomed, at least by public opinion, after it was revealed that Armstrong had asked the publisher for a pre-publication copy of the book. Armstrong's letter concealed that he had already acquired one from a confidential source whose identity he felt bound to protect. Instead of admitting from the witness box that such minor deceptions are commonplace in security operations, he told the court, 'It contains a misleading impression, not a lie. It was being economical with the truth.' That subtle distinction, enunciated by Edmund Burke two centuries earlier, provoked both press and public to brand

Armstrong an unscrupulous liar. The final judgement of the court, however, allowing Wright to publish *Spycatcher* in Australia, took a more measured view. While treating much of Armstrong's evidence 'with considerable reserve', it acquitted the Cabinet Secretary of having deliberately set out to mislead.

Wright was fortunate in his counsel as was his counsel in the trial judge. Malcolm Turnbull, no more than thirty-one when briefed to represent the author of the as yet unpublished *Spycatcher* in the High Court of New South Wales, had taken a law degree at Sydney University, dabbled in journalism and made his name as in-house lawyer to the newspaper owner Kerry Packer. Turnbull's aggressive tactics in defending his client from allegations of murder and drug-smuggling drove him to exchange the vocation of barrister for that of solicitor. It gave him the same right of audience in the courts without obligation to accept the gentler etiquette of the Bar.

The assignment of His Honour Justice Powell to the case was another bonus for Wright. He was beyond doubt learned, industrious and only occasionally impatient. Yet there were moments when he and Turnbull, incidentally a leading republican, seemed to be acting in collusion to tweak the tail of an English Establishment epitomised by the urbane, self-confident Armstrong. Turnbull astutely positioned his lectern so that Armstrong faced the distraction of a press gallery who (as Turnbull wrote) 'were laughing at him and some were sneering too'. Few other Australian judges would have allowed such contrived disorder in their courts.

A cosy relationship developed between a judge who fancied himself as a wit and a counsel alert to every possible advantage of ingratiation. To read their exchanges is to recall Oliver Goldsmith on the schoolmaster and his pupils:

> *Full well they laughed with counterfeited glee*
> *At all his jokes, for many a joke had he.*

Some of them were good. As a mountain of books and newspapers cited by the defence piled up on his desk, Powell observed, 'I do not want to stop you, Mr Turnbull, but please remember that in 13 years, 11 months and 14 days I reach the statutory age of judicial senility.' Small wonder that Turnbull wrote of the trial, 'It was an enormous lark and I enjoyed every minute of it.'

Armstrong's evidence seems to have implanted in the judge a distaste not only for Margaret Thatcher's Cabinet Secretary but for Cabinet secretaries in general. Michael Codd, the Australian holder of that office, testified that if Wright were to publish *Spycatcher* in Australia, the intelligence agencies of friendly countries, including the United Kingdom, would be reluctant to exchange secrets. Although Codd's evidence carried the authority of the federal government in Canberra and the approval of the Australian security services, the judge dismissed it out of hand as 'complete and utter moonshine'. Chapman Pincher, who was not in court, later alleged that Powell had described it as 'codswallop'. On matters of such sophistication, His Honour may perhaps be given the benefit of the doubt.

When the trial opened in November 1986, six years had passed since the three conspirators had set in motion the *Spycatcher* saga and Victor's shadowy role seemed likely to remain secret for the rest of his life. Then, in the pre-trial discussions with his client, Turnbull heard with near incredulity how Victor had introduced Pincher to Wright as the ghostwriter of *Their Trade Is Treachery*. Wright's argument seemed plausible enough:

> I knew Lord Rothschild to be an intimate confidant of successive heads of British intelligence establishments. I could not conceive of him embarking on such a project without knowing it had the sanction, albeit unofficial, of the authorities.
>
> I sensed I was being drawn into an authorised but deniable operation which would enable the Hollis affair and other MI5 scandals to be placed in the public domain as the result of an apparently inspired leak.
>
> All I know about Lord Rothschild and the ease with which *Their Trade Is Treachery* was published leads me to the inescapable conclusion that the powers that be approved of the book.

Here indeed was a robust weapon with which to defend the publication of *Spycatcher*. For if the British government had deliberately refrained from taking action against *Their Trade Is Treachery*, was it not hypocritical to seek a worldwide ban on *Spycatcher*?

Yet Turnbull hesitated. Even with some form of official cognisance, why would a seventy-year-old peer of the realm, a pillar of Establishment respectability with an honoured name, a striking record of public service and a chestful of medals and decorations, risk so much for so little? Ten years earlier he had warned MI5 that Wright, dissatisfied with his pension, was threatening to write vengeful memoirs. MI5 had shown little interest in Victor's anxiety. Why then should he have subsequently engaged in a murky plan to do MI5's dirty work? Then the light dawned on Turnbull. 'He was a spook once, wasn't he? That's how those blokes think.'

Before Turnbull could deploy Wright's defence in detail, he had a further obstacle to overcome: his client's conscience. 'I don't want to get Victor involved,' Wright told Turnbull. 'He was very good to me. He is an old man. It could kill him.' Turnbull was not to be deflected by such tearful sentiments. He impressed on Wright that if he did not tell the truth about Rothschild, he would lose the case. Here is Turnbull's account of how Wright at last agreed to betray his patron and friend:

> Finally Wright went silent and nursed his whisky glass for a full minute. He took a deep swig of his drink and held the empty glass up as if for a toast. An almost theatrical tone of resolve took over his old man's voice, with a sad and weary undertone of one who knows the dreadful consequences of what he was about to say.
>
> 'Oh well, poor dear Victor,' he intoned, deliberately replacing the glass down on the desk. 'Throw him to the wolves!'

Before examining Wright's evidence at the *Spycatcher* trial, let us pause to consider whether Victor had acted alone or had been manipulated by the authorities in bringing together Wright and Pincher. Victor and I retraced that sequence of events several

times after Wright's betrayal of his benefactor in the Sydney courtroom, analysing his tainted testimony. One day, almost casually,
that most secretive of men made a startling admission. The
scheme had not been his own brainchild but that of a friend who
had visited him during his weeks in hospital between February and
April 1980. Having enquired about Peter Wright and heard from
Victor that the ex-MI5 man was writing a dangerous and vengeful
book of memoirs, the visitor suggested the plan that culminated in
the publication of Pincher's *Their Trade Is Treachery*.

'Who was the visitor?' I asked Victor.

He replied, 'I cannot tell you his name because of the Official
Secrets Act. But he was a friend of importance and known
integrity who had good reason to understand the obligations of
confidentiality. He was not the sort of man to make the deflection
proposal rashly.' Victor continued, 'Some may think it was uncharacteristic behaviour on my part, some that I was being advised or
even led by the nose.' Then he clammed up.

Did the hospital visitor exist or was he, like Oscar Wilde's
Bunbury, a ghost character to whom Victor could conveniently
transfer moral responsibility for all that sprang from the supposed
bedside chat? The patient had just undergone severe cardiac
surgery followed by bacterial endocarditis and the prospect of
blindness; he was also suffering from the nervous strain and fear
of Boyle's book about Blunt.

I nevertheless set about tracking down Victor's persuasive
friend, inferring that he must be a senior officer, past or present,
of the security services. Why otherwise would Victor have felt
inhibited by the Official Secrets Act from revealing his name? (It
was striking how punctiliously Victor obeyed the minutiae of the
Official Secrets Act while appearing to breach its broad principles
of confidentiality in the Wright–Pincher affair.) Who, except
within the restricted circle of spookdom, would have known about
the as yet obscure Peter Wright? And who in that world would
have been incautious enough to risk both his own reputation and
Victor's had the stratagem become public knowledge?

Two of Victor's intimates to whom I spoke on separate occasions were Dick White and Robert Armstrong. Each denied his

own involvement; each suggested that the most likely candidate was Sir Maurice Oldfield, a close friend of both Victor and Pincher. Oldfield came from an unusual background. One of eleven children of a Derbyshire tenant farmer, he had won a scholarship from a local school to Manchester University, where he studied history under A. J. P. Taylor and might himself have followed an academic career but for the war. He joined the Intelligence Corps and in 1946 was recruited by MI6. Appointed White's deputy director-general in 1965, Oldfield had every hope of succeeding him three years later. White, however, refused to recommend him for promotion, fearing that he would be too unstable, too insecure for so exacting a post. He finally reached the top of MI6 in 1973, serving with distinction until his retirement in 1978, when he received the highest grade in the Order of St Michael and St George.

Oldfield was called out of retirement by the new Prime Minister, Margaret Thatcher, in 1979 to become co-ordinator of security intelligence in Northern Ireland, again against the advice of White. Perhaps there was substance in White's misgivings. In June 1980, some months after supposedly visiting Victor in hospital, Oldfield was relieved of his post on confessing that he had tried to conceal his homosexual past when being positively vetted; but there was no suggestion that his sexual tastes had ever prejudiced security. He died of cancer in 1981.

With his long experience of covert operations, his range of friendships and his colourful imagination, Oldfield could well have offered Victor a solution to the problem of Wright's menacing book as he lay in hospital in 1980. Was he not reputed to be the prototype of John le Carré's inscrutable George Smiley? It was not until after Victor's death in 1990 that White and Armstrong led me to identify him. I then searched my memory to recall whether Victor had ever mentioned Oldfield's name to me.

There was a single occasion, one I had cause to remember. In November 1986, a few days after Turnbull had browbeaten Peter Wright into 'throwing poor dear Victor to the wolves', his damaging testimony began to leak into the British newspapers. 'Rothschild paid for secret Wright trip', trumpeted the *Observer*.

Victor telephoned me in some agitation, 'What was the date', he asked, 'of Maurice Oldfield's death?' I looked it up: March 1981, a year after he had visited Victor in hospital. Was Victor already planning his defence? A straw in the wind, perhaps. But then Maurice Oldfield's world was not built on granite.

Turnbull waged war against the British government on three fronts: in the high court of New South Wales, in the press and in the House of Commons. Even before the full trial began after much legal skirmishing, Wright's allegations against MI5, some true, others false, were selectively leaked. Turnbull denied that he had been responsible, but it was in the interest of his client that both the government and MI5 should be publicly reviled. Pincher had told *The Times* how Wright had received more than £30,000 of the royalties of *Their Trade Is Treachery*. Turnbull reacted indignantly to this wholly truthful but hitherto concealed report of Wright's motives:

> The revelation was potentially very dangerous for us. Our whole strategy against Havers [the Attorney-General] was dependent on the Labour Party attacking him and Thatcher in the Commons. Kinnock [leader of the Labour Party] was rightly suspicious of being used by us and he would be even less likely to help if Wright was perceived as a greedy old man, rather than a genuine (if a little misguided) patriot.

Wright's counsel responded by persuading his client to hold a press conference – such are the ways of Australian justice – in which every shred of Victor's conduct was thrown to the wolves: his summoning of Wright from Tasmania to England, the introduction to Pincher in Cambridge, the secret transmission of Wright's royalties supposedly by NMR.

The galvanic effect of the press conference was followed by a further shock to public opinion: Wright's long affadavit which he read out in court. It did not altogether deviate from the truth, but it was embellished by false interpretation, picturesque fantasy and downright lies.

One damaging assertion was that Victor had channelled half the royalties of *Their Trade Is Treachery* to Wright in Tasmania through a Swiss bank account, so bribing the former MI5 man to break the Official Secrets Act and incidentally incriminating himself. The correspondence between Wright and Pincher during their collaboration on the book seemed to prove Victor's involvement. In reply to one of Wright's repeated demands for cash, Pincher told him in January 1981, 'Five [thousand pounds] is on the way by the V-channel.' There were further references to 'our intermediary' and 'our mutual friend'.

The truth was less sinister. Responding to Wright's plea for anonymity, Victor asked a colleague in N. M. Rothschild to arrange for successive instalments of Wright's half-share of the royalties to be paid through a Swiss bank to Wright's agent in Tasmania. That was the limit of Victor's involvement in what Pincher loosely called 'the V-channel'. As for 'our intermediary' and 'our mutual friend', they were coded references not to Victor but to the London publisher, who alone controlled the frequency and amounts of the payments. The transactions were entirely legal, there being no exchange controls at the time, and could have been carried out under the same seal of secrecy by the publisher's own bank. If Wright mistakenly exaggerated Victor's role, it was nevertheless incautious of Victor to have linked himself and his bank, however tenuously, to Wright's subterranean finances.

There were flights of fancy, too, in Wright's evidence that fed his self-importance but also branded Victor as the man who had lured an innocent patriot into disloyalty. 'Victor was always very secretive,' he swore, 'and it was not done to ask him questions. He loved intrigue and conspiracies and was always engaged in secret deals and arrangements, especially with politicians. He loved to exert influence behind the scenes.' We have already looked at two such improbable examples related by Wright, both from Victor's years as head of the Think Tank. One depicts Edward Heath poking his head round the door of Victor's room in the Cabinet Office and finding Wright there. The other is of Victor at Chequers, taking Heath for a walk in the gardens and persuading the Prime Minister to reject Whitehall's candidate for a new director-general of MI5. Victor dismissed both episodes as fiction.

Wright also alleged in his affadavit that Victor had once said to him in the flat in St James's Place, 'You know Mrs Thatcher was sitting on this couch only a few days ago. She doesn't understand intelligence.' That supposed conversation, too, was denied by Victor. The Prime Minister, he told me, had never been to his flat; and the only time she had visited his house in Cambridge was for tea after looking round a laboratory. She had been escorted by her husband and her parliamentary private secretary, and intelligence was not on the menu.

The most lurid of Wright's untruths was that 'up to 30 officers of MI5' had plotted to destabilise Harold Wilson's government of 1974–6 in the belief that he was a Soviet spy. Turnbull swallowed the story uncritically on Wright's word alone. 'This was treason of the worst kind,' he wrote in his account of the trial. 'The agency chartered to defend the realm was trying to undermine it.' His client, he argued, far from betraying the operational secrets of MI5, had first tried to thwart the plot; and when Hanley, the effete director-general, refused to take his warning seriously, Wright had been driven by selfless patriotism to make public this threat to the nation.

Throughout the long cross-examination of Sir Robert Armstrong, Turnbull belaboured him again and again on the failure of the British authorities to act against the conspirators. 'Your real motive and your government's motive in trying to stop *Spycatcher*', he argued, 'is that it provides first-hand evidence of the plot against Wilson ... You have created a privileged class of criminal in the security service, haven't you?'

Justice Powell was as gullible as Turnbull: 'Mr Wright went to see Sir Michael Hanley and told him, and there was some dressed-up little inquiry that got nowhere. Michael Hanley took a degree of delight in its getting nowhere.' Neither learned counsel nor learned judge paused to consider a more obvious reason why the inquiry got nowhere. It was that the thirty conspirators did not exist. In 1988, having won the right to publish *Spycatcher* in Australia, Wright confessed to a BBC *Panorama* programme that far from trying to crush the anti-Wilson plot, he had been its ringleader and that the conspirators numbered not thirty but two, himself and a single colleague. Such was the self-proclaimed patriot who tarnished the reputation of his country's security service worldwide in return for money. Such was the friend who so cheerfully threw Victor to the wolves. Such was the Titus Oates of MI5.

In retrospect it seems supine of the British government's legal team, led by Theo Simos QC, neither to have investigated Wright's testimony in depth nor to have exposed its flaws in court. But Simos had been told that Wright might drop dead in the witness box were he exposed to stress. His cross-examination was short and perfunctory. He lived for another nine years.

Defendant's counsel was less chivalrous. When Turnbull telephoned Neil Kinnock to secure his help in denouncing Thatcher, Havers, Armstrong, Pincher and Rothschild on the floor of the House of Commons, the Labour leader reacted cautiously. He reminded Turnbull that both Havers and Rothschild were old and sick, and that the proposed campaign could kill them. Turnbull replied, 'Oh well, Comrade, everyone has to make sacrifices for the revolution. Why not start with Havers and Rothschild?' It was just another of his little jokes, Turnbull assured a shocked Kinnock. Despite his scruples, the Leader of the Opposition was persuaded to put several embarrassing questions to the Prime Minister, precisely in the form suggested by Turnbull. When however, the Conservatives accused him of a lack of patriotism in trying to undermine Britain's case in the Australian high court, he withdrew from the fray.

Other Labour MPs, none of them of the first rank, agreed to carry on the dirty war. Rothschild became the target of a vicious campaign from the left. He had all the vices. He was titled, rich, successful, arrogant – what Australians contemptuously call a tall poppy, needing to be cut down to size. Day after day, he and his supposed fellow conspirators were vilified in debate or by insultingly hostile parliamentary questions and motions on the order paper inspired by Wright's flawed testimony.

MPs claim absolute privilege in making such assertions; their victims have no protection either inside or outside the House. One outraged Conservative MP asked the Speaker, 'Is there no vicious or slanderous calumny that cannot be put on the order paper without your having any control over it?' Mr Speaker's logic-chopping reply could have graced the pages of *Alice in Wonderland*. 'Every question and every early-day motion on the order paper has been carefully screened by the Table Office to ensure that it meets the rules. If it did not meet the rules, it would not be on the order paper.'

So provocative motions continued to be put down on the order paper about the plot to destabilise the Wilson government, about Victor's sinister meeting with Thatcher in his flat, about his pay-out of money to Wright to reveal secrets that breached national security. All were accepted as the truth; all were false. The little band of Labour tormentors, as unctuous as they were nasty, resurrected an earlier smear. They called on the Prime Minister 'to state whether the security services ever carried out an investigation into suspicions, which surfaced at the time and of which Lord Rothschild was aware, that he was a Soviet spy and the fifth man'.

For Victor it was an indignity that demanded an immediate riposte. Exactly a century earlier the first Lord Rothschild was rumoured to have been given budget secrets by his friend Lord Randolph Churchill. He shrugged off the whispers in silence. His grandson received the same advice when he consulted James Callaghan. 'Rise above it,' the former Labour prime minister told him. Others also counselled him to ignore his spiteful antagonists, skulking behind the protection of parliamentary privilege.

Lord Goodman, the solicitor, who might have been expected to protect his client from injustice, offered little comfort. Having experienced Victor's overbearing manner, he thought that his head had been turned by the awe and adulation that so often greeted the name Rothschild. 'He was *incredulous*', Goodman asserted, 'when the government did not instantly endorse his patriotism.'

Yet his rage and frustration were understandable. Had he not been positively vetted, the most stringent test of security, giving as the names of his referees those pillars of integrity Sir Dick White and Sir Michael Hanley? Had not his past also been raked over again and again on appointment to the Think Tank and to Whitehall committees on such exceptionally secret themes as the future of the British nuclear deterrent? Had he not alerted MI5 to the existence of two Soviet agents, Watson and Philby? The ghost of Blunt nevertheless returned to haunt him.

Perhaps the only man who might have persuaded both MI5 and the Prime Minister publicly to proclaim Victor's innocence was Dick White. But he had become estranged after Victor's failure to consult him about the plot to bring together Wright and Pincher. 'The reason Victor did not ask my advice', White told me after Victor's death, 'was that he knew I should not approve. He wrote me a terrible letter when I protested. His mind had become inconsistent and fragmented. He went with the wind. There was no strength at the centre.' White also discerned that his friend of more than forty years had never ceased to feel threatened by anti-Semitism, a prejudice that regarded this most assimilated of Jews as an exotic if not an outsider.

White was magnanimous enough to tell *The Times* in December 1986, 'I haven't the slightest doubt that Lord Rothschild was not a Soviet spy.' It was a view held unanimously by the security services and by an overwhelming majority of MPs. Yet the government resisted all private entreaties to clear him, at least while the *Spycatcher* case continued.

Another bout of ill health was also a factor as Victor pondered the options open to him. Persistent pain in one leg had to be relieved by endarterectomy, the removal of the diseased inner layer of an artery. He described it to me as a 'rather bad but not sinister operation'. It may, however, have affected the judgement of a man in his seventy-seventh year suffering from other ailments.

After a fresh rash of references to him had appeared on the Commons order paper, he wrote a letter to the *Daily Telegraph* that was splashed across its front page and picked up by every other national newspaper. It displayed the anguish and anger of Zola's *J'accuse* in defence of Captain Dreyfus but not its literary appeal.

Dear Editor and Readers,
    Since at least 1980 up to the present time there have been innuendoes in the Press to the effect that I am 'the 5th man', in other words a Soviet agent.

The Director General of MI5 should state publicly that it has unequivocal, repeat unequivocal, evidence that I am not, and never have been, a Soviet agent. If the 'regulations' prevent him making such a statement which, in the present climate I doubt, let him do so through his legal adviser or through any other recognizably authoritative source.

I am constrained by the Official Secrets Act but I write this letter lest it be thought that silence would be an indication of anything other than complete innocence.

I shall not make any other public statement to the Press until further notice.

> Yours truly,
> Rothschild

The opening of his *cri de coeur* is clumsily phrased, as if translated from French or German. The next paragraph may be thought bombastic, ambiguous and shaky on syntax. The third is both moving and dignified, and should have concluded the letter. The final lines are otiose and bathetic.

There was a significant omission from the letter. While vehemently demanding to be cleared of having been a Soviet spy, Victor made no mention of more recent allegations that he had brought Wright and Pincher together to produce *Their Trade Is Treachery*, so breaching the Official Secrets Act and perhaps national security. Wright's account given to the courts in Australia thus stood unchallenged. Victor's silence about the Cambridge meeting in 1980 in no way confirmed the slanderous accusations that he had been the Fifth Man, but it did intensify the mystery of what this distinguished man had been up to in the shadier reaches of espionage. Even the *Daily Telegraph*, on the morning it published Victor's letter, suggested that sooner or later he must give some public explanation of his dealings with Wright and his motives for them.

Scarcely anyone except a few journalists and backbench parliamentarians with self-serving motives believed that Victor had been a Soviet agent; certainly no member of the security services or of the government. So it was naive of him to demand a declaration of his innocence on the strength of what he called 'unequivocal, repeat unequivocal, evidence'.

He was referring, he let it be known, to the help he had given the security services in unmasking Alister Watson and Kim Philby. He was, in fact, neither the first nor the only witness to have reported doubts about their loyalty and his part in identifying them, while strengthening the probability of his own patriotism, did not conclusively prove it. In the shadowy world of espionage it is not at all uncommon for one agent to throw another of the same allegiance to the wolves, as a few days earlier Wright had thrown Victor. Guilt can be proved, innocence hardly ever.

There were other puzzling aspects of the letter. As its purpose was to evoke an endorsement of Victor's patriotism, why did he not openly and confidently appeal to the Prime Minister, the head of the security services, rather than to the director-general of MI5 and his acolytes, faceless men whose existence was all but denied by Whitehall? She may have been loathed and feared by Labour's 'maniacal rabble', as Victor called them. But she was widely trusted, respected and admired, especially by readers of the *Daily Telegraph*.

MI5, by contrast, had been much diminished in public esteem by the unsavoury allegations of Wright and other authors: Soviet penetration, plots to destabilise a prime minister, bugging and burgling, sanctified incompetence. No statement from that quarter would have inspired public confidence in Victor or in anyone else. In any case MI5 by tradition never commented on its policy or personalities. The Prime Minister (or occasionally a senior Cabinet colleague) spoke on its behalf in Parliament. She was Victor's best, indeed his only, court of appeal.

How inept of him, then, to have sprung his challenge on her without warning and through the pages of a newspaper. It also happened to be an exceedingly strenuous day for her, even by the standards of that Stakhanovite prime minister: ministerial meetings all the morning followed by parliamentary questions, a gladiatorial contest requiring meticulous preparation. That left her no time to consult MI5 files on Victor's helpful role after the defection of Burgess and Maclean more than thirty years before.

Five times that afternoon she was asked in the Commons to give Victor a public assurance that he had not been a Soviet spy. Five times she refused. She confined herself to this bleak reply: 'The letter was published this morning. I have seen it. The letter is being studied in government and I cannot add anything further at this stage.' There was an explosion of anger, genuine on the part of many MPs of all parties, brazen hypocrisy from those Labour backbenchers who wept crocodile tears for the pain they had caused Rothschild by their own malevolence.

It was noted that Edward Heath, who might have been expected to speak on behalf of the man he had made head of his Think Tank, remained silent. Rarely helpful to the woman who had supplanted him as leader of the Conservative party, on this occasion he showed a too-sensitive appreciation of her need for caution.

Like all prime ministers, she disliked the failings of the security services to be discussed in Parliament. Ministerial condemnation of the guilty – Burgess and Maclean, Philby and Blunt – evoked the persistent question 'How many more?' and left a shadow of mistrust over the services they had betrayed. Nor did the posthumous rehabilitation of the innocent, such as Hollis, disarm the persistent, almost professional critics. For any government, silence was the best policy; if that proved unacceptable to the House, then as few words as possible must suffice.

Mrs Thatcher was also haunted by an unfortunate precedent. In 1955 Harold Macmillan, as Foreign Secretary, was asked in the Commons whether Philby was the Third Man – spycatchers had not yet learned to count up to five – who had tipped off Burgess and Maclean to flee the country in 1951. Macmillan replied, 'I have no reason to conclude that Mr Philby has at any time betrayed the interests of his country or to identify him with the so-called "Third Man", if indeed there was one.' After several more years as a Soviet agent, Philby ended up in Moscow.

A generation later, the Prime Minister was convinced both by personal knowledge of Victor and by the results of repeated interrogation of him by MI5 that he had never been a Russian spy. But MI5 advised her that she must take no chances. Hence her bleak response to Victor's open letter of 4 December 1986. Within twenty-four hours, however, she gave way to public pressure and issued this statement from Downing Street:

> I have now considered more fully Lord Rothschild's letter in the *Daily Telegraph* yesterday in which he referred to innuendoes that he had been a Soviet spy.
>
> I consider it important to maintain the practice of successive governments of not commenting on security matters. But I am willing to make an exception on the matter raised in Lord Rothschild's letter.
>
> I am advised that we have no evidence that he was ever a Soviet spy.

According to the practice of the security services, that curt last sentence was an adequate, almost fulsome vindication. Yet there was widespread anger in press and Parliament that it seemed to record a verdict of 'not proven' rather than 'not guilty'. The Prime Minister was also found wanting in evading any reference to Rothschild's years of outstanding public service. The criticism stung her. 'This is clearance,' she insisted. 'Leave it at that and don't go on.' She stressed that her words, at first sight ungraciously negative, meant that no shadow of guilt hung over him and that the government accepted his innocence; the media, she insisted, not her government, were responsible for the 'innuendo' of his having been a Soviet spy. And she added a dewdrop of sympathy at the 'anxiety' caused him.

Scarcely any of his friends had expected so satisfactory a conclusion when he exploded his bombshell in Downing Street. Isaiah Berlin spoke for many in a letter to the present writer: 'There are few mistakes, it seems to me, that that very intelligent man has in this case failed to make.' Yet against all the odds, Victor had removed the taint of treason from his name.

Brian Sedgemore, one of the Labour MPs who had skulked behind parliamentary privilege to smear his patriotism, flippantly conceded that he was not 'the Fifth Man or Sixth Man or Seventh Man or indeed any Soviet agent at all'. Another, Dale Campbell-

Savours, whose conduct I had castigated in the *Sunday Telegraph*, assured me by telephone that it was not his intention to pursue a vendetta against Lord Rothschild, but to use allegations against him to smash the Official Secrets Act. 'I have wrestled with my conscience over this,' he went on in sorrowful tones, 'and have considered writing to Lord Rothschild to explain my motives.'

Neither MP, however, offered him a word of apology or regret, and they continued to dance to Turnbull's tune. After Wright had won his case to publish *Spycatcher* in Australia, Campbell-Savours initiated a debate in the Commons to dissuade the government from appealing. Ostensibly shocked by 'the undignified spectacle of Britain being hauled over the coals in an Australian court action' – an undignified spectacle which at Turnbull's urging he had earlier encouraged with relish – he disclosed his true motive:

> There is concern about the delay that any appeal may have on the decision whether to prosecute Lord Rothschild under section 7 of the Official Secrets Act 1920 for soliciting Mr Peter Wright, by means of an offer of money, to pass to Mr Pincher documents known or believed to contain official secrets relating to the security services.

Campbell-Savours spoke with two voices on the subject of leaking official secrets. He urged the government not to appeal against the verdict of the Australian courts that allowed Wright to publish the secrets of MI5 in *Spycatcher*. He simultaneously demanded the criminal prosecution of Lord Rothschild for having supposedly solicited Wright to leak the same or similar secrets into Pincher's *Their Trade Is Treachery*. In an assembly more rational and discerning than Westminster, the double standards of Campbell-Savours would have been exposed and derided.

As it was, public opinion accepted both the good faith of the Labour MP and the flawed testimony of Peter Wright at their face value. Presented with a prima facie case that Victor had breached the Official Secrets Act, the Serious Crimes Squad of Scotland Yard invited him to help them with their enquiries. Once more Victor had been thrown to the wolves.

The two senior officers of the Serious Crimes Squad who questioned Victor assured him at the outset that he was not under
arrest or obliged to remain in their company. He could bring each
session of the interrogation to an end whenever he pleased: a
welcome concession to an ailing man about to undergo yet another
operation to relieve a painful obstruction of the left femoral artery.
He was also allowed to have his lawyer present. Having lost confidence in Lord Goodman, he chose Sir Max Williams, a solicitor
also from the top rank of his profession. Some friends urged
Victor to remain silent, as was his right; but he cared too much for
his name and reputation to run away. He would instead demonstrate both his innocence and his patriotism. And as always, the
former head of the Think Tank with an IQ of 184 would not shirk
a battle of wits.

The shadow of disgrace nevertheless left him apprehensive
throughout the investigation, which lasted from January to April
1987. To regain strength before the ordeal he took a winter
holiday with Tess in South Africa, but was too distracted to enjoy
it and returned after nine days.

Victor was conscious of one psychological advantage. The
dozen or so hours of questioning took place not in an intimidating
police station but in his eyrie at the top of Dollie de Rothschild's
house in St James's Place. One of the detectives later recalled with
wonder how austere an apartment Lord Rothschild inhabited: the
smallness of the creaking lift that bore him high above his cousin's
sumptuous quarters; the lavatory that led directly – surely in
defiance of planning regulations – out of his sitting room.

'Everything', William Waldegrave reminded the mourners at
Victor's memorial service, 'was a clue to some part of him.' There
were the books that he and his children had written, a piano dedicated to the genius of Art Tatum, a diagram of the disembowelled
German sabotage bomb that had won him a George Medal, a solitary little side table in *le style Rothschild*, a television set the cables of
which snaked across the floor to keep visitors on their toes. Such
were the *lares et penates* that brought their polymathic owner solace
in time of stress.

The first session of the interview went badly. He did not find nicotine-impregnated chewing gum an adequate substitute for the heavy cigarettes he had given up on medical advice and his nerves suffered accordingly. He was impatient of the clerkly procedure by which his answer to each question put to him by one policeman was recorded in pen and ink by another. And the questions themselves he thought 'tricky and muddled'.

How could it have been otherwise? The only evidence of his having allegedly breached the Official Secrets Act was contained in that given by Wright during the *Spycatcher* case in Australia. Hardly any of it had been tested by cross-examination in court or corroborated by other witnesses. Yet Scotland Yard, under pressure from Campbell-Savours and his ilk, treated it with the reverence accorded to Holy Writ. The interrogation of Victor, retracing the pattern of Wright's testimony, leapt haphazardly from one point to another. Some of them, having been made in open court and reported in the newspapers, were familiar to Victor; others, made in closed session, were sprung on him. He feared that his answers had not always done himself justice.

The chief superintendent seemed suspicious that a professional relationship between the head of Shell Research and the innovative technician of MI5 should have blossomed into friendship. Why, he asked, was Wright so frequent a visitor to St James's Place and what did the two men talk about? Here there seems to have been a lingering Victorian assumption of the rich man in his castle, the poor man at his gate – at least out of office hours.

A persistent line of questioning implied that over the years Victor had used his money and influence to put Wright under an obligation. Why had he tried to secure him an improved pension from MI5? Why had he offered him a well-paid consultancy at N. M. Rothschild? Why, after Wright's retirement to Tasmania, had Victor sent him a first-class return air ticket to England? (Victor insisted it was economy class, and produced a receipt to prove it.) He resented that his kindness should be made to seem patronising and perhaps part of a devious design.

At this early stage of the investigation the interrogators had no means of distinguishing fact from fantasy in Wright's testimony. They asked Victor whether in 1965 he had given a dinner party in

Cambridge to bring together Wright and Lord Adrian, the Master of Trinity; whether Peter Kapitza, the respected Soviet scientist who spent thirteen years in the Cavendish Laboratory, Cambridge as a protégé of Lord Rutherford, had also been a guest; whether Victor had introduced Wright to other men of influence, including Roy Jenkins, James Goldsmith and Shapoor Reporter. Victor replied that he had introduced none of them to Wright; but that after Blunt's confession in 1964 he had suggested to Wright, by now an MI5 spycatcher, some names of Blunt's associates, including possible suspects. None of the dinner guests was among them.

Wright's account of the part played by Victor in the appointment of a new director-general of MI5 provoked a sharp exchange with the chief superintendent:

Do you think it was your function to manipulate who should be appointed?

I do not accept the word manipulate. I gave my opinion, confirmed by someone with far greater knowledge, Sir Dick White.

They clashed again over Victor's appeal to Wright for a list of his services to MI5 to refute rumours that he had been a Soviet agent:

Why ask Wright? Why not ask MI5?

I did not know whether MI5 had all the information that Wright had.

At least you could have asked MI5 to say whether suppositions that you were a possible spy were without foundation?

Your assertion is incorrect because MI5 never to my knowledge made such statements, even in regard to their ex-employees.

Did you ask them?

No.

Why not?

See above answer.

An offensive innuendo about the origins of *Their Trade Is Treachery* once more enraged Victor.

> Your cautiousness in respect of government security matters is well known. Yet now you throw caution to the winds and suggest to Wright that this dossier should be turned into a book?
>
> Rubbish! I have always been extremely cautious about confidential, secret and top secret matters, and still am.
>
> Who in fact suggested that the book should be written?
>
> I don't know. It must have been Pincher or Wright or conceivably Pincher's publisher.

Such studied ignorance did not go down well with the men from the Yard. 'What is the outlook?' I asked him one day.

'Black,' he replied.

Victor decided on a change of tactics. Rather than continue to answer a barrage of questions, many of them repetitive, he prepared a written statement for Scotland Yard to refute accusations that he had breached the Official Secrets Act or behaved with any lack of patriotism. Violating the Act did not in itself imply moral turpitude. Its prohibitions included both leaking nuclear secrets to a foreign power and publishing the menu in the Ministry of Defence canteen. Victor's conduct was seen by his interrogators to be at the more serious end of the scale.

Whatever Victor's patriotic motives in deflecting Wright's as yet unpublished memoirs, the police seemed bewildered, even scandalised, that an eminent scientist, government adviser and banker should have brought together a disaffected former member of MI5, with stolen documents in his possession, and a journalist and author hungry for lucrative scoops.

Victor's first line of defence was unconvincing. Introducing Wright to Pincher, he said, had been suggested by a friend of 'importance and known integrity' who visited him in hospital in the early months of 1980 (see pages 264–266). Victor did not name him and the police were unimpressed. Nor could they have sought corroboration of Victor's tale, for what it was worth. The friend had died six years earlier. Victor alone had to bear the responsibility.

He returned in his statement to the Cambridge meeting, but it was no more lucid or wholly credible than what he had said under interrogation. His plan had been to bring together two near strangers. Wright would then learn of Pincher's extensive knowledge of security matters, agree to relinquish his own unfinished book and instead collaborate with Pincher on a more anodyne work. All this, according to Pincher, who had been summoned from Berkshire to Cambridge, a journey of some hundred miles, at five minutes' notice, was agreed between 8 p.m. and a late dinner one summer evening, without preliminary planning. No two merchant bankers could have done as well.

Victor did not, however, intrude on his friends' negotiations or show vulgar curiosity about their financial arrangements. 'I was not present during their talks. Nor did I discuss with Pincher any "deal" he might make with Wright. I did not discuss with Wright his conversation with Pincher. Nor was I involved in any arrangement on royalty payments, then or at any time.' It is rare in these pages to find that most inquisitive of men cast in the role of Trappist.

That Victor was not involved in any arrangement of royalty payments was untrue. What he must have meant is that he was not involved in funding the collaboration. His statement later admits that he did ask a colleague in NMR to find a way, quite legally, of transmitting Wright's half-share of the royalties of *Their Trade Is Treachery* from the London publisher to Wright's agent in Australia. 'I took no interest in the mechanics of the transaction or in the final details, which I did not then know. Therefore there was never any question of me inducing, let alone bribing Wright to violate the Official Secrets Act.'

That last sentence seems to clear him of one of the gravest charges made by Campbell-Savours in the Commons. Whoever was prepared to pay a near-bankrupt Wright substantial royalties to disgorge MI5 secrets to Pincher, it was not Victor.

He ended his statement to Scotland Yard on a note of triumph:

The deflection operation was a success and in the national interest. Wright was deflected from writing his book for seven years.

Pincher wrote a book far less damning. The authorities did not suppress Pincher's book, nor was he prosecuted under the Official Secrets Act. Nor was there any action to delay publication of *Their Trade Is Treachery*.

Victor was made to wait several months before learning whether he would be prosecuted. The delay was callous and unnecessary. Both the Director of Public Prosecutions and the Attorney-General, to whom he was obliged to pass the report of the Serious Crimes Squad, should have seen at a glance that the proposed prosecution failed both the necessary tests. There was no 'realistic prospect of conviction', nor would it have been 'in the public interest' to try.

As has been noted again and again, the only evidence against Victor was the tainted testimony of Wright in the *Spycatcher* case. No English court would accept it unless the ex-MI5 man agreed to submit himself to cross-examination in the witness box. Otherwise there was not a ghost of a chance of Rothschild's conviction. Yet Wright was determined to remain in Australia, for the rest of his life if need be, rather than risk prosecution under the OSA on his own account.

The test of 'public interest' was equally inhibiting. No prosecuting counsel would dare to put Victor, much less Wright, in the witness box after the government's humiliation in Sydney. Their evidence could well damage national security, prestige and relations with foreign states. Both men knew too much.

Sir Michael Havers, the Attorney-General, had already seen his reputation mauled, albeit unfairly, by Malcolm Turnbull during the *Spycatcher* case. To put Victor on trial would provoke another storm of controversy in Parliament and press that could affect the result of the next general election in June.

He had more to lose than other Conservative ministers. It was widely and correctly forecast that if Mrs Thatcher were returned, she would appoint him to supersede the aged Lord Hailsham in the historic office of Lord Chancellor, with a salary and pension far exceeding those of the Prime Minister. Crushed between the conflicting pressures of judicial duty, electoral prospects and honourable ambition, Havers procrastinated. Yet again Victor had been thrown to the wolves.

So the weeks turned into months; Margaret Thatcher won the general election of June 1987 and Havers duly became Lord Chancellor, although obliged to retire through ill health not long afterwards. Still there was no word from the office of his successor, Sir Patrick Mayhew. Victor's friends rallied round. Robin Butler, about to take over from Robert Armstrong as Cabinet Secretary, arranged a reunion dinner at a Chinese restaurant for the original members of the Think Tank at which there was much mockery of the Official Secrets Act and its costive guardians. And Robert Rhodes James, as MP for Cambridge, protested at the distress inflicted on the Rothschild family by the continuing uncertainty.

At last, in a letter to me dated 6 July, Victor wrote, 'For the next ten days or so I am somewhat distressed because I think things are coming to the boil for me, but I will get in touch with you.' Three days later, in a written parliamentary answer (which unlike an oral answer does not permit the government to be questioned on the floor of the House) the new Attorney-General announced,

> Allegations made against Lord Rothschild and also against Mr Chapman Pincher have been investigated by the police. The Director of Public Prosecutions has now decided that the investigation has not disclosed evidence justifying the bringing of proceedings against either Lord Rothschild or Mr Chapman Pincher. The Director has consulted me and I have agreed with his decision.

So ended this deplorable charade. Pincher, more experienced than Victor in the arts of self-defence, not all of them under Queensberry Rules, spoke for them both in the book he wrote about the case, *The Spycatcher Affair* (1987):

I was gratified to have been cleared but felt that it had been ludicrous for exceptionally able officers of the Serious Crimes Squad to spend several months talking to me and others simply to pacify one or two mischievous back-benchers seeking to make political capital and to support Wright. They had been required to chase the fantasies of Peter Wright and Campbell-Savours, and much public money, apart from their time, had been wasted in the sterile process.

The embers continued to smoulder to the end of Victor's life. From time to time some insulting reference would catch his eye and he would send me a draft reply for my comments. One contained a favourite passage of scatological invective by Aristippus, the companion of Socrates and teacher of rhetoric. I dissuaded him from sending it off to the paper only after pleading that ancient Greek was not much read either on the Labour benches of the Commons or in MI5.

CHAPTER 13

Last Years

Victor spent his sunset years destroying the past. It was a family failing. The first Lord Rothschild, consulted by every statesman of his age from Disraeli to Lloyd George, bequeathed to the flames bundle after bundle of their confidences. (His son Charles, a collector of autographs, was allowed to keep a single envelope in Dizzy's hand, but not the letter it had enclosed.) A generation later, the conflagration that followed the death of Victor's Uncle Walter consumed a lifetime's meticulously kept records of his natural history collections. Miriam borrowed an epigraph from *Macbeth* to describe this wilful depletion of history: 'The primrose way to the everlasting bonfire'. Only the royal family could match the Rothschilds in a zealous pyromania that saw the immolation of Queen Victoria's journals by her obedient daughter Princess Beatrice.

It is tragic that Walter's successor, Victor, having rescued and renovated what remained of the nineteenth-century Rothschild archives, should have obliterated so many of his own. His chosen instrument was not fire but an electric shredding machine. Amschel, chief executive of Rothschild Asset Management from 1990, discovered that it had been in systematic use for at least three years before his father's death, when certain files he needed could not be found. Even earlier, Amschel said, Victor would destroy the working papers of a project once he had completed it.

Some, however, did escape the voracious shredder. 'I am sending you a few snippets I have come across when clearing out my papers,' he wrote to me in December 1988. 'A few snippets' was an inadequate description of the many letters, memoranda and dictated recollections he contributed to the present volume. Yet they were tantalisingly incomplete. Having early in my researches been allowed by him to read his sparkling exchange of letters with Duff and Diana Cooper, I longed to roam the rest of his archives rather than be tossed a succession of ragbags.

One day, for instance, a promising bundle arrived, labelled 'Letters from important people'. Most of Victor's correspondents represented in the selection had indeed found a place in *Who's Who* and many in *The Dictionary of National Biography*. Their letters, however, were by no means of uniform interest, likely to be coveted less by Victor's biographer than by a dealer in autographs. The names of the great and the good came tumbling out: Queen Elizabeth the Queen Mother, Winston Churchill, G. M. Trevelyan, Bertrand Russell, Isaiah Berlin, Maynard Keynes... But the harvest was sparse, often no more than a two-line invitation to dine or a brief acknowledgement of a favour.

The use of such a category as 'important people' implies an unexpected awe on Victor's part: not at all the way in which a *grand seigneur* files his letters. It can be found more predictably in James Boswell's *London Journal* two centuries earlier: 'The correspondence of distinguished men is very much to be valued. It gives a man a dignity that is very desirable.' The Germans have a word for it: *Geltungsbedürfnis*, or the need for admiration.

While trying to regain peace of mind after the long nightmare of the *Spycatcher* case, Victor suffered a double blow. Dollie de Rothschild died in December 1988 at the age of ninety-three. He mourned not only a cousin of rare intellect and sweetness of character but also an indulgent landlady who for more than thirty years had allowed him and Tess to live rent-free on the top floor of her London house in St James's Place. It had been rumoured in the family that she would leave her fortune to the unassuming Amschel. In the event, much of her estate of £93 million went to Jacob, and with it the lease of her valuable London property. Gazing down from his London flat one day, Victor saw Dollie's wine cellar loaded into vans and driven away. Would he and Tess, too, be ejected?

In spite of efforts by such intimate friends as Stuart Hampshire and Marcus Sieff, Victor had never made his peace with Jacob. I, too, thought that Victor would have been a happier man had he shown more generosity of spirit. He would refer to Jacob as 'Granite' and judge his motives with harsh cynicism. Jacob, by contrast, I never heard disparage his father, though he sometimes mocked his foibles. When a friend asked Jacob to subscribe to an obscure overseas charity, he replied, 'I will give you £1000 if you can get £10 out of my father.'

Within months of Dollie's death, Jacob had let her house to his business associate, James Goldsmith. Victor feared for the worst. Jacob's response, however, was filial, although it could have been managed more gracefully. He came up to the flat one evening and, ignoring Victor, said to Tess, 'It may improve relations between us if I say that you and Victor can remain here for as long as you wish.' Nothing was said about rent. A few days later Jacob reappeared: 'It would be better if you paid a rent, and I suggest £5000 a year.' That sum was well below the market level and one that Victor could comfortably afford. The immensely rich Jacob might on reflection have spared Victor an irritant that added comparatively little to his own income.

Victor, so secretive about himself, so inquisitive about others, told me a few months later that he had just made a furtive tour of Dollie's old rooms to appraise the new tenant's decor. 'But first', he admitted with childish glee, 'I made sure Goldsmith was away.'

At the end of 1990, after Victor's death, chance drew me for the last time to 23 St James's Place. The French embassy in Kensington Palace Gardens had gone up in flames during routine repairs and the ambassador, M. Luc de La Barre de Nanteuil, per-suaded Jacob to let his government take over Goldsmith's lease. I was invited to luncheon and I asked my host whether I could see the third-floor flat. Victor's comfortable clutter had given way to Gallic elegance. I should not have recognised it; but I did leave a little of my heart behind.

During those last years Victor's thoughts turned, not very con-vincingly, to the simple life. On the Rushbrooke estate in Suffolk he built what he called 'my old people's home': a white-painted, two-room cottage, run on electricity from its own generator. There was a tip-up bed, a bath, a circular desk and of course a shredding machine. The views from its windows, marred only by pylons, were of rich farmland over which Amschel and his friends shot partridges. 'I shall sleep between blue satin sheets, live off microwave food and do sums,' Victor said. It was the retreat of a wealthy man with other houses, a pastoral image dependent on modern technology. He did not often use it.

Victor grew up in a world that smoked tobacco without guilt. Most Rothschilds did so; even his mother, a cigarette clinging to the very edge of her lower lip, an inch of ash defying both gravity and decorum. In any well-to-do family a silver cigarette case was an almost obligatory present to a boy on his eighteenth birthday. By the time Victor had weaned himself from the habit sixty years later, he calculated he had smoked thirty-two miles of them. A favourite photograph in middle age depicts him in profile, gazing through a delicate wisp of smoke such as hangs over Vesuvius on a quiet day.

Baron Henri de Rothschild, the French cousin he most admired – he left an unfinished memoir of him at his death – was even more stylishly photographed in frock coat and silk hat, ecstatically applying a match to his cigarette. He was making up for lost time; his martinet of a mother rationed him to one a day, with an injunction never to drop ash out of the window in case he 'set fire to the garden'. The inveterate smoker became a highly esteemed physician specialising in children's ailments.

From his years in a Cambridge laboratory, Victor took as much interest in the physical imperfections of *homo sapiens* as in the mating exertions of the sea urchin. Serving in MI5 during the war, he found time to correspond with Aldous Huxley in California about the treatment of defective vision by psycho-physical education. Should any of his friends fall ill, he was always at hand to recommend a trusted specialist or a newly discovered remedy (He drew the line, however, at visiting the sick, which upset him.) While awaiting an operation in hospital, he was curious enough to extract from a nurse a list of the twenty-five procedures to be followed before the scalpel descended.

So he must have been aware of the expanding programme of research seeking to establish a link between cigarette smoking and the incidence of lung cancer, heart disease and obstruction of the arteries. As a student of statistics, Victor cannot have failed to accept the evidence that increasingly confirmed the researchers' first tentative assumptions. Yet he either would not or could not stop smoking, even when obliged to seek surgical relief for atherosclerosis.

By August 1986 the pain in his left leg was so acute that he could walk no more than fifty metres without developing claudication, or limping. The specialist whom he consulted said, 'I wish you had come to see me three years ago.' Their conversation continued:

'I note that you smoke quite a lot.'

'How do you know?'

'Because your clothes stink. You are risking gangrene and amputation. You must stop smoking at once.'

'Okay, but I think it would be a good thing to taper off gradually so as not to get withdrawal symptoms.'

'I agree, but the tapering off must be finished by the time you leave this room.'

That was the sort of man Victor could do business with. He agreed to stop smoking immediately. The specialist also recommended that he chew gum containing a little nicotine. It brought some relief but in turn another problem; how to stop using it without suffering lesser withdrawal symptoms. It was a battle he did not live to win. He also discovered that his house smelled of dry rot. Others said it was stale tobacco. One of his friends alleged that to ease the pangs of withdrawal, Victor engaged a hypnotist. As the only part of the day Victor could spare was the early morning he invited the hypnotist to breakfast. It was too much for the visitor. He fainted.

To exercise his legs and expand his arteries, Victor acquired an electric walking machine. It worked on the treadmill principle, requiring the user to walk briskly or risk being swept off it. To relieve the boredom of those joyless jogs, Victor played tapes of the great jazz pianist Art Tatum. Then, fearing the noise might disturb his fellow tenant of St James's Place, he moved the machine down to New Court. Nothing quite like it had ever been heard there before, but there were no complaints. By a bizarre whim of fate, the phenomenon fulfilled a prophecy made by his friend Brendan Bracken as long ago as 1932, when the young MP wrote to Victor in mock disapproval of his research into fertilisation, 'The sort of work you are engaged upon is distinctly unedifying. You certainly know too much for your tender years. I look forward to the time when you are at New Court and that ark of respectability will be turned into a jazzing harlotry.'

Another gadget which Victor acquired in his fight against ill health was his own set of machines for registering blood pressure. His doctors demurred. Patients who produce their own diagnoses are never popular. In any case, the machines were not standardised, so frequently gave misleading results. Victor also convinced himself that he was suffering from cancer of the throat in spite of strong denials by his medical men.

Advised to ease the strain on heart and legs by losing weight, he first submitted himself to three hours of lying motionless on his back in the human calorimeter of the Medical Research Council. The ordeal prompted him to commission a drawing of himself in his cramped cell wearing monogrammed pyjamas that seemed to have shrunk in the wash. It was to illustrate a small book he decided to write entitled *Too Fat?*.

He assembled the familiar depressing statistics on losing weight. One set listed foods that were forbidden except as an occasional treat, such as mayonnaise and peanut butter; there were extra black marks for saturated fat and cholesterol. Another set recorded human energy expenditure during certain timed activities. More used to mental work (3.5 in the scale) than to wrestling (490), Victor had a lot of thinking to do before shedding so much as a gram. The proposed book, too technical in its measurements for the layman, too unoriginal for the scientist, was never published. Victor did not shirk a penitential diet of bran, turnip tops and

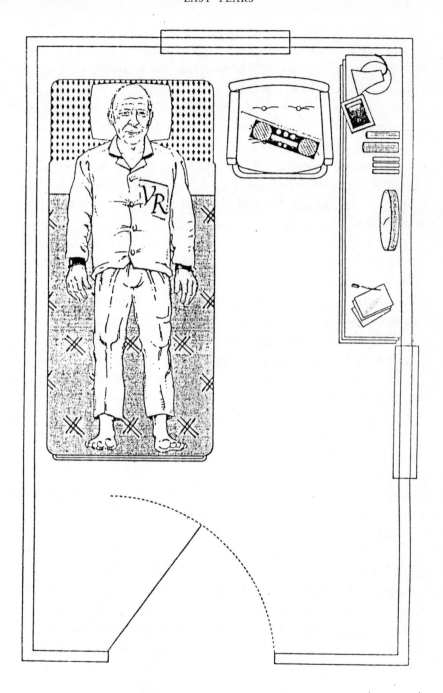

Figure 6
The MRC's HUMAN CALORIMETER

other lowering dishes. But when staying with the Rothschilds in Cambridge I could not fail to notice how, on his way out of breakfast, he would with artful absent-mindedness gobble up the three remaining sausages on the sideboard.

By October 1989 he had lost nearly three stone in weight; perhaps by a disciplined regime, but more likely, his friends feared, through the decline of a hard-driven physique. Colleagues at New Court noticed that his memory was no longer reliable. Others shared my experience of receiving a packet of letters to be used in his biography which he had earlier lent me and which I had returned to him only a month before.

The clouds, however, could swiftly roll away. He was in exuberant spirits when I dined with him and Tess just before Christmas at a somewhat pretentious restaurant. He ordered a tinsel-festooned flower arrangement to be removed from the table, gave minute instructions about the cooking of this dish and that (none of which seemed to have penetrated to the kitchen), waved away a propitiatory leather-bound pocket diary stamped with a golden R (I appropriated it). At ease in each of the two cultures, he castigated the Foreign Office for needlessly forbidding on health grounds the use at its overseas missions of aluminium pots and pans; then lacerated the judges of a well-known literary prize for having withheld it from a writer whom he admired. That was Victor's way: to leave the field strewn with corpses.

On the evening of 20 March 1990, while watching the television news with Tess at the flat in St James's Place, he suffered a sudden heart attack and died.

There was no surprise among the initiated that Victor had so arranged his finances as to leave an estate of only £270,410 net. Rich testators often outmanoeuvre the tax inspector. What did dismay family and friends was the deliberate omission from his Will of the son and two daughters of his first unhappy marriage. It is true that in his lifetime he had settled varying amounts of money and property on the children of both marriages; and that Jacob had also inherited a large part of Dollie's estate of £93 million. Sarah and Miranda, however, were not at all well off, even by non-

Rothschild standards, and were now to suffer public humiliation, too.

Both in earlier settlements and under the Will, the principal ben-eficiaries were Tess and her son Amschel; she left some £4 million at her death in May 1996 and Amschel £18 million at his death a few weeks later. Tess had also been appointed an executor of the Will. In a well-meant gesture to soften Victor's exclusion of her three stepchildren, she gave each a memento purporting to have been chosen by him. For Jacob there was the modern replica of a Treasury inkstand given to Victor after he had presided over the Royal Commission on Gambling. Sarah received a gold-mounted agate *nécessaire* or workbox bearing the motto '*L'Espoir de ta fidelité fait ma seul felicité*'. Miranda was assigned a clock that stood on the desk of her father's office. A cynic may smile at the choice of these gewgaws from the possessions of a Croesus; but Tess did not have that sort of mind and doubtless proffered them in good faith.

Victor's friends had received many imaginative presents while he lived; two alone were remembered in his Will. For William Waldegrave there was a pair of red ministerial despatch boxes said to have belonged to Disraeli; as Victor's grandfather had been Dizzy's executor, the attribution was plausible. Rumour had it that Waldegrave would find one or both stuffed with banknotes. Neither, however, yielded so much as a Suez Canal Company share certificate.

The only other beneficiary was Marcus Sieff, to whom Victor bequeathed a pair of decanters, each large enough to hold a magnum. I had last seen them a few years earlier in Herschel Road filled with Château Lafite 1870 at a birthday party for Dadie Rylands. He, however, to his dismay, received no parting mark of affection.

Victor left instructions that his remains were to be buried next to those of Nathan Mayer Rothschild, the founder of the English branch of the family, in a Jewish cemetery in the East End of London disused since 1858. To reopen its gates, where his great-great-grandfather had been buried in 1836, involved him in several years of negotiation with authorities as various as the Privy

Council, which made the necessary Order on 8 February 1984; the Beth Din, or rabbinic court; and Tower Hamlets Borough Council. He could also count on the guidance of William Waldegrave, by then Minister of State for the Environment. It was an administrative feat requiring the same grasp of detail that he had brought to more festive occasions, such as the Roxburghe Club dinner in Trinity or the tea party for Margaret Thatcher at New Court.

For Victor, New Court was as much a shrine to its founder as a counting house; with what pride he displayed the relics of the dynasty in its corridors. He paid another tribute to NM in *The Shadow of a Great Man*, depicting those qualities of his ancestor he most admired and perhaps saw reflected in his own life: mental agility, industry and patriotism. The monograph made scarcely any mention, however, of NM's having been a Jew.

His desire to mingle his earthly dust with that of his ancestor was similarly accompanied by emphatic instructions that the religious rites should be of the simplest, lasting no more than ten minutes and including neither psalms nor hymns. That posthumous gesture was both defiant and unexpected, for in his last years he had seemed more reconciled to the traditions of Judaism. He ensured that his newly built retirement cottage at Rushbrooke bore a *mezuzah* on its doorpost: a small parchment scroll inscribed in Hebrew with passages from *Deuteronomy*, revered by the Orthodox as a permanent blessing on the house. Even more striking by a man who shunned any display of emotion in public was his final choice on the popular radio programme *Desert Island Discs*: the rendering by a cantor of that melancholy Jewish lament from Psalm 137, 'By the waters of Babylon we sat down and wept'. He had included it, he explained, 'to remind me that I am what I am'.

Victor also insisted that his funeral should exclude any opportunity for a demonstrative farewell or recognition of his achievements. NM's cortège to the same cemetery in 1836 had consisted of seventy-five carriages that took fifteen minutes to pass any point along a route lined with mourners. Victor's remains were carried to the graveyard in secrecy, attended by a handful of kinsmen.

Those dismayed by Victor's perfunctory funeral were reassured

At the Court at Buckingham Palace

THE 8th DAY OF FEBRUARY 1984

PRESENT,

THE QUEEN'S MOST EXCELLENT MAJESTY
IN COUNCIL

Whereas by the Burial Act 1855 it was amongst other things enacted that it should be lawful for Her Majesty, by and with the advice of Her Privy Council, from time to time to vary any Order in Council made under any of the Acts recited in the said Act, as to Her Majesty, with such advice aforesaid, might seem fit:

And whereas an Order in Council was made on the 21st day of May 1855 (hereinafter referred to as "the principal Order") directing the discontinuance of burials in the New Synagogue Jewish Burial-ground (now known as the Jewish Cemetery at Brady Street, Whitechapel, in the London Borough of Tower Hamlets);

And whereas it seems fit to Her Majesty, by and with the advice of Her Privy Council, that the principal Order should be varied;

Now, therefore, Her Majesty, by and with the said advice, is pleased to order, and it is hereby ordered, that notwithstanding anything in the principal Order, the burial may be allowed in the said Cemetery, at his decease, of the body of Nathan Mayer Victor, Baron Rothschild, G.B.E., G.M., F.R.S., subject to the condition that the coffin containing the body shall be interred in a vault having walls, lined throughout with impermeable material, extending to a depth of not less than two feet below the level of the adjoining ground and, after the interment, filled with earth and surmounted by a stone slab hermetically cemented to the vault; and provided further that nothing in this Order shall be construed as authorising the disturbance of any laterally adjacent grave, or of human remains heretofore interred in the said Cemetery.

N. E. Leigh

Printed in England for Her Majesty's Stationery Office by Bemrose Printing, Confidential and Information Products, Derby. (Dd. 5053400) (3420017) 5903-2

(1-1-25)

by the elaborate memorial service arranged by the family in the West London Synagogue some weeks later. Three prime ministers and a large part of the Establishment echoed the passage from *Ecclesiasticus* that begins, 'Let us now praise famous men'. A wealth of sacred music was leavened by a few bars of a tape by Victor's beloved pianist Art Tatum, the man with three extra fingers.

There were several addresses. Lord Swann FRS, who had worked with Victor at a marine biological station on the Clyde estuary, described in all too vivid detail how they had induced multitudes of sea urchins to impregnate the objects of their desire with spermatozoa under photographic scrutiny: a scientific tour de force that left some of the congregation feeling faint.

William Waldegrave roamed confidently through Victor's life with the affection and humour of a colleague, a confidant and a surrogate son. 'He was a Rothschild,' Waldegrave proclaimed, 'and a glory to that name.'

It was left to Lennie Hoffmann, the only Jewish eulogist of the three, to guide Victor back into the Jewish fold. He did not disguise his friend's antipathy to beliefs and ritual, but commended his essentially Jewish regard for intellect and learning. Above all, he insisted, Victor had never lost touch with his roots:

> He was proud of being Jewish rather in the way Disraeli was; he saw the romantic and tragic history of the Jews as conferring upon them a natural aristocratic lineage. And he regarded the princely role which his family have played among the Jewish people as a source of both pride and responsibility.

Thus by a few deft words did the crown of thorns that in life had long encumbered Victor's consciousness become in death the victor's garland.

Source Notes

Each reference to a quotation or allusion consists of a catch-phrase for identification of the subject, the surname of the author, the title of the book or article, the volume number (where necessary) and the page. The full name of the author (or editor) of the book, the title, the publisher and the date of publication are listed alphabetically under the author's surname in BIBLIOGRAPHY.

Abbreviations

When there are several quotations from the same book I have sometimes abbreviated the title. Thus Victor Rothschild's *Meditations of a Broomstick* becomes simply *Meditations*.

Frequently quoted names in the source notes are also abbreviated. Victor Rothschild becomes VR. Other members of the family are referred to by their first names or sobriquets: Natty for the 1st Lord Rothschild, Walter for the 2nd Lord Rothschild, Tess for Victor's second wife Teresa, Jacob for Victor's elder son, Tory for Victor's daughter Victoria. All can be found in the family tree (pp. xvi–xvii). I have similarly abbreviated references to one or two of Victor's intimates: Duff for Duff Cooper and Dadie for George Rylands.

The word 'Archives' in a source reference indicated that the letter quoted or alluded to comes from the archives of N.M.Rothschild & Sons Ltd in New Court, London.

I have generally applied the formula 'VR to author, 6 November 1982' to letters and conversations alike.

Introduction

p.1 line 21 Grooves of change. Tennyson. *Locksley Hall.* 181.
p.2 line 2 Capital of £20,000. Buxton. *Memoirs.* 160–161.
line 26 My own business. Lucien Wolf. *Essays in Jewish History.* 283–284.
line 34 Prince Pückler Muskau. *Gentleman's Magazine.* November 1871. 734.

p.3   line 2   Very amusing. Buxton. *Op.cit.* 290.

p.4   line 8   Ancestor's probity. VR. *Shadow of a Great Man. Passim.*

      line 27   Deathbed transactions. Archives. c/1/57–68.

      line 30   Will. Ferguson. *The World's Banker.* 323.

p.5   line 8   Anthony's baronetcy. Hannah to Lionel [ND]. Archives. 109/58/1.

      line 26   He can't take his seat. Greville. *Memoirs.* 13 July 1847. v. 460.

p.6   line 11   Paul Veronese. Disraeli to Charlotte. 2 January 1867. Archives. c/2/6.

      line 18   To speak with him. Lionel to Charlotte. 16 July 1848. Archives. c/4/49.

      line 21   Hypocrisy. Natty to Lionel. [ND] Archives. c/3/90.

p.7   line 29   Dustbin of history. Monypenny & Buckle. *Disraeli.* v. 446.

p.8   line 11   Transaction. VR. *You have it, Madam. Passim.*

      line 22   All tailors. Nat to Mayer. 21 Nov 1840. Archives. 104/0/129.

      line 29   Minnows escape. *Jewish Chronicle.* 5 October 1877.

p.9   line 5   Tottenham Court Road. Eva Lady Rosebery to author. Mentmore, 24 November 1974.

      line 15   Hold something. Everard Primrose to Mary Ponsonby. 20 December 1874. *Mary Ponsonby.* 154.

      line 25   Three panelled rooms. Dorothy de Rothschild. *Waddesdon Manor.* 28.

      line 34   Preferable to this. Morrell. *Early Memories* (1909). 170.

p.10   line 5   Waddesdon kitchens. Dorothy de Rothschild. *Op.cit.* 49.

      line 19   Civil and attentive. Hannah to Charlotte. 22 November 1841. Archives. c/1/14.

      line 28   Bowled at legs. Natty to Lionel [ND]. *Ibid.* c/3/133.

      line 28   Loser at whist. *Ibid.* c/3/93.

      line 29   Bullying the weak. *Ibid.* c/3/117.

      line 32   Master of the Horse. *Ibid.* c/3/8.

      line 36   Madingley. *Ibid.* c/3/8.

p.11   line 8   Ripened early. Davis. *The English Rothschilds.* 122.

      line 13   Vive l'Empereur. Goncourt. *Journal.* 21 December 1862. v. 232.

      line 20   Guessing. Lionel to Leo. 25 May 1867. Archives. c/4/325.

      line 22   Bed at six. *Ibid.* 29 May 1867. c/4/326.

      line 27   Old silver things. *Ibid.* 3 November 1863. c/4/328.

      line 29   Fine old plate. *Ibid* [ND]. c/4/348.

p.12   line 3   We have decided. Miriam. *Dear Lord Rothschild.* 12.

      line 17   Sign a cheque. Palin. *Rothschild Relish.* 43.

      line 23   Required to resign. Morton. *The Rothschilds.* 164.

      line 29   Proportion of things. Constance, Lady Battersea. *Reminiscences.* 42.

      line 33   Ayer's dismissal. Ayer. *Part of My Life.* 16–17.

p.13   line 6   Affronted Emma. Miriam. *Op.cit.* 11.

      line 16   Red and yellow. Gaucher. *Les Jardins de la Fortune.* 132.

      line 23   Poussins Haltonnais. Cornwallis-West. 135.

      line 27   Future Messiah. Monypenny & Buckle. *Op.cit.* II 333.

line 35 Young man's salary. Palin. *Op.cit.* 7.

p.14 line 2 Water and glass. 26 April 1962.

line 7 The Prime Ministers. Jolliffe. *Raymond Asquith.* 105,111.

line 11 'Welcome as ever?' Hart-Davis. *Cartoons of Max Beerbohm.* 37.

line 21 Too many Rothschilds. Disraeli to Leo. 11 December 1880.

p.15 line 7 To be made a peer. Natty to Lionel. 28 January 1863. Archives. c/3/36.

line 11 Could not consent. Queen Victoria to Earl Granville. 22 August 1869. Guedalla (Ed.). *The Queen and Mr Gladstone.* 198.

line 20 Democratic camp. Granville to Queen Victoria. 23 August 1869. *Ibid.* 199–200.

line 23 Harm instead of good. Queen Victoria to Granville. 24 August 1869. *Ibid.*

line 37 Weather and influence. Queen Victoria to Gladstone. 1 November 1869. *Ibid.* 207.

p.16 line 22 From the menu. Miriam. *Op.cit.* 29.

line 28 Half the county. Prince of Wales to Carrington. 10 May 1889. Lincolnshire Papers.

p.17 line 18 Growing consternation. Crawford. *The Crawford Papers.* 22 July 1939. 509.

line 21 Sandhurst. W.S. Churchill to Lady Randolph Churchill. 21 October [1893]. *Churchill CV. I. i.* 422.

line 26 Annual fish bill. Miriam. *Op.cit.* 30.

line 29 Game pie. *Ibid.* 49.

p.18 line 6 Owed the bank £66, 902. Foster. *Lord Randolph Churchill.* 394.

line 13 Battleship from Brazil. Miriam. *Op.cit.* 42. (One of the few letters from Lord Rothschild's papers to have survived destruction, having been given to his son Charles for his autograph album).

line 25 Persecution of the Jews. Lee. *King Edward VII.* II. 594–595.

line 29 Mortgage on Sandringham. Allfrey. *Edward VII and his Jewish Court.* 191.

p.19 line 2 Distinction of this kind. Natty to Lionel. [ND]. Archives. c/3/82.

line 22 To sit in judgement. Churchill. *W S Churchill.* II. 82.

p.20 line 3 Found it fun. Miriam. *Op.cit.* 50.

line 10 No questions asked. Haldane. *Autobiography.* 163.

line 12 One year's salary. Palin. *Op.cit.* 39.

line 20 Make you a partner. VR to author. 23 November 1989.

line 23 Large transactions. Nevill. *My Own Times.* 170.

line 27 Cause had been traced. Goncourt. *Op.cit.* 9 June 1879. xii. 27.

line 33 Too large to float. VR. Speech to Weizmann Institute. *The Times,* 22 November 1968.

p.21 line 1 Floating batteries. Natty to Lionel [1862] Archives. c/3/68.

line 7 Work it out. Palin. *Op.cit.* 102.

p.22 line 19 Whores and jockeys. Edmund de Rothschild. *A Gilt-edged life.* 85.

line 31 Sympathetic biography. Miriam. *Dear Lord Rothschild: Birds, Butterflies and History.* She also wrote a privately printed memoir of her father, Nathaniel Charles Rothschild, known as Charles. The present author is much idebted to both volumes.

p.24 line 24 Xendpsylla Cheopis. Miriam. *Nathaniel Charles Rothschild.* 9.

line 33 Skill in taxidermy. Jolliffe. *Raymond Asquith.* Letter dated 22 March 1903. 103.

p.25 line 2 Lost an ear. Miriam. *Dear Lord Rothschild.* 98.

Chapter 1 – Youth

p.26 line 17 Any scientist. VR. *Meditations.* 11.

line 13 Stoatly different. Miriam. *N C Rothschild.* 10.

p.27 line 11 High Street. Miriam. *Dear Lord R.* 291.

line 24 Railway line. VR. *Meditations.* 12.

line 31 'Dirty Little Jew'. *Ibid.* 13.

p.28 line 3 Schoolboy letters. 5 October 1919 – 5 December 1920. Tess Rothschild's Papers.

line 18 Spreading germs. Miriam to author.

line 28 Hunters and the hunted. Miriam. *Op.cit.* 90.

line 34 Mawkish forgiveness. *Ibid.* 91.

line 15 Significant association. Tyerman. *A History of Harrow School.* 463.

line 29 More than unhelpful. *Ibid.* 463–64.

p.30 line 3 Madness and suicide. Miriam to author.

line 13 Particular circumstances. VR. *Meditations.* 13.

line 37 From then onwards. *Ibid.* 14.

p.31 line 3 Put on weight. Sir Anthony Lambert to author. 3 May 1991.

line 15 Runnymede. Tyerman. *Op.cit.* 217.

line 32 Most destructive. Miriam to author.

line 36 Stay the course. VR. *Meditations.* 14–15.

p.32 line 11 Husband's successors. Miriam. *Dear Lord R.* 18, 288.

line 13 Family houses. Miriam to author.

line 22 Lavatory door. VR. *Meditations.* 14.

line 25 Never got one. *Ibid.* 12.

p.33 line 13 Learnt his cricket. *The Times.* 29 August 1929.

line 30 Designs on him. Miriam to author.

p.34 line 7 He had gone. Tyerman. *Op.cit.* 510.

line 28 Two teams of Trinity men. Rylands to author. 24 March 1991.

p.35 line 5 Hands in your pockets. VR. *Meditations.* 17.

line 18 Noisy disturbance. H.A. Hollond to VR. [ND] 1932.

p.36 line 10 Gracefully puritanical. David Newsome. *On the Edge of Paradise.* 360.

line 26 Flanks of a doe. Woolf. *A Room of One's Own.* 1996 edition. 10.

p.37 line 6 Forty-nine minutes. Marcus Sieff to author. 31 July 1990.

line 25 With his winnings. VR to author. 13 May 1989.

p.38 line 13 Where it is needed. VR. *Meditations*. 17.
    line 35 Doubled his money. VR to author. 14 August 1987.
p.39 line 7 Pound of butter. VR to author. *Ibid.*
    line 23 Admirable clarity. VR to author. 14 September 1979.
    line 26 Tidied up. Sir Steven Runciman to author. 21 November 1988.
p.40 line 5 Fellowship last night. VR. *Meditations*. 22.
    line 15 King George V and frogs' eggs. VR to author. 15 May 1988.
p.41 line 4 That impression. H. A. Hollond to VR. 24 September 1948.
    line 20 After some elections. *Ibid.* 27 September 1948.
    line 31 Affectionate verdict. VR to author. 12 December 1989.
    line 36 Popular board game. *Ibid.*
p.42 line 7 Another great man. VR. *Meditations*. 19.
    line 21 Cambridge friends. *Ibid.* 16.
p.43 line 6 Retainer. Miriam to author; Isaiah Berlin to author, 1 April 1989.
    line 16 Pornographic literature. Hearnden. *A Life of Robert Birley.* 65 – 66.
p.44 line 18 Homosexual and Communist. Rees. *Chapter of Accidents.* 110–11.
    line 27 Entirely lacking. *Ibid.* 114.
p.45 line 2 Fallen angel. Straight. *After Long Silence.* 94.
    line 17 Will be for me. Burgess to Churchill. 2 October 1938. Gilbert. *WSC.* CV v. 3. 1193–6.
    line 31 Not political. VR. *Meditations*. 16.
p.46 line 12 Appalling news. VR. *Random Variables.* 203.
p.47 line 18 Unnecessary and irrelevant. *Ibid.* 203–04.
    line 26 In his veins. Miriam to author.
p.48 line 1 Sold for £192,500. VR. *Meditations*. 204: author's correspondence with VR, Sir Hugh Leggatt and Professor Michael Jaffe.
    line 27 Soviet spies. Costello. *Mask of Treachery.* 189.
p.49 line 14 Committed. Rees. *Op.cit.* 116.
    line 25 Room above. Straight. *Op.cit.* 145.
p.50 line 19 Just as delightful. VR to Maynard Keynes. [1934] Skidelsky. II. 516.
    line 26 Suffer any indignity. Trevor-Roper. *The Philby Affair.* 21.
p.51 line 3 Member of the C.P. *Sunday Telegraph.* 20 June 1991.
    line 13 In those days. Rupert Allason to author. 23 November 1993.
    line 32 Supportive of Communism. Anon to author. 24 March 1994.

Chapter 2 – Marriage

p.52 line 18 On the sofa. 7 November 1931. This and subsequent extracts from the diary of Barbara Hutchinson, whom Victor married in 1933, are reproduced by permission of her elder daughter, Sarah Daniel.
p.53 line 3 Being treated. *Ibid.* 12 March 1932.
    line 15 Pre-war perfection. *Ibid.* 22 June 1932.
p.54 line 54 Crystallised Pru. Miriam to author.
    line 22 Did not dine together. Barbara's diary. 16 November 1931.

line 25 Might have a stroke. Jack (later Lord) Donaldson's diary. 15 February 1933.

p.55 line 9 Nice and limp. Barbara's diary. 1 April 1932.

line 12 Talking of a saint. Jacob Rothschild to author. 7 March 1992.

p.56 line 6 Sovereign. VR. *Shadow of a Great Man.* 8.

line 28 Run or two. VR to author. 13 May 1989.

p.58 line 3 Without a pang. Hinks. *Journal.* 17 April 1937. 35.

line 12 Height of footmen. Madan. *Notebooks.* 92.

line 14 Quite elated. *The Times.* 23 April 1937.

line 34 On your dividends. VR to author. 6 November 1982.

line 37 Pol Roger 1921. VR to WSC. 16 March 1937. Gilbert. *WSC* CV.v. iii. 624–25.

p.59 line 16 Feelings of other Jews. VR to Diana Cooper. 23 September 1952.

p.60 line 16 That country. VR. Speech at Mansion House. 9 December 1938.

line 25 Decisions. VR. Speech. 27 October 1938.

p.61 line 10 We know nothing. Neville Chamberlain. *The Times.* 28 September 1938.

line 26 Times of distress. Message from Pope Pius XI. 9 December 1938.

line 36 Stilton cheese. Cardinal Hinsley to VR. 21 December 1938.

p.62 line 22 Like Nazi Germany. *News Chronicle.* 9 August 1934.

line 24 Age of change. Miriam to author. 27 June 1999.

line 33 You are different. VR to author (conversation). 4 September 1985.

line 37 Liberal-minded. *Ibid.* (letter) 17 September 1985.

p.63 line 7 Real Christian. Dorothy de R to author. 16 March 1987.

line 18 Ben Gurion and de Gaulle. Isaiah Berlin to author. 21 December 1985.

Chapter 3 – War

p.64 line 14 In the country. Duff to VR. 5 October 1938.

line 37 Private meeting. Theodore C. Achilles, State Department, Washington, to VR. 2 March 1939.

p.65 line 17 Just fifty. VR. *Meditations* 16.

line 11 Chemical warfare. Sir Henry Dale to VR. 3 November 1939.

line 27 Wise selection. Masterman. *On the Chariot Wheel.* 212.

line 35 Prima donnas. Sir Dick White to author. 29 June 1991.

p.66 line 23 Retreating Germans. Much of this account of VR's work in counter-sabotage comes from MI5 file KV4/23, now in Public Record Office, supplemented by author's personal interviews and correspondence.

p.67 line 33 Technical man. VR to author. 18 October 1989.

p.68 line 6 Well-padded armchair. VR talk to Press Club, London. 7 September 1997.

p.69 line 11 All safe now. Transcript reproduced in *Meditations.* 29–32.

line 16 To keep them sweet. VR to Duff. 17 April 1944.
line 27 External correspondence. *DNB* 1961–70.
p.70 line 17 Civil Service life. VR to Duff. 17 April 1944.
line 28 Independent witnesses. *Ibid.* 28 February 1944.
p.71 line 17 The whole business. VR to J P Hudson. 12 April 1944.
line 23 Nervous system. Diana Cooper to Duff. 4 April 1944. *Double Fire.* 307.
line 27 Oranges. VR to author. 14 March 1981.
p.72 line 11 To take offence. *Ibid.* 17 October 1989.
line 22 Two subordinates. VR to Duff. 17 April 1944.
line 30 Judy Montagu. Clementine Churchill to VR. 1 February 1944.
p.73 line 17 Great success. VR to Duff. 28 February 1944.
p.74 line 5 Original twelve. VR. *Meditations.* 25–26.
line 22 To the ranks. Duff to VR. 16 February 1944.
line 25 Piles of rubble. VR to Duff. 28 February 1944.
line 30 Chelsea flat. Sir Dick White to author. 29 January 1991.
p.75 line 12 As good as ever. VR to Duff. 17 April 1944.
line 18 Eggs and olive oil. Waugh. *Unconditional Surrender.* 20.
line 20 Invariable reply. William Waldegrave to author.
line 28 Wine cellar. Herbert Hart to Jenifer Hart. ND [1944].
p.76 line 11 Brown paper. Miriam to author.
line 21 Not to visit again. VR to Duff. 30 March 1944.
line 30 Sent empty away. *Ibid.* 23 August 1944.
p.77 line 2 Camouflage colours. Solly Zuckerman to author. 11 July 1992.
line 14 Racecourse. Lord Dalmeny to author. 4 June 1992.
line 31 Ailment. Sir Stuart Hampshire to author. 29 November 1991.
p.78 line 17 Fly home unscathed. VR to author. 27 April 1989.
line 25 Her brother. Miriam to author. 6 April 1991.
p.79 line 2 Poles and residues. VR. *Meditations.* 25.
line 5 Frightfully hard. Natty to Lionel [ND]. Archives. c/3/110–11.
line 12 Bored to distraction. VR to Duff. 30 March 1944.
line 20 Recruit staff. VR to Woolton. 14 December 1944; Woolton to VR. 17 December 1944.
line 23 Onion marmalade. VR to Duff. 7 February 1944.
line 35 Own language. *Ibid.* 23 August 1944.
p.80 line 17 Psychological laboratory. VR. *Random Variables.* 63.
line 37 Co-operation. *Daily Telegraph.* 13 April 1946.
p.81 line 5 Nor a Christian. John Julius Norwich to author. 15 July 1990.
line 17 Little luxuries. Cahen d'Anvers. *Baboushka Remembers.* 241–42.
line 27 Bicycle. Liliane de R to author. 9 June 1989.
p.82 line 17 Iron Cross. VR to author. 12 December 1989.
line 37 Acquitted. *Ibid.* 13 December 1989.
p.83 line 14 Think it over. Duff to VR. 15 August 1944.
line 26 Mitterrand. Guy de Rothschild. *The Whims of Fortune.* 272.
line 28 Rejected appointment. Duff to VR. 15 August 1944.

p.84 line 35 Dictating memoranda. Muggeridge. *Chronicles of Wasted Time*. Vol 2. *The Infernal Grove*. 222.

p.85 line 2 Bullet holes. VR to author. 16 April 1975.

line 32 Britain stood alone. Muggeridge. *Op.cit.* 106–07.

p.86 line 12 Letter box. Bower. *The Perfect English Spy*. 63.

line 22 Total poppycock. C. Harmer to author. 31 March 1995.

p.87 line 37 As all endings are. Muggeridge. *Op.cit.* 215.

p.88 line 18 As themselves. Rees. *Op.cit.* 154–55.

line 37 Possibilities of peace. *Ibid.* 155.

p.89 line 4 Professional. VR to author. 25 July 1984.

line 21 All four. Memoranda by VR on 5 Bentinck Street. 21 January 1987.

p.90 line 3 Calm and gaiety. Drogheda. *Double Harness*. 67–68,

line 4 Disintegrates. Miriam to author.

line 6 Wronged. Rylands to author. 11 November 1990.

line 19 Forgotten myself. Hodgkin. *Chance and Design*. 308.

line 24 Humdrum existence. *Ibid.* 253.

line 31 Written. VR. *Meditations*. 20.

line 32 Intellectual Aristocracy. Annan. *Studies in Social History*. 241–287.

p.91 line 14 Cold and damp. Hodgkin. *Op.cit.* 260.

line 22 Each night. Hodgkin to author. 11 November 1990.

line 24 Tahitian girl. Hodgkin. *Op.cit.* 125.

line 26 Quaker upbringing. *Ibid.* 70.

line 31 My old flame. *Ibid.* 259.

line 36 Newspaper. VR to author. 18 October 1989.

p.93 line 4 Land or money. *Daily Telegraph*. 21 March 1961.

Chapter 4 – Collector

p.94 line 5 To start collecting. VR to author. 14 August 1987.

line 11 Second handle. Illustrated in Miriam, *Dear Lord R*, between pages 232 and 233.

line 17 Builds too small. Dorothy de R. *Op.cit.* 20.

line 21 Giant tortoises. Miriam. *Op.cit.* 149.

line 22 The Louvre. *Ibid.* 110.

p.95 line 1 Second time. Henri de R. Unpublished memoirs of Arthur de R.

line 3 1500 learned papers. Miriam. *Op.cit.* 121 and *Passim*.

line 5 Live parakeets. *Ibid.* 232.

line 19 Decadent. VR to author. 18 October 1989.

line 25 Total of £1.44 million. Christie's Sale. 20 November 2001.

line 28 Frankfurt branch. Christie's Sale. 30 June 1982.

p.96 line 2 David and Heffer. *Rothschild Library*. ix.

line 7 Learned from me. Rylands to VR. 26 June 1983.

line 13 Beneficiary. Munby. *Phillipps Studies*. V. 99.

line 16 Swift books and manuscripts. *Ibid.*

line 21 Customers. Wolf. *Rosenbach.* 394.

line 26 Repentance. *Ibid.* 400.

line 29 33,000 dollars. *Ibid.* 457

line 34 Edward Gibbon's Library. A.R.C. Carter. *Daily Telegraph.* 21 December 1934.

line 37 Revived its fortunes. Wolf. *Op.cit.* 445.

p.97 line 10 Patient laying. Carter. *Taste and Technique.* 65.

line 26 No monetary dividend. VR. *Random Variables.* 53–55.

line 30 Gabriel Wells. VR. *The History of Tom Jones.* I. *et seq.*

line 37 29,000 dollars. Wolf. *Op.cit.* 310.

p.98 line 30 Cheque for £3,500. VR. *Tom Jones.* 4.

line 35 Two identical cheques. *Ibid.* 73.

p.99 line 22 Set of volumes. *Ibid.* 10.

p.100 line 14 St John Hutchinson. VR to author. 2 December 1976.

p.101 line 23 Forger's art. VR. *Random Variables.* 52.

line 33 Wrapping paper. Robert S. Pirie to author. 4 February 1992.

p.102 line 14 Previous cases. Lord Gardiner to VR. 1 April 1970.

line 25 Getty Museum. Author. *Sunday Telegraph.* 7 July 1991.

p.103 line 5 Catalogue of my library. VR to Duff Cooper. 25 April 1946.

line 22 Eighteenth-century books. Waldegrave. Memorial address. 15 May 1990.

line 25 Vintage flower show. David Holland. *Book Collector.* 1955. 29.

line 30 Reynolds to Garrick. *Ibid.* 31.

p.104 line 17 The Poussin. VR to author. Memorandum. Undated.

line 20 In his Will. Rylands to author. 11 November 1990.

p.105 line 6 Sufficient interest. VR to Robert S. Pirie. 4 May 1988.

line 10 Man or beast. *Quo* Rhodes James. *Rosebery.* 212.

p.106 line 28 Wren library. VR. *Random Variables.* 21.

p.107 line 8 Respect and affection. VR to Trevelyan. 1 October 1948.

line 10 Bitter regrets. VR to author. 16 April 1975.

line 31 Sixteen years. VR. *Open Letter.* 10 August 1985.

p.108 line 30 Unimportant manuscript. VR to author. 5 December 1989.

p.109 line 9 In his words. *Ibid.*

line 24 What he hears. VR. *Rylands.* 7.

line 31 Infinity. VR to Rylands. 9 October 1987.

line 34 Hock-loving epicene. VR. *Open Letter.* 13.

Chapter 5 – Post-War World

p.111 line 4 Always be here. Duff to VR. 15 August 1946.

line 7 Red Tess. Harry, 6th Earl of Rosebery, for instance. VR to author. 15 May 1988.

p.112 line 8 Competition, *et seq.* Tess to author. 3 April 1991.

line 21 Cold fire. Straight. *Op.cit.* 82.

line 32 Leicester University. Nöel Annan to author. 4 June 1990.

p.113 line 20 London house. Tess to author. 3 April 1991.

line 21 In one room. *Daily Express.* 15 August 1946.

line 26 Labour party. *The Times.* 12 November 1945.

line 29 Individualistic views. Miriam. *Dear Lord R.* 225.

line 34 Arouse criticism. Duff to VR. 15 October 1946.

p.114 line 2 Shared with Tess. VR to Duff. 28 February 1944, 17 April 1944.

line 17 On the Government. VR. Interview. *Reynolds News.* 20 January 1948.

p.115 line 5 He would be welcome. *Ibid.*

line 23 More scientific and modern. *Ibid.*

line 31 Pasteurisation of milk. House of Lords. 10 April 1946.

p.116 line 2 Killed twice every year. VR to Duff. 25 April 1946.

line 5 Palpitating interest. Duff to VR. 20 May 1946.

line 22 Overruled Duff. VR to Duff. 9 October 1946; Duff to VR. 15 October 1946.

line 29 Stern Gang. House of Lords. 21 July 1946.

line 34 Minister's neck. VR to Duff. 18 Feb 1947.

line 37 Shyness and shame. Waugh. *Diary.* 7 January 1948.

p.117 line 16 Expenditure *et seq.* Wood. *The Groundnuts Affair.* Thomas. *John Strachey.*

p.118 line 10 Unavailable. Daily Telegraph. 22 November 1948.

line 23 Concerns myself. VR to Duff. 23 May 1949.

p.119 line 8 In the trade. Surtees. *Hillingdon Hall.* (1844, reprinted 1921). 249.

line 20 30 Shillings. VR to author. 25 June 1983.

line 24 Lost in handling. Miriam. *Op.cit.* 211.

line 30 Farm operations. VR to author. 22 August 1978.

line 35 Exclaimed. *Ibid.* 5 December 1985.

p.120 line 16 Fastidious customer. Lord Rayner to author. 10 November 1992.

line 31 Became legal. Tess to author. 20 November 1991.

p.121 line 13 The pigman. VR. Lecture. Long Ashton Research Station. 1953.

line 21 Mouldy peanuts. Sir Gordon Cox to author. 2 December 1992.

line 25 Experience and judgement. *Ibid.* 2 December 1992.

p.122 line 3 Ministry of Agriculture. Zuckerman. *Monkeys.* 162.

line 10 Strong swimmer. VR. *Meditations.* 24.

line 14 Act of 1956. Cox to author. 2 December 1992.

line 30 Would affect. *Ibid.*

p.123 line 7 Destroy or harm. *Ibid.*

line 28 Food in peacetime. VR lecture. 1953.

line 34 Make a killing. VR to author. 11 August 1980.

p.124 line 18 Government support. VR. *The Times.* 15 November 1974.

line 20 Levied on farms. Alister Sutherland. *The Times.* 5 October 1979.

line 23 Academic economists. VR. *The Times.* 10 October 1979.

line 26 Cambridge laboratory. 'Desert Island Discs'. 7 July 1984.

line 34 Taken seriously. *Ibid.*

p.125 line 11 Disproportionately. VR to author. 1 February 1989.

line 21 Spermatozoa. VR. *Meditations.* 23.

p.126 line 8 Spermatozoon. VR to author. 13 April 1989.

line 12 A delicacy. Lady Anne Tree to author. August 1995.

line 22 In Cambridge. Professor John Davenport to author. 8 October 1994.

line 29 A Love Story. Duff to VR. 21 April 1952.

p.128 line 3 Why cubical? VR to Duff. 8 May 1952.

line 5 Rejected. Duff to VR. 10 May 1952.

line 11 Genetic information. VR to author. 13 April 1989.

line 14 Spider and leech. VR. *Scientific American.* November 1956.

line 25 Whore's egg. VR. *A Classification of Living Animals.* vii.

p.129 line 8 Solved her problem. VR. *Meditations.* 23.

line 25 Rich amateur. Miriam. *Op.cit.* 132.

line 27 Sir Roy Lankester. *Ibid.* 228, 229.

line 30 Mad genius. *Ibid.* 214.

p.130 line 3 Victor's sister. Miriam to author. 6 April 1991.

line 5 Agility. *Ibid.*

line 13 Turned him down. VR to author. 22 June 1974.

line 29 Election. Lord Salisbury to VR. 24 March 1971.

p.131 line 2 When to stop. VR. *Meditations.* 23–24.

line 29 Grew with the years. Noël Annan to author. 18 November 1991.

Chapter 6 – Well-ordered Life

p.132 line 16 Midnight celebrations. Jenkins. *European Diary.* 31 December 1977. 193.

line 20 Full of bombs. Ziegler. *Diana Cooper.* 220.

p.133 line 2 Meals in the garden. *Ibid.* 221.

line 4 In the family. Sarah to author.

line 15 Manservant. Duff to VR. 29 November 1951.

line 23 Remained untasted. Daniel. *Favourite Recipes.* 5 *et seq.*

p.134 line 24 Joan of Arc. Liliane de R to author. 9 June 1989.

line 30 Nevile's Court. 22 June 1964. VR to author. 30 May 1989.

line 32 Humble potato dish. Pommes Victor: small roast potatoes, each half-dipped in glaze.

line 34 North Sea gas. VR. *Risk.* 16.

p.135 line 2 Ambrosial dish. VR to author. 14 August 1987.

line 10 Sole Murat. HM Queen Elizabeth the Queen Mother to VR. 11 December 1977.

line 21 To give one's loader. Harold Macmillan. 15 December 1983.

line 36 Body or mind. Duff to VR. 28 December 1937.

p.136 line 12 Two. VR to author. 8 December 1976, 13 November 1977.

line 18 Top of the bottle. VR to author. 6 September 1978.

line 31 Bells and buzzers. Marshall. *Life's Rich Pageant.* 176.
p.137 line 3 Much in demand. Rylands to author. 11 November 1989.
line 23 Since he was. *Daily Telegraph.* 5 March 1962.
£100,000 in 1962: perhaps £1.2million in 2002.
p.138 line 7 Before saying yes. VR to author. 4 November 1989.
line 25 Israeli Parliament. Dorothy de R. *Op.cit.* 93.
p.139 line 2 Eastern Europe. *Ibid.*
line 25 100 to 1. In 1898 the Derby winner was Jeddah.
p.140 line 22 As a pastime. Dorothy de R to author. 24 February 1987.
line 33 Her dying day. Isaiah Berlin. *Independent.* 12 December 1988.
p.141 line 13 As long ago as 1895. Dorothy de R to author. 15 April 1987.
line 30 Fiery fanaticism. Isaiah Berlin. 1 April 1989.
p.142 line 3 Natural beauty. Sir Joshua Rowley to author. 10 September 1986.
line 12 De Beers. Jacob to author. 4 November 1992.
line 21 Governor of the Bank. *Ibid.* They were Lord Faringdon and Luke Meinertzhagen, both of Cazenove & Co.
p.143 line 3 Touché. Elie de R to author. 12 April 1986.
line 19 Inaccurate and vulgar. VR to author. 14 August 1987.
line 29 Pyjamas in ribbons. Liliane de R to author. 12 April 1986.
p.144 line 3 Best companies. Elie de R. 12 April 1986.
line 30 I have no income. Lovelock. *Op.cit.* 167–68.
p.145 line 16 Acceptable as the gift. VR to Duff. 23 August 1944.
line 36 Made her future. Mary Hutchinson to VR. 4 August 1943.
p.146 line 2 Perhaps I shall. Duff to VR. 8 January 1947.
line 9 On its screen. VR to John Hayward. 15 April 1947.
p.147 line 3 Left. VR to author. 4 November 1989.

Chapter 7 – Sons and Daughters

p.149 line 11 Age of three. Tory to author. 16 November 1999.
line 23 Why not. Hart. *Ask Me No More.* 107.
line 30 Ham sandwich. Tory to author. 16 November 1999.
p.150 line 7 Like a knell. Diana Cooper to VR. 22 July 1947.
line 25 This fancy. VR to Duff. 26 July 1947.
p.151 line 4 Order of the day. Winston S. Churchill to author.
line 15 Sometimes malicious. Tam Dalyell, quoted in *Eton Voices* (Ed. Danny Danziger). 81.
line 22 Plead for leniency. Jacob to author. 7 March 1992.
line 34 Humiliating his son. David Pryce-Jones to author. 4 February 1992.
p.152 line 4 Making an officer. Andrew Parker-Bowles to author. 5 November 1997.
line 8 Window. Jacob to author. 18 January 1993.
line 30 Agreed. Graham C. Greene to author. 18 November 1991.

p.153 line 6   Lacking in warmth. Hugh Trevor-Roper (Lord Dacre) to author. 20 November 1990.

p.154 line 16   Board game of Monopoly. Sarah to author.

line 18   Reavealing his own. Sir Stuart Hampshire to author. 7 December 1991.

line 31   Garbo's elusive magic. Sarah. Scrapbook.

line 33   Little catt. Cecil Beaton's unpublished diary. Oct 1956.

line 35   Leaving the rest *et seq*. Sarah to author.

p.156 line 21   Bengal tiger. Shakespeare. *Bruce Chatwin*. 247.

p.157 line 25   Of years alone. *et seq*. Tory to author.

p.161 line 4   It isn't very pleasant. Vickers. *Loving Garbo*. 206–207.

line 23   What a whopper. Lady Anne Tree to author. 2 August 1995.

line 26   Lord Spoiltchild. Sir John Astor to author. 24 March 1991.

line 34   Return his call. Marcus Sieff to author. 2 August 1995.

p.162 line 6   Pat of butter each. VR memoranda to author. Undated.

Chapter 8 – Shell

p.163 line 14   £500 million. John H. Loudon to author. 2 March 1992.

line 21   That distinction. VR. Farewell dinner. 14 September 1970.

p.164 line 27   Methane. VR. *Back to the Bio-Board*. Annals NY Academy of Sciences. 1979.

p.165 line 13   Too many toes. John H. Loudon to author. 13 November 1991.

line 26   Binding advice. VR. Farewell dinner. 14 September 1970.

p.166 line 34   Most treasured possession. VR memorandum on industrial relations. Undated.

p.167 line 26   Even his thanks. VR memorandum. 19 July 1989.

p.168 line 28   Change for centuries *et seq*. Sir Denis Wright to author, 5 December 1991; Sir Shapoor Reporter to author, 2 January 1992; Kenneth Dick to author, 25 January 1993.

p.170 line 22   Israelis will mend it. Reporter to author. 2 January 1992.

line 27   Crown Prince. Jacob to author. 18 June 1993.

p.171 line 6   Financial backers. Kenneth Dick to author. 25 January 1993.

Chapter 9 – Think Tank

p.173 line 8   Outside Whitehall. Kenneth Dick to author. 25 January 1993.

p.174 line 4   Candidates. Lord Jellicoe to author. 15 June 1992.

p.175 line 3   Any other points. VR talk at Press Club, London. 7 September 1977.

line 6   In the future. Hurd. *An End to Promises*. 39.

line 15   Civil Service. Edward Heath. 'Downing Street and Whitehall'. *Daily Telegraph*. 13 April 1975.

line 28 Average age 35. Blackstone & Plowden. *Inside the Think Tank.* 28.

p.176 line 13 Ended his career. Private information.

line 26 Most difficult men. William Waldegrave to author. 13 July 1976.

p.177 line 16 Departmental three-deckers. Waldegrave. Memorial address. 15 May 1990.

p.178 line 4 Round and round. VR. *Random Variables.* 81.

line 14 What do we do now? Sir Robin Butler to author. 16 December 1991.

line 28 Success from the start. Hurd. *Op.cit.* 38.

p.179 line 9 Abrogated. VR. 'A Useful Exercise with Interest'. *The Times.* 2 July 1983.

line 18 Can't stay out. Lord Plowden to VR.

line 26 Worst of both worlds. Hurd. *Op.cit.* 39.

line 32 Self-criticism. Sir Robin Butler to author. 16 December 1991.

p.180 line 12 Commercial disaster. Sir Robert Wade-Gery to author, during one of our frequent meetings over the years, which I have not thought it necessary to date.

line 26 Private cellar. William Waldegrave to author. Again, I have not thought it necessary to date our many conversations.

line 37 To the Cabinet. Heath. *The Course of My Life.* 316.

p.181 line 3 Taking an interest. VR. *Variables.* 82.

line 10 In later years. Lord Hunt of Tanworth to author. 7 June 1989.

line 31 Astounded Cabinet. Waldegrave. Memorial address. 15 May 1990.

line 37 Presenting the results. *Quo.* Hennessy. *Whitehall.* 226.

p.182 line 3 Uncomfortable. Sir Robert Armstrong to author. 26 August 1990.

line 13 Coloured in red. VR. Israel Sieff memorial lecture. 4 May 1976.

line 24 Green paper. *A Framework for Government Research and Development.* HMSO 1971.

p.183 line 9 Before delivery. Original draft of address to Letcombe laboratory of the Agriculture Research Council. 24 September 1973.

line 37 Not even a Sollypsism. VR Talk at Press Club, London. 7 September 1977.

p.184 line 5 Of course. Zuckerman. *Monkeys, Men and Missiles.* 450.

line 23 Relations remained cool. *Ibid.* 461.

line 31 Glorious stuff. Heath to VR. Letter dated 2 February 1972.

p.185 line 7 American oil consultant. Walter J. Levy to author. 19 November 1991.

line 19 11 dollars. Blackstone & Plowden. *Op.cit.* 76–77.

line 32 World crisis. Sir Shapoor Reporter to author. 2 January 1992.

p.187 line 4 97 out of 100. VR to author; *The Times* 24 December 1974; Hennessy. *Op.cit.* 248.

line 13 Denied to Think Tank. Sir Robert Armstrong to author. 26 August 1990.

line 21 Irreverent. Lord Jellicoe to author. 15 January 1992.

line 28 The other was sober. Sir Robert Wade-Gery to author.

p.188   line 4   Sir John Hunt. *Ibid.*
        line 15   Bureaucracy. VR to Margaret Thatcher. Draft letter, unsent. July
                  1984.
        line 22   Knew our business best. Sir Patrick Nairne to author. 9 July
                  1990.
        line 24   Years at No.10. Heath. *The Course of My Life.* 316.
        line 31   From Edward Heath. VR to author. 21 June 1974.
p.189   line 2   Party politic. Sir Robin Butler to author. 16 December 1991.
        line 7   Safety equipment. John Guinness to author. 17 August 1998.
p.190   line 4   At the same time. VR address to ARC. 25 September 1973.
        line 7   Spain and Portugal. *Daily Telegraph.* 25 September 1973.
        line 12   Television sets. *Daily Telegraph.* 26 September 1973.
        line 28   Closed. Heath. Answer to Parliamentary Question. 18 October
                  1973.
p.191   line 5   August. VR to author. 3 October 1973.
        line 15   144 per cent. Author. *Sunday Telegraph.* 1 May 1977.
        line 20   Solly Zuckerman. VR to author. 3 October 1973.
p.192   line 9   Concordia. Author. *Sunday Telegraph.* 7 October 1973.
        line 25   Falsely friendly. VR to author. 21 June 1974.
        line 29   Economics. VR. Israel Sieff memorial lecture. 4 May 1976.
p.193   line 9   Dangerous enemy. Tony Benn. *Diary.* 2 June 1974.
        line 13   More loyal. *Ibid.* 24 April 1974.
        line 19   Your administration. *Quo.* VR to author. 25 September 1977.
p.194   line 14   Social division. VR. *The Times.* 13 October 1974.
        line 17   Chaos. CPRS. *Unfinished Business.* 1974.
        line 25   Very busy people. Sir Robert Wade-Gery to author.
        line 26   Made us think. VR. Dimbleby lecture. 1978.

Chapter 10 – Chairman of NMR

p.195   line 10   Cardinal. Elie de R to author. 12 April 1986.
        line 14   Arbiter. VR to author. 4 September 1985.
        line 22   £8 million. Ferguson. *Op.cit.* 1042.
p.196   line 5   Settle her debts. *Ibid.* 1011–1012.
        line 16   Talk to us. Palin. *Op.cit.* 187.
        line 22   Mrs Lionel. *Ibid.* 25.
        line 37   Exbury village. Holland & Edmund de R. *Our Exbury.* 19.
p.197   line 3   Rough woodland. Palin. *Op.cit.* 118.
        line 6   Estate duty. Edmund de R. *Op.cit.*
        line 9   Irritable. Palin. *Op.cit.* 66
        line 27   Perhaps too much. Leo de R to author. 12 June 1991.
p.198   line 7   There before. Jacob Rothschild. Quo. Barbara Amiel. *The Times
                  Saturday Review.* 11 August 1990.
        line 12   NMR itself. *Ibid.*

line 24 You wouldn't. Edmund de R. *Op.cit.* 137.
line 34 Counting house. *Ibid.* 190.
p.199 line 23 His legitimacy. VR. Press Club, London. 7 September 1977.
p.200 line 5 After his father's death. Edmund de R. *Op.cit.* 165; Ferguson. *Op.cit.*1011.
line 26 Public occasions. VR to author. 4 September 1985.
p.201 line 19 Classical lines. Author. *Sunday Telegraph.* 10 December 1989.
p.202 line 17 Of my age. VR to Sarah. 17 June 1976.
line 33 It is infinite. VR to Hoffmann. 28 April 1982.
p.203 line 5 Stretch his mind. Evelyn de R to author. 16 July 1991; Leo de R to author. 12 June 1991; John Loudon to author. 10 October 1993.
line 8 Gossip. Jeremy Soames to author. 21 November 1991.
line 16 Comrade. VR to author. 20 October 1987.
line 22 What lies beneath. *Ibid.* 11 August 1975.
line 29 Would amuse you. Leo de R to author. 31 October 2000.
line 34 Like everyone else. Elie de R to author. 12 April 1986.
p.204 line 6 Plain square ones. Sir Robert Armstrong to author. 26 April 1990.
line 13 Charged to NMR. Evelyn de R to author. 16 July 1991.
line 17 Perfunctory. Norman Lamont to author. 21 December 1989.
line 33 Over-reaction. Evelyn de R to author. 16 July 1991.
p.205 line 15 Over 12 years. Sieff to author. 31 July 1990 and 1 October 1990.
line 18 Forms and documents. Sieff. *Don't Ask the Price.* 155.
line 26 Bargain basement levels. Sieff to author. 31 July 1990.
line 31 Just relax. VR to Kenneth Dick. 30 November 1978.
line 37 Rothschild Asset Management. Sir Robert Armstrong to author. 26 February 1992.
p.208 line 23 £1.5 million. *Ibid.* 26 August 1990
p.207 line 10 Contents inaccessible. Memorandum by Yvonne Clarke of NMR. 14 April 1986.
p.208 line 4 Commit to paper. Ferguson. *Op.cit.* 30–31.
p.209 line 6 Done his Herrick. VR to Duff. 15 April 1944.
line 25 More daggers. VR to author. 24 October 1977.
line 31 Maniacal rabble. *Ibid.* 5 or 6 March 1985.
p.210 line 18 BBC official. Edward Mirzoeff to VR. 22 June 1978.

Chapter 11 – Employed on Commission

p.211 line 20 £7 billion. Hoffmann to author. 21 February 1992.
line 37 Never backed a horse. *Ibid.*
p.212 line 16 Institutions. *Royal Commission on Gambling: Final Report* II. 527–35.
line 22 Boring duties. VR to author. 10 June 1977.
line 25 To bribe a Rothschild. Hoffmann to author. 21 February 1992.
line 37 Outdoor sports. *Report.* I. 50.

p.213 line 7 What they may win. *Report.* I. 5.
     line 14 Analytical mind. *Report.* II. 457.
     line 17 4am. *Report.* II. 302.
     line 21 £100 or less. *Report.* I. 83.
     line 27 Except bookmakers. *Report.* I. 30.
     line 31 General education. *Report.* I. 193.
     line 33 17, 000 clubs. *Report.* II. 363.
p.214 line 4 Drinks and lavatories. *Report.* I. 53.
     line 13 Civil war. *Report.* I. 213.
     line 17 10 per cent. *Report.* II. 435.
     line 27 Succinctly presented. Roy Jenkins to VR. 27 August 1978.
     line 36 Worthwhile. VR. 'The doubtful honour of being employed on commission.' *The Times.* 5 December 1979.
p.215 line 14 £20 less. VR to author. 10 July 1978.
p.216 line 5 Which kind she ate. Dr Pat Altham to author. 10 November 1990.
     line 17 Printer's error. Dorothy de R to author. 16 March 1987.
     line 23 In the heavens. VR to author. 20 May 1987.
     line 26 Pure mathematics. 'Desert Island Discs'. 7 July 1984.
     line 35 Prime numbers. VR to author. 18 October 1989.
p.217 line 5 Poll tax. VR to author. 12 December 1989.
     line 19 Un-conservative. Thatcher. *The Downing Street Years.* 644.
     line 24 Services they provided. *Ibid.* 645–46.
p.218 line 17 How you like it. VR to Hoffmann. 5 June 1986.
p.219 line 5 Serious objections. Hoffmann. *Local Government Finance.* 4.
     line 14 Regressive tax. *Ibid.* 4–5.
     line 20 Marvellously lucid. VR to Hoffmann. 15 April 1985.
     line 36 Unusually silent. Hoffmann to author. 21 February 1982.
p.220 line 13 Cabinet Secretary. *Ibid.*
     line 22 Abolish the rates. Michael Crick & Adrian Van Klaveren. 'Poll Tax'. *Journal of Contemporary British History.* v.3. 409. Winter 1991.
p.221 line 5 An apology. Caroline Waldegrave to author. 8 February 1988; Anthony Mayer to author. 30 June 1992.

Chapter 12 – Spies and Spycatchers

p.224 line 12 At that time. Rees. *A Chapter of Accidents.* 171. Rees writes that Kinsey's work was hidden in the safe of the Foreign Secretary himself, an improbable adornment to the story.
     line 28 On his desk. Greenhill. *More by Accident.* 73.
     line 34 Innocent eccentricity. Sir Alexander Cadogan to Brian Urquhart quo. Urquhart's *A Life in Peace and War.* 117.
p.225 line 30 Potsdam conference. Modin. *My Five Cambridge Friends.* 191.
p.226 line 30 Shaken them off. Boyle. *The Climate of Treason.* 117.

p.228　line 32　Britain's humiliation. Modin. *Op.cit.* 197–198.

p.229　line 28　Trade agreement. Robert Cecil. *Quo.* Costello. 547.

p.231　line 11　Victor's unofficial role. White to author. 29 January 1991.

p.232　line 9　Yes. Blunt interview. *The Times.* 21 November 1979.

　　　　line 22　Letter of recommendation. White to author. 29 January 1991.

p.233　line 13　Even after thirty years. VR. *Random Variables.* 204.

　　　　line 25　Two masters. Robert Cecil. *Quo.* Costello. 396.

　　　　line 29　Thousands of documents. Modin. *Op.cit.* 132.

p.234　line 1　To the Russians. Pincher. *Too Secret Too Long.* 351.

　　　　line 16　A man can receive. Lees-Milne. *Prophesying Peace.* 16 November 1944. 132.

　　　　line 26　Ushered in. Millar. *The Queen's Pictures.* 215.

　　　　line 37　Never reached Paris. Duff to VR. 8 January 1947. VR to Duff. 18 February 1974.

p.235　line 1　Very good actor. Blunt. *Slow on the Feather.* 243.

　　　　line 3　Our Russian spy. HRH the Duke of Kent to author. 25 February 1992.

　　　　line 5　Blunt's hidden past. Private information.

　　　　line 28　Counter-espionage service. Modin. *Op.cit.* 180.

　　　　line 35　Leisurely travel. *Ibid.* 204.

p.236　line 5　Lame excuse. Blunt interview. *The Times.* 21 November 1979.

　　　　line 36　Straight's evidence. *After Long Silence. Passim.*

p.237　line 17　Catalogues of its contents. Dorothy de R. *Op.cit.* 162.

　　　　line 34　In 1984. VR. *Random Variables.* 203–05.

p.238　line 28　House guests. Jenkins. *A Life at the Centre.* 185.

p.239　line 6　Sort of girl-friend. Miriam to author. 8 February 1991.

　　　　line 12　Official Secrets Act. VR to author. 7 April 1983.

　　　　line 18　Best friend. Sir John Astor to author. 24 March 1991.

p.240　line 10　No justification. VR. *Random Variables.* 204.

p.241　line 12　Police state. White to author. 10 January 1991.

　　　　line 17　Man of action. *Ibid.* 2 April 1991.

　　　　line 24　Inferiority complex. VR to Duff. 17 April 1944.

p.242　line 8　'Bastards!' Pincher. *Too Secret Too Long.* 133.

　　　　line 36　Legendary. Wright. *Spycatcher.* 117.

p.243　line 3　Long periods. *Ibid.* 118.

　　　　line 4　Arcane practices. Lovelock. *Homage to Gaia.* 169.

　　　　line 14　Anywhere else. Wright. Affidavit. Para 68. 8 November 1986.

　　　　line 24　He grunted. Wright. *Spycatcher.* 366.

　　　　line 31　Poky lift. Waldegrave to author. 11 November 2001.

　　　　line 33　Complete fiction. VR to author. 15 May 1988.

p.244　line 8　Links with Russian. Wright. *Spycatcher.* 364 et seq.

　　　　line 14　All that good. White to author. 29 January 1991.

　　　　line 28　Bend his ear. Wright. *Spycatcher.* 351.

　　　　line 37　In the coup. White to author. 29 January 1991.

p.245　line 6　Extended farewell. Wright. *Spycatcher.* 357.

line 8   Fruitless quest. *Ibid.* 375.

line 34   Repaid as promised. Wright. Affidavit. Para 74. 8 November 1986.

p.246   line 5   Ought to write it. Wright to VR. 3 November 1976.

line 14   Danger. VR to Hanley. 15 November 1976.

line 14   Nonchalantly. Hanley to VR. 10 December 1976.

line 16   Official Secrets Act. VR to Hanley. 20 December 1976.

line 21   Resentment behind him. Hanley to VR. 29 April 1977.

line 23   Examine the case. VR to Wright. 17 May 1977.

line 29   Russian threat. Wright to VR. 12 July 1977.

line 34   He'll be in touch. Tess to Wright. Undated. Private source.

p.247   line 3   Andrew Boyle. *Ibid.*

line 26   Nor does A. *Ibid.*

p.248   line 13   Embarassment. Strong. *Diaries.* 28 November 1979. 246.

line 18   Tom Brocklebank. Wilfrid Blunt. *Op.cit.* 162.

line 35   Unhealthy life. Jenkins. *European Diary.* 542.

p.245   line 2   I am all right. VR to author. 10 April 1979.

line 17   Second World War. *The Times.* 6 June 1980.

line 32   Starting to get rough. VR to Wright. 25 June 1980. Private source.

line 36   The Spectator. 14 June 1980.

p.250   line 18   Cabinet offices. White to author. 2 April 1991.

line 29   His dagger. Quo. by VR to author. 14 August 1987.

line 30   Private party. Lady Avon to author.

p.251   line 2   Dismissive. Sir Robert Armstrong to author. 2 May 2001.

line 5   Phalanx of hostility. White to author. 29 January 1991.

line 7   Director-General of MI6. *Ibid.*

line 17   Ceased to consult me. *Ibid.*

line 28   Cancer in our midst. Wright to VR. 12 June 1980.

p.252   line 6   My beloved England. *Ibid.*

line 20   Think about it. VR to Wright. 25 June 1980.

line 18   Deemed suitable. Wright. Affidavit. Para 65. 8 November 1986.

line 23   Mr Rossetti. Beerbohm. *Rossetti and his Circle.*

p.255   line 7   September afternoon in 1980. *et seq.* Pincher. *The Spycatcher Affair*, Pincher to author. *Passim.*

p.256   line 14   To the Press. *The Times.* 9 October 1982; 2 July 1983.

line 37   History as a whole. Pincher. *Op.cit.* 28.

p.257   line 37   Without comment. Pincher. Pincher papers.

p.258   line 21   Russian intelligence service. Margaret Thatcher. House of Commons. 26 March 1981.

line 24   Remaindered. Pincher. *Op.cit.* 82.

p.260   line 27   Wright's defence team. For this account of the trial I have relied largely on court transcripts and on *The Spycatcher Trial* by Wright's counsel, Malcolm Turnbull. I also had the benefit of helpful talks with Mr Turnbull, as well as with Sir Robert (now Lord) Armstrong.

p.261 line 5   Set out to mislead. Turnbull. *The Spycatcher Trial.* 132.

p.262 line 3   Every minute of it. *Ibid.* 'Acknowledgements'.

      line 13 Moonshine. *Ibid.* 149.

p.263 line 32 To the wolves. *Ibid.* 102.

p.264 line 31 Wright-Pincher affair. Sir Robin Butler to author. 16 December 1991.

p.265 line 2   Oldfield. Sir Robert Armstrong to author. 26 August 1990; Sir Dick White to author, 2 April 1991.

      line 37 The *Observer.* 23 November 1986.

p.266 line 25 Patriot. Turnbull. *Op.cit.* 133.

p.267 line 31 Behind the scenes. Wright. Affidavit. Para 82. 8 November 1986.

p.268 line 11 Not on the menu. VR to author. 15 May 1988.

      line 17 Undermine it. Turnbull. *Op.cit.* 28.

      line 29 Haven't you? Court transcript. 28 November 1986.

      line 39 Getting nowhere. *Ibid.* Comment of Justice Powell.

p.269 line 3   Single colleague. Wright, questioned by John Ware on BBC 'Panorama', 13 October 1988.

      line 20 Havers and Rothschild. Turnbull. *Op.cit.* 117.

      line 24 Suggested by Turnbull. *Ibid.* 118.

p.270 line 7   Order paper. Exchange between Patrick Nicholls MP and Mr Speaker, House of Commons. 26 November 1986.

      line 17 Soviet spy and the fifth man. Motion by Brian Sedgemore MP, Dale Campbell-Savours MP and others. House of Commons. 1 December 1986.

      line 21 In silence. Miriam. *Op.cit.* 29.

      line 23 Former Labour prime minister. James Callaghan to author. 27 September 1991.

      line 31 His patriotism. Lord Goodman to author. 13 December 1988.

      line 35 Sir Michael Hanley. VR to author. Undated note. VR added: 'I understand this caused some confusion...'

p.271 line 14 Anti-Semitism. White to author. 24 May 1991.

      line 18 Not a Soviet spy. *The Times.* 5 December 1986.

      line 26 Sinister operation. VR to author. 3 March 1987.

p.272 line 13 'Yours truly, Rothschild'. *Daily Telegraph.* 4 December 1986.

p.273 line 27 30 years before. Sir Robin Butler to author. 16 December 1991.

p.274 line 6   At this stage. *Daily Telegraph.* 4 December 1986.

      line 32 If indeed there was one. House of Commons. 7 November 1955.

p.275 line 27 Anxiety caused him. *Daily Telegraph.* 6 December 1986.

      line 32 Failed to make. Sir Isaiah Berlin to author. 24 April 1989.

p.276 line 6   Explain my motives. Dale Campbell-Savours. Telephone call to author. 2 March 1987.

      line 21 Security services. House of Commons. 16 March 1987.

p.277 line 3   Interrogation. January to April 1987. My account of VR's interrogation by the Serious Crimes Squad of Scotland Yard rests largely, but not entirely, on the records he kept and on the

retrospective comments he made to me about it. The humiliating
memory persisted until his death nearly three years later.

p.284   line 8   Sterile process. Pincher. *The Spycatcher Affair.* 209.

Chapter 13 – Last Years

p.285   line 1   Destroying the past. Tess to author. 20 December 1991; Amschel
to author 26 June 1995.

        line 6   Dizzy's hand. Miriam. *Op.cit.* 296.

        line 11   Everlasting bonfire. *Ibid.* 245.

        line 37   Clearing out my papers. VR to author. 20 December 1988.

p.287   line 21   His own income. VR to author. 3 April 1989.

        line 25   Goldsmith was away. *Ibid.* 2 July 1989.

p.288   line 6   Do sums. *Ibid.* 12 March 1986.

        line 25   Set fire to the garden. Baron Henri de Rothschild. *Croisières autour de mes souvenirs.*

        line 31   Psycho-physical education. Aldous Huxley to VR. 25 May 1942.

        line 37   Scalpel descended. VR. *Variables.* 71.

p.289   line 22   Leave this room. VR and Victoria Rothschild. *Vicnic and Nicvic.* Privately printed. 1989.

p.290   line 5   No complaints. VR to author. 11 May 1989.

        line 12   Jazzing harlotry. Brendan Bracken to VR. 19 February 1932.

        line 17   Misleading results. Dr D. M. Krikler to author. 4 June 1996.

p.294   line 29   I am what I am. 'Desert Island Discs'. 7 July 1984.

p.296   line 2   Some weeks later. 15 May 1990.

Acknowledgements

My most enduring debt is to Victor, 3rd Baron Rothschild and the subject of this biography, without whose friendship and encouragement it could not have been written. Over the years he talked to me freely about his life, lent me letters and other papers from his private archives, dictated memoranda for my use on particular topics and in a correspondence of nearly 200 letters commented drily on the human comedy of our times.

I am scarcely less indebted to his eldest sister, Dame Miriam Rothschild FRS (Mrs George Lane) whose friendship has made my task all the more delightful and whose memory remains undimmed well into her tenth decade.

All other members of the family whom I consulted were unsparing of their time, often buttressing their recollections with letters and other documents.

They include his widow Teresa (Tess) Lady Rothschild and the six children of his two marriages. In chronological order of birth they are Sarah Daniel, Jacob 4th Baron Rothschild, Miranda, Emma, Victoria (Tory) and Amschel, who died in 1966. (See family tree, p.xiv–xvii).

Among Victor's cousins to whom I am indebted are Sir Evelyn de Rothschild, Edmund de Rothschild, Baron Elie de Rothschild and his wife Liliane, Sybil Marchioness of Cholmondeley and Eva Countess of Rosebery.

I thank the many others who have helped me in their various ways, not all of whom have lived to read these words. I apologise if any have been inadvertently omitted:

Dr Patricia Altham; Noël (later Lord) Annan; Sir Robert Armstrong (later Lord Armstrong of Ilminster); Sir John Astor; the Countess of Avon; the Duke of Beaufort; Sir Isaiah Berlin; Sir Robin Butler (later Lord Butler of Brockwell); Lord Callaghan of Cardiff; Winston S. Churchill; Sir Gordon Cox; Lord Dalmeny; Professor Sir John Davenport; Sir Robin Day; Kenneth Dick; Professor David Dilks; Lord Donaldson of Kingsbridge; Dean Godson; Graham C. Greene; Paul Greengrass; John Grigg; Lord Goodman; Sir John Guinness; Professor Sir Stuart Hampshire; C. Harmer; Mrs Jenifer Hart; Alisdair Hawkyard Mrs Drue Heinz; Sir Alan and Lady Hodgkin; Professor J.P. Hudson; Sir John Hunt (later Lord Hunt of Tanworth); Professor Michael Jaffé; Mrs Mary James; Earl Jellicoe; HRH the Duke of Kent; Dr D.M. Krikler; Sir Anthony Lambert; Norman (later Lord) Lamont; Sir Stephen Lander; Sir Hugh Leggatt; Walter J. Levy; Miss Judy Lloyd; Jonkheer John Loudon; Anthony Mayer; Sir Patrick Nairn; Viscount Norwich; Brigadier Andrew Parker-Bowles; Robert S. Pirie; David Pryce-Jones; Lord Rayner; Sir Shapoor Reporter; Sir Francis Richards; Andrew Roberts; Sir Joshua Rowley; Sir Steven Runciman; Dr George ('Dadie') Rylands; Lord Sieff; Jeremy Soames; Mrs Jack Steinberg; Chief Superintendent K.H.W. Thompson; Lady Anne Tree; Hugh Trevor-Roper (Lord Dacre of Glanton); Sir Alan Urwick; Hugo Vickers (as a literary executor of Sir Cecil Beaton); Sir Robert Wade-Gery; William Waldegrave (later Lord Waldegrave of North Hill); John Ware; Sir Dick White; Harry Williams-Bulkeley; Sir Denis Wright; Lord Zuckerman.

Four members of the staff of the Archives of N.M. Rothschild & Sons were exceptionally welcoming and helpful in my research over the years: Miss Simone Mace, Miss Julia Harvey, Dr Victor Gray and Miss Melanie Asper.

I am also much indebted to the Weidenfeld & Nicolson editorial team that includes Ion Trewin, Victoria Webb, Ilsa Yardley, Helen Smith and Laura Carnwath.

My gratitude also goes to Mrs Mary Clapison, Keeper of Western Manuscripts and Special Collections of the Bodleian Library, Oxford; and to the staff of the London Library and of the Royal Borough of Kensington and Chelsea Public Library.

Bibliography

Books by Victor, 3rd Baron Rothschild

The History of Tom Jones, A Changeling, privately printed at the Cambridge University Press, 1951.

The Rothschild Library: A Catalogue of the Collection of Eighteenth-Century Printed Books and Manuscripts formed by Lord Rothschild (2 volumes), privately printed at the CUP, 1954.

Fertilisation, Methuen, 1956.

A Classification of Living Animals, Longmans, 1961.

A Framework for Government Research and Development, HMSO, 1972.

Royal Commission on Gambling: Final Report (2 volumes), HMSO, 1977.

Meditations of a Broomstick, Collins, 1977.

Risk (The Dimbleby Lecture), BBC, 1978.

You have it, Madam: The Purchase, in 1875, of Suez Canal Shares by Disraeli and Baron Lionel de Rothschild, printed by W & J Mackay, 1980.

The Shadow of a Great Man: Nathan Mayer Rothschild, Rothschild Archive, New Court, St Swithin's Lane, London, 1982.

An Enquiry into the Social Science Research Council, HMSO, 1982.

Random Variables, Collins, 1984.

An Open Letter to the Master of Trinity College, Cambridge, privately printed, 1985.

(With N. Logothetis) *Probability Distributions,* John Wiley & Sons, New York, 1986.

The Rothschild Family Tree, Rothschild Archive, London, 1988.

Rylands, Stourton Press, Hackney, 1988.

(With Victoria Rothschild) *Vicnic and Nicvic,* privately printed, 1989.

I am grateful to the authors, publishers and copyright holders of the following books for permission, where necessary, to quote from them. Each individual mention is acknowledged in SOURCE REFERENCES:

Allfrey, Anthony, *Edward VII and his Jewish Court*, Weidenfeld & Nicolson, 1991.

Annan, Noël, 'The Intellectual Aristocracy', in *Studies in Social History*, ed. J.H. Plumb, Longmans Green, 1955.

Ayer, A.J., *Part of My Life*, Collins, 1977.

Battersea, Constance, Lady, *Reminiscences*, Macmillan, 1922.

Beerbohm, Max, *Rossetti and His Circle*, Heinemann, 1922.

Benn, Anthony, *Against the Tide, Diaries 1973-76*, Hutchinson, 1989.

Blackstone, Tessa, & Plowden, William, *Inside the Think Tank: Advising the Cabinet*, Heinemann, 1988.

Blunt, Wilfrid, *Slow on the Feather*, Russell, 1986.

Bower, Tom, *The Perfect English Spy*, Heinemann, 1995.

Boyle, Andrew, *The Climate of Treason*, Hutchinson, 1979; revised edition, Coronet Books, 1979.

Buxton, Charles, *Memoirs of Sir Thomas Fowell*, Buxton, Bart, Murray, 1872.

Cahen d'Anvers, Yvonne, *Baboushka Remembers*, privately printed, 1972.

Carter, John, *Taste and Technique in Book Collecting*, Private Libraries Association, 1969.

Churchill, Randolph S., *Winston Spencer Churchill, Companion volume I, part 1*, Heinemann, 1967.

Churchill, Randolph S., *Winston Spencer Churchill, volume II*, Heinemann, 1969.

Cooper, Artemis (Ed.), *Double Fire: The Letters of Duff and Diana Cooper*, Collins, 1983.

Cornwallis-West, George, *Edwardian Hey-Days*, Putnam, 1930.

Costello, John, *The Mask of Treachery*, Collins, 1988.

Crawford, Earl of, *The Crawford Papers*, Manchester University Press, 1984.

Daniel, Sarah, *Lord Rothschild's Favourite Recipes*, Stourton Press, 1989.

Danziger, Danny (Ed.), *Eton Voices*, Viking, 1988.

Davis, Richard, *The English Rothschilds*, Collins, 1983.

Dictionary of National Biography, 1961-1970, Oxford University Press, 1981.

Drogheda, Lord, *Double Harness*, Weidenfeld & Nicolson, 1978.

Elon, Amos, *Founder: Meyer Amschel Rothschild and his Time*, HarperCollins, 1996.

Ferguson, Niall, *The World's Banker: The History of the House of Rothschild*, Weidenfeld & Nicolson, 1998.

Foster, Roy, *Lord Randolph Churchill*, OUP, 1981.

Gaucher, Marcel, *Les jardins de la fortune*, Hervé, Paris, 1985.

Gilbert, Martin, *Winston Spencer Churchill, Companion volume V, Part 3*, Heinemann, 1982.

Goncourt, Edmond & Jules, *Journal: Mémoires de la vie littéraire*, L'Imprimerie Nationale de Monaco, 1956-57.

Greenhill, Denis, *More by Accident*, Wilton 65, 1992.

Greville, Charles, *The Greville Memoirs*, ed. Lytton Strachey and Roger Fulford, Macmillan, 1938.

Guedalla, Philip (Ed.), *The Queen and Mr. Gladstone*, Hodder & Stoughton, 1933.

Haldane, Viscount, *Autobiography*, Hodder & Stoughton, 1929.

Hart, Jenifer, *Ask Me No More*, Peter Halban, 1998.

Hart-Davis, Rupert, *A Catalogue of the Caricatures of Max Beerbohm*, Macmillan, 1972.

Hearnden, Arthur, *Red Robert: a Life of Robert Birley*, Hamish Hamilton, 1984.

Heath, Edward, *The Course of My Life*, Hodder & Stoughton, 1998.

Hennessy, Peter, *Whitehall*, Secker & Warburg, 1989.

Hinks, Roger, *The Gymnasium of the Mind, Journals 1933-36*, Ed. John Goldsmith, Michael Russell, 1984.

Hodgkin, Sir Alan, *Chance and Design*, CUP, 1992.

Hoffmann, L.H., *Local Government Finance*, privately printed, 1985.

Holland, A.J., & Rothschild, Edmund de, *Our Exbury*, Paul Cave Publications, Southampton, 1982.

Hurd, Douglas, *An End to Promises*, Collins, 1979.

Jenkins, Roy, *European Diary*, Collins, 1989.

Jenkins, Roy, *A Life at the Centre*, Macmillan, 1991.

Jolliffe, John, *Raymond Asquith, Life and Letters*, Collins, 1980.

Lee, Sidney, *King Edward VII*, Macmillan, 1927.

Lees-Milne, *Prophesying Peace*, Faber, 1977.

Lovelock, Sidney, *Homage to Gaia*, OUP, 2000.

Madan, Geoffrey, *Notebooks*, OUP, 1981.

Marshall, Arthur, *Life's Rich Pageant*, Hamish Hamilton, 1984.

Masterman, J.C., *On the Chariot Wheel*, OUP, 1975.

Millar, Oliver, *The Queen's Pictures*, Weidenfeld & Nicolson/BBC, 1977.

Modin, Yuri, *My Five Cambridge Friends*, Headline Press, 1994.

Moneypenny, W.F. and Buckle, G.E., *The Life of Benjamin Disraeli*, Murray, 1929.

Morrell, Lady Ottoline, *Early Memories*, Faber, 1963.

Morton, Frederic, *The Rothschilds*, Secker & Warburg, 1962.

Muggeridge, Malcolm, *Chronicles of Wasted Time: The Eternal Grove*, Collins, 1973.

Muhlstein, Anka, *James de Rothschild*, Gallimaud Press, Paris, 1981.

Munby, A.N.L., *The Disposal of the Phillipps Library*, CUP, 1960.

Nevill, Lady Dorothy, *My Own Times*, Methuen, 1912.

Newsome, David, *On the Edge of Paradise*, A.C. Benson, Murray, 1980.

Palin, Ronald, *Rothschild Relish*, Cassell, 1970.

Pincher, Chapman, *Too Secret Too Long*, Sidgwick & Jackson, 1984.

Pincher, Chapman, *The Spycatcher Affair*, Sidgwick & Jackson, 1988.

Ponsonby, Magdalen, *Mary Ponsonby*, Murray, 1927.

Pope-Hennessy, James (Ed.), *Baron Ferdinand de Rothschild's Livre d'Or*, printed for presentation to members of the Roxburghe Club, Cambridge, 1957.

Rees, Goronwy, *A Chapter of Accidents*, Chatto, 1972.

Reeve, Susan, *Nathaniel Mayer, Victor Rothschild, Third Baron Rothschild*, Royal Society, 1993.

Rothschild, Dorothy de, *The Rothschilds at Waddesdon Manor*, Collins, 1979.

Rothschild, Edmund de, *A Gilt-Edged Life*, Murray, 1998.

Rothschild, Guy de, *The Whims of Fortune*, Granada, 1985.

Rothschild, Baron Henri de, *Crosières autour de mes souvenirs*, Paris, 1932.

Rothschild, Miriam, *Nathaniel Charles Rothschild*, privately printed by CUP, 1979.

Rothschild, Miriam, *Dear Lord Rothschild: Birds, Butterflies and History*, Hutchinson, 1983.

Sieff, Marcus, *Don't Ask the Price*, Weidenfeld & Nicolson, 1986.

Shakespeare, Nicholas, *Bruce Chatwin*, Harvill and Cape, 1999.

Skidelsky, Robert, *John Maynard Keynes*, Macmillan, 1992.

Straight, Michael, *After Long Silence*, Collins, 1983.

Strong, Roy, *Diaries*, Weidenfeld & Nicolson, 1997.

Surtees, John, *Hillingdon Hall*, Harrap, 1844; reprinted, 1931.

Thatcher, Margaret, *The Downing Street Years*, HarperCollins, 1993.

Thomas, Hugh, *John Strachey*, Eyre Methuen, 1973.

Trevor-Roper, Hugh, *The Philby Affair*, Kinber, 1968.

Turnbull, Malcolm, *The Spycatcher Trial*, Heinemann, 1988.

Tyerman, Christopher, *A History of Harrow School*, OUP, 2000.

Urquhart, Brian, *A Life in Peace and War*, Weidenfeld & Nicolson, 1987.

Vickers, Hugo, *Loving Garbo*, Cape, 1994.

Waugh, Evelyn, *Unconditional Surrender*, Chapman & Hall, 1951.

Waugh, Evelyn, *Diaries*, ed. Michael Davie, Weidenfeld & Nicolson, 1976.

Wolf, Edwin, with Fleming, John F., *Rosenbach*, Weidenfeld & Nicolson, 1960.

Wolf, Lucien, *Essays in Jewish History*, The Jewish Historical Society of England, 1934.

Wood, Alan, *The Groundnuts Affair*, Bodley Head, 1950.

Woolf, Virginia, *A Room of One's Own*, Vintage, 1966.

Ziegler, Philip, *Diana Cooper*, Hamish Hamilton, 1981.

Zuckerman, Solly, *Monkeys, Men and Missiles*, Collins, 1988.

I am also grateful to the editors of *The Times*, the *Daily Telegraph*, the *Sunday Telegraph*, the *Independent*, the *Daily Express*, the *Book Collector*, the *Jewish Chronicle*, *Scientific American* and *Parliamentary Debates: Official Report* (Hansard). Each individual mention is acknowledged in SOURCE REFERENCES.

Index

Blair, William, 212
Blake, William: *Poetical Sketches*, 104; *Songs of Innocence and Experience*, 104
Bletchley Park, 75–6, 85, 111
Bloomsbury, 36, 54, 55, 90
Blunt, Anthony: family background, 46; education, 46, 242; VR's association with, xiii, 46–7, 222, 223, 231; Miriam Rothschild's impression of, 47; member of Apostles, 48, 49; receives book from VR, 104; receives money from VR to purchase painting by Poussin, 47, 104; fails to gain Fellowship at King's, 46; elected Fellow of Trinity, 39, 46; Barbara Rothschild dislikes frequent visits of, 55; at Bentinck Street, 87, 89, 238; volunteers for army, 231; works for MI5, 231–4; spying activities, 222, 233, 235; career as art historian, 39, 46, 231, 234, 236, 237; edits Waddesdon catalogue, 142, 237; involved in defection of Burgess and Maclean, 235, 236; suspicions about, 236; role of Straight in unmasking, 44, 236–7; secret confession, 237; VR's reaction to confession, 46, 237–8; VR and wife continue as friends of, 238–9; retirement, 237; Wright proposes to write about, 246; and publication of Boyle's book, 247, 249; exposed as Soviet agent, xiii, 42, 247–8; denounced in House of Commons, 248; interviewed by journalists, 231–2, 235–6; death, 47, 248; brief mentions, 35, 50, 75, 151, 223, 240, 250, 251, 254, 257, 271, 274, 279 Boccaccio, Giovanni: *Decameron*, 104
Boer War, 19
Bordeaux, 120, 135, 167
Boswell, James: *An Account of Corsica*, 103; *London Journal*, 286
Boumaza, Boudjemaa, 156
Boumaza, Da'ad, 156
Bower, Tom: *The Perfect English Spy*, 86
Bowra, Maurice, 44, 90
Boyle, Andrew, 247–8, 250, 264; *The Climate of Treason*, 247, 249
Bracken, Brendan, 240, 290
Braddyll family (picture), 61
Braque, Georges, 95
Bridges, Sir Edward, 69
British American Tobacco (BAT), 201
British Broadcasting Corporation *see* BBC
British Gas, 204
British Limbless Ex-Servicemen's Association, 93
British Museum, 58, 63, 111, 152
British Overseas Airways Corporation, 117
Brocklebank, Tom, 151, 248
Bruno (chef), 134
Buchenwald, 81
Buckingham, Duke of, 8

Buckingham Palace, 14, 21, 71, 146–7, 235, 236, 237, 247
Burgess, Guy: and Eton, 43–4, 242; as student at Cambridge, 43, 45, 48; VR's friendship with, xiii, 42, 45, 222, 223–4; relationship with VR's mother, 42–3; descriptions of, 42–3, 44–5, 87; sexual life, 43, 44, 45, 88, 228; political views, 43, 44, 45, 222; visits Churchill, 45; career, 224; lives at Bentinck Street, 87, 88, 89; outrageous behaviour, 223, 224, 228; helps Philby to join MI6, 225; Philby's role in planned defection, 227, 274; and role of Blunt, 235, 236, 238; Charleston visit, 228; recalled to London, 228; defection, xiii, 46, 223, 229, 230, 249, 273; death, 229; brief mentions, 50, 226, 247, 274
Burn, Micky, 45
Burney, Frances (Fanny): *Evelina*, 108
Burns, Robert: *Poems, chiefly in the Scottish Dialect*, 108
Butler, Sir Robin, 176–7, 178, 179, 181, 283
Butler family, 90
Buxton, Sir Thomas, 2–3
Byron, Lord, 34

CPRS (Central Policy Review Staff) *see* Think Tank
Cabinet, xi, 7, 64, 173, 175, 176, 178–9, 180, 181, 185, 218, 241
Carnarvon, George Edward Herbert, 5th Earl of, 12, 196
Cahen d'Anvers, Yvonne, 81
Cairncross, John, 223, 242
Cairo, 227
Callaghan, James, 270
Cambridge: Barbara visits VR in, 52, 53; VR takes lease on Merton Hall, 55; VR lodges with the Hodgkins in, 91; VR makes early book purchases in, 95–6; VR's domestic life with Tess in, 132–7; VR moves to new house in, 137; Pincher and Wright meet in, 255, 256, 257, 266, 281; brief mentions, xii, 37, 62, 84, 99, 110, 143, 144, 154, 155, 238, 243, 268, 272, 279; *see also* Cambridge University
Cambridge University: Blunt at, 42, 46–7, 48, 49, 222, 231; Burgess at, 42, 43, 45, 48, 222; Cairncross at, 242; Communism at, 48–51; and intellectual aristocracy, 90; Maclean at, 42; Philby at, 225; Rothschild family members at, 10, 11, 18, 23, 138, 197; VR at, xi, 32, 33, 34–51, 124–5, 126, 131, 247; VR's wife (Tess) at, 112–13; brief mentions, 31, 65; *see also* Apostles; Cavendish Laboratory; King's College; Newnham College; St John's College; Trinity College; Trinity Hall
Campbell-Savours, Dale, Lord, 275–6, 278, 281, 284

and espionage, 77–8, 79–80, 82; brief
mentions, xiii, 18, 20, 48, 113
Getty, J. Paul, 201
Getty Museum, Malibu, 102
Ghika, Nico, 92
Gibbon, Edward, 87, 88, 96
Gibbons, Grinling, 92
Gibraltar, 66–7
Gladstone, W. E., 7, 15, 18, 105
Goderich, Frederick John, Viscount, 140
Goldsmid, Sir Isaac, 5
Goldsmith, Sir James, 201, 279, 287
Goldsmith, Oliver, 261
Goodman, Arnold, Lord, 249, 250, 270, 277
Gordievsky, Oleg, 223, 252
Gosford, Lady, 104
Gramont, Duc de, 139
Grant, Duncan, 54
Granville, Earl, 15
Gray, Sir James, 39, 125, 131, 145
Gray, Simon, 158
Gray, Thomas: *Elegy*, 96, 109
Great Crash (1929), 143
Great Cumbrae, Isle of, 126
Great War (First World War), 23, 26, 195–6
Greene, Graham C., 152
Greengrass, Paul, 259 *see also Spycatcher*
(Wright and Greengrass)
Greg, Sir Walter, 103
Gresham's School, Holt, 242
Gretton, John Frederick, Lord, 132
Greuze, Jean Baptiste, 13
Greville, Charles, 5
Grossstephen Snr (chef), 17
Grosvenor House, London, 165
Grote, George, 111
Grote, John, 111
Guardi, Francesco, 9
Guinness, Anita, 159
Guinness, James, 159
Guinness, John, 178
Gunnersbury Park, 4
Gutenberg Bible, 108

Haldane, J. B. S., 129, 146
Haldane, Richard Burdon, Lord, 20
Haldane family, 90
Halton, 13, 17, 196
Hampshire, Sir Stuart, 77, 154, 161, 208, 287
Hampton Court, 237
Hanadiv, 159
Hanley, Sir Michael, 244–5, 246, 251, 268, 270
Harcourt, Sir William, 105
Hardy, G. H., 34, 78
Harmer, Christopher, 86
Harrow School, 23, 28–34, 45, 62, 65, 150, 176, 242
Hartley, Sir Harold, 65, 117
Havers, Sir Michael, 266, 269, 282–3

Haxton, Gerald, 37
Hay, Philip, 235
Hayward, John, 96, 99, 101–2, 103, 146
Heath, Sir Edward: wartime service, 70; and
Think Tank, xi, 173–5, 176, 177, 180, 181,
182, 184, 186, 188–92, 193, 239, 243, 244,
267–8; appoints Thatcher as shadow
Environment Secretary, 217; Wright's
apocryphal stories about, 243, 244, 267–8;
stays silent on allegations against VR, 274;
brief mentions, 146, 220
Heffer's bookshop, Cambridge, 96
Heinemann (publishers), 259
Heron Bay, Barbados, 137
Hesse-Cassel, Elector of, 2
Hilliard, Nicholas, 95, 159
Hinks, Roger, 57
Hinsley, Arthur, Archbishop of Westminster,
61
Hodgkin, Sir Alan, 90–1, 107, 123 183, 194
Hodgkin, Marni, 91
Hoffmann, Leonard, 202, 208, 211–12, 213,
218, 219, 296
Hogarth Press, 36
Holland, David, 103
Hollis, Sir Roger, 241, 242, 244, 254, 257–8,
260, 274
Hollond, Professor H. A., 40–1
Holocaust, xiii, 81–2
Hooch, Pieter de, 58
Hood, Sammy, Viscount, 42
Hoover, J. Edgar, 64, 79–80
Hopkins, Sir Frederick Gowland, 34
Houghton, 143
House of Commons *see* Commons, House
of
House of Lords *see* Lords, House of
Housman, A. E., 34, 49, 109
Howard, Brian, 53
Howe, Geoffrey, 190
Hudson, Major J. P., 71
Hull, Cordell, 64
Hunt, Sir John, 188
Hurd, Douglas, 175, 178, 179
Hutchinson, Barbara *see* Rothschild (*née*
Hutchinson), Barbara (VR's first wife)
Hutchinson, Jeremy, 145
Hutchinson, Mary, 54, 64, 114, 145
Hutchinson, St John, 53–4, 64, 100, 114
Huxley, Aldous, 146, 288
Huxley, Sir Andrew, 107
Huxley, Ena Mary *see* Prentice (*née* Huxley),
Ena Mary ('Mrs P.')
Huxley, Maria, 146
Huxley family, 90

Iran, 168–72, 185, 205
Ironside, General Sir Edmund (later Lord
Ironside), 169
Isle of Great Cumbrae (Scotland), 126